THE ILLUSTRATED
ENCYCLOPEDIA OF
FIGHTERS

THE ILLUSTRATED ENCYCLOPEDIA OF
FIGHTERS

Editor-in-chief BILL GUNSTON

MACDONALD

Contents

Introduction

FEW of man's creations have changed so much in the half-century from the 1930s to the 1980s as fighter aircraft. Some of the basic tenets of air combat, such as getting on the tail of an enemy aircraft and shooting it down with guns fixed to fire directly ahead, have remained applicable throughout. Almost all other rules about methods of use, weapons, and above all the aircraft themselves, have changed. Indeed today many aircraft that look like fighters, and are called such by the media, are actually used only to attack surface targets and have little or no capability against hostile aircraft.

The first half of this volume deals with the major fighters of World War II. Many of them were designed in the first half of the 1930s, when designers – often in the teeth of opposition from fighter pilots – were trying to bring in fast monoplane fighters. These tended to have engines of up to 1000 hp, compared with 450 to 850 hp for the biplanes and early braced monoplanes. They were much more expensive, with complicated electric and hydraulic systems working retractable landing gear, flaps and variable-pitch propellers. They had heavier armament of groups of machine-guns or cannon instead of the twin machine-guns that had become standard in 1916. At first they were a handful to fly. They landed too fast for the small bumpy grass fields, pilots forgot to put down the landing gear, and they complained they could not see out of enclosed cockpits nor manoeuvre as tightly as in the light fabric-covered biplanes.

Innumerable combats soon proved that the future lay with the fast monoplane, but there was ample scope for diversity. In the Soviet Union designers saved precious aluminium by making fighters mainly from wood, and strove to obtain high performance and agility by making them small – which in turn restricted the armament to (typically) a single cannon and two machine-guns. By far the most important German fighters, the old Bf 109 and new Fw 190, were as small as the Russian types but far more heavily armed; in fact the 190 could even carry a bomb weighing 1800 kg (3968 lb)! Italy tried to stick to biplanes and poor undergunned monoplanes, and only built good fighters when it was about to capitulate. Japan began with a smash hit, the A6M Zero; subsequently it failed to meet the ever-tougher opposition with better successors.

Britain began with two winners. The Hurricane was an ancient but tough and easily repaired aircraft which could carry an assortment of weapons – including heavy cannon for 'tank-busting' – and did more than any other Allied aircraft to stem the tide of the mighty Luftwaffe in the dark early days. The trim Spitfire was more difficult to make and to repair but not only combined every quality needed in a fighter but also had amazing potential for development, so that in 1945 it was every bit as competitive as the first had been in 1936. As for the Americans, their mainstream types – the tough P-40, superb P-51, mighty P-47, radical P-38 and the first-class Navy F4F, F6F and F8U – were so good that shoals of new prototypes never got into production.

In the late 1930s the new class of big twin-engined escorts were overlooked by the RAF, which hastily put a battery of guns in Blenheim bombers and then, thanks to initiative at Bristol, received the great radar-equipped Beaufighter, first of the purpose-built night-fighters able to stalk quarries in the dark. Ever since, fighters have tended to be divided into nimble machines intended for close combat, such as the MiG-21 and F-16, and large long-range interceptors carrying powerful radars and long-range missiles and able to kill at distances of tens of kilometres.

The switch to jet propulsion naturally transformed the flight performance of fighters and, because of this, led to a few unusual shapes including the tailless delta (triangular) aircraft which in the latest Mirages survive to this day, both with and without canards (horizontal control surfaces ahead of the wing, instead of at the back as in a tail). To get the best of both low-speed and high-speed worlds some designers have gone for the swing-wing, able to pivot to different angles of sweepback. No aircraft with a wing of fixed shape can be as good in all regimes of flight, though it might be at least as good in one particular situation. The most amazingly manoeuvrable dogfighters today do not have swing-wings, but large broad wings (often with long forward root extensions) and tremendous surplus engine thrust.

The idea of dogfighting in the 1980s would have seemed incredible 25 years ago. Then it was thought by some that fighters would soon be replaced by missiles; and even the fighters that did get built had all-missile armament. It was the Vietnam war that showed – as the top-scoring US pilot, Col Robin Olds, put it – "A fighter without a gun is like a bird without a wing". Violent arguments continue to rage about whether a small agile fighter is better than a big heavy machine able to carry more fuel, engines, guns and missiles, and also the vital electronics that enable modern combat aircraft to do their job and survive in hostile airspace. Some modern warplanes do nothing but pump out electronics, jammers, flares and chaff (billions of slivers of reflective foil) to protect other friendly aircraft.

Perhaps the chief unresolved question concerns V/STOL (vertical or short take-off and landing). Air forces have consistently preferred to spend astronomic sums on aircraft absolutely tied to fixed concrete runways which can be wiped off the map in a split second by hostile missiles. The V/STOL can be dispersed in thousands of locations on land or sea, and thus could not be caught in a pre-emptive attack. People who are tied to runways will regret it.

Bill Gunston

Contributors: Bernard
Fitzsimons, David Scallon,
Michael J Gething

Colour illustrations: John
Batchelor, Kai Choi, Mike
Roffe
Line illustrations: Jerry
Banks, Nick Farmer, Ray
Hutchins
Retouching: Tony
Hannaford
Cutaways: © Pilot Press
Ltd
Three-view drawings:
© Pilot Press Ltd,
© Macdonald Phoebus
Publishing Company

Phototypeset by
Tradespools Limited,
Frome, Somerset, England

Printed in Great Britain by
Redwood Burn Limited,
Trowbridge, Wiltshire

ISBN 0 356 07569 9

FK.58, Koolhoven

FIRST FLIGHT 1938

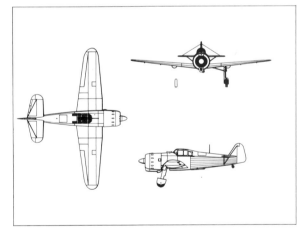

CONSTRUCTED in the Netherlands on the eve of World War II, powered by a French engine and armed with Belgian guns, the FK.58 saw service only with the French air force and was flown mainly by Polish pilots. As might be expected in the circumstances, not many were built. A collaborator on the 1912 Deperdussin racers, and subsequently responsible for a number of famous aircraft for the British firms of Armstrong Whitworth and BAT, Frederik 'Cully' Koolhoven returned after World War I to Holland, where the 58th design to carry his initials (the actual designer was E Schatzki, who had also designed the D.XXI for Fokker) appeared in prototype form in mid 1938.

Powered by a 1080-hp Hispano-Suiza 14Aa 10, the FK.58 was a compact monoplane of mixed construction. In October 1938 it was demonstrated at the French test centre at Villacoublay, with the result that in January 1939, 50 were ordered for service in French colonies. The first flight of a second prototype took place in February, and the following month the Dutch government ordered a further 36, to be powered by 1080-hp Bristol Taurus III engines, and the construction of ten of the French machines was sub-contracted immediately to SABCA in Belgium.

Deliveries to France began in June 1939, the first four being FK.58s with the original powerplant. The remainder were to be FK.58As, using the 1080-hp Gnome-Rhône 14N/16, and 13 of these had been delivered by September 1939. No more were delivered to France – the Belgian machines were assembled but no engines had been supplied for them by the time of the German invasion in May 1940, exports from Holland had been banned on the outbreak of war, and the absence of the intended engines also prevented any of the Dutch machines being completed.

By this stage the French government had more pressing concerns than the supply of fighters to Indo-China, and in May 1940 the FK.58As were issued to Patrouilles de Protection to be flown principally by Polish pilots who had escaped to France. Charged with defending industrial centres, the Patrouilles de Protection were ad hoc units of whose activities little record was kept. The FK.58s had been in storage for several months, were largely unserviceable, and saw little action.

FK.58

Type: single-seat monoplane fighter
Maker: NV Koolhoven Vliegtuigen; Société Anonyme Belge de Constructions Aéronautiques (SABCA)
Span: 11 m (36 ft 1 in)
Length: 8.7 m (28 ft 6½ in)
Height: 3 m (9 ft 10 in)
Wing area: 17.21 m² (185.25 sq ft)
Weight: maximum 2750 kg (6063 lb); empty 1795 kg (3957 lb)
Powerplant: one 1080-hp Hispano-Suiza 14Aa 10 14-cylinder two-row air-cooled radial
Performance: maximum speed 504 km/h (313 mph) at 4500 m (14 764 ft); range 750 km (466 miles); service ceiling 10 400 m (34 121 ft)
Armament: four 7.5-mm (0.295-in) FN-Browning machine-guns
Crew: 1
Production: 4 (80 other airframes completed)

Above: A Koolhoven FK.58 of the Armée de l'Air showing the underwing fairing for a pair of 7.5-mm (0.295-in) machine-guns

1

Bf 109, Messerschmitt

FIRST FLIGHT 1935

WILLI Messerschmitt's Bayerische Flugzeug-werke seemingly had little chance of meeting the requirement for a new fighter issued by the Luftwaffe in 1933: he had proved his ability as a designer, but was so out of favour with the new administration that he was officially advised to abandon aircraft manufacture and take up an academic career. Nevertheless, he persevered, to be vindicated in 1936 when comparative trials between prototypes of his Bf 109 and the Heinkel He 112 resulted in the Messerschmitt fighter being selected for production.

The first production model, deliveries of which began in February 1937, was the B-1, powered by a 635-hp Junkers Jumo 210D and armed with three 7.92-mm (0.312-in) MG 17S in the nose. Only a few B-1s were built, and they were succeeded by mid 1937 by the B-2, with a variable-pitch propeller replacing the B-1's fixed-pitch type and, in later examples, with a 640-hp Jumo 210G engine. Two squadrons of 109Bs served with the Legion Condor in Spain from mid 1937, proving markedly superior to the Republican fighters.

By early 1938 deliveries of the C-1 had started, with a redesigned nose housing two MG 17s, two more being added in the wings. The C-2 incorporated a fifth machine-gun in the nose, firing through the propeller hub.

Production was now being carried out by Arado, Erla, Fieseler and Focke-Wulf as well as Messerschmitt, as the Bayerische Flugzeugwerke was now known, and by the end of 1938 virtually all

Below: A Bf 109G-10/U4 of the last Croatian Jagdstaffel at Eichwalde, November 1944. This was a Croatian unit under command of the East Prussia Fighter Command. The Bf 109 was supplied to Axis allies such as the Hungarians, Romanians and Bulgarians; it also served after the war in Spain, Czechoslovakia and Israel

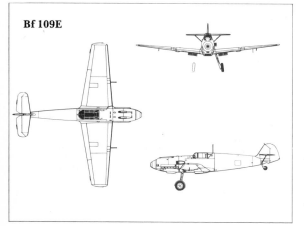

Bf 109E

Bf 109B-2

Type: single-seat fighter
Maker: Bayerische Flugzeugwerke; Messerschmitt AG; Erla; Fieseler; Focke-Wulf and others
Span: 9.87 m (32 ft 4½ in)
Length: 8.55 m (28 ft 0¾ in)
Height: 2.45 m (8 ft 0½ in)
Wing area: 16.4 m² (176.53 sq ft)
Weight: maximum 2150 kg (4740 lb); empty 1505 kg (3318 lb)
Powerplant: one 680-hp Junkers Jumo 210Da 12-cylinder liquid-cooled engine
Performance: maximum

speed 465 km/h (289 mph) at 4000 m (13 120 ft); range 692 km (430 miles); operational ceiling 8199 m (26 900 ft)
Armament: three 7.9-mm (0.31-in) MG 17 machine-guns
Crew: 1
Production: approx 34 000 (all types)

Bf 109D-1

Specification similar to the Bf 109B-2 except in the following particulars:
Length: 8.6 m (28 ft 2½ in)
Height: 2.56 m (8 ft 4¾ in)

Weight: maximum 2420 kg (5335 lb); empty 1798 kg (3964 lb)
Powerplant: one 986-hp Daimler-Benz DB 600Aa inverted-V liquid-cooled engine
Performance: maximum speed 574.5 km/h (357 mph) at 3500 m (11 480 ft); range 560 km (348 miles); operational ceiling 10 000 m (32 810 ft)
Armament: one 20-mm (0.79-in) MG FF/M cannon; two 7.9-mm (0.31-in) MG 17 machine-guns

Germany's 21 Jagdgruppen were equipped.

The next major step in Bf 109 development was the installation of the Daimler Benz DB 600 engine, with a three-blade propeller. Limited production of D-1s with this powerplant and an armament of two MG 17s and an MG FF began in late 1937. But the D-1s service career, like its production run, was short: by the end of 1938 the first E-1s had appeared, with a fuel-injected 1175-hp DB 601A engine and two wing-mounted MG FFs in addition to two MG 17s in the nose. Deliveries to service units began in February 1939.

By September 1, 1939, when the German invasion of Poland signalled the start of World War II, new production facilities in Austria were coming into use. Over 1000 109Es had been produced since the beginning of the year.

The beginning of 1940 saw the Jagdgruppen receiving the E-3, whose 1175-hp DB 601A engine had provision for an MG FF firing through the propeller hub, though it was not often carried. Other changes included a new cockpit canopy and armour protection for the pilot. Even without the extra weapon, combat losses during the invasion of western Europe were not particularly heavy, though the rapid advance through the Low Countries and France saw fighter strength eroded.

The Battle of Britain brought new problems. The 109s over England were fighting at the limit of their range, with the additional responsibility of protecting their bombers, against Hurricanes and Spitfires which were far from being outclassed.

Bf 109E-1

Specification similar to the Bf 109B-2 except in the following particulars:
Length: 8.65 m (28 ft 4½ in)
Height: 2.5 m (8 ft 2⅓ in)
Weight: maximum 2505 kg (5523 lb); empty 1840 kg (4056 lb)
Powerplant: one 1100-hp Daimler-Benz DB 601A inverted-V 12-cylinder liquid-cooled engine
Performance: maximum speed 550.4 km/h (342 mph) at 4000 m (13 120 ft); range 660 km (410 miles); operational ceiling 10 500 m (34 450 ft)

Armament: two 20-mm (0.79-in) MG FF cannon; two 7.9-mm (0.31-in) MG 17 machine-guns

Bf 109F-4

Specification similar to the Bf 109B-2 except in the following particulars
Span: 9.9 m (32 ft 5¾ in)
Length: 8.85 m (29 ft 0⅓ in)
Height: 2.59 m (8 ft 6 in)
Wing area: 16.2 m² (174.376 ft)
Weight: maximum 2900 kg (6393 lb); empty 2390 kg (5269 lb)
Powerplant: one 1350-hp

Daimler-Benz DB 601E-1 inverted-V 12-cylinder liquid-cooled engine
Performance: maximum speed 624.4 km/h (388 mph) at 6500 m (21 325 ft); range 711 km (442 miles) with drop-tank; operational ceiling 12 000 m (39 370 ft)
Armament: one 20-mm (0.79-in) MG 151 cannon and two 7.9-mm (0.31-in) MG 17 machine-guns

Bf 109G-6

Specification similar to the Bf 109B-2 except in the following particulars:

Span: 9.92 m (32 ft 6½ in)
Length: 8.85 m (29 ft ½ in)
Height: 2.50 m (8 ft 2½ in)
Wing area: 16.20 m² (174⅓ sq ft)
Weight: maximum 3398 kg (7491 lb); empty 2673 kg (5893 lb)

Powerplant: one 1475-hp Daimler-Benz DB 605AM inverted V-12 liquid-cooled engine
Performance: maximum speed 621 km/h (386 mph) at 6900 m (22 640 ft); range 560 km (348 miles); operational ceiling 11 550 m (37 894 ft)
Armament: one 30-mm

(1.18-in) MK 108 or 20-mm (0.79-in) MG 151/20 cannon; two 13-mm (0.51-in) MG 131 machine-guns

Right: Bf 109E-3 with British serial AE479 which was originally in service with I/JG 76. After careful evaluation it was passed to the USA where it was written off

Centre: A Bf 109F pilot starts his pre-take-off checks in 1940. His life jacket indicates operations over the English Channel

Far right: A Bf 109E-3 with the markings of 6/JG 26. 'Yellow-nose Messerschmitts' were famous in the Battle of Britain, but most staffeln used other colours

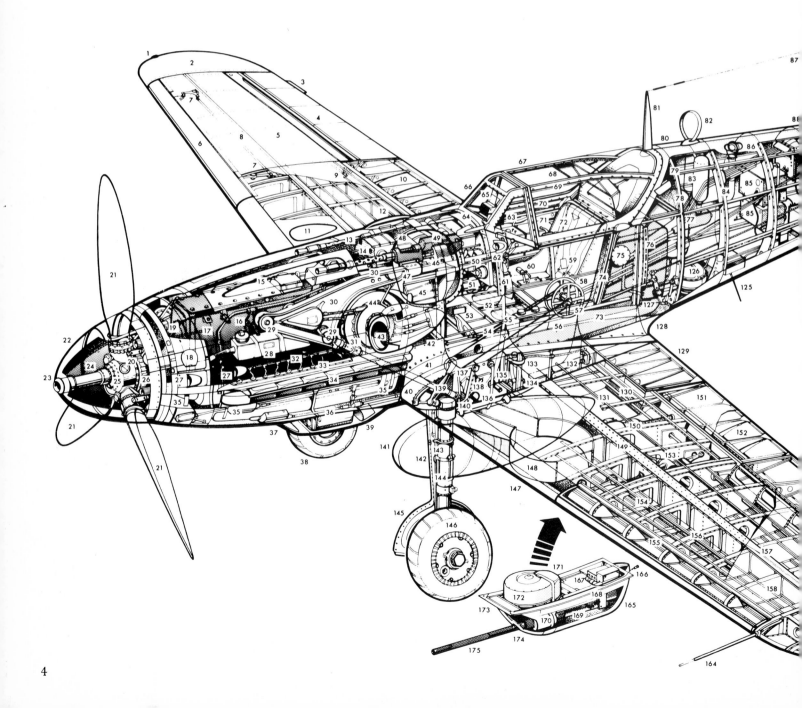

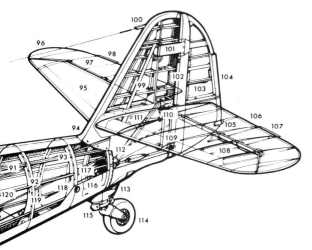

Bf 109G-14/U4

1 Right navigation light
2 Right wingtip
3 Fixed trim tab
4 Right Frise-type aileron
5 Flush-riveted stressed wing-skinning
6 Handley Page leading-edge automatic slot
7 Slot control linkage
8 Slot equalizer rod
9 Aileron control linkage
10 Fabric-covered flap section
11 Wheel fairing
12 Left fuselage machine-gun ammunition-feed fairing
13 Left Rheinmetall Borsig 13-mm MG 131 machine-gun
14 Engine accessories
15 Right machine-gun trough
16 Daimler Benz DB 605Am inverted V-12 liquid-cooled engine
17 Detachable cowling panel
18 Oil filler access
19 Oil tank
20 Propeller pitch-change mechanism
21 VDM electrically-operated constant-speed propeller
22 Spinner
23 Engine-mounted cannon muzzle
24 Blast tube
25 Propeller hub
26 Spinner back plate
27 Auxiliary cooling intakes
28 Coolant header tank
29 Anti-vibration rubber engine-mounting pads
30 Elektron forged engine bearer
31 Engine bearer support strut attachment
32 Plug leads
33 Exhaust manifold fairing strip
34 Ejector exhausts
35 Cowling fasteners
36 Oil cooler
37 Oil cooler intake
38 Right mainwheel
39 Oil cooler outlet flap
40 Wing root fillet
41 Wing/fuselage fairing
42 Firewall/bulkhead
43 Supercharger air intake
44 Supercharger assembly
45 20-mm cannon magazine drum
46 13-mm machine-gun ammunition feed
47 Engine bearer upper attachment
48 Ammunition feed fairing
49 13-mm Rheinmetall Borsig MG 131 machine-gun breeches
50 Instrument panel
51 20-mm Mauser MG 151/20 cannon breech
52 Heelrests
53 Rudder pedals
54 Undercarriage emergency retraction cables
55 Fuselage frame
56 Wing/fuselage fairing
57 Undercarriage emergency retraction handwheel (outboard)
58 Tail trim handwheel (inboard)
59 Seat harness
60 Throttle lever
61 Control column
62 Cockpit ventilation inlet
63 Revi 16B reflector gunsight (folding)
64 Armoured windshield frame

65 Anti-glare gunsight screen
66 90-mm armourglass windscreen
67 'Galland'-type clear-vision hinged canopy
68 Framed armourglass head/back panel
69 Canopy contoured frame
70 Canopy hinges (right)
71 Canopy release catch
72 Pilot's bucket-type seat (8-mm back armour)
73 Underfloor contoured fuel tank
74 Fuselage frame
75 Circular access panel
76 Tail trimming cable conduit
77 Wireless leads
78 MW 50 (methanol/water) tank
79 Handhold
80 Fuselage decking
81 Aerial mast
82 D/F loop
83 Oxygen cylinders (three)
84 Filler pipe
85 Wireless equipment packs (FuG 16zy communications and FuG 25a IFF)
86 Main fuel filler cap
87 Aerial
88 Fuselage top keel (connector stringer)
89 Aerial lead-in
90 Fuselage skin plating sections
91 'U'-stringers
92 Fuselage frames (monocoque construction)
93 Tail trimming cables
94 Tailfin root fairing
95 Right fixed tailplane
96 Elevator balance
97 Right elevator
98 Geared elevator tab
99 All-wooden tailfin construction
100 Aerial attachment
101 Rudder upper hinge bracket
102 Rudder post
103 Fabric-covered wooden rudder structure
104 Geared rudder tab
105 Rear navigation light
106 Left elevator
107 Elevator geared tab
108 Tailplane structure
109 Rudder actuating linkage
110 Elevator control horn
111 Elevator connecting rod
112 Elevator control quadrant
113 Tailwheel leg cuff
114 Castoring non-retractable tailwheel
115 Lengthened tailwheel leg
116 Access panel
117 Tailwheel shock-strut
118 Lifting point
119 Rudder cable
120 Elevator cables
121 First-aid pack
122 Air bottles
123 Fuselage access panel
124 Bottom keel (connector stringer)
125 Ventral IFF aerial
126 Master compass
127 Elevator control linkage
128 Wing root fillet
129 Camber-changing flap
130 Ducted coolant radiator
131 Wing stringers
132 Wing rear pick-up point
133 Spar/fuselage upper pin joint (horizontal)
134 Spar/fuselage lower pin joint (vertical)

135 Flaps equalizer rod
136 Rüstsatz 3 auxiliary fuel tank ventral rack
137 Undercarriage electrical interlock
138 Wing horizontal pin forward pick-up
139 Undercarriage retraction jack mechanism
140 Undercarriage pivot/bevel
141 Auxiliary fuel tank (Rüstsatz 3)
142 Mainwheel leg fairing
143 Mainwheel oleo leg
144 Brake lines
145 Mainwheel fairing
146 Left mainwheel
147 Leading-edge skin
148 Left mainwheel well
149 Wing spar
150 Flap actuating linkage
151 Fabric-covered control surfaces
152 Slotted flap structure
153 Leading-edge slot actuating mechanism
154 Slot equalizer rod
155 Handley Page automatic leading-edge slot
156 Wing stringers
157 Spar flange decrease
158 Wing ribs
159 Flush-riveted stressed wing-skinning
160 Metal-framed Frise-type aileron
161 Fixed trim tab
162 Wingtip construction
163 Left navigation light
164 Angled pitot head
165 Rüstsatz 6 optional underwing cannon gondola
166 14-point plug connection
167 Electrical junction box
168 Cannon rear mounting bracket
169 20-mm Mauser MG 151/20 cannon
170 Cannon front mounting bracket
171 Ammunition feed chute
172 Ammunition magazine drum
173 Underwing panel
174 Gondola fairing
175 Cannon barrel

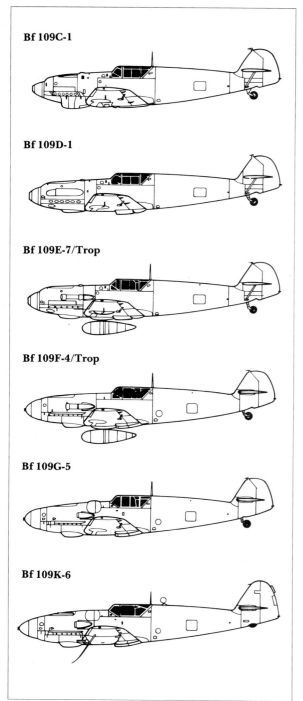

Bf 109C-1

Bf 109D-1

Bf 109E-7/Trop

Bf 109F-4/Trop

Bf 109G-5

Bf 109K-6

The various sub-types of the G series were powered by DB 605A or 605D engines and armament was increased to one 30-mm (1.18-in) MK 103 or 108, or one 20-mm (0.79-in) cannon where these were not available, plus two 13-mm (0.51-in) MG 131s in the nose, while additional cannon were often carried in gondolas. The G-6 was designed to accept a variety of DB 605 engines and a range of operational conversions kits, the G-8 was a reconnaissance fighter, and the G-12 a trainer.

The projected high-altitude H series never progressed beyond the development stage, and the 'twin' 109Z was never built, but the 109K series began production in late 1944 with an MK 103 and two MG 151/15s in the nose. The final variant was the K-14, some with the DB 605L engine.

Total Bf 109 production amounted to some 34 000: the fighter was used by all Germany's Allies during World War II, and by Spain and Switzerland, and many continued in service after 1945 with a number of air forces. Although only 610 109Es were lost, compared with 1172 British fighters, German losses also included 235 Bf 110 escort fighters and 947 bombers.

Further 109E sub-types included the E-4, which finally abandoned the engine-mounted cannon; the E-5 and E-6 reconnaissance fighters, with no wing cannon and a fuselage-mounted camera, the E-6 having a high-compression 1200-hp DB 601N; the E-7, with provision for a drop-tank or a 250-kg (551-lb) bomb; and the E-8 and E-9, respectively equivalent to the E-7 and E-5 but with 1350-hp DB

Above left; The development of the Bf 109, ending in the K, which was the final production series and had a taller vertical tail. The Bf 109E-7/Trop and the 109F-4/Trop are fitted with 300-litre (66-Imp gal) drop-tanks

Above: A Bf 109E-4/Trop of I/JG 27 flies over scrub-covered desert in Cyrenaica in 1941. The Trop versions were fitted with filters against sand and grit. They were used not only in North Africa but also in dusty areas of the Soviet Union

601E engines. Fighter-bomber and tropical modifications of these models were also produced, while the E-7/Z introduced the GM-1 nitrous oxide booster used on many later variants. The E-1 also formed the basis for the Bf 109T carrier fighter.

So far the basic airframe had been left more or less alone, but during 1940 extensive redesign went into the 109F, which was given a bigger spinner, new nose, improved air collection for the supercharger and radiators, different ailerons, rounded wingtips, a smaller rudder, unbraced horizontal tail and fully retracting tailwheel. It was also intended to have the 1350-hp DB 601E, but because of a shortage of this powerplant the F-1 entered service in January 1941 with the DB 601N. No wing armament was carried, two MG 17s and

an MG FF being mounted in the nose, but the F-2 substituted a 15-mm (0.59-in) MG 151/15 for the MG FF.

The F-3 introduced the DB 601E engine early in 1942, and the F-4 added a 20-mm MG 151/20 and greater pilot protection. The F-5 and F-6 were reconnaissance fighters, the former losing its cannon and the latter carrying no armament. As with the E series, fighter-bomber conversions were produced, while some Fs were given a pair of MG 151/20s in a gondola below the fuselage.

Over 2000 Fs had been produced by the end of 1941, when the G series began to take over. A total of 23 000 109Gs were built, over 14 000 of them in 1944 alone – an astonishing number for a fighter already past its peak.

Above: The Bf 109B-1 which was first delivered to JG 132 Richthofen in February 1937. The B was nicknamed Bertha by its crews, and these names stuck with each sub-type, so the C became Clara, the D Dora, the E Emil, and the G Gustav; the F does not appear to have been named

Hurricane, Hawker
FIRST FLIGHT 1935

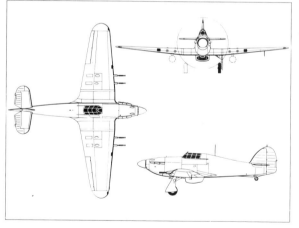

THE development of the RAF's first monoplane fighter, not counting the RFC's excellent Bristol M.1C of 1917, began in 1933 with the projected Fury Monoplane. This was intended as a four-gun, fixed-landing gear single-wing conversion of the Hawker Fury biplane to be powered by a 660-hp steam-cooled Goshawk engine. Anticipation of the Rolls-Royce PV.12 (later named Merlin) engine caused the Fury conversion to be abandoned, and a new 'Interceptor Monoplane' was planned to meet a revised specification for a four-gun fighter.

Hawker were given the go-ahead for construction of a prototype in February 1935, but by the time the prototype flew in November that year, British licence production of the Browning machine-gun in 0.303-in (7.7-mm) calibre had been agreed, and the design was further revised to accommodate eight in the wings.

Trials in early 1936 showed a top speed of 507 km/h (315 mph), and with minor revisions to the controls, landing gear and sliding canopy, 600 production aircraft were ordered in July 1936, the same month that the name Hurricane was bestowed. First deliveries were to No 111 Squadron at the end of 1937, and Nos 3 and 56 Squadrons were equipped in 1938. This was entirely because in January 1936, long before the Air Ministry had even hinted at an order, the Hawker Siddeley board had tooled up to make 1000 at Kingston and a new factory at Langley, near Slough.

The decision to adopt the eight-gun armament led to the development of an all-metal stressed-skin wing as early as 1935, but production aircraft

delivered before the autumn of 1939 were fitted with the traditional fabric-covered wing. Meanwhile, trials had also been carried out with variable-pitch propellers, which offered much improved take-off and climb performance, and DH and Rotol variable-pitch models became standard in 1940.

The installation of the 1260-hp Merlin XX engine was the basic distinguishing feature of the Mk II, a converted Mk I flying for the first time with this powerplant in June 1940. New wings with different armament options resulted in a number of sub-series. The IIA retained the Mk I wing, but the IIB had twelve wing-mounted Brownings, the IIC four 20-mm (0.79-in) Hispano-Suiza drum-feed cannon and the IID, which first flew in

Hurricane IIC

Type: monoplane fighter and fighter-bomber
Maker: Hawker Aircraft Ltd; Gloster Aircraft Co Ltd
Span: 12.19 m (40 ft)
Length: 9.81 m (32 ft 2¼ in)
Height: 2.67 m (8 ft 9 in)
Wing area: 23.93 m² (257.6 sq ft)
Weight: maximum 3649 kg (8044 lb); empty 2566 kg (5658 lb)
Powerplant: one 1260-hp Rolls-Royce Merlin XX V-12 liquid-cooled engine
Performance: maximum speed 529 km/h (329 mph) at 5487 m (18 000 ft); range 740 km (460 miles); operational ceiling 10 851 m (35 600 ft)
Armament: four 20-mm (0.79-in) Hispano-Suiza cannon; 454 kg (1000 lb) of bombs
Crew: 1
Production: 4711

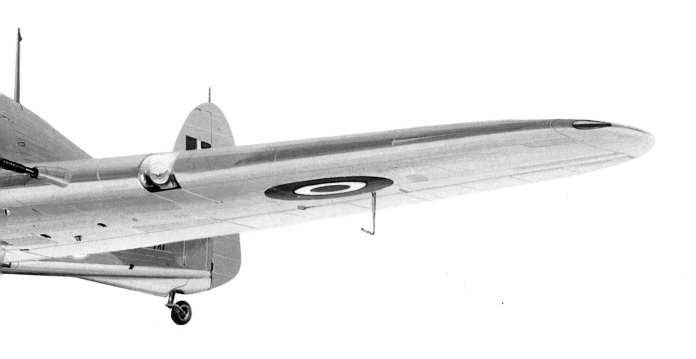

Top: The Hurricane IIC was first delivered to the RAF in June 1941. It served not only in Europe but also in North Africa and the Far East
Far left: The 'tin opener' tank-busting IID with 40-mm (1.57-in) cannon
Above: One of the few surviving IICs of the RAF Memorial Flight
Left: The Hurricane production line at Kingston; this comparatively old fighter destroyed more enemy aircraft in the Battle of Britain than all other fighters and the AA guns combined

September 1941, carried a pair of 40-mm (1.57-in) Vickers S cannon for anti-tank work in North Africa. The last three could also accommodate a 113-kg (250-lb) or 227-kg (500-lb) bomb under each wing, on hardpoints which from late 1941 were plumbed for drop-tanks.

This multiplicity of armament options was rationalized in the Hurricane IV, originally designated Mk IIE, whose wings provided stations for 40-mm cannon, bombs or rockets; the powerplant was a 1620-hp Merlin 24 or 27, driving a four-blade propeller and 794 were produced, including 270 IIEs. The Mk III was an unbuilt version with the Packard-built Merlin, and the two Mk Vs were Hurricane IV conversions with Merlin 32s driving four-blade propellers. The Canadian Car and Foundry company began building Hurricane Is in 1939, and remaining designations covered CCF Hurricanes using Packard-built Merlin 28 or 29 engines. The Mk X and XI corresponded to the IIB, the latter having Canadian equipment, and the Mk XII and XIIA (Merlin 29) were distinguished by the number of guns, respectively eight and twelve Brownings.

Total Hurricane production amounted to 14 233, the majority by Hawker but including 2750, principally Mk Is, supplied by Gloster and 1451 built by CCF. The only other firms to build the fighter were Avions Fairey in Belgium, who contributed two of the above total, and Rogožarski in Yugoslavia, who built another handful to back up 24 supplied by Britain. Although most exports, which included orders from Turkey, Poland and Iraq, were cur-

tailed by the war, over 100 found their way to overseas customers, and there were postwar sales to Portugal and Iran, included in which were various tandem dual trainers.

This bare summary of Hurricane development and production gives little hint of the type's astonishing versatility. In its original role of interceptor it saw heavy fighting in Norway and France in 1940, before forming the mainstay of Fighter Command during the Battle of Britain, in which no fewer than 1715 examples took part, outnumbering the combined total of all other RAF aircraft, and claiming nearly four-fifths of the 1792 German aircraft destroyed.

It continued to serve in the home-defence role when the Luftwaffe switched to night raids, at the same time expanding its sphere of operations to the Mediterranean, North Africa and the Middle East during 1940, and to the Far East in 1941. In August 1941, the first of an eventual total of 2952 Mks II and IV were despatched to the Soviet Union. Hurricanes generally delivered their various ordnance loads to telling effect in all their many theatres of operations. They proved particularly valuable in Burma and also carried out second-line tasks.

Finally, not the least of the Hurricane's contributions to Allied victory came at sea. Surplus Mk Is were fitted with catapult spools for use aboard Catapult Armed Merchantmen for convoy protection as Sea Hurricane IAs, from early 1941. Thereafter arrester hooks were added to enable Sea Hurricanes to operate from aircraft carriers.

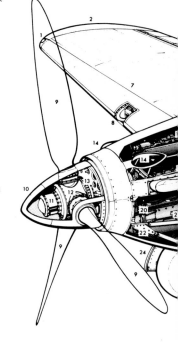

Mk IIC

1 Right navigation light
2 Right wingtip
3 Aluminium alloy aileron
4 Ball-bearing aileron hinge
5 Aft wing spar
6 Aluminium alloy wing skinning
7 Forward wing spar
8 Right landing light
9 Rotol three-blade propeller
10 Spinner
11 Propeller hub
12 Pitch-control mechanism
13 Spinner back plate
14 Cowling fairings
15 Coolant pipes
16 Rolls-Royce Merlin XX engine
17 Cowling panel fasteners
18 'Fishtail' exhaust pipes
19 Electric generator
20 Engine forward mounting feet
21 Engine upper bearer tube
22 Engine forward mount
23 Engine lower bearer tubes
24 Right mainwheel fairing
25 Right mainwheel
26 Low-pressure tyre
27 Brake drum (pneumatic brakes)
28 Manual-type inertia starter
29 Hydraulic system
30 Bearer joint
31 Auxiliary intake
32 Carburettor air intake
33 Wing root fillet
34 Engine oil drain collector/breather
35 Fuel pump drain
36 Engine aft bearers
37 Magneto
38 Two-stage supercharger
39 Cowling panel attachments
40 Engine RPM indicator drive
41 External bead sight
42 Aluminium alloy cowling panels
43 Engine coolant header tank
44 Engine firewall
45 Fuselage (reserve) fuel tank
46 Exhaust glare shield
47 Control column
48 Engine bearer attachment
49 Rudder pedals
50 Control linkage
51 Centre-section fuel tank

52 Oil system piping
53 Pneumatic system air cylinder
54 Wing centre-section
55 Engine bearer support strut
56 Oil tank
57 Dowty undercarriage ram
58 Left undercarriage well
59 Wing centre-section girder frame
60 Pilot's oxygen cylinder
61 Elevator trim tab control wheel
62 Radiator flap control lever
63 Entry footstep
64 Fuselage tubular framework
65 Landing lamp control lever
66 Oxygen supply cock
67 Throttle lever
68 Safety harness
69 Pilot's seat
70 Pilot's break-out exit panel
71 Map case
72 Instrument panel
73 Cockpit ventilation inlet
74 Reflector gunsight
75 Bullet-proof windscreen
76 Rear-view mirror
77 Rearward-sliding canopy
78 Canopy frames
79 Canopy handgrip
80 Plexiglas canopy panels
81 Head/back armour plate
82 Harness attachment
83 Aluminium alloy decking
84 Turnover reinforcement
85 Canopy track
86 Fuselage framework cross-bracing
87 Radio equipment (TR9D/TR133)
88 Support tray
89 Removable access panel
90 Aileron cable drum
91 Elevator control lever
92 Cable adjusters
93 Wing/fuselage fillet
94 Ventral identification lights
95 Footstep retraction guide
96 Radio equipment (R3002)
97 Recognition apparatus
98 Handhold
99 Diagonal support
100 Fuselage fairing
101 Dorsal identification light
102 Aerial mast
103 Aerial lead-in
104 Recognition apparatus cover panel

105 Mast support
106 Wire-braced upper truss
107 Wooden fuselage fairing formers
108 Fabric covering
109 Radio antenna
110 All-metal tailplane structure
111 Elevator balance
112 Right elevator
113 Tailfin metal leading-edge
114 Fabric covering
115 Tailfin structure
116 Diagonal bracing struts
117 Built-in static balance
118 Aerial stub
119 Fabric-covered rudder
120 Rudder structure
121 Rudder post
122 Rear navigation light
123 Balanced rudder trim tab
124 Wiring
125 Elevator trim tab
126 Fixed balance tab
127 Fabric-covered elevator
128 Tailplane rear spar
129 Tailplane front spar
130 Rudder lower hinge
131 Rudder operating lever
132 Connecting rod
133 Control pulleys
134 Elevator operating lever
135 Tailplane spar attachments
136 Aluminium alloy tailplane
137 Tailwheel shock-strut
138 Angled frame rear structure
139 Sternpost
140 Ventral fin
141 Dowty oleo-pneumatic tailwheel
142 Fin framework
143 Handling-bar socket
144 Fabric covering
145 Swaged tube and steel gusset fitting
146 Upper tube/longeron
147 Rudder cables
148 Wooden stringers
149 Elevator cables
150 Aluminium alloy formers
151 Diagonal brace wires
152 Lower tube/longeron
153 Aluminium alloy former
154 Retractable entry footstep
155 Wingroot fillet
156 Flap rod universal joint
157 Aileron cables

158 Wing rear spar girder attachment
159 Main wing fuel tank
160 Glycol radiator and oil cooler
161 Front spar wing fixings
162 Cannon forward mounting bracket
163 Cannon fairing
164 Recoil spring
165 Cannon barrels
166 Undercarriage retraction jack
167 Undercarriage fairing
168 Low-pressure tyre
169 Left mainwheel
170 Mainwheel shock-strut
171 Oleo-pneumatic cylinder
172 Landing gear drag strut
173 Leading-edge armament doors
174 Landing gear pivot point
175 Undercarriage sliding joint
176 Armament access plates
177 Rear spar wing fixing
178 Magazine blister fairings
179 Gun heating manifold
180 Breech-block access plates
181 Metal flaps
182 Cannon breech-blocks
183 Ammunition magazine drum
184 Left outer 20-mm Hispano cannon
185 Spar section change
186 Left landing light
187 Leading-edge structure
188 Front main spar
189 Forward intermediate spar
190 Stringers
191 Rib formers
192 Aluminium alloy wing skinning
193 Rear intermediate spar
194 Rear spar
195 Aileron control pulley
196 Aileron inboard hinge
197 Aluminium alloy aileron
198 Aileron control gear main pulley
199 Self-aligning ball-bearing hinge
200 Aileron outboard hinge
201 Detachable wingtip
202 Left navigation light

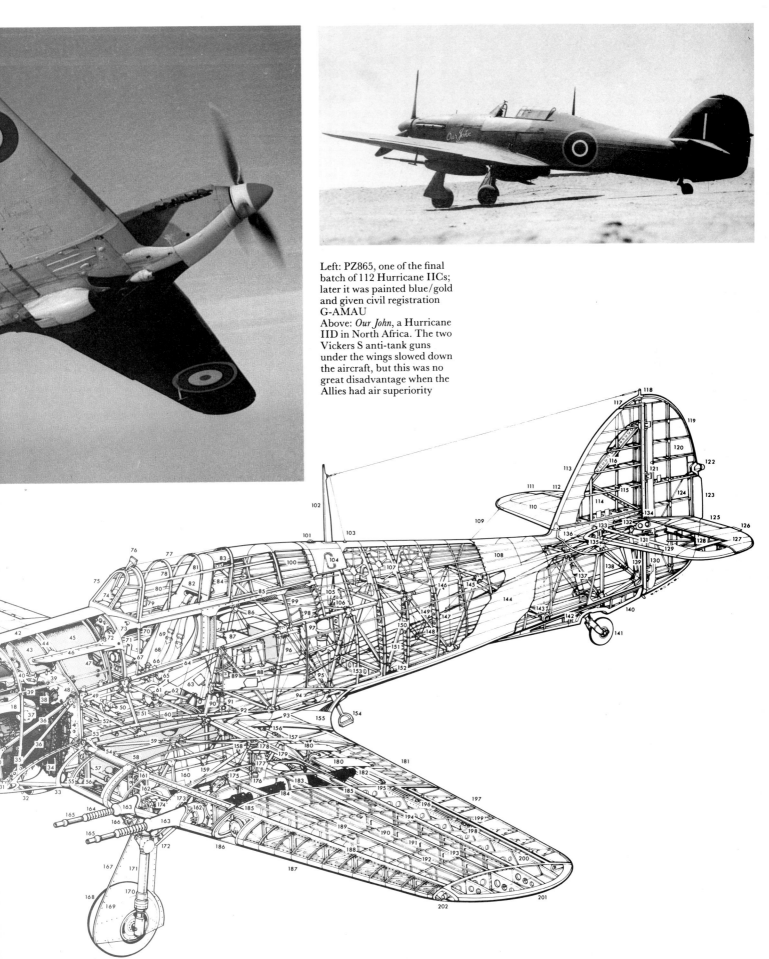

Left: PZ865, one of the final batch of 112 Hurricane IICs; later it was painted blue/gold and given civil registration G-AMAU

Above: *Our John*, a Hurricane IID in North Africa. The two Vickers S anti-tank guns under the wings slowed down the aircraft, but this was no great disadvantage when the Allies had air superiority

Spitfire, Supermarine

FIRST FLIGHT 1936

THE name Spitfire was first applied – unofficially – to the Supermarine Type 224, a low-wing monoplane completed in 1933 with fixed undercarriage, a machine-gun in each wing root and each wheel fairing, and a 660-hp Rolls-Royce Goshawk III engine. Armament and engine had been stipulated by a 1930 specification, but Supermarine designer Reginald Mitchell was already having further thoughts which materialized in late 1935 as the Type 300. The Type 224's inverted gull wings were replaced by straight-taper elliptical wings housing outward-retracting undercarriage and the eight Browning machine-guns called for by subsequent specifications, while power was provided by a 990-hp Rolls-Royce Merlin C engine. Successful trials and a top speed of 562.5 km/h (349½ mph) led to a first order for 310 Spitfire Is, and deliveries to 19 Squadron began in mid 1938.

The 1583 Spitfire Is included early examples with only four machine-guns, and a small number of Mk IBs, with four machine-guns and a pair of drum-fed Hispano-Suiza 20-mm (0.79-in) cannon, the eight-Browning type becoming the Mk IA: powerplant was a 1030-hp Merlin II or III. The 920 Mk IIA and IIB which followed were similarly differentiated by armament, changes including the use of the 1175-hp Merlin XII driving a three-blade constant-speed propeller and the provision of modest armour protection, substantially increased on later models. The Mk III was an experimental machine, while the Mk IV was the first of a series of photographic reconnaissance variants, and the next production fighter version was the Mk V. This was numerically the most important Spitfire, a total of 6479 being produced.

Among the improvements were structural strengthening and the use of 1470-hp Merlin 45, 50 and 50A, and 1415-hp Merlin 46 engines. Again, VA (94 built) and VB (3923 built) were distinguished by the armament carried, while the VC introduced a new wing capable of accommodating either of the above options or two cannon and a 113-kg (250-lb) bomb; alternatively, a drop-tank or a 227-kg (500-lb) bomb could be carried below the fuselage. As their role switched from interception to ground attack many Mk Vs had their wingtips removed and 1585-hp Merlin 45M, 50M or 55M engines fitted to become LF IX low-altitude fighters.

In contrast, the Mk VI was a high-altitude Mk VB development, featuring enlarged wings of 12.24 m (40 ft 2 in) span, a 1415-hp Merlin 47 engine driving a four-blade propeller and cabin pressurization, which increased the operational ceiling to 12 192 m (40 000 ft). Only 100 were built, these being followed from April 1942 by 140 of the more specialized Mk VIIs, whose length was increased to 9.54 m (31 ft 3½ in) to accommodate a 1520-hp Merlin 61 or 1710-hp Merlin 64. Most of the 1658 Mk VIIIs were low-altitude, clipped-wing versions of the Mk VII without cabin pressurization and powered by the 1720-hp Merlin 66, though 267 F VIIIs had the standard wing and Merlin 61 or 63 and 160 were HF VIIIs with extended wings and Merlin 70 engines.

Meanwhile, the orderly development of aircraft and engine was disrupted towards the end of 1941

Left: A Spitfire IX; this aircraft preserved in the USA has a modern VHF antenna behind the original mast. The Mk IX was never planned at all; it was a hasty lash-up to get the two-stage Merlin 61 into the Mk V airframe. It kept being re-ordered, keeping out the definitive Mk VIII

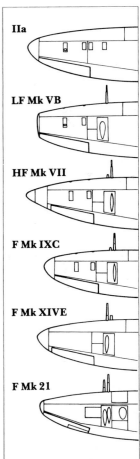

Above: The elliptical wing shape of the Spitfire altered a little during its life. Some marks were clipped for fast low level flight, the wings being not only stronger with this shape, but allowing the aircraft to make tight rolls. The long tapered points on types like the HF VII were for high-altitude interceptors which could tackle German reconnaissance aircraft. The armament changed with a mix of cannon and machine-guns. It is a tribute to the wings and airframe that the Spitfire could be fitted with more powerful engines and weapons

13

Spitfire I

Type: interceptor and fighter-bomber
Maker: Supermarine Division of Vickers-Armstrongs Ltd in factories at Southampton, Winchester, Swindon and Castle Bromwich, and numerous subcontractors
Span: 11.23 m (36 ft 10 in)
Length: 9.12 m (29 ft 11 in)
Height: 2.69 m (8 ft 10 in)
Wing area: 22.48 m^2 (242 sq ft)
Weight: maximum 2623 kg (5784 lb); empty 2102 kg (4810 lb)
Powerplant: one 1030-hp Rolls-Royce Merlin II or III V-12 liquid-cooled engine
Performance: maximum speed 571 km/h (355 mph) at 5791 m (19 000 ft); range 636 km (395 miles) operational ceiling 10 363 m (34 000 ft)
Armament: eight 7.7-mm (0.303-in) machine-guns (IA) or four machine-guns and two 20-mm (0.79-in) cannon (IB)
Crew: 1
Production: 1583

Mk VC

Specification similar to Spitfire I except in following particulars:
Height: 3.48 m (11 ft 5 in)
Weight: maximum 3078 kg (6785 lb); empty 2313 kg (5100 lb)
Powerplant: one 1470-hp Rolls-Royce Merlin 45 V-12 liquid-cooled engine
Performance: maximum speed 602 km/h (374 mph) at 3963 m (13 000 ft); range 756 km (470 miles); operational ceiling 11 278 m (37 000 ft)
Armament: two 20-mm (0.79-in) Hispano-Suiza cannon; four 0.303-in (7.7-mm) Browning machine-guns or four 20-mm cannon; 227 kg (500 lb) of bombs
Production: 2447 (6479 all Mk Vs)

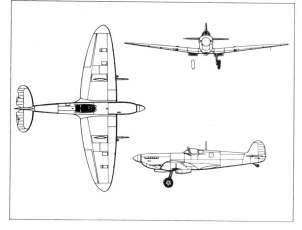

Mk XVI

Specification similar to Spitfire I except in the following particulars:
Span: 9.98 m (32 ft 8 in)
Length: 9.55 m (31 ft 4 in)
Height: 3.86 m (12 ft 8 in)
Wing area: 23.04 m^2 (248 sq ft)
Weight: maximum 3311 kg (7300 lb); empty 2631 kg (5800 lb)
Powerplant: one 1720-hp Packard Merlin 266 liquid-cooled engine
Performance: maximum speed 652 km/h (405 mph) at 6706 m (22 000 ft); range 698 km (434 miles); operational ceiling 12 192 m (40 000 ft)
Armament: two 20-mm (0.79-in) cannon; four 7.7-mm (0.303-mm) machine-guns; provision for 454 kg (1000 lb) of bombs or rockets
Production: 1054

Mk XIV

Specification similar to Spitfire I except in the following particulars:
Length: 9.95 m (32 ft 8 in)
Height: 3.86 m (12 ft 8 in)
Wing area: 22.67 m^2 (244 sq ft)
Weight: maximum 4663 kg (10 280 lb); empty 2994 kg (6600 lb)
Powerplant: one 2050-hp Rolls-Royce Griffon 65 engine
Performance: maximum speed 721 km/h (448 mph) at 7925 m (26 000 ft); range 1368 km (850 miles); operational ceiling 13 564 m (44 500 ft)
Armament: two 20-mm (0.79-in) Hispano Mk II cannon; two 0.5-in (12.7-mm) Browning machine-guns; provision for 454 kg (1000 lb) of bombs
Production: 957 (total Spitfires of all types excluding Seafires 20 351)

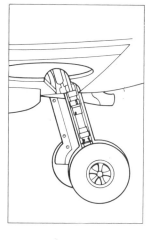

Above: Built to specification F.4/40, DP 845 was a special prototype for the Spitfire III, IV and Griffon-engined XX in succession
Left: A close up of the narrow, outward retracting landing gear of the Spitfire; despite a variety of changes to the powerplant and airframe, the landing gear remained geometrically the same in all marks
Right: The prototype Type 502, a postwar two-seat conversion of the Spitfire 8. Six similar machines went to the Irish Air Corps for pilot training

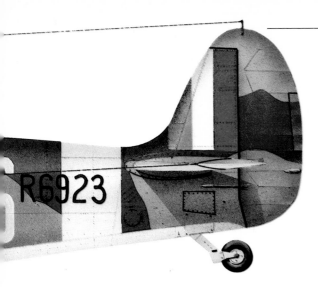

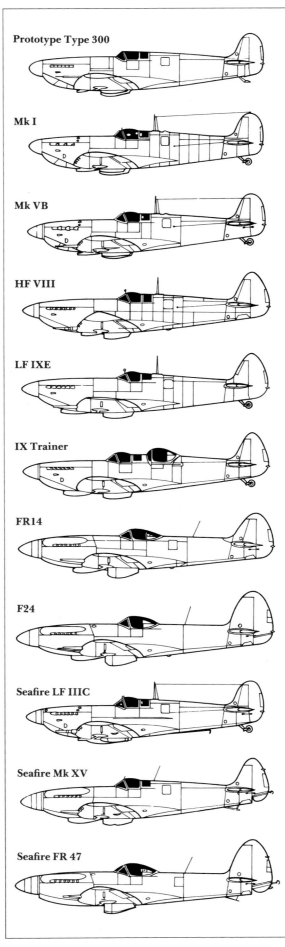

Prototype Type 300

Mk I

Mk VB

HF VIII

LF IXE

IX Trainer

FR14

F24

Seafire LF IIIC

Seafire Mk XV

Seafire FR 47

Far left: The Spitfire V was one of the most widely produced types. This version, the VB, normally received a Merlin 45 or 50, but one captured aircraft was powered by a DB 605A. This aircraft retained its radiator and oil-cooler and with its German engine flew in comparative tests against the Bf 109G. Though slower than the Bf 109 it was more manoeuvrable, had a greater rate of climb and superior ceiling

Left: The changing shape of the Spitfire; not only did the engines become more powerful, but the canopy was improved to better all-round visibility and a whip antenna replaced the earlier mast. Four of the eight machine-guns were replaced by two cannon and aircraft were given underwing points to take bombs or rockets. Despite all these changes the aircraft remained a Spitfire, and one of the best fighters of World War II

Above: A Spitfire IA which was brought up to Mk V standard during the war and subsequently fitted with a non-standard four-blade propeller and six-stub exhausts. The access to the cockpit is open – it allowed pilots to climb quickly into the narrow confine of the cockpit

by the appearance of the Focke-Wulf Fw 190. The superiority of the new German fighter was such that the outclassed Mk V was given the 60-series Merlin as the Mk IX: intended as a temporary expedient, production of this variant reached a total of 5665, mainly LF IXs but including 1255 F IXs and 400 HF IXs. Deliveries began in mid 1942, and in 1944 a new wing was introduced to carry one 12.7-mm (0.5-in) machine-gun and one cannon. Last of the Merlin-powered Spitfire fighters were the 1054 Mk XVIs, which used the 1705-hp Packard-built Merlin 266 and were fitted with a bubble canopy.

Another Mk V development was the Seafire. In 1941 a Mk VB was fitted with an arrester hook for carrier landing trials, and the success of these led to 170 being converted as Seafire Mk IBs, with catapult attachment points and naval equipment for carrier service. A further 372 Mk IICs were purpose-built naval versions of the Spitfire VC, 110 being low-altitude versions with the 1645-hp Merlin 32. The 1250 Seafire IIIs introduced folding wings and had provision for rocket-assisted take-off gear; the powerplant was the Merlin 55.

Further Spitfire variants were based on the Rolls-Royce Griffon engine. First was the F XII, with 1735-hp Griffon III or IV and four-blade propeller, and this was followed by 957 F XIVs with 2050-hp Griffon 65 or 67 and five-blade propeller. Strengthened fuselage and undercarriage and increased fuel capacity distinguished the 100 F XVIII and 200 camera-equipped FR XVIII, and the F 21 (122 built) finally dispensed

with the elliptical wing in favour of a new wing, mounting two cannon, which was also used on the 278 F 21s and 54 F 24s. The last three versions used the Griffon 61 or 85, the latter driving contra-rotating six-blade propellers, similar engines being used by the Seafire F 45, F 46 and F 47. Total Seafire production was 2622 and included 434 F XVs and 232 F XVIIs with Griffon VIs: later models were produced after the war, and only 164 were built before production ended in March 1949. The last F 24 was delivered in February 1948.

The Spitfire's achievements are legion: its exploits during the Battle of Britain have made it one of the most famous of all fighters, and it was the only Allied fighter to remain in continuous production throughout World War II.

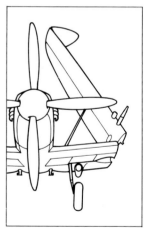

Above: The wingfold on the Mk III Seafire. This modification resulted in a small loss in torsional rigidity and fall-off in performance, but allowed the Spitfire to go to sea and gave the Fleet Air Arm a potent interceptor
Above left: The Seafire F 46, with contra-rotating propellers, was the penultimate version

MS.406, Morane-Saulnier

FIRST FLIGHT 1937

Left: A Morane-Saulnier MS. 406 in Vichy markings; these yellow and red bands distinguished the aircraft as non-combatant, though they were used by the French against the Allies in North Africa and Syria

Below left and right: The MS. 406 was exported to Turkey, Lithuania, Poland and China, though not all reached their destination. The Germans supplied the Finns with numerous MS. 406s, some being re-engined with the Soviet 1300-hp Klimov M-105P and called LaGG-Moranes or Super-Moranes. They saw action in 1944

IN response to a 1934 Armée de l'Air specification, the first prototype MS.405 flew in August 1935 and was followed by a revised second prototype in February 1937, by which time 15 pre-production aircraft had been ordered. Instead of earlier versions of the Hispano-Suiza 12Y engine one pre-production machine was fitted with the 860-hp 12Y-31 engine which incorporated a 20-mm (0.79-in) Hispano-Suiza cannon mounted between the cylinders and firing through the propeller hub, to become the prototype MS.406. Others were modified to become the parachute trials MS.407LP; the MS.408 and 411 which served as prototypes for the Swiss licence-built D-3800 and D-3801 versions; the MS.409 with a new radiator installation; and the MS.410 with four 7.5-mm (0.295-in) MAC 1934 machine-guns in the strengthened wings.

Production for the Armée de l'Air was of the MS.406, with a single machine-gun in each wing, and after evaluation during 1938 a total of 955 were ordered. Construction was carried out by the Ouest, Midi and Centre divisions of SNCA (Société Nationale de Constructions Aéronautiques, the nationalized French aircraft industry) as well as by Morane-Saulnier. However, by September 1939 only 572 had been delivered.

The total had risen to 961 by the end of the year and 1098 by the time of the French surrender in June 1940, which included a number built for export but not delivered. Finland and Turkey each received the 30 they had ordered, but the first 50 of a Polish order for 160 were still in transit when that

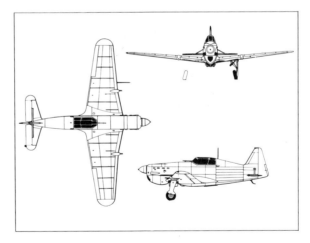

country was occupied by Germany in September 1939. Another 12 for China were taken over by the French on their arrival in Indo-China; 13 for Lithuania and 20 for Yugoslavia were not delivered.

The MS.406 equipped four Groupes de Chasse in France at the start of World War II, and during the months of preliminary skirmishing a number of deficiencies became apparent, particularly in the matter of armament, which proved too light and prone to failure. A few were modified to MS.410 standard with an extra pair of guns. Although the 406 was numerically the most important French fighter, its combat record was poor and by the Armistice it was being replaced by other fighters. The Germans transferred 20 MS.406s to Finland and 36 to Croatia after the occupation.

MS.406

Type: monoplane fighter
Maker: Morane-Saulnier; Société Nationale de Constructions Aéronautiques
Span: 10.61 m (34 ft 9¾ in)
Length: 8.17 m (26 ft 9¾ in)
Height: 3.25 m (10 ft 8 in)
Wing area: 16 m² (172.23 sq ft)
Weight: loaded 2540 kg (5600 lb); empty 1895 kg (4178 lb)
Powerplant: one 860-hp Hispano-Suiza 12Y-31 V-12 liquid-cooled engine
Performance: maximum speed 490 km/h (304.5 mph) at 4500 m (14 764 ft); range 720 km (447 miles); operational ceiling 10 000 m (32 808 ft)
Armament: one 20-mm (0.79-in) Hispano-Suiza cannon; two 7.5-mm (0.295-in) MAC machine-guns
Crew: 1
Production: 1098 (all types)

C.714, Caudron
FIRST FLIGHT 1938

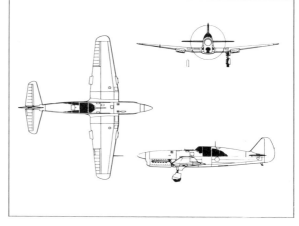

THE Caudron-Renault racers that competed in the French Coupe Deutsch de la Meurthe air races in the early 1930s inspired a whole series of experimental military aircraft characterized by extreme lightness. The C.690 trainer, with a 240-hp Renault six-cylinder inline, was followed in 1936 by the C.710 prototype fighter, powered by a 450-hp Renault 12 RoI. Both of these had fixed landing gear, but the C.713, first flown in December 1937, introduced retractable landing gear. By the following September further refinement had produced the C.714.

This was tested by the Armée de l'Air in the autumn of 1938, and 100 production aircraft were ordered. A great attraction of the type was the primarily wooden construction which required only a minimum of building time. A second order followed for a similar quantity of export aircraft intended for Finland and Yugoslavia, but the Armée de l'Air reconsidered its decision and cancelled its order on the grounds of poor climb-rate.

Meanwhile, a 730-hp Isotta-Fraschini Delta RC40 had been installed in the further revised C.715, subsequently re-designated CR.760, which added a further pair of machine-guns to the four 7.5-mm (0.295-in) weapons carried by the C.714. Two prototypes were tested in early 1940, while a third was given an 800-hp Renault 626 inverted-vee 16-cylinder engine as the CR.770. This was flown briefly in May 1940, but proved to have a faulty engine installation. The projected CR.780, intended to have a 500-hp Renault 468, was never built. These lightweight fighters had shown great promise before the abandonment of the programme, the CR.760 having proved extremely manoeuvrable and reached 540 km/h (335.5 mph) at 5000 m (16 404 ft).

However, production of the C.714 had gone ahead on the strength of a revised order from Finland for 70, though only six had reached Finland when the Winter War against the Soviet Union ended in March 1940. A number were also acquired by the Armée de l'Air, which had received 47 by the beginning of March. These were issued to a Polish unit, GC I/145, assigned to the defence of Paris, and on June 2, 1940, the squadron claimed two Bf 109s shot down. More successes were achieved in the next few days, before the survivors were abandoned as unserviceable.

C.714

Type: lightweight fighter
Maker: Avions Caudron-Renault
Span: 8.95 m (29 ft 4½ in)
Length: 8.53 m (27 ft 11¾ in)
Height: 2.87 m (9 ft 5 in)
Wing area: 12.5 m² (134.55 sq ft)
Weight: loaded 1750 kg (3858 lb); empty 1400 kg (3086 lb)
Powerplant: one 450-hp Renault 12 RoI inverted V-12 air-cooled engine
Performance: maximum speed 490 km/h (304.5 mph) at 4000 m (13 123 ft); range 900 km (559 miles); operational ceiling 9100 m (29 856 ft)
Armament: four 7.5-mm (0.295-in) MAC 1934 M39 machine-guns
Crew: 1
Production: approx 150 completed

D.520, Dewoitine

FIRST FLIGHT 1938

WHEN the D.513 had proved inferior to the prototype of the Morane-Saulnier MS.405, Emile Dewoitine's design bureau began work on a new fighter, the D.520 (the designation reflecting the speed of 520 km/h (323 mph) required by the air ministry and embodied in a January 1937 specification). In March 1937 Dewoitine joined SNCA du Midi, where work was continued, and by the time a government contract was placed in April 1938, the prototype D.520 was nearing completion.

Its first flight came in October 1938, a second prototype appeared in January 1939 and a third flew in March 1939, shortly before the first of a total of 1280 production aircraft were ordered. By April 1940 the quantity had been increased to 2320, including 120 for the Aéronavale, to be delivered at a rate of 350 per month. The production aircraft were longer than the prototypes and carried four instead of two 7.5-mm (0.295-in) machine-guns in the wings.

Unfortunately, a number of problems were experienced with the first production D.520, flown in November 1939: only 13 had been delivered by the end of the year, and it was not until April 1940 that a hasty modification programme had cured all the faults. The result was that D.520s were operational with only one Groupe de Chasse on May 10, when the westward German advance began, though by June 25, with 437 machines completed, four more Groupes had begun operations and another two were in the process of conversion to the new fighter.

The armistice was not the end of the D.520's career. Four Groupes de Chasse and two

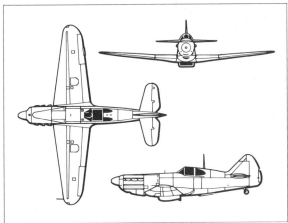

Aéronavale squadrons of the Vichy air forces operated the type in North Africa, and in mid 1941 production of the type was resumed by SNCASE, another 349 being completed, 197 of them with 12Y-49 engines. Further units were equipped with them, and many saw action against the RAF in North Africa and Syria in 1941–42. In March 1943 the Germans occupied the remainder of France, and the D.520 was taken over by Luftwaffe training units, some serving on the Eastern Front and others being allocated to Italy, Romania and Bulgaria. Another change of side came in 1944, when French units were formed to fight in support of the re-occupying Allies, and some remained in service as dual-control trainer conversions until 1953.

D.520

Type: monoplane fighter
Maker: Société Nationale de Constructions Aéronautiques du Midi, de Sud-Est
Span: 10.2 m (33 ft 5½ in)
Length: 8.76 m (28 ft 8¾ in)
Height: 2.57 m (8 ft 5 in)
Wing area: 15.95 m² (171.69 sq ft)
Weight: loaded 2676 kg (5900 lb); empty 2092 kg (4612 lb)
Powerplant: one 920-hp Hispano-Suiza 12Y-45, or 910-hp 12Y-49, V-12 liquid-cooled engine
Performance: maximum speed 535 km/h (332.4 mph) at 5500 m (18 045 ft); range 890 km (553 miles); operational ceiling 11 000 m (36 089 ft)
Armament: one 20-mm (0.79-in) Hispano-Suiza HS 404 cannon; four 7.5-mm (0.295-in) MAC machine-guns
Crew: 1
Production: 786

Bloch 152

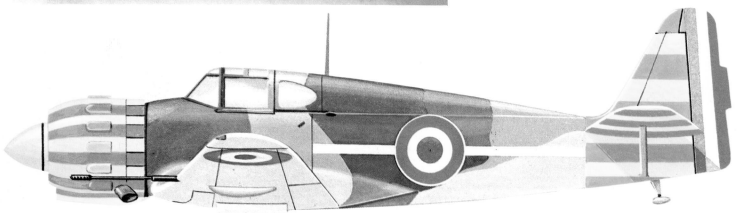

Left: The Bloch MB-151 No 1, the first pre-production machine with close-fitting cowling
Below: An MB-152 in Vichy markings; there were six Groupes de Chasse in unoccupied France equipped with the MB-151 and MB-152. Some 95 machines were modified with long-range tanks to enable them to escape to North Africa – but the plan was discovered by the German monitoring teams

THE air ministry specification of July 1934, which gave rise to the Morane-Saulnier MS.405 and 406 resulted in a number of other prototypes, among them the Marcel Bloch 150. Powered by a 930-hp Gnome-Rhône 14Kfs radial and armed with two wing-mounted HS 404 cannon, the 150 was abandoned after proving unable to take off in July 1936. However, the design was revised during 1937, and with new wings, engine and landing gear the prototype finally flew in September of that year. Performance was modest, but with the Armée de l'Air desperately short of modern fighters three new prototypes using more powerful engines were requested.

The first prototype 151 to fly, with an 870-hp Gnome-Rhône 14N11 and four wing-mounted machine-guns, was one of the pre-production batch, and its first flight in August 1938 was followed in December by that of the first prototype 152. Overheating limited its 1000-hp Gnome-Rhône 14N25's speed to under 500 km/h (311 mph). The second prototype, designated Bloch 153, used a Pratt & Whitney Twin Wasp and flew in April 1939, but the planned Wright Cyclone-powered 154 was never completed.

Deliveries did not begin until the spring of 1939, and although the orders were increased on the outbreak of war, control problems and lack of parts, usually from sabotage, delayed their service introduction, and many of the 151s were relegated to training duties. The 151 order was completed in early 1940, but further modifications were considered necessary before the 152s were considered

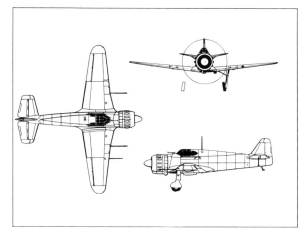

suitable for operational service: orders were reduced again, some being amended to cover a new development, the Bloch 155, which had increased fuel capacity and extra pair of machine-guns. The 157 had the exceptional speed of 709 km/h (441 mph).

Deliveries by the time of the armistice totalled 699, comprising 60 151s, and 639 152s, in addition to the single 153 and nine 155s. In action the 152 proved extremely tough, with amazing ability to survive battle damage. It was sweet to handle, had outstanding manoeuvrability and could even overtake a Bf 109E in a dive. It was also a very steady gun platform. In 1942 the Germans discovered a plan to fit long-range tanks to allow 152s to escape to North Africa.

Bloch 152

Type: monoplane fighter
Maker: Société Nationale de Constructions Aéronautiques de Sud-Ouest
Span: 10.54 m (34 ft 7 in)
Length: 9.1 m (29 ft 10¼ in)
Height: 3.03 m (9 ft 11¼ in)
Wing area: 17.32 m² (186.44 sq ft)
Weight: maximum 2800 kg (6172 lb); empty 2103 kg (4636 lb)
Powerplant: one 1000-hp Gnome-Rhône 14N25 14-cylinder two-row radial
Performance: maximum speed 515 km/h (320 mph) at 4000 m (13 129 ft); range 580 km (360 miles); operational ceiling 10 000 m (32 808 ft)
Armament: two 20-mm (0.79-in) Hispano-Suiza HS 404 cannon; two 7.5-mm (0.295-in) MAC machine-guns
Crew: 1
Production: 639

Blenheim IF, Bristol

FIRST FLIGHT 1935

Left: An AI-equipped Blenheim IF night-fighter of No 614 Squadron. Blenheim bombers were converted using a gun pack built by Southern Railways Ashford factory. With this installation they were known as IF – interim fighters
Below left: The bomber prototype which was as fast as contemporary fighters and had the popular name of *Britain First*
Below: The pilot's position in the bomber. With the gun and radar installation it became the first British night-fighter

IN 1938 it was decided to convert a number of Type 142M Blenheims as Mk IF long-range and night-fighter – a class of aircraft entirely absent from the RAF's procurement plans – by adding ventral gun packs containing four 0.303-in (7.7-mm) Browning machine-guns with 500 rounds of ammunition for each gun.

The packs, complete with magazines were sub-contracted to the Southern Railway workshops at Ashford, Kent, and were carried in addition to the standard bomber armament of one forward-firing Browning in the left wing, and a Vickers K in a retractable dorsal turret. The 200 Blenheims converted in this way equipped a total of 11 home and three overseas fighter squadrons during the early stages of World War II, until their replacement by the Bristol Beaufighter.

The Blenheim was the first night-fighter ever equipped with the British invention of AI (Airborne Interception) radar. It was the only fighter available with room for the bulky and temperamental equipment and its operator, a third crew-member. The first installations, of AI Mk III sets, were made in July 1939. The plan was that Blenheims would be directed to the general vicinity of hostile aircraft detected by ground radar stations, at which point the airborne radar would take over for the final stages of the interception.

The reality was rather different. For a start, the positions supplied by the ground controllers were inevitably imprecise, while ground interference tended to obscure the image received by the AI set, whose range was thus limited to a distance equiva-

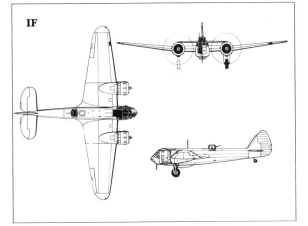

IF

lent to the aircraft's height. Even worse, because of interference from the transmitting aerial, the minimum effective range was around 1.6 km (1 mile), which was of little use in darkness. A great improvement was made with the AI Mk IV set, which had a minimum effective range of 336 m (1100 ft), but the Blenheim was in any case poorly armed and too slow to have much chance of catching an intruder. The first operational kill using AI radar was made in July 1940 by a Blenheim of the experimental Fighter Interception Unit, but there were not many more. Some Blenheim IVs were also fitted with dorsal gun packs and, after brief service as interceptors, were passed to Coastal Command for use against shipping.

Blenheim IVF

Type: long-range and night-fighter
Maker: Bristol Aeroplane Co
Span: 17.17 m (56 ft 4 in)
Length: 12.98 m (42 ft 7 in)
Height: 3.05 m (10 ft)
Wing area: 43.57 m^2 (469 sq ft)
Weight: maximum 6580 kg (14 500 lb); empty 4173 kg (9200 lb)
Powerplant: two 920-hp Bristol Mercury XV 9-cylinder air-cooled radials
Performance: maximum speed 418 km/h (260 mph) at 3658 m (12 000 ft); range 2350 km (1460 miles); operational ceiling 7498 m (24 600 ft)
Armament: five 0.303-in (7.7-mm) Browning machine-guns; one or two 0.303-in Vickers K machine-guns
Crew: 2 to 3
Production: 3983

G.1, Fokker

FIRST FLIGHT 1937

DESIGNED and built in secrecy, and transported to France by boat, the Fokker G.1 was officially unveiled by its manufacturers at the Paris Air Show of November 1936, where its novel configuration aroused considerable interest. A central nacelle housed the pilot and rear gunner, plus the armament of two 23-mm (0.91-in) cannon and two 7.92-mm (0.312-in) machine-guns in the nose and a third machine-gun on a flexible mount aft. The two engines were 750-hp Hispano-Suiza 80-02 radials, and the horizontal tail was carried on booms and incorporated a single tailwheel. Provision for a 400-kg (882-lb) bombload, and for a radio operator to be carried in place of the fuselage fuel tank, gave the aircraft a multirole capability.

The G.1's first flight was made in March 1937

and test flights proved satisfactory, but after a demonstration the following month the Dutch army air service asked for a number of modifications. The principal change requested was to the engines, as standardization was desirable. The prototype was re-engined with 750-hp Pratt & Whitney Twin Wasp Juniors later in 1937, becoming the G.1b, and in November the army air service ordered 36 G.1as, to be of increased overall dimensions, with two Bristol Mercury VIII engines and a revised armament of eight nose and one tail machine-guns, plus a radio operator.

Deliveries began in October 1938. The fourth aircraft had a glazed gondola in place of the bomb bay under the crew nacelle, but this was not adopted and Dornier Do 215s were ordered from

Below left: The first prototype Fokker G.1 which was later rebuilt as a G.1b for the Spanish government but never exported
Below: The first production G.1a in army air force insignia
Below right: A rear view showing the tailcone position. It housed a single machine-gun which was operated by the radio operator. One machine was also fitted with an experimental observation cupola beneath the fuselage

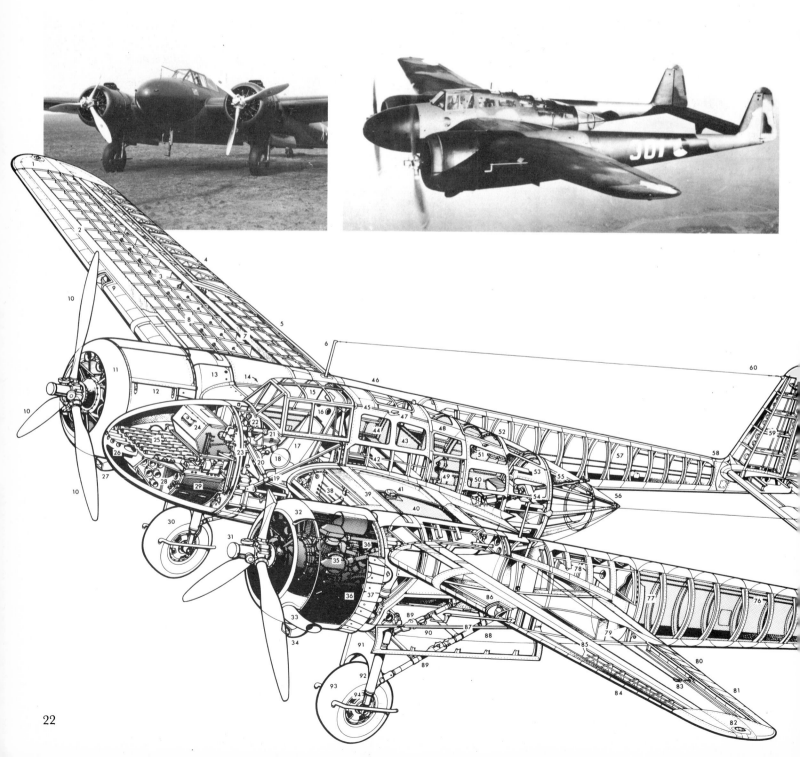

Germany (though never delivered) to fulfil the reconnaissance role. Another 1a had hydraulically operated dive brakes under the outer wings.

Meanwhile, foreign interest in the G.1 had led to the development of the Twin Wasp Junior G.1b, closely based on the original prototype, whose design was finalized in early 1939. The first order, from the Spanish Republicans, was embargoed by the Dutch government (Estonia tried desperately to buy the same aircraft and may have been acting as a Spanish agent), where they were to be fitted with 20-mm (0.79-in) Oerlikon cannon; Sweden ordered 18, with Bofors cannon and machine-guns; and licence production was planned in Denmark. By late 1939 all the 'Estonian' G.1bs had been test-flown, but the two 23-mm Madsen cannon (plus two 7.92-mm FN) were absent from their noses.

On May 10, 1940, when the German invasion began, 23 G.1as were airworthy with the 3rd and 4th Fighter Groups of the 1st Air Regiment, another two having been lost previously. Most were destroyed on the ground, but the former unit succeeded in destroying 14 German bombers on the first day of fighting. Three of the G.1bs were given an armament of four machine-guns.

Before the war ended further development there had been plans to exploit the design's multirole potential. A mock-up was prepared of the four-man G.2, to combine the fighter, bomber and reconnaissance functions; another derivative, the T-6 bomber, would have had an enlarged nacelle with a glazed nose, but German occupation halted progress with these designs.

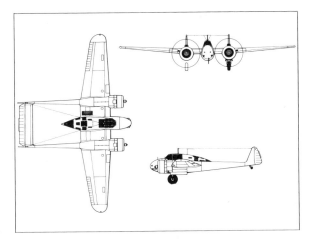

G.1a

Type: heavy fighter and close-support aircraft
Maker: NV Vliegtuigenfabriek Fokker
Span: 17.15 m (56 ft 3 in)
Length: 11.5 m (37 ft 8¾ in)
Height: 3.4 m (11 ft 1¾ in)
Wing area: 38.3 m² (412.2 sq ft)
Weight: loaded 4800 kg (10 582 lb); empty 3360 kg (7407 lb)
Powerplant: two 830-hp Bristol Mercury VIII 9-cylinder air-cooled radials
Performance: maximum speed 475 km/h (295 mph); range 1410 km (876 miles); operational ceiling 9300 m (30 512 ft)
Armament: nine 0.312-in (7.92-mm) FN-Browning machine-guns; 400 kg (880 lb) of bombs
Crew: 2 to 3
Production: 36

G.1

1 Right navigation light
2 Forward spruce-and-ply mainspar
3 Plywood former ribs
4 Fabric-covered welded steel-tube aileron (statically and dynamically balanced)
5 Hydraulically-operated duralumin landing flap
6 Right aerial mast
7 Rear mainspar
8 Control runs
9 Right landing light
10 Three-blade Hamilton Standard two-piston airscrew
11 Cowling spring
12 Nacelle panel quick-release catches
13 Duralumin boom skinning
14 Right fuel tank
15 Centre-hinged canopy roof
16 Pilot's headrest
17 Pilot's adjustable seat
18 Circular vision port
19 Welded chrome-molybdenum steel tube forward fuselage structure
20 Throttle controls
21 Control column
22 Instrument panel
23 Forward bulkhead
24 Ammunition tank (4000 rounds)
25 Battery of eight 7.9-mm (0.311-in) FN-Browning M-36 machine-guns
26 Gun ports
27 Carburettor air intake
28 Gun support frame
29 Case collector box
30 Right mainwheel
31 Airscrew pitch-control mechanism
32 Exhaust collector ring
33 Exhaust pipe
34 Carburettor air intake
35 Bristol Mercury VIII air-cooled radial engine
36 Engine bearers
37 Controllable cooling gills
38 Mainspar inboard section (integral with fuselage nacelle)
40 Left fuel tank
41 Fuel filler cap
42 Rear spar carry-through
43 Aft bulkhead
44 Centre fuselage (accommodating radio equipment)
45 Plywood monocoque fuselage nacelle centre section
46 Right tailboom
47 Hinged entry hatch
48 Duralumin rear fuselage construction
49 Rear gunner's couch
50 Gimbal-suspended 7.9-mm (0.311-in) FN-Browning M-36 machine-gun
51 Ammunition racks
52 Hinged entry hatch
53 Handholds
54 Gun support bar
55 Inward-hinged tailcone section
56 Perspex tailcone
57 All-metal monocoque tailboom structure
58 Tailboom/fin fairing fillet
59 Integral duralumin tailfin structure
60 Aerials
61 Welded chrome molybdenum steel-tube fabric covered rudder
62 Rudder tab
63 Fabric-covered steel-tube elevator
64 Elevator hinge fairing
65 Elevator tab
66 Tailwheel leg fairing
67 Swivelling tailwheel
68 Dural tailplane structure (duraplat sheet skinning)
69 Steel-tube elevator structure (fabric skinning)
70 Duraplat tailfin skinning
71 Tail navigation light
72 Left rudder
73 Rudder tab
74 Rudder hinge fairing
75 Metal monocoque tailboom construction
76 Control runs
77 Bolted joint between wooden (integral with wing centre section) and duralumin monocoque tailboom portions
78 Wooden tailboom strujcture
79 Wing rearspar
80 Aileron tab (left side only)
81 Left aileron (fabric-covered welded steel-tube)
82 Left navigation light
83 Aileron control linkage
84 Leading-edge construction
85 Forward spruce-and-ply mainspar
86 Left landing light
87 Pitot tube
88 Mainwheel doors
89 Mainwheel retraction members
90 Mainwheel well
91 Mainwheel leg cover plate
92 Mainwheel leg
93 Left mainwheel
94 Shock absorbers

Gladiator, Gloster

FIRST FLIGHT 1934

THE 1930 Air Ministry specification for a 402-km/h (250-mph) four-gun fighter anticipated trials of the resulting aircraft taking place in 1932. Unfortunately for a number of firms which responded quickly the recommended powerplant (the steam-cooled Rolls-Royce Goshawk) proved a failure, and the trials were postponed repeatedly.

This worked to the advantage of Gloster, which was too busy with the Gauntlet to respond to the new specification until 1933, when it was decided to develop the Gauntlet to meet the requirement. Strengthened single-bay wings, a single-strut landing gear with Dowty internally-sprung wheels, and a more powerful Bristol Mercury engine were expected to provide the necessary improvement in performance. The armament requirement was met by adding to the two Vickers on the fuselage sides a pair of drum-fed Lewis guns in fairings under the lower wings. The prototype, designated SS.37, flew in September 1934, and with a 645-hp Mercury VIS was subjected to official trials the following year. It was selected for production as the Gladiator in July 1935.

Production Gladiators featured an enclosed cockpit and four belt-fed Browning machine-guns. Deliveries did not begin until early 1937. Nevertheless, delays in the supply of more modern fighters led to the last two dozen of the 231 Gladiator Is that had been ordered being modified to Mk II standard, and another 350 Mk IIs being ordered. The main change was the replacement of the Mk I's 840-hp Mercury IX by an 890-hp Mercury VIIIA. By this time the Royal Navy had selected the Gladiator as a replacement for the Hawker Nimrod, and 98 Gladiator IIs were completed as Sea Gladiators with arrester hooks, ventral dinghy and other naval equipment.

Despite its obsolescence, it saw combat on almost every front during the first two years of World War II, and won an enduring reputation.

Gladiators saw their first action in 1938, with the Chinese air force and with the RAF in Palestine. Two of the AAF squadrons went to France towards the end of 1939, where their aircraft were lost or destroyed, like the Belgian Gladiators, in the face of the German invasion of May 1940. The previous month, Gladiators had taken part in the resistance to the invasion of Norway, the RAF's 163 Squadron achieving fame for its attempts to operate the fighter from the frozen Lake Lesjaskogsvatn after flying in from HMS *Glorious*.

Subsequent action for the type came in the contrasting conditions prevailing in the Mediterranean, the Middle East and North and East Africa, with Australian and South African units.

Although home-based Gladiators had been relegated to second-line duties by the end of 1940, a few of the naval version remained in service aboard HMS *Courageous* and *Eagle* until 1941. It was the Sea Gladiators that provided the most famous individual examples. In June 1940, four Sea Gladiators were assembled from crated, spare airframes on Malta. For three weeks, with only three of the fighters serviceable at any one time, they provided the island's only fighter defences, becoming known in the process as *Faith, Hope* and *Charity*.

Above: The third of the first batch of 23 production aircraft in 1936
Right: A briefing for Fleet Air Arm pilots on the wing of a Sea Gladiator
Centre: A Gladiator banks to the right, with full 'top rudder'. The cockpit position gave the pilot fair visibility
Far right: A pre-war Gladiator patrols the Suez Canal – its serial number has been deleted by the censor
Top right: The Gladiator has the distinction of being the last biplane fighter to serve in the RAF

24

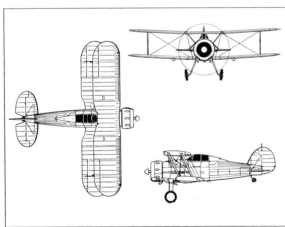

Gladiator II

Type: biplane fighter
Maker: Gloster Aircraft Co Ltd
Span: 9.83 m (32 ft 3 in)
Length: 8.36 m (27 ft 5 in)
Height: 3.23 m (10 ft 7 in)
Wing area: 30.01 m² (323 sq ft)
Weight: loaded 2206 kg (4863 lb); empty 1745 kg (3847 lb)
Powerplant: one 890-hp Bristol Mercury VIIIA 9-cylinder air-cooled radial
Performance: maximum speed 414 km/h (257 mph) at 4450 m (14 600 ft); range 715 km (444 miles);

operational ceiling 10 211 m (33 501 ft)
Armament: four 0.303-in (7.7-mm) Browning machine-guns
Crew: 1
Production: 768 (all types)

Fulmar, Fairey

FIRST FLIGHT 1940

IN late 1937, delays in the development of the Blackburn Roc led the Royal Navy to seek another fighter. The prime requirements were accommodation for a radio operator and long range, rather than speed, as its duties were expected to be restricted to escorting strike aircraft and dealing with enemy reconnaissance aircraft.

The Fairey P.4/34 light bomber proved readily adaptable to the Royal Navy's purpose. Among the changes needed for naval operations were an increase in fuel capacity to provide the necessary range, the addition of catapult hooks and an arrester hook, and wing-folding mechanism.

The powerplant remained a Rolls-Royce Merlin and armament was to be the new standard of eight 0.303-in (7.7-mm) machine-guns: the prototype

bombers had their bomb racks buried in the wings, so accommodation was readily available for the guns and a generous 750 rounds of ammunition for each.

One of the two P.4/34s was converted to become the prototype of the new fighter, and with the name Fulmar the first production example made its maiden flight in January 1940. Performance with a 1060-hp RM3M (modified Merlin III) was not encouraging, the maximum speed achieved on official trials being 411 km/h (255.4 mph) at 732 m (2400 ft). Climb rate and ceiling were equally disappointing, but handling and manoeuvrability were good, and by April the first Merlin III-powered production Fulmar had been completed. By the end of 1940, 159 had been delivered, and

Above: The Fulmar with its long greenhouse canopy proved to be slow and vulnerable to attack from the rear. However in more specialized roles, such as night intrusion and Airborne Interception radar training, it enjoyed some success. It also did well against Italian aircraft

Above right: A Fulmar II in April 1942; this aircraft is armed with eight machine-guns, but some machines received heavier guns for attacking the larger German bombers

Fulmar I

1 Right navigation light
2 Deck-handling hold
3 Right wingtip
4 Aileron control linkage
5 Aileron torque tube
6 Underwing pitot head
7 Right wing gun ports
8 Aileron control rod
9 Wing rib
10 Right aileron
11 Aileron trim tab
12 Right flap
13 Flap operating mechanism
14 Trailing-edge wing-fold mechanism
15 Wing-fold hinge line
16 Camera gun access
17 Camera gun left
18 Three-blade Rotol constant-speed propeller
19 Spinner
20 Coolant header tank
21 1080-hp Rolls-Royce Merlin VIII engine
22 Coolant pipes
23 Ejector exhaust mainfold
24 Engine bearing frame support
25 Engine accessories
26 Propeller speed control unit
27 Engine bearer strut
28 Oil/coolant intake
29 Right mainwheel fairing
30 Right mainwheel
31 Carburettor air intake
32 Intake duct
33 Oil radiator (centre)
34 Coolant radiators (left and right)
35 Firewall bulkhead
36 Rudder pedal mounting
37 Control column
38 Exhaust glare shield
39 Oil tank
40 Windscreen
41 Reflector gunsight
42 Rear-view mirror
43 Aft-sliding cockpit canopy
44 Sling shackle
45 Pilot's fire extinguisher (hand-held)
46 Pilot's seat
47 Seat harness
48 Arrester hook release
49 Underfloor control linkage

50 Fuselage/main spar attachment
51 No 1 fuselage frame
52 Transmitter/receiver
53 Accumulator
54 Dry battery
55 Canopy track
56 Receiver
57 Fuselage fuel tank
58 Hydraulic header tank
59 Aerial mast
60 Observer's auxiliary instrument panel (ASI/altimeter)
61 ARI.5003 indicator
62 Indicator cradle
63 Fire extinguisher
64 Sliding chart table
65 Oxygen cylinders, (left and right)
66 Observer's swivel seat
67 Oxygen supply tube
68 ARI.5003 transmitter unit
69 Compass mounting
70 Compass
71 Observer's canopy section (forward-sliding)
72 Fixed aft canopy
73 Dorsal identification light
74 Aerial lead-in
75 Break-out window panels
76 Signalling lamp stowage
77 Signal cartridge stowage
78 CO$_2$ cylinder (dinghy inflation)
79 First-aid kit
80 Dinghy stowage
81 Jettisonable panel
82 Aerials
83 Aft canopy fairing
84 Right tailplane
85 Right elevator
86 Elevator trim tab
87 Fin leading edge
88 Fin structure
89 Rudder trim tab control
90 Rudder upper hinge
91 Rudder frame
92 Rudder trim tab
93 Rear formation light
94 Rear navigation light
95 Tail cone
96 Rudder lower hinge
97 Aft fuselage frame (No 22)
98 Rudder pivot
99 Elevator cross-shaft control
100 Elevator trim tab

101 Elevator frame
102 Tailplane structure
103 Fixed tailwheel
104 Tailwheel shock-absorber
105 Fuselage frame (No 20)/tailfin attchment
106 Rudder cables
107 Dinghy release cord (external)
108 Fuselage structure
109 Elevator cables
110 Arrester hook tunnel
111 Arrester hook
112 Catapult spool
113 Arrester hook pivot
114 Arester hook shock-absorbing damper
115 TR.1133/1143 aerial
116 Sea marker flares/smoke-float chute
117 Flare/float chute
118 Entry foot/handholds
119 Aft cockpit floor level
120 Wingroot fillet
121 Flap section
122 Flap structure
123 Left aileron trim tab
124 Aileron frame
125 Deck-handling hold
126 Left navigation light
127 Outer wing ribs
128 Rear spar
129 Forweard spar
130 Leading-edge ribs
131 Four 0.303-in (7.7-mm) Browning machine-guns
132 Machine-gun barrels (blast tubes omitted)
133 Gun ports
134 Diagonal bracing ribs
135 Ammunition box stowage
136 Strengthened wing rib (No 10)
137 Diaphragms
138 Outer wing (hinge) diagonal frame
139 Stringers
140 Rear spar attachment
141 Inboard rib
142 Intermediate (oinboard) strut
143 Landing gear retraction link
144 Left mainwheel well
145 Radiator shutters
146 Mainwheel inner fairing
147 Rib cut-outs
148 Landing gear catch/lock
149 Landing gear pivot

150 Toggle spring
151 Retraction lever
152 Wing hinge
153 Landing gear rear bearing strut
154 Landing lamp
155 Mainwheel leg outer cylinder
156 Side bracing
157 Mainwheel leg fairing
158 Sliding member
159 Mainwheel fairing
160 Left mainwheel

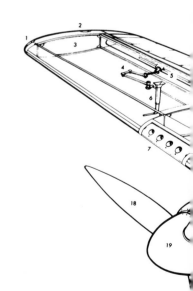

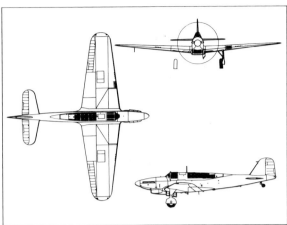

Fulmar II

Type: shipboard fighter
Maker: Fairey Aviation Ltd
Span: 14.14 m (46 ft 4¾ in)
Length: 12.24 m (40 ft 2 in)
Height: 4.3 m (14 ft 1¼ in)
Wing area: 31.77 m² (342 sq ft)
Weight: loaded 4387 kg (9672 lb); empty 3924 kg (8651 lb)
Powerplant: one 1300-hp Rolls-Royce Merlin 30 V-12 liquid-cooled engine
Performance: maximum speed 438 km/h (272 mph) at 2210 m (7251 ft); range 1255 km (780 miles); operational ceiling 8291 m (27 201 ft)
Armament: eight 0.303-in (7.7-mm) Browning and one 0.303-in Vickers K machine-guns; light bombs
Crew: 2
Production: 602 (both models)

one of these had been completed as a Fulmar II, with 1300-hp Merlin 30 engine and a 159-kg (350-lb) reduction in maximum weight. These changes resulted in a slightly improved level speed and a considerably better rate of climb, so from the beginning of 1941, production switched to the Mk II, almost 450 of this model being built out of a production total of 602. Approximately 100 of these were converted to the night-fighter role, with Airborne Interception radar, and others were completed with provision for four 12.7-mm (0.5-in) Brownings instead of the eight 0.303-in weapons which had proved ineffective against German anti-shipping aircraft.

The type's relatively low speed made a rearward-firing gun desirable, and many Fulmars were so fitted with a pillar-mounted machine-gun, while most Mk IIs had provision for a drop-tank or light bombload to be carried under the fuselage.

The first Fulmars to enter service joined 806 Squadron in June 1940, and the type eventually equipped 14 first-line squadrons. It served aboard the aircraft carriers *Illustrious*, *Ark Royal*, *Formidable*, *Victorious*, *Argus*, *Furious* and *Indomitable*, on Fighter Catapult Ships and various shore stations.

The night-fighter conversions were used mainly for training. The Fulmar's shipboard service as a day fighter had ended by mid 1942, when the last examples were replaced by Seafires, though a few remained in service with shore-based fighter squadrons until the following spring. In 1945 it was replaced by the Firefly.

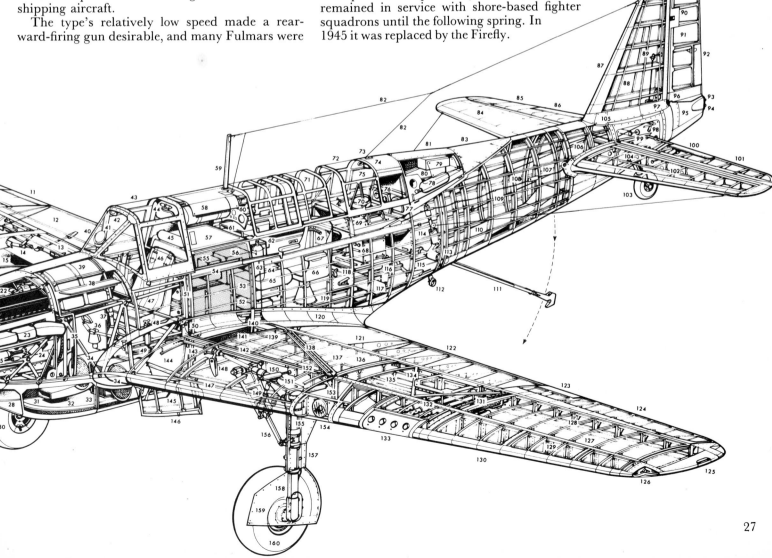

Defiant, Boulton Paul
FIRST FLIGHT 1937

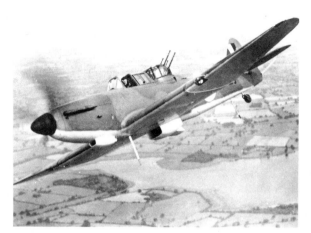

IN April 1935 the Air Ministry issued a specification for a two-seat fighter with the endurance to fly standing patrols, a performance comparable to that of contemporary single-seat fighters, and an armament of multiple machine-guns in a powered turret. Boulton Paul had done considerable work on aircraft gun turrets, and their proposal, along with that of Hawker, was accepted. Although the prototype Defiant did not fly until August 1937, 87 production aircraft were ordered in April of that year, and in February and May, 1938, a further 363 were ordered.

The prototype Hawker Hotspur was not completed until mid 1938, and no orders were placed. The Defiant turret carried four Brownings with 600 rounds per gun; elevation and traverse were hydraulically powered, and fairings fore and aft were automatically retracted to allow the guns to pass.

The first prototype Defiant, K8310, with a 1030-hp Merlin I engine, showed a top speed of 486 km/h (302 mph), but the second prototype, K8320, did not fly until May 1939. Deliveries of production aircraft were only beginning at the start of World War II: 264 Squadron, the first to use the type, did not receive them until December 1939.

The Defiant had been intended to fly standing patrols, using its guns to attack bombers from below, but the shortage of fighters in May 1940 led to it being used as a normal interceptor. It enjoyed some early success in this role when flown in company with Hawker Hurricanes. Once the German pilots became aware of the turrets, they attacked head-on; heavy losses were suffered and

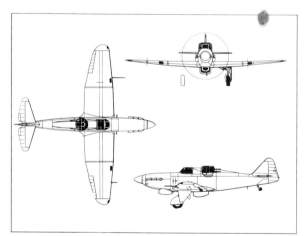

the aircraft was withdrawn from the Battle of Britain. They were then switched to night-fighting, and by May 1941 seven night-fighter squadrons were equipped with Defiants, but without radar.

Meanwhile, by the summer of 1940 another 480 Mk Is had been ordered, but from May 1941 production switched to the Mk II. The last of the Mk Is ordered were completed as Mk IIs with the 1280-hp Merlin XX engine. Small airborne interception (AI) radar sets had been developed by 1941, and towards the end of the year AI Mk IV and Mk VI sets began to be installed in Defiants.

From mid 1942 Defiants were relegated to other duties, including target towing, gunnery training and air-sea rescue searches. The last 40 Mk IIs were completed as TT.I target tugs.

Defiant I

Type: two-seat fighter
Maker: Boulton Paul Aircraft
Span: 11.99 m (39 ft 4 in)
Length: 10.77 m (35 ft 4 in)
Height: 3.45 m (11 ft 4 in)
Wing area: 23.23 m² (250 sq ft)
Weight: maximum 3900 kg (8600 lb); empty 2757 kg (6078 lb)
Powerplant: one 1030-hp Rolls-Royce Merlin III V-12 liquid-cooled engine
Performance: maximum speed 489 km/h (304 mph) at 5182 m (17 000 ft); range 748 km (465 miles); service ceiling 9251 m (30 350 ft)
Armament: four 0.303-in (7.7-mm) Browning machine-guns
Crew: 2
Production: 723

Potez 63

FIRST FLIGHT 1936

THE Armée de l'Air's 1934 specification for a twin-engined three-seat fighter envisaged an aircraft capable of operating as a two-seat day and night interceptor or escort fighter and as a command fighter with the third man aboard. By April 1936, Potez had flown their model 63.01 (subsequently re-designated 630.1) prototype designed to meet this requirement.

Subsequent derivatives of the basic design included ground-attack and reconnaissance aircraft, but the fighter developments were based on the first and second prototypes. The latter was completed in March 1937 and designated 631.01, being powered by two 580-hp Gnome-Rhône 14Mars engines in place of the earlier model's similarly-rated Hispano-Suiza 14Hbs.

In 1937 Potez was absorbed by the Nord (northern) division of the nationalized French aircraft industry, and received production orders for 80 P.630s and 140 P.631s. The armament originally specified was two 20-mm (0.79-in) Hispano-Suiza cannon in the nose, and a 7.5-mm (0.295-in) machine-gun on a flexible mount in the rear of the crew compartment. However, shortages of the cannon led to early examples having a nose battery of four machine-guns – either way, this was rather light armament for such a big aircraft.

Deliveries of the 631 began in 1938, and by the end of the year two night-fighter squadrons had been equipped with the type. Unfortunately, the Hispano-Suiza engines that powered the 630 proved unreliable, and this model was relegated to training duties, being replaced in operational units

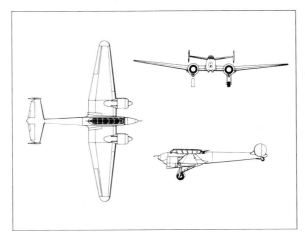

by the 631, orders for which had been increased to a total of 210. In pursuit of the command fighter idea, small numbers of 631s were allocated to each of 20 single-seat fighter squadrons, while others formed autonomous squadrons. Early in 1940 it was decided to augment the 631's armament by the addition of three guns under each wing.

When Germany invaded in May 1940, eight squadrons were equipped with the Potez 631, all but one in northern France. During the resistance to the German invasion some of these engaged in ground-attack missions, suffering heavy losses, while others were mistaken for Bf 110s and shot down by Allied fighters. The bulk of the survivors remained in the occupied zone after the armistice, though some were evacuated to Tunisia.

Potez 631

Type: multirole fighter
Maker: Société Nationale de Constructions Aéronautiques du Nord
Span: 16 m (52 ft 6 in)
Length: 11.07 m (36 ft 3¾ in)
Height: 3.6 m (11 ft 9¾ in)
Wing area: 32.70 m² (352 sq ft)
Weight: loaded 4500 kg (9921 lb); empty 2960 kg (6526 lb)
Powerplant: two 660-hp Gnome-Rhône 14M 14-cylinder two-row radials
Performance: maximum speed 445 km/h (276.5 mph) at 4000 m (13 123 ft); range 1220 km (758 miles); operational ceiling 9000 m (29 528 ft)
Armament: two 20-mm (0.79-in) Hispano-Suiza cannon; seven 7.5-mm (0.295-in) MAC 1934 machine-guns
Crew: 2 to 3
Production: approx 1360 (all types)

Above: The Potez 63.0 No 02; the first prototype had demonstrated its good flying qualities when it landed safely after the loss of one engine
Far left: One of the two 630s purchased by the Swiss in February 1938. Other buyers included Czechoslovakia and the Finns. Potez 633s went to Romania, China and Greece
Left: A war-weary Potez 63-11, the mass-produced reconnaissance version, showing the glazed nose

Havoc, Douglas

FIRST FLIGHT 1940

IN the second half of 1940 the first Douglas DB-7 bombers began to arrive in Britain, where they were named Boston. The Boston I (DB-7) was used for training, and the Mks II (DB-7A) and III (DB-7B) were distinguished by 1200-hp Pratt & Whitney R-1830 Twin Wasp and 1600-hp Wright R-2600 Cyclone engines respectively.

The most common conversion involved the replacement of the glazed bombing nose with a solid nose housing eight or twelve 7.7-mm (0.303-in) Browning machine-guns, along with Airborne Interception Mk IV or V radar sets; approximately 100 each of the Havoc Mk I (R-1830, small fin) and Mk II (R-2600, large fin) were produced. In addition, a number of Havoc IVs – later Havoc I (Intruder) – retained the glazed nose and bomb

bay and were used as night intruder aircraft.

While only one squadron, No 85, operated the Havoc as a normal night-fighter, using the type from early 1941 until September 1942, considerable effort was devoted to the development of less conventional interception techniques. The first of these involved the use of the Long Aerial Mine, or 'Pandora', which consisted of a small explosive charge suspended on a 610-m (2000-ft) length of piano wire attached to a small parachute. The idea was that curtains of these mines should be dropped in the path of approaching bombers: on snagging a wing, the parachute would drag the mine onto the aircraft, where it would explode.

No 93 Squadron was formed to operate the Havoc I (Pandora) at the end of 1940, and

Top: Bomber turned night-fighter; the first Douglas DB-7s were an ex-French contract that was diverted to Britain in 1940. Radars were then still bulky but the DB-7 could carry one as well as heavy armament
Above left: A Douglas Havoc II with 12-gun nose and AI.IV radar in October 1941
Above: Fresh from the factory, one of the first DB-7s in 1939
Above right: An A-20 Havoc at a USAAF training base

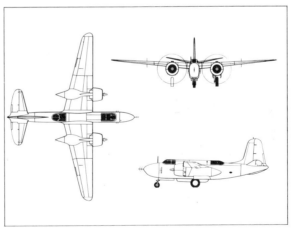

P-70

Type: night-fighter
Maker: Douglas Aircraft Co
Span: 18.7 m (61 ft 4 in)
Length: 14.5 m (47 ft 7 in)
Height: 5.36 m (17 ft 7 in)
Wing area: 43.11 m² (464 sq ft)
Weight: loaded 9645 kg (21 263 lb); empty 7272 kg (16 032 lb)
Powerplant: two 1600-hp Wright R-2600-11 14-cylinder two-row radials
Performance: maximum speed 529 km/h (329 mph) at 4267 m (14 000 ft); range 1706 km (1060 miles); operational ceiling 8611 m (28 250 ft)
Armament: four 20-mm (0.79-in) cannon
Crew: 2
Production: 60

although one probable and one definite kill were claimed, the device proved both ineffective and dangerous to use. Accordingly, towards the end of 1941 the squadron was disbanded to form one of ten flights operating the Havoc I (Turbinlite).

The Turbinlite was a 2700-million candlepower searchlight mounted in the nose of an unarmed Havoc. This time the plan was to use the radar to locate a target, then illuminate it with the search-light, whereupon an accompanying Hurricane could shoot it down. Although 70 Havocs were modified to use the device, the difficulty of co-ordinating Havoc and Hurricane at night, and the ease with which the target could escape the beam, meant that by the time Turbinlite squadrons were disbanded in January 1943 only two enemy aircraft

plus a Stirling had been destroyed, while 17 Havocs had been lost in accidents.

The RAF's use of the Havoc inspired the USAAF to order similar conversions while awaiting the Northrop P-61 Black Widow. Accordingly, 63 A-20s were given flame-damping exhausts, matt black finish and British AI-IV radar to become P-70s. These were armed with four 20-mm (0.79-in) cannon in a ventral tray. The cannon were replaced by six 12.7-mm (0.5-in) machine-guns in the P-70A-1. Sub-sequent models had a similar armament mounted in the nose. These included 65 P-70A-2s and 106 P-70Bs, the latter using SCR-520 radar.

Some of the earlier conversions saw operational service in the Pacific, throughout 1943–44, but most were used for crew training.

Beaufighter, Bristol

FIRST FLIGHT 1940

IN the autumn of 1938 the Bristol company suggested a fighter version of their new Beaufort torpedo bomber. The conversion involved using Hercules instead of Taurus engines, with propellers of increased diameter, and redesigning the entire fuselage. The pilot sat centrally in a very short nose. Four prototypes were ordered in 1939, the first flying in July, 1940.

Production of the Beaufighter I, with 1560-hp Hercules III or XI, reached 915, while another 450 Mk IIs used the 1280-hp Rolls-Royce Merlin XX to guard against the possible shortage of the Hercules. An early modification was the provision of six 7.7-mm (0.303-in) machine-guns in the wings (four on the right, two on the left), and after the first 400 had been completed a belt feed was introduced for the cannon. Other modifications were aimed at curing problems of stability, particularly evident in the Mk II, and after various solutions had been tried, dihedral was added to the tailplane.

By early 1942 the Mk VI was in production, with 1595-hp Hercules VI or XVI engines. A total of 1732 Mk VIs were built, and of these 50 were torpedo-carrying conversions designated Mk VI (ITF) as interim torpedo fighters. Dive-brakes were fitted, and in the 2205 production TF.Xs that followed, low-altitude Hercules XVII engines were used and a torpedo-aimer's position was provided just aft of the pilot's cockpit.

The Beaufighter X was frequently equipped with wing racks for rockets or bombs, as was the

Below left: A Beaufighter TF. X converted to a (TT.10) target tug after the war
Below: A Beaufighter Mk II in overall black with wing and nose mounted AI. Mk IV radar for night interception. The 'Beau' was a very effective night-fighter with a big enough fuselage to take radar and sufficient range to stay airborne for long periods
Bottom: A well-used Bristol Beaufighter VIF takes off in North Africa. It appears to have a non-standard nose, with a large ram inlet in the centre instead of a camera or radar aerial

final British production version, the Mk XI, which dispensed with the torpedo capability: 163 Mk XIs were built. When production by the Government Aircraft Factory began in Australia in 1943 the designation Beaufighter 21 was used. Powerplant was two Hercules XVIII engines, and wing armament was changed to four 12.7-mm (0.5-in) machine-guns; otherwise the 364 built were based on the Mk X, but without the torpedo capacity.

The Beaufighter's initial service was as a night-fighter. The first squadron deliveries were made in September 1940. AI Mk IV airborne interception radar was installed as sets became available. From early 1942 the centimetric AI Mk VII and VIII were installed, with the aerial in thimble fairings on Mk VIF night-fighters. By early 1943 four United States Army Air Force night-fighter squadrons were operating Beaufighters alongside RAF units in the Mediterranean.

Meanwhile, the Mk IC had entered service with Coastal Command in early 1941, the night-fighter designation being amended to Beaufighter IF. The Mk IC dispensed with the wing armament in favour of additional fuel tanks, roughly two-fifths of the Mk Is being adapted in this way. All the Mk IIs were delivered as night-fighters, but 693 Mk VICs had the extra wing fuel tanks, and many of these were also given the Vickers K gun in the rear cockpit that became standard on the TF.X.

The range of armament options made the Beaufighter a potent ground-attack and anti-shipping aircraft, while its gun armament was one of the heaviest carried by any wartime fighter.

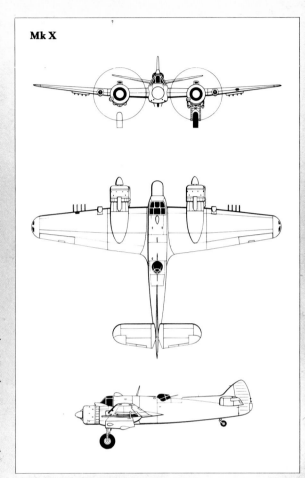

Mk X

Beaufighter IF

Type: multirole fighter
Maker: Bristol Aeroplane Co
Span: 17.63 m (57 ft 10 in)
Length: without radar 12.6 m (41 ft 4 in)
Height: 4.83 m (15 ft 10 in)
Wing area: 46.73 m² (503 sq ft)
Weight: maximum 9470 kg (21 100 lb); empty 6382 kg (14 070 lb)
Powerplant: two 1560-hp Bristol Hercules III or XI 14-cylinder sleeve-valve radials
Performance: maximum speed 520 km/h (323 mph) at 4572 m (15 000 ft); range 1883 km (1170 miles); operational ceiling 8077 m (26 500 ft)
Armament: four 20-mm (0.79-in) Hispano cannon; six 0.303-in (7.7-mm) Browning machine-guns
Crew: 2
Production: 525 (5564 all types)

CR.42 Falco, Fiat

FIRST FLIGHT 1939

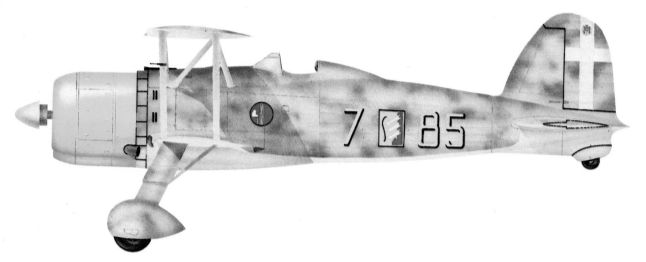

THE last of Celestino Rosatelli's classic biplane fighters retained the characteristic lines of his CR.32, from which it was developed during the late 1930s via the experimental CR.33, 40 and 41. By early 1939, when test flights of the prototype Falco began, biplane fighters were already something of an anachronism. However, manoeuvrability, undoubtedly one of the CR.42's strong points, was a prime consideration in the Regia Aeronautica, as was an open cockpit. Production was authorized, despite the fact that a top speed of 440 km/h (273 mph) and an armament of only two machine-guns – one 7.7-mm (0.303-in) and one 12.7-mm (0.5-in) – must have appeared unlikely to prove adequate in combat.

Substantial numbers were exported: 50 went to Hungary, 34 to Belgium, and 72 to Sweden, where they were designated J 11 and served until 1945.

On June 10, 1940, Italy joined Germany in declaring war on the Allies. By this time over 300 Falcos were operational. Following the armistice between France and Germany the Corpo Aereo Italiano was formed to assist the Luftwaffe in its attempted destruction of British air power. Including 50 Falcos on its strength, the corps moved to Belgium in October 1940, but only two missions were mounted and little was achieved.

The Falco saw more extensive service as a bomber escort in the Mediterranean and as a ground-attack aircraft in North Africa, in the latter role being fitted with tropical equipment and wing racks for two 100-kg (220-lb) bombs and given the

Above: The Fiat CR.42 in standard desert camouflage with unit markings. The last remaining example of the Falco is in England – it was shot down during the Battle of Britain, repaired and test flown

Above right: The ICR.42, an experimental floatplane version

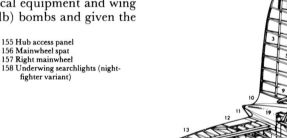
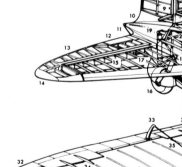

CR.42

1 Rudder balance
2 Rudder upper hinge
3 Rudder frame
4 Rudder post
5 rudder hinge
6 Tailfin structure
7 Tailfin front spar
8 Tailfin frame support
9 Rudder actuating hinge
10 Tailcone
11 Tail navigation light
12 Elevator tab
13 Right elevator
14 Elevator balance
15 Tailplane structure
16 Fixed tailwheel
17 Hinged tailwheel spat
18 Tailwheel leg assembly
19 Tailwheel shock absorber
20 Fuselage end post frame
21 Fuselage/tailfin frames
22 Tailfin leading edge
23 Left elevator
24 Elevator balance
25 Left tailplane
26 Rudder cable turnbuckles
27 Fuselage dorsal decking formers
28 Elevator tab control cables
29 Fuselage upper frame
30 Fuselage fabric stringers
31 Lifting point
32 Right aileron
33 Aileron hinge
34 Aileron leading-edge balances
35 Aileron control cable
36 Wing fabric covering
37 Right upper wingtip
38 Right navigation light
39 Aileron control cable turnbuckle
40 Aileron control cable run
41 Wing ribs
42 Wing rear spar
43 Fuselage framework
44 Elevator control rod linkage
45 Rudder cables
46 Fuselage cross-frame members
47 Pilot's headrest fairing
48 Pilot's headrest
49 Cockpit coaming
50 Oxygen cylinder
51 Fire extinguisher

52 Pilot's seat
53 Compressed air cylinder
54 Air cleansing filter
55 Compressor
56 Pilot's seat support frame
57 Rudder bar assembly
58 Control column
59 Instrument panel
60 Gunsight
61 Windscreen
62 Windshield frame
63 Pilot's entry handhold
64 Wing structure
65 Generator for underwing searchlights (night-fighter variant)
66 Fuselage/upper wing rear strut (aileron cable run)
67 Interplane strut attachment
68 Upper wing rear spar
69 Internal cross-brace wires
70 Wing ribs
71 Left aileron
72 Aileron leading-edge balances
73 Aileron hinge
74 Interplane outer strut attachment
75 Wing outer ribs
76 Left upper wingtip
77 Left navigation light
78 Wing leading-edge
79 Upper wing front spar
80 Aileron control cable turnbuckle
81 Interplane cross-brace wires
82 Pitot head
83 Interplane outer struts
84 Left lower wing
85 Strut lower attachment
86 Lower wing rear spar
87 Wing skinning
88 Gun muzzles
89 Fuselage/upper wing strut assembly
90 Strut/upper wing centre join
91 Internal brace
92 Upper wing centre-section profile
93 12.7-mm (0.5-in) machine-gun
94 Ammunition feed chute
95 Ammunition magazine
96 Fuselage supplementary fuel tank
97 Cartridge collector box
98 Fuselage main fuel tank
99 Fuselage frame
100 Strut attachment point
101 Machine-gun blast tube
102 Access panels

103 Fuel filler point
104 Oil filler point
105 Gun muzzle troughs
106 Gun synchronization control
107 Supplementary oil tank
108 Engine bearer attachment
109 Compressor
110 Main oil tank
111 Firewall/bulkhead
112 Cooling gills
113 Filter
114 Engine cowling ring
115 Exhaust collector ring
116 Cowling panelling
117 Fiat A.74R radial engine
118 Cylinder head fairings
119 Cowling nose profile
120 Propeller control mechanism
121 Propeller hub
122 Fiat three-blade propller
123 Spinner
124 Wheelspat strakes (servicing access)
125 Carburettor intake
126 Left wheelspat
127 Left mainwheel
128 Carburettor intake trunking
129 Exhaust outlet
130 Radiator wingroot intake
131 Intake duct
132 Right oil radiator assembly
133 Wingroot exhaust
134 Lower wing end rib/fuselage attachment
135 Landing gear attachment
136 Landing gear rear strut attachment
137 Lower wing structure
138 Interplane inner struts
139 Pitot head
140 Interplane outer struts
141 Lower wing trailing edge
142 Rear spar
143 Interplane strut attachment
144 Wing ribs
145 Front spar
146 Landing gear leg rear strut
147 Landing gear leg
148 Brace strut
149 Leg/trouser attachment
150 Landing gear trouser join
151 Torque strut
152 Axle
153 Brake line
154 Wheelspat stakes (servicing access)

155 Hub access panel
156 Mainwheel spat
157 Right mainwheel
158 Underwing searchlights (night-fighter variant)

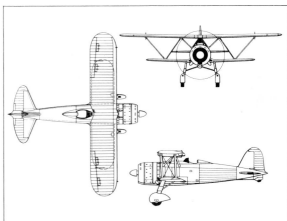

CR.42 Falco

Type: biplane fighter
Maker: Aeronautica D'Italia SA (Fiat)
Span: 9.7 m (31 ft 10 in)
Length: 8.25 m (27 ft 0¾ in)
Height: 3.06 m (10 ft 0½ in)
Wing area: 22.4 m² (241.12 sq ft)
Weight: loaded 2283 kg (5033 lb); empty 1782 kg (3929 lb)
Powerplant: one 840-hp Fiat A74.RC38 14-cylinder two-row air-cooled radial
Performance: maximum speed 430 km/h (267 mph) at 5330 m (17 487 ft); range 775 km (482 miles); operational ceiling 10 200 m (33 465 ft)
Armament: one 12.7-mm (0.5-in) and one 7.7-mm (0.303-in), or two 12.7-mm Breda-SAFAT machine-guns
Crew: 1
Production: 1781 (all types)

designation CR.42AS (*Africa Settentrionale*, or North Africa). Armament of later production CR.42s was increased to two 12.7-mm (0.5-in) machine-guns. The only other production version of the Falco, the CR.42*bis*, had a further pair of 12.7-mm guns under the wings to augment the original pair on top of the forward fuselage.

Experimental versions included the twin-float ICR.42 (*Idrovolante*, or seaplane), a single example of which was built by CMASA in 1940, and the CR.42B of 1941, another one-off prototype powered by a 1010-hp Daimler-Benz DB 601 liquid-cooled engine: maximum speed with this powerplant was 520 km/h (323 mph).

CR.42s fought in Ethiopia until mid 1941, when the airlift of supplies to the Italian forces there petered out. They were heavily involved in the battles for Greece and Crete during 1940, and subsequently saw considerable action in the desert fighting in North Africa. By 1943 the Falco had been switched to other tasks, including anti-shipping strikes. Towards the end of 1941 the CR.42CN (*Caccia Notturna*, or night-fighter) conversion had appeared, equipped with radio and a pair of searchlights below the wings, but the night-fighter Falcos proved of little use.

Of the 1781 Falcos produced, only 113 were left in Italian service when Italy surrendered in September 1943: a few were used by the co-belligerent air force and survived as trainers until the end of the decade. Handling and manoeuvrability were outstanding.

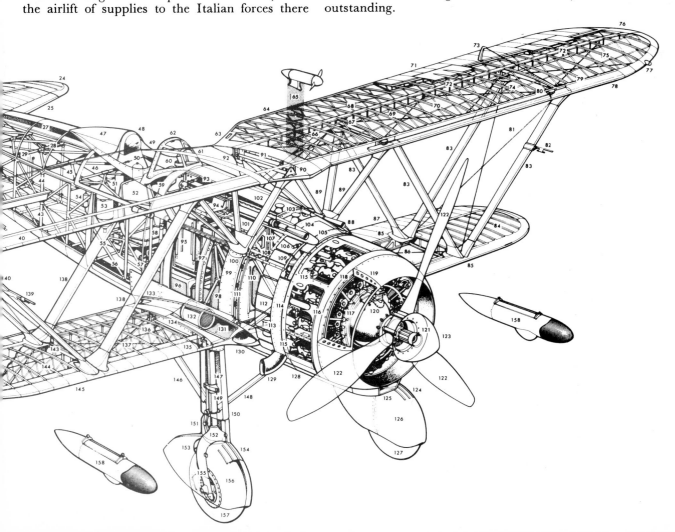

P-43 Lancer, Republic

FIRST FLIGHT 1940

THE last of the 76 P-35s built for the United States Army Air Corps were completed to a revised design as the AP-4. Delivered to the army in 1938 as the XP-41, this aircraft was powered by a turbo-supercharged 1200-hp Pratt & Whitney R-1830-45 Twin Wasp engine in a reworked cowling. It also featured a new landing gear whose main units retracted inwards into the wings, rather than backwards into large 'trouser' fairings. The span showed a slight increase, but overall length remained the same as that of the P-35, and performance was sufficient for 13 service-test machines to be ordered with the designation YP-43.

The company was re-organized to become Republic Aviation in October 1939, and the first examples were delivered in September 1940. Further redesign resulted in a simplified landing gear and cleaner fuselage lines, and an increase in armament to two 0.5-in (12.7-mm) machine-guns in the nose and one 0.3-in (7.62-mm) gun in each wing. Although gross weight of the YP-43 was almost 40% greater than that of the P-35, with a consequent adverse effect on rate of climb, the new fighter retained the great range of its predecessor. The turbo-supercharger improved altitude performance to give it a top speed of 562 km/h (349 mph) at 7620 m (25 000 ft) compared with the P-35's 452 km/h (281 mph). Fifty-four production P-43 Lancers were ordered by the USAAC at the end of 1940.

The AP-4J was based on the new 1400-hp Pratt & Whitney R-2180 Twin Hornet, and in October 1939 the USAAC ordered 80 examples of this new fighter to be designated P-44. However, in mid 1940 the P-44 order was dropped in favour of the P-47 Thunderbolt. To keep the line open 80 P-43As which used the R-1830-39 engine but were otherwise similar to the P-43, were substituted for the 1939 order for 80 P-44s.

The final P-43 production version was the P-43A-1, whose R-1830-57 engine gave it a top speed of 579 km/h (360 mph). The 0.5-in guns were moved to the wings. An order for 125 was made in 1941 for supply to the RAF under Lend-Lease. These were eventually rejected by the British, and the majority (108) went instead to the Chinese Nationalist air force. The rest of the P-43s and P-43As (150 in all) were then equipped with cameras for use as USAAF P-43B reconnaissance aircraft. Two had different camera installations and were designated P-43C; P-43D and P-43E were also allocated for photo-reconnaissance conversions of the P-43 and P-43A-1. The 17 remaining P-43A-1s were supplied to the Royal Australian Air Force after conversion.

Republic's modest start in fighter production was to lead to greater things, and perhaps the main significance of the P-43 was its place in the evolution of the later P-47 Thunderbolt, one of the most successful fighter-bombers of World War II. Lancers were never used as fighters by the USAAF, and the relatively small orders placed at a time of general rearmament may be seen as encouragement for Republic's progression towards the Thunderbolt; ultimate development of the line begun with the P-35. They were also a means of keeping the production line functioning.

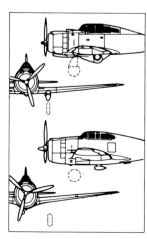

Top: The P-43 in wartime camouflage. The Lancer saw little service with the Western Allies, but did operate successfully with the Chinese
Above: A P-43A; this aircraft had an R-1830-49 engine but was otherwise very similar to the P-43
Right: The change in landing gear in the YP-43 from a rearward retracting design to an inward retracting system on the P-43
Far right: Family resemblance to the first P-47 Thunderbolt can be seen in this P-43

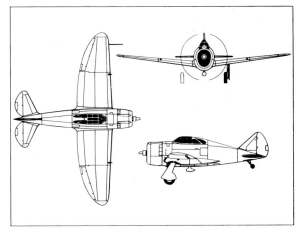

P-43 Lancer

Type: fighter and photo-reconnaissance aircraft
Maker: Republic Aviation Corporation
Span: 10.97 m (36 ft)
Length: 8.69 m (28 ft 6 in)
Height: 4.27 m (14 ft)
Wing area: 20.72 m² (223 sq ft)
Weight: loaded 3543 kg (7810 lb); empty 2565 kg (5654 lb)
Powerplant: one 1200-hp Pratt & Whitney R-1830-49 14-cylinder air-cooled radial
Performance: maximum speed 562 km/h (349 mph) at 7620 m (25 000 ft); range

1287 km (800 miles); operational ceiling 11 582 m (38 000 ft)
Armament: two 0.5-in (12.7-mm) and two 0.30-in (7.62-mm) Browning machine-guns
Crew: 1
Production: 272 (all types)

IAR 80

FIRST FLIGHT 1939

Left and below: The Romanian IAR.80 was the only indigenous design to be built by the national aircraft industry. It was used both as a fighter and fighter-bomber on the Eastern Front, and is seen here with the yellow fuselage band of Axis aircraft operating in that theatre

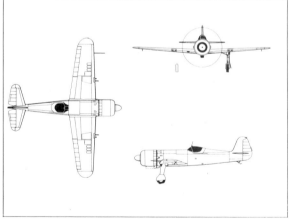

THE Industria Aeronautica Romana, at Brasov, had produced a few of its own designs during the 1930s, but was concerned mainly with the construction under licence of Polish types, including the PZL P.11 and P.24 fighters. In 1937, when the rights to build the P.24E were acquired IAR began the design of a new fighter, which was intended to use as many P.24E components as possible. In fact, the prototype, which made its first flight in 1939, used the rear fuselage, tail and engine installation of the Polish fighter allied to a new forward fuselage, and low-mounted wings instead of the characteristic PZL gull type. Another new feature was a retractable landing gear, and the wings also housed four 7.92-mm (0.312-in) machine-guns. Before production, began, it was decided to substitute the 1025-hp IAR K14-1000A (Gnome-Rhône) engine, and new wings of increased span and a lengthened fuselage.

The IAR 80 finally succeeded the P.24E in production in 1941, and a total of 50 of the original model were followed by 90 IAR 80As, which had an extra pair of wing-mounted machine-guns, and 31 IAR 80Bs with improved radio and a pair of 13.2-mm (0.52-in) machine-guns along with four of the lighter weapons. The IAR 81 was a dive-bomber development of the 80A, whose slightly lengthened wings could carry two 50-kg (110-lb) bombs each in addition to a 250-kg (551-lb) bomb below the fuselage. Fifty were built, and were followed by 29 IAR 81As, with six 7.92-mm machine-guns. The 81B carried fuel tanks in place of the bombs under the wings. It was armed with

the standard four 7.92-mm guns plus two Oerlikon (Ikaria) MG FF or Mauser MG 151 20-mm (0.79-in) cannon, a similar armament being fitted to the 38 IAR 81Cs, with bomb racks.

The 81C was the last version produced, as the IAR factory turned to assembly of the Messerschmitt Bf 109G in early 1943 and continued in this work until it was destroyed by bombing in the spring of 1944. The various 80/81 models were used by home defence squadrons of the Romanian air force until 1947, and as ground-attack fighters on the Eastern Front in 1942–43. Some of the survivors were converted to two-seat IAR 80DC dual-control trainers after World War II, while the remaining operational fighters were replaced by Soviet La-7s and Yak-9s from 1948.

IAR 80A

Type: single-seat fighter
Maker: Industria Aeronautica Romana
Span: 10.5 m (34 ft 5½ in)
Length: 8.9 m (29 ft 2½ in)
Height: 3.6 m (11 ft 9¾ in)
Wing area: 15.97 m² (171.9 sq ft)
Weight: maximum 2490 kg (5489 lb); empty 1783 kg (3931 lb)
Powerplant: one 1025-hp IAR (Gnome-Rhône) K14 14-cylinder air-cooled radial
Performance: maximum speed 510 km/h (317 mph) at 4000 m (13 123 ft); range 940 km (584 miles); operational ceiling 10 500 m (34 450 ft)
Armament: six 0.312-in (7.92-mm) FN-Browning machine-guns
Crew: 1
Production: 90

F4F Wildcat, Grumman

FIRST FLIGHT 1937

Left: A Grumman F4F-4
Wildcat touches down on a
US carrier. Though inferior in
some respects to the Japanese
Zero, the F4F was much
tougher and had a kill ratio of
6.9:1. However, many of these
victories were against
bombers and transports
Below: Thumbs up from
Lieutenant O'Hare before
take-off. He was credited with
five kills against Japanese
aircraft

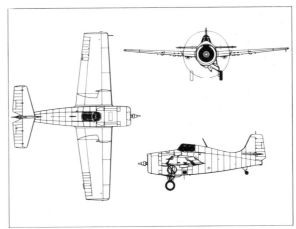

IN 1935 the US Navy ordered prototypes of two new fighters, the monoplane Brewster XF2A-1 and the biplane XF4F-1 from Grumman. Subsequent trials with a number of new monoplanes convinced the navy that the biplane had had its day. In any case Grumman's previous F3F-2 offered performance almost equal to that expected from the new design. In July 1936 the Grumman contract was cancelled in favour of a new order for a monoplane designated G-18 by the company and XF4F-2 by the navy. The first prototype flew for the first time in September 1937, powered by a 1050-hp Pratt & Whitney R-1830-66 Twin Wasp but after a long series of trials had revealed a top speed of 467 km/h (290 mph), problems with the engine caused the Grumman design to be rejected in favour of the Brewster F2A. However, a modified version, the G-36, was ordered as the XF4F-3, which flew in February 1939. Square-tipped wings of increased span and a two-stage supercharger for the R-1830-76 engine resulted in a top speed of 537 km/h (333.7 mph), and in August 1939, 54 production F4F-3s were ordered.

The first of these flew for the first time in February 1940, and the second in the following July. By the time production of the -3 ended in 1941, 185 had been built, though 21 unarmed F4F-7 reconnaissance versions were built in 1942, and 100 F4F-3 trainers in 1943, during which year one F4F-3 was tested as a twin-float seaplane.

Meanwhile, orders were placed in 1939 by France and Britain for 81 G-36As and 100 G-36Bs respectively. The French version used a 1200-hp Wright R-1820 Cyclone engine and was to be armed with six 7.5-mm (0.295-in) Darne machine-guns. However the first example was not completed until May 1940, and so the remaining G-36As were supplied to Britain and named Martlet I. Two of the US Navy's F4F-3s were also tested with the Cyclone as XF4F-5s, and one was designated XF4F-6 as an engine-trials aircraft. Another 95 F4F-3As were ordered with R-1830-90 engines using single-stage superchargers. Thirty of these were despatched to Greece in March 1941, but taken over by the Fleet Air Arm after the defeat of Greece and used as Martlet IIIs in North Africa.

Martlet II was the designation of a new version developed for the Fleet Air Arm and substituted for the G-36B originally ordered. Featuring folding

F4F-4

Type: shipboard fighter
Maker: Grumman Aircraft Engineering Corporation
Span: 11.58 m (38 ft)
Length: 8.84 m (29 ft)
Height: 3.45 m (11 ft 4 in)
Wing area: 24.16 m² (260 sq ft)
Weight: maximum 3607 kg (7952 lb); empty 2624 kg (5785 lb)
Powerplant: one 1200-hp Pratt & Whitney R-1830-86 Twin Wasp 14-cylinder two-row radial
Performance: maximum speed 515 km/h (320 mph) at 5730 m (18 800 ft); range 1336 km (830 miles); operational ceiling 10 364 m (34 003 ft)
Armament: six 0.5-in (12.7-mm) Browning machine-guns
Crew: 1
Production: 7344 (all types)

wings, except on the first ten, six 12.7-mm (0.5-in) machine-guns and a Cyclone powerplant, 100 Martlet IIs were delivered by April 1941. Folding wings and a similar armament were also used on the US Navy's next production version, the F4F-4, using the R-1830-86 fitted to later F4F-3s. Grumman built 1169 F4F-4s, plus 220 Cyclone-powered Martlet IVs for the Royal Navy.

From 1942 the Eastern Aircraft Division of General Motors built another 839 with four guns and the designation FM-1, in addition to 312 Cyclone-powered Martlet Vs. Grumman concentrated on the F6F Hellcat from 1943, leaving Wildcat construction to Eastern, and in that year production switched to the FM-2 (XF4F-8), with 1350-hp R-1820-56 Cyclone engine and many other changes included a taller fin and four-gun armament: 4407 FM-2s were built for the US Navy, and 370 Martlet VIs for the Fleet Air Arm.

In December 1941, 245 Wildcats were in US service. For the next two years the F4F was the main US Navy and Marine Corps fighter, and when the type began to be replaced aboard aircraft carriers by Hellcats in 1943 it saw extensive service aboard the new escort carriers, for which the lightened FM-2 was developed. The British Martlets, the Fleet Air Arm's first monoplane fighters, were renamed Wildcats in 1944.

Although not in the front rank in terms of performance, the Wildcat was strong and well armed. In the hands of an experienced pilot it proved the equal of the Japanese A6M Zero. However, over 1800 Wildcats were lost in 1940–45.

Above: An FM-2 in pre-1942 markings operated by the Confederate Air Force at an air display in 1976
Right: The engine mounting, in this case for the Wright R-1820 Cyclone
Centre right: An FM-2 prepares to take-off; this final version was known as the Wildcat VI by the British who received 340, the USN total being 4127. The FM-2s were standard equipment for escort carriers until the end of the war

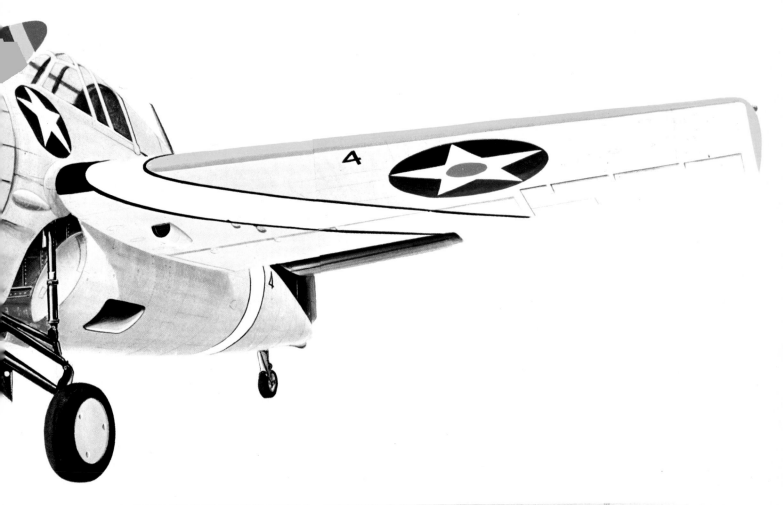

Top: An F4F in the striking
markings of the USN in early
1942. The landing gear
retracting into the fuselage
was typical of the Grumman
designs of the 1930s
Above: Royal Navy Martlets
(as the F4F was at first known
in British service) on the deck
of an escort carrier
Left: In British markings a
batch of aircraft await
delivery. The type first saw
action against the Germans
off the coast of Britain in late
1940

G.50 Freccia, Fiat

FIRST FLIGHT 1937

THE contemporary of the Macchi C.200 and Reggiane Re 2000, Giuseppe Gabrielli's G.50 became the first of the trio to fly in February 1937. It was also the Regia Aeronautica's first all-metal monoplane fighter, though with an 840-hp Fiat A74 engine it was somewhat underpowered. Also, its armament of two 12.7-mm (0.5-in) machine-guns, with only 150 rounds each, could hardly be considered adequate.

Nevertheless, 45 Freccias were ordered from CMASA. In January 1938, the first 12 were despatched to Spain for operational evaluation with the Italian forces fighting on the Nationalist side in the civil war, following which another 200 were ordered with open-topped cockpits. In 1939 another 35 were ordered by Finland, and after being delayed in Germany en route they were delivered in 1940.

The first flight of an unarmed two-seat trainer, the G.50B took place in April 1940, and the following September it was joined by the prototype G.50*bis*, which incorporated a number of detail improvements. Next came the G.50*ter*, first flown in July 1941 with a 1000-hp Fiat A76 engine, but development of this version was halted by the cancellation of the A76 programme. More radical redesigns resulted in the G.50V, powered by the liquid-cooled Daimler-Benz DB 601A, and the single G.50*bis*-A two-seat fighter-bomber, first flown in October 1942 and intended for carrier service. The prototype G.50V flew in August 1941, but a planned production version designated G.52 was abandoned in favour of the G.55, and the

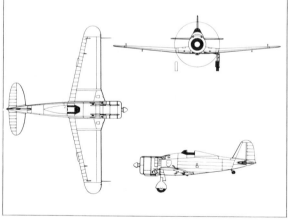

G.50*bis*-A became redundant when the planned aircraft carriers failed to materialize.

The final total of 774 Freccias built for the Regia Aeronautica included 108 trainers and 421 of the G.50*bis*, nine of which went to the Croatian air force. By June 1940, when Italy joined World War II, 118 G.50s were in service, equipping one fighter Stormo; a number of these went to Belgium with the Corpo Aereo Italiano later that year. Others took part in the Greek, Balkan and North African campaigns as fighters and ground-attack aircraft, before being replaced in the last-named theatre by the G.50*bis* from late 1940. Freccias were also used as bomber and convoy escorts in the Mediterranean, while the aircraft supplied to Finland gave good service against the Soviet Union.

G.50*bis*

Type: monoplane fighter
Maker: Costruzioni Meccaniche Aeronautiche SA (Fiat)
Span: 11 m (36 ft 1 in)
Length: 8.29 m (27 ft 2½ in)
Height: 3.6 m (11 ft 9¾ in)
Wing area: 18.25 m² (196.45 sq ft)
Weight: loaded 2500 kg (5511 lb); empty 2015 kg (4442 lb)
Powerplant: one 840-hp Fiat A74.RC38 14-cylinder two-row radial
Performance: maximum speed 486 km/h (302 mph) at 6000 m (19 685 ft); range 1000 km (621 miles); operational ceiling 10 750 m (35 269 ft)
Armament: two 12.7-mm (0.5-in) Breda-SAFAT machine-guns
Crew: 1
Production: 421 (774 all types)

G.55 Centauro, Fiat

FIRST FLIGHT 1942

THE main deficiencies of the Fiat G.50, shortage of power and poor armament, were successfully remedied by the G.55 development, the prototype of which flew for the first time in April 1942. The Freccia's underpowered radial gave way to the 1475-hp Daimler-Benz DB 605A-1 liquid-cooled engine, and its two 12.7-mm (0.5-in) machine-guns were augmented in the prototype and pre-production G.55/0 by a 20-mm (0.79-in) Mauser MG 151/20 cannon firing through the propeller hub. At the same time, the airframe itself was considerably refined, and on the first production model, the G.55/I, a further two MG 151/20s were added in the wings.

Unfortunately for the Regia Aeronautica, squadron deliveries were only just beginning when the armistice between Italy and the Allies was signed in September 1943. Most of Italy was still under German occupation at the time, however, and it was decided that the G.55 would be used to equip the Aviazione della Repubblica Sociale Italiana the air arm of the puppet regime established under the nominal leadership of Mussolini. Large orders were placed with Fiat, most of whose factories were also in the German-occupied area. These orders could hardly be considered realistic as shortages of both the DB 605A-1 and the Fiat licence-built version, the RA.1050 RC.58 Tifone, reduced production to a trickle. By the time German resistance in Italy ended in April 1945, only 105 Centauros had been completed, and these had been issued to various fighter units of the RSI air force.

Meanwhile, 1944 had seen two more G.55

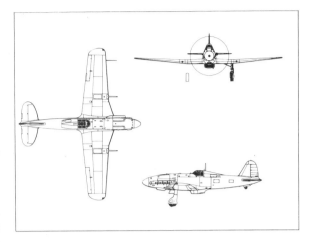

developments take to the air. The G.55/II dispensed with the nose machine-guns, adding a second pair of MG 151/20s in the wings; and the G.55S (*Silurante*, or torpedo-carrier) replaced the ventral radiator with underwing radiators to accommodate a torpedo below the fuselage. Also flown in 1944 was the prototype of the G.56, which was powered by the 1750-hp DB 603A and achieved a top speed of 685 km/h (426 mph), but there was no prospect of sufficient DB 603s being available for production to be undertaken. Production of the G.55 was resumed after the war, with a total of 85 being built in two versions, the G.55A fighter and G.55B two-seat trainer. It was one of the best of all piston-engined fighters and a complete contrast to the G.50.

G.55/I Centauro

Type: monoplane fighter/ fighter-bomber
Maker: Aeronautica D'Italia SA (Fiat)
Span: 11.84 m (38 ft 10½ in)
Length: 9.37 m (30 ft 9 in)
Height: 3.13 m (10 ft 3¼ in)
Wing area: 21.11 m² (227.27 sq ft)
Weight: maximum 3710 kg (8179 lb); empty 2630 kg (5798 lb)
Powerplant: one 1475-hp Daimler-Benz DB 605A-1 or Fiat RA.1050 RC58 Tifone V-12 liquid-cooled engine
Performance: maximum speed 620 km/h (385 mph) at 7000 m (22 966 ft); range 1200 km (746 miles); operational ceiling 13 000 m (42 651 ft)
Armament: three 20-mm (0.79-in) Mauser MG 151/20 cannon; two 12.7-mm (0.5-in) Breda-SAFAT machine-guns
Crew: 1
Production: approx 200 (all types)

Above: A G.55 in the colours of the German-controlled Aviazione della RSI (Repubblica Sociale Italiana)
Far left: A production G.55/0 powered by a DB 605A-1 engine. This German powerplant was made under licence by Fiat
Left: The radiator intake beneath the fuselage of the G.55 was replaced by twin intakes under the wings on the torpedo-carrying versions

C.200, Macchi

FIRST FLIGHT 1937

TOGETHER with the Fiat G.50 and Reggiane Re 2000, the Macchi C.200 was produced for the Regia Aeronautica's expansion programme of the late 1930s. Like its contemporaries, it was handicapped by the necessity of using a relatively low-powered engine, in this case the 840-hp Fiat A74. While performance was better than its rivals, and manoeuvrability was excellent, armament was restricted to only two machine-guns.

Designed by Mario Castoldi, the first prototype C.200 was flown in December 1937, and the following year production began with an order for 99 machines. These used a more powerful version of the A74, and later production batches had an open-topped cockpit instead of the original clumsy-looking enclosed canopy. The wings had to be modified at an early stage after they were found to be responsible for a dangerous susceptibility to high-speed stalls, and the last C.200s to be built were fitted with the wings of the C.202, thus gaining a pair of 7.7-mm (0.303-in) machine-guns.

Altogether, 1143 C.200s were built, 395 by Macchi and the rest by SAI-Ambrosini and Breda. The C.201 development was planned to have the more powerful A76.RC40 engine. But the A76 was abandoned and the C.201 was in any case rendered unnecessary by the appearance of the C.202 Folgore, the prototype of which flew in August 1940, the same month as the C.201 prototype.

By June 1940, 156 C.200s were in Regia Aeronautica service, (with the name Saetta) though in the initial period of Italy's participation in World War II they were grounded as a result of

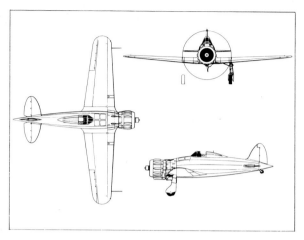

fatal crashes, many caused by high-speed stalls. The type's main service was in the various theatres around the Mediterranean, though two Gruppi served with the Italian expeditionary force on the Eastern Front. Its poor armament was compensated for by exceptional climb and turn performance. It also proved an adaptable aircraft: early service as an interceptor was followed by employment as a bomber and convoy escort, for which drop-tanks could be fitted to give a 300-km (186-mile) increase in range. The later stages of its career saw it adopting a fighter-bomber role, able to carry a bombload of up to 320 kg (705 lb). Finally, after the Italian armistice of September 1943, a small number served as trainers with the Allied co-belligerent air force.

C.200 Saetta

Type: monoplane fighter
Maker: Aeronautica Macchi; SAI Ambrosini; Società Italiana Ernesto Breda
Span: 10.58 m (34 ft 8½ in)
Length: 8.2 m (26 ft 10¾ in)
Height: 3.51 m (11 ft 6¼ in)
Wing area: 16.8 m² (180.84 sq ft)
Weight: maximum 2328 kg (5132 lb); empty 1894 kg (4175 lb)
Powerplant: one 870-hp Fiat A74. RC38 14-cylinder two-row radial
Performance: maximum speed 503 km/h (313 mph) at 4500 m (14 764 ft); range 570 km (354 miles); operational ceiling 8900 m (29 200 ft)
Armament: two 12.7-mm (0.5-in) Breda-SAFAT machine-guns
Crew: 1
Production: 1143

Far left: A C.200 preserved in Italy in the colours of 22° Gruppo Autonomo Spauracchio which served in the USSR in World War II
Left: The prototype C.200 (MM 336) first flown in 1937 and winner of the fighter trials at Guidonia in 1938
Below: An early production C.200, with fully-enclosed cockpit. This machine has the non-retracting tailwheel and no propeller spinner

C.202 Folgore, Macchi
FIRST FLIGHT 1940

Left: A C.202 AS (Africa Settentrionale) Serie III. The Macchi Folgore (Lightning) served in Africa, the USSR and Italy
Below left: A Folgore in Co-Belligerent markings
Below: The C.202 was superior to the Hurricane and P-40 but no match for the Spitfire or P-51

WITH their C.200 Saetta in production for the Regia Aeronautica, Macchi set about realizing the design's full potential by replacing its under-powered Fiat A74 engine with a Daimler-Benz DB 601A-1 to produce the prototype C.202 Folgore. This flew in August 1940, and in trials registered a top speed of 599 km/h (372 mph) – 96 km/h (59.7 mph) better than the production C.200 – while retaining its predecessor's exceptional climb rate and responsiveness. Since it was based on a type in production, assembly lines could be established relatively quickly.

Consequently, production of the C.202, both by Macchi and licensees, was authorized. Arrangements were made for licence production of the engine by Alfa Romeo, though deliveries of the powerplant consistently failed to keep pace with demand. The first Folgores entered service in mid 1941, and production continued until September 1943. A total of 11 sub-series were distinguished by variations of detail and equipment, some of the last examples having racks for 100- or 150-litre (22- or 33-Imp gal) drop-tanks or 50-, 100- or 150-kg (110-, 220-, or 331-lb) bombs under the wings. Aircraft of the sixth and subsequent series carried a 7.7-mm (0.303-in) machine-gun in each wing in addition to the Saetta's standard armament of two 12.7-mm (0.5-in) guns in the top of the forward fuselage.

Even greater improvement was offered by the 1475-hp DB 605A-1 engine, and in April 1942 a converted Folgore with this powerplant was flown for the first time. Maximum speed with the new

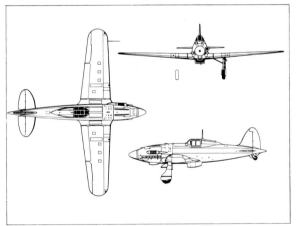

engine was 642 km/h (399 mph) but, again, production was hampered by shortage of the Italian licence-built version, the Fiat RA1050 RC58 Tifone.

The C.205V Veltro (Greyhound), as the new fighter was designated, made its operational debut in July 1943, but by the time of the Italian armistice in September of that year only 66 were in service. Most of these remained in service with the Repubblica Sociale Italiana air force, and subsequent production of the Veltro brought the total built to 262. Original armament of the type corresponded to that of the bomb-carrying C.202, but the wing machine-guns were replaced on later examples by 20-mm (0.79-in) Mauser MG 151/20 cannon.

C.202 Folgore

Type: monoplane fighter
Maker: Aeronautica Macchi; Società Italiana Ernesto Breda; SAI Ambrosini
Span: 10.58 m (34 ft 8½ in)
Length: 8.85 m (29 ft 0½ in)
Height: 3.5 m (11 ft 5¾ in)
Wing area: 16.8 m² (180.84 sq ft)
Weight: loaded 2930 kg (6459 lb); empty 2490 kg (5490 lb)
Powerplant: one 1075-hp Alfa Romeo RA1000 RC411 V-12 liquid-cooled engine
Performance: maximum speed 595 km/h (370 mph) at 6000 m (19 685 ft); range 765 km (475 miles); operational ceiling 11 500 m (37 730 ft)
Armament: two 12.7-mm (0.5-in) and two 7.7-mm (0.303-in) Breda-SAFAT machine-guns
Crew: 1
Production: approx 1500

Re 2000, Reggiane

FIRST FLIGHT 1938

Left: The Re 2000 during the 1938 trials at Guidonia when it was pitted against the Macchi C.200. Flown by Commandante De Bernadi it was superior even to the Bf 109E. The only reservations concerned the supposedly vulnerable wing fuel tanks
Below: A Hungarian Re 2000, known as the Héja and later powered by a Wright Cyclone GR-1280-G2 engine. This installation slightly increased the fuselage length

THE prototype of this, the first of a famous series of fighters, was flown in 1938, only three years after the Officine Meccaniche Italiane Reggiane was taken over by the Caproni organization. It would appear also that the rapidity of its completion was not connected with its pronounced resemblance to the contemporary Seversky P-35. Comparative trials with the Macchi C.200 showed the Falco, as Reggiane named their aircraft, to be superior in handling and performance, but doubts about the vulnerability of the wing-mounted fuel tanks prevented its adoption by the Regia Aeronautica. However, as universal rearmament in 1939 limited availability of modern fighters, the company decided to speculate.

Their judgement was vindicated by an order, in December 1939, from Hungary for 70 complete aircraft together with a manufacturing licence. Deliveries began in April 1940 and the Re 2000 entered Hungarian service as the Héja, though it was late 1942 before MAVAG in Hungary flew their first example. The Hungarian-built aircraft, designated Héja II, used the 930-hp Weiss-Manfred WMK-14 licence-built version of the Gnome-Rhône K14 Mistral Major instead of the unreliable 985-hp Piaggio PXI RC40 installed in the Italian aircraft. Gebauer machine-guns replaced the Italian Breda-SAFATs.

Total Hungarian production was 192, and Héjas served on the Eastern Front during 1942, and thereafter as home-defence fighters and advanced trainers. Sweden was another customer, ordering 60 in November 1940: these were delivered the

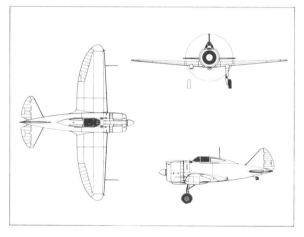

following year and served as interceptors with the Swedish air force under the designation J20.

Potential orders from other European countries, including Britain, were frustrated by Italy's involvement in the war, and the remaining 38 from the Reggiane production line were used by the Italians. A few were modified with increased fuel tankage in the wings with the object of flying them to Ethiopia, but the collapse of the Italian campaign there frustrated the scheme. More aircraft were fitted with the tanks and based in Sicily in 1941–42, to act as maritime-patrol and escort fighters. Some had catapult hooks but had to land on airfields. Trials were completed successfully, but the curtailment of Italian naval activity prevented their becoming operational.

Re 2000

Type: monoplane fighter
Maker: Officine Mechaniche Italiane Reggiane SA
Span: 11 m (36 ft 1 in)
Length: 7.99 m (26 ft 2½ in)
Height: 3.2 m (10 ft 6 in)
Wing area: 20.4 m² (219.59 sq ft)
Weight: loaded 2880 kg (6349 lb); empty 2070 kg (4563 lb)
Powerplant: one 985-hp Piaggio PXI RC40 14-cylinder two-row radial
Performance: maximum speed 530 km/h (329 mph) at 5000 m (16 404 ft); range 1150 km (715 miles); operational ceiling 9500 m (31 168 ft)
Armament: two 12.7-mm (0.5-in) Breda-SAFAT machine-guns
Crew: 1
Production: 170 (plus 192 Héja)

Re 2001, Reggiane

FIRST FLIGHT 1940

THE Re 2001 Falco II was produced by combining the German Daimler-Benz DB 601A-1 engine with a refined Re 2000. After promising trials with the prototype in August 1940, new wings were designed to replace the type that had been found unacceptable on the Re 2000.

This was the beginning of a series of new designs, as delays in the supply of licence-built DB 601s by Alfa Romeo led to the substitution of other powerplants. The Re 2002 Ariete (Ram) reverted to a radial engine, the 1175-hp Piaggio P.XIX RC.45. After making its first flight in October 1940 it underwent official trials the following year, and despite problems with the new powerplant a total of 700 were ordered. Again, the engine manufacturers could not keep up with the required production rate, and the final Reggiane design to fly used the 1475-hp DB 605A-1.

The new fighter, the Re 2005 Sagittario (Archer), also introduced a much heavier armament, replacing the twin nose 12.7-mm (0.5-in) and two wing 7.7-mm (0.303-in) machine-guns with a 20-mm (0.79-in) MG 151/20 firing through the propeller hub plus a similar weapon and a 7.7-mm machine-gun in each wing. The prototype was flown for the first time in May 1942 and subjected to official trials in July and August, but in spite of an impressive top speed of 678 km/h (421 mph) at 6950 m (22 802 ft) no production was authorized until the following February.

Meanwhile, deliveries of production Re 2001s had begun in September 1941. When production ended two years later 224 had been built. Of these,

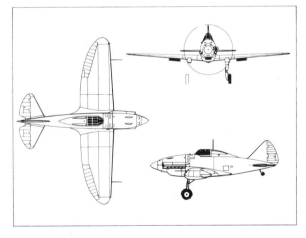

39 2001CBs had a rack below the fuselage for a 640-kg (1410-lb) bomb. Another 124 were completed as night-fighters, with two 20-mm cannon in underwing gondolas. Fourteen were navalized for catapult trials as part of Italy's abortive aircraft-carrier programme. They were used in the Mediterranean in 1942–43, and a few served with the co-belligerent and Repubblica Sociale Italiana air forces after the Italian armistice.

Production Re 2002s began to reach the Regia Aeronautica in mid 1942, and by September 1943, 147 had been completed. Some 40 of these were used by the Co-Belligerent Air Force, and another 76 were built subsequently for the Luftwaffe. Most of the 36 Re 2005s completed were commandeered by the Germans after the armistice.

Re 2002 Ariete

Type: monoplane fighter
Maker: Reggiane; Caproni
Span: 11 m (36 ft 1 in)
Length: 8.16 m (26 ft 9½ in)
Height: 3.15 m (10 ft 4 in)
Wing area: 20.4 m² (219.59 sq ft)
Weight: maximum 3240 kg (7143 lb); empty 2390 kg (5269 lb)
Powerplant: one 1180-hp Piaggio P.XIX RC.45 14-cylinder air-cooled radial
Performance: maximum speed 530 km/h (329 mph) at 5500 m (18 045 ft); range 1100 km (684 miles); operational ceiling 11 000 m (36 089 ft)
Armament: two 12.7-mm (0.5-in) and two 7.7-mm (0.303-in) Breda-SAFAT machine-guns; 950 kg (2095 lb) of bombs or one torpedo under fuselage plus 320 kg (706 lb) under-wing bombs
Crew: 1
Production: 227 (total Re 2001 Falcos, 237)

Buffalo, Brewster

FIRST FLIGHT 1937

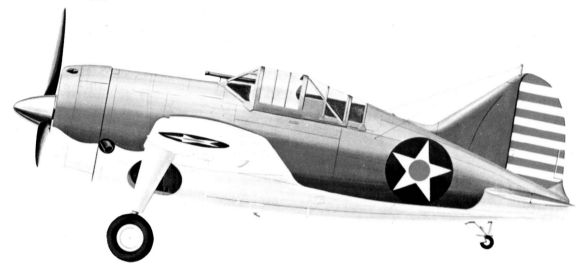

CONSTRUCTED in response to the same US Navy competition of 1935 that gave rise to Grumman's biplane XF4F-1, the Brewster Model 39 was flown for the first time in December 1937 with the designation XF2A-1. Powered by a 950-hp Wright R-1820-22 Cyclone, it underwent a long series of refinements before 54 F2A-1s were ordered in June 1938.

After crashing during landing trials, the prototype was re-engined with a 1200-hp R-1820-40, its first flight in July 1939 coinciding with deliveries of the first production F2A-1s. Subsequently, 43 F2A-2s were built with the new engine, and the final production version for the US Navy, the F2A-3, used the same powerplant. Although the weight of additional armour and equipment reduced speed, ceiling and climb rate, 108 were built.

Only 11 F2A-1s went to the US Navy; the remainder, designated B-239, were sent to Finland, where they fought throughout the war against the Soviet Union. Export models were also produced for Belgium, which ordered 40 B-339Bs in 1939; Britain, which ordered 170 B-339Es the following year; and the Dutch East Indies requested 72 B-339Ds and 20 B-439s later in 1940. The B-339s were equivalent to F2A-2s without naval equipment, and the B-439 was derived from the F2A-3.

After the German invasion of Belgium, most of the B-339Bs were diverted to Britain, where they saw limited service under the name Buffalo I. The B-339Es were delivered to the Far East, where they equipped two Royal Air Force, two Royal Australian Air Force and one Royal New Zealand Air

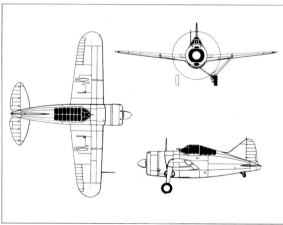

Force squadrons. Most of the aircraft of these and the four Dutch colonial squadrons formed with the type were destroyed over Burma, Singapore, Malaya and Java in the early months of fighting against the Japanese in the weeks following December 1941. Their inferiority to the Japanese fighters, even with all non-essential equipment removed to reduce weight, was such that the survivors, plus a small number diverted to Australia, saw no further operational service.

After brief service aboard US Navy carriers *Saratoga* and *Lexington* in 1940–41, most F2A-3s were used for training, though some saw action over Midway with US Marine Corps squadron VMF-221 in June 1942, when 11 were shot down by fighters escorting a Japanese bomber force.

F2A-3

Type: shipboard fighter
Maker: Brewster Aeronautical Corporation
Span: 10.67 m (35 ft)
Length: 8.12 m (26 ft 7½ in)
Height: 3.47 m (11 ft 4½ in)
Wing area: 19.41 m² (208.9 sq ft)
Weight: maximum 3247 kg (7159 lb); empty 2146 kg (4732 lb)
Powerplant: one 1200-hp Wright R-1820-40 Cyclone 9-cylinder radial
Performance: maximum speed 467 km/h (290 mph) at 5029 m (16 500 ft); range 1553 km (965 miles); operational ceiling 7620 m (25 000 ft)
Armament: four 0.5-in (12.7-mm) Browning machine-guns
Crew: 1
Production: 509 (all Buffalos)

MiG-3, Mikoyan-Gurevich
FIRST FLIGHT 1940

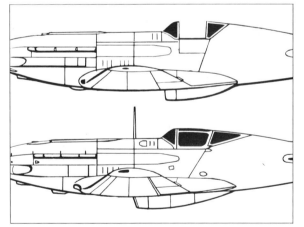

THE 1938 VVS (*Voenno-vozdushniye Sily*, or Soviet air forces) requirement for a high-performance, high-altitude fighter was taken up by the new Mikoyan-Gurevich design bureau. Having selected the heavy but powerful Mikulin AM-35A supercharged engine, the designers were forced to use the lightest, and consequently smallest, possible airframe, with the cockpit well aft to balance the engine's weight. Construction was of wood, except for the forward fuselage and wing centre section, and the armament comprised two 7.62-mm (0.30-in) and one 12.7-mm (0.5-in) machine-guns in the nose.

Trials of the prototype MiG-1 in 1940 revealed the impressive level speed of 649 km/h (403 mph) at 6900 m (22 638 ft), but the size constraints had resulted in extremely awkward handling, compounded by limited forward view. Nevertheless, assembly of the production batch of 100 went ahead. However, because of changes to the design, the rate of completion averaged only five per month during the last third of 1940, and the inclusion of the armour protection and armament that had been omitted from the original prototype resulted in a further deterioration of flying qualities. The level speed performance was also reduced, and other deficiencies included lack of range because of limited fuel capacity.

The reports of fighter units and the findings of wind-tunnel tests resulted in such a large number of changes to aircraft built after the first 100, that the new designation MiG-3 was applied.

Among the changes were an increase in fuel capacity, modification of the supercharger intakes and ventral radiator, increased dihedral on the outer-wing panels and the provision of a sliding canopy and extended glazing aft of the cockpit. Production MiG-1s dispensed with the folding canopy of the prototype. A second production line was established, and the first examples of the MiG-3 appeared in March 1941.

Over 3300 examples were delivered in little more than a year. Unfortunately, although range and handling had been improved, the MiG-3 was at its best at high altitudes, whereas most combat was taking place at lower levels. Although the armament was clearly below standard, the weight of the AM-35A engine was such that there was no scope for carrying more weapons.

Above: MiG-3s of the 12 IAP, the fighter aviation unit assigned to the defence of Moscow in early 1942. The picture was taken when the unit was raised to Guards standard
Left: The prototype MiG-1 was designed with a sideways opening cockpit. This was later replaced by a sliding canopy on production models to allow pilots to fly with the cockpit open

There were a number of projected developments of the MiG-3. The MiG-3D was intended to use the 1700-hp AM-39 engine, but when MiG-3 production ended in the spring of 1942, this still had not flown. The imminent termination of AM-35A production towards the end of 1941 resulted in the I-210, with a 1540-hp Shvetsov M-82 radial.

This proved unstable and deficient in performance, and when these problems were solved with the 1650-hp M-82FN-powered I-211, it had been rendered unnecessary by production of the Lavochkin La-5. Subsequent derivatives with later Mikulin engines in the I-220 and I-230 series achieved exceptional speeds.

When Germany invaded the Soviet Union in June 1941 a number of fighter divisions had been equipped with the MiG-3, though there was apparently some initial reluctance on the part of less-experienced units even to attempt to fly the type. During the early stages of the war, a combination of poor manoeuvrability, insufficient experience and inadequate low-altitude performance placed the MiG-3 at a considerable disadvantage in combat with the Bf 109E and F.

As an interceptor, moreover, the MiG-3 was hampered in its attacks on bombers by its lack of firepower, and as other new fighters became available the MiG-3 was gradually replaced in front-line formations by the LaGG-1 and Yak-1. Large numbers remained in service with second-line fighter units and many were fitted with cameras for service as high-speed reconnaissance aircraft.

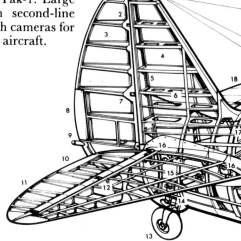

MiG-3

1 Aerial attachment
2 Rudder upper hinge
3 Fabric-covered metal-framed rudder
4 Wooden tailfin structure
5 Rudder post
6 Rudder control cables
7 Rudder centre hinge
8 Rudder tab
9 Rear navigation light
10 Elevator tab
11 Fabric-covered metal-framed elevator
12 Tailplane structure
13 Fixed tailwheel
14 Tailwheel leg fairing
15 Tailwheel shock absorber
16 Tailplane spar attachment points
17 Fuselage aft frame
18 Left elevator
19 Left tailplane
20 Aerials
21 Control cable runs
22 Upper longeron
23 Fuselage stringers
24 Lower longeron
25 Fuselage frame
26 Frame strengthening brace
27 Radio compartment access
28 Aft-vision glazing
29 Pilot's headrest
30 Aft-sliding cockpit canopy
31 One-piece moulded windscreen
32 PBP-1a reflector gunsight
33 Instrument panel shroud
34 Control column
35 Fuselage metal frame
36 Pilot's seat
37 Back armour
38 Fuselage wood/metal construction joint
39 RSI-3 radio receiver
40 Radio equipment rack
41 Fairing attachment
42 Trim handwheels
43 Underfloor fuel tank
44 Wing root fairing
45 Formers
46 Right flap inboard section
47 Flap pushrod
48 Right flap outboard section
49 Rear spar
50 Fabric-covered metal-framed aileron
51 Wing stiffeners
52 Wing outer section ribs
53 Right navigation light
54 Leading-edge ribs
55 Forward spar
56 Mainspar
57 Wing inboard/outboard section attachments
58 Strengthened rib
59 Mainwheel leg pivot
60 mainwheel leg flap hinged upper section
61 Brake line
62 Mainwheel fairing
63 Torque links
64 Right mainwheel
65 Cooling louvres
66 Oleo shock absorber sleeve
67 Inboard leading-edge structure
68 Rib cut-outs
69 Right wing fuel tank
70 Ventral radiator bath
71 Rear spar/fuselage attachment
72 Rudder pedals
73 Bulkhead
74 Fuselage forward fuel tank
75 Fuel filler access
76 Cooling louvres
77 Angled aerial mast
78 Machine-gun breeches
79 Gun cooling intake scoops
80 Ammunition tanks
81 Fuselage forward frame
82 Main spar/fuselage attachment
83 Intake duct
84 Induction air intake
85 Left mainwheel
86 Engine accessories
87 Intake fairing
88 Oil cooler air intake
89 Intake scoop
90 Exhaust stubs
91 Cowling release catches
92 Mikulin AM-35A 1/82-cylinder liquid-cooled engine
93 One 7.62-mm (0.30-in) ShKAS machine-gun left and right and one 12.7-mm (0.5-in) UB machine-gun
94 Mainspar (outboard section)
95 Aileron control linkage
96 Aileron tab (left wing only)
97 Left aileron
98 Plywood outer panel wing skinning
99 Left navigation light
100 Forward spar (outboard section)
101 Gun troughs
102 Coolant tank
103 Spinner back plate
104 Reduction gear housing
105 Auxiliary intake
106 VISh-22E (later VISh-61) all-metal variable-pitch three-blade propeller
107 Spinner

Far left: A MiG-3 in winter camouflage. Pilots complained that, though it could compete with enemy aircraft at 5000 m (16 400 ft), it was no match for fighters at low levels and was heavy on the controls

Left: The MiG-1 differed from the MiG-3 with its hinged cockpit cover, landing-gear leg design and hinged wheel covers. At the time of its introduction into service the Russians claimed that it was the fastest military aircraft in production in the world

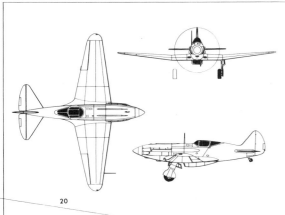

MiG-3

Type: single-seat interceptor and reconnaissance aircraft
Maker: State aircraft factories
Span: 10.3 m (33 ft 9½ in)
Length: 8.15 m (26 ft 8¾ in)
Height: 2.62 m (8 ft 7 in)
Wing area: 17.44 m² (187.73 sq ft)
Weight: maximum 3350 kg (7385 lb); empty 2699 kg (5950 lb)
Powerplant: one 1350-hp Mikulin AM-35A V-12 liquid-cooled engine
Performance: maximum speed 640 km/h (398 mph) at 7800 m (25 591 ft); range 1250 km (777 miles); operational ceiling 12 000 m (39 370 ft)
Armament: one 12.7-mm (0.5-in) Berezin UB and two 7.62-mm (0.3-in) ShKAS machine-guns
Crew: 1
Production: 3322

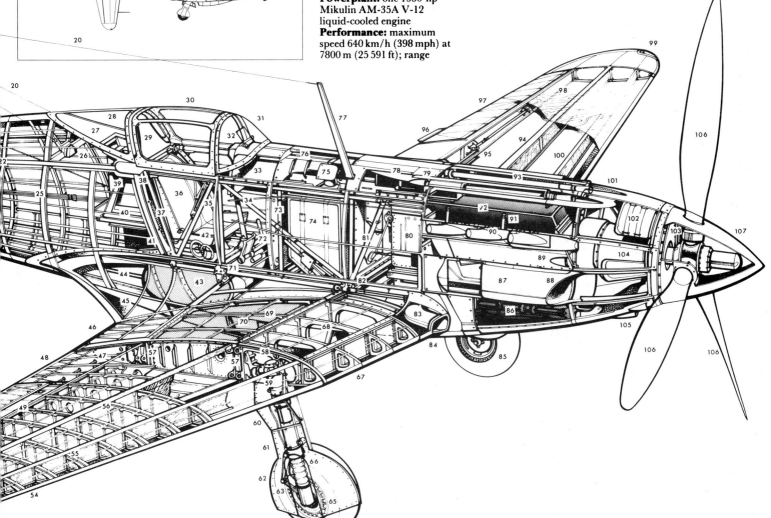

LaGG-3, Lavochkin

THE Soviet air force fighter specifications issued in 1938 for a less specialized tactical machine optimized for combat at around 3500 m (11 483 ft), led to proposals being submitted by the design bureaux of Lavochkin and Yakovlev. These were selected for further development, with the respective designations I-22 and I-26.

The I-22 used the 1100-hp Klimov M-105P engine, with provision for a cannon to be mounted between the cylinder banks, and while the low-wing monoplane configuration was conventional, the all-wood construction used an unorthodox compound birch ply. Metal was used only in the nose, which housed two 12.7-mm (0.5-in) machine-guns, and on movable control surfaces.

The first of a number of prototypes, soon to be designated LaGG-1, flew for the first time at the end of March 1940. It gave a maximum speed of 600 km/h (373 mph) at 5000 m (16 404 ft) but other aspects of performance as well as general flying qualities were extremely poor. However, the pressing need for new fighters, and the fact that the bureau had already established a production line for its design, led to a programme of improvements to salvage the design rather than scrap it.

Amendments to the control systems, lightening of the structure, the use of 7.62-mm (0.30-in) machine-guns and the replacement of the original 23-mm (0.91-in) VYa cannon with a 20-mm (0.79-in) ShVAK, as well as the incorporation of extra fuel tanks in the wings cured the worst of the problems. Production of the revised design designated LaGG-3 began in January 1941.

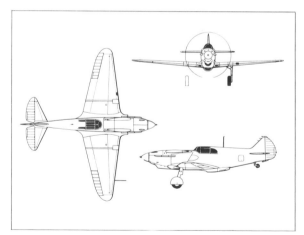

By the end of the year 2463 examples had been completed, and another 4065 followed before production ended in the second half of 1942. A number of changes were introduced, the major improvement being the 1260-hp M-105PF.

Armament was subject to numerous variations, the original 23-mm cannon often being used, and one or both of the 7.62-mm machine-guns being replaced by the 12.7-mm BS. Standard external stores attachment points allowed six RS-82 rockets, up to 200 kg (441 lb) of bombs or an additional pair of machine-guns to be carried under the wings, with the alternative of drop-tanks for escort missions. At one stage a new version mounting a 37-mm (1.46-in) cannon was considered. Other abortive developments included using more powerful

LaGG-3

Type: tactical fighter
Maker: State aircraft factories
Span: 9.8 m (32 ft 2 in)
Length: 8.81 m (28 ft 11 in)
Height: 4.4 m (14 ft 5¼ in)
Wing area: 17.5 m² (188.37 sq ft)
Weight: maximum 3180 kg (7231 lb); empty 2620 kg (5776 lb)
Powerplant: one 1100-hp Klimov M-105P or 1260-hp M-105PF V-12 engine
Performance: maximum speed 570 km/h (354 mph) at 4000 m (13 123 ft); range 700 km (435 miles) with drop-tanks; operational ceiling 9600 m (31 496 ft)
Armament: one 23-mm (0.91-in) Volkov VYa-23 or 20-mm (0.79-in) Shpitalny ShVAK cannon; two 7.62-mm (0.3-in) ShKAS and 12.7-mm (0.5-in) UB machine-guns; two 100-kg (220-lb) bombs or six RS-82 rockets
Crew: 1
Production: 6528

Klimov engines and fitting a ramjet booster.

The service introduction of the LaGG-3 in the first half of 1941 caused general dismay among the pilots called upon to fly it. The basic shortcomings of early models was compounded by poor finishing of production examples. In combat, the type proved markedly inferior to contemporary German fighters, and even the soundness of its construction was vitiated by the vulnerability of the radiator and wing tanks and the minimal armour protection for the pilot.

After being switched in increasing numbers to the ground-attack role, to which it proved better suited, the LaGG-3 was replaced in both production and service from 1942 by the radial-engined La-5.

Top: The LaGG-3 was built extensively from plywood with bakelite bonding agents between layers of birch skin
Above left: A captured aircraft evaluated by the Finns
Left: The top two aircraft are early production versions with rudder and fuselage-gun modifications and fixed tailwheel. The lower two have improved windscreens and the bottom aircraft is fitted with an extended radiator duct
Above: The single 20-mm cannon of the LaGG-3 was mounted between the engine cylinder blocks

Yak-1, Yakovlev

FIRST FLIGHT 1940

THE Yakovlev I-26, ordered along with the Lavochkin I-22 (LaGG-1) as a prototype low-level tactical fighter at the beginning of 1939, began flight tests in March 1940. Like its counter-part from Lavochkin, the I-26 used the 1100-hp Klimov M-105P engine with 20-mm (0.79-in) cannon firing through the propeller hub. Two 7.62-mm (0.30-in) ShKAS machine-guns were fitted above the cowling. Though wood was used in its construction it was confined to the wings, which also carried the fuel tanks, the fuselage being of welded steel tubes. Service evaluation began in June 1940, and by October deliveries had begun of pre-series aircraft. The early examples proved slightly heavier, and consequently slower than expected. But performance was good enough for production to begin almost immediately under the designation Yak-1.

By the end of the year a total of 64 had been completed, and another 335 followed in the first half of 1941. Early production was accompanied by the development of a lightened airframe with boosted 1260-hp M-105PF engine, flown in June 1941, demonstrating an increase in top speed from 540 km/h (336 mph) to 580 km/h (360 mph). Before production of the new model could gather momentum, however, the factory was evacuated from the Moscow area, but production was re-sumed rapidly at new factories in the east. By this time the two machine-guns had been replaced by a single 12.7-mm (0.5-in) UB, and from January 1943 a new cockpit canopy with improved rear view was introduced to produce the Yak-1M,

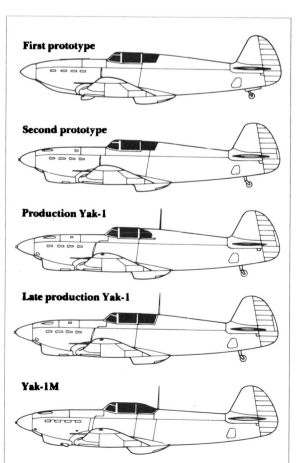

First prototype

Second prototype

Production Yak-1

Late production Yak-1

Yak-1M

Top: The Yak-9D was the long-range version
Centre left: The Yak-1M prototype
Centre right: The Yak-1M had improved rear view
Above: A Yak-3 squadron; this close dogfighter was derived from the lightweight Yak-1M. Though lightly armed and armoured by western standards, it handled superbly and was superior to the Bf 109G and Fw 190A at low and medium altitudes
Left: Variations of the Yak-1

54

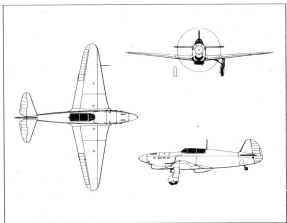

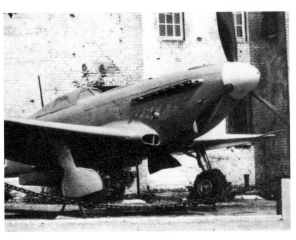

Top: A Yak-9D flown by M V Avdyeyev of an élite Guards Regiment over the Crimea in May 1944. The fin bears his six kills while the nose has the Guards badge and Order of the Red Banner (Military)
Above: A Yak-9P captured in the Korean war and flown by the USAF for evaluation
Left: The Yak-9U was virtually a new aircraft with an all-metal skin. It saw action in the closing months of the war and equipped Soviet satellite countries after the war

Yak-3

Type: tactical fighter
Maker: State aircraft factories
Span: 9.2 m (30 ft 3 in)
Length: 8.5 m (27 ft 11 in)
Height: 2.96 m (9 ft 8½ in)
Wing area: 14.85 m² (159.8 sq ft)
Weight: loaded 2660 kg (5864 lb); empty 2105 kg (4641 lb)
Powerplant: one 1290-hp Klimov VK-105PF-2 liquid-cooled engine
Performance: maximum speed 655 km/h (407 mph) at 3300 m (10 820 ft); range 900 km (560 miles)

Armament: one 20-mm (0.79-in) Shpitalny ShVAK cannon; two 12.7-mm (0.5-in) Berezin UBS machine-guns
Crew: 1
Production: 4848 (all Yak-3s)

which also used a new wing which increased wing span to 10.25 m (33 ft 7½ in).

Before production of the Yak-1 had begun, a UTI-26 two-seat trainer version was built. This carried only a single rifle-calibre machine-gun, and had the increased-span wing used on later Yak-1s. The desirability of a conversion trainer led to production of this version, designated Yak-7V and using the M-105PF engine, beginning in 1941. The success of the Yak-7V ensured that a single-seat version was developed, armament of which was increased to include two 12.7-mm machine-guns as well as the 20-mm cannon. Extra fuel was carried in the rear cockpit space, and aerodynamic refinement led to maximum speed being increased to 613 km/h (381 mph), and production of the Yak-7

single-seater began in early 1942. By the second half of the year production had switched to the improved Yak-7B single-seater which used the Yak-1M cockpit canopy.

A variety of derivatives of the Yak-7 were produced. The two-seat Yak-7K omitted the dual controls and was used for liaison; some Yak-7Vs had a fixed landing gear which could be fitted with skis. Experimental versions were tested with radial engines, underwing ramjets, pressurized cabins and 37-mm (1.46-in) anti-tank cannon. The most important derivative however, was the Yak-7D, flown in July 1942, which had a new wing of light-alloy structure and enlarged fuel capacity. Pre-series examples were built with the designation Yak-7DI, but when full-scale production started in

Yak-1

1 Muzzle of 30-mm (0.79-in) Shpital'ny-Vladimirov cannon
2 Propeller spinner
3 VISh-61P variable-pitch metal propeller
4 Pitch control mechanism
5 Engine coolant tank
6 Filler cap
7 Electrical distributors
8 Auxiliary intake scoop
9 Oil cooler intake
10 Oil cooler
11 Right mainwheel
12 Radiator outlet
13 Cowling lower panel line
14 Engine bearers
15 Coolant piping
16 Outlet
17 Klimov M-105PF liquid-cooled V-12 engine
18 Ejector exhaust stubs
19 Gun troughs
20 Cowling frames
21 Blast tubes
22 Right mainwheel leg position indicator
23 Fuel filler cap
24 Right outboard fuel tank
25 Plywood wing skinning
26 Box spar structure
27 Right navigation light
28 Right metal-framed fabric-skinned aileron
29 Aileron hinge fairing
30 Flap profile
31 Gun cocking mechanism
32 Shpital'ny-Komaritsky 7.62-mm (0.30-in) machine-gun (left and right)
33 Ammunition feed (375 rpg)
34 Gun support tray
35 Breech of 20-mm (0.79-in) Shpital'ny-Vladimirov cannon
36 Oil tank
37 Mainspar/fuselage forward frame member
38 Spar/fuselage attachment bracket
39 Ammunition box
40 Rudder pedal assembly
41 Control column
42 Instrument panel
43 PBP-1a reflector sight
44 Optically-flat armourglass windscreen
45 Aft-sliding (non-jettisonable) canopy
46 Turnover bar
47 Armoured headrest
48 Cockpit aft glazing
49 Accumulator
50 Single-channel RS⅛-3 radio
51 Back armour
52 Pilot's seat
53 Harness
54 Rear-spar carry-through frame
55 Oxygen cylinder
56 Coolant radiator housing
57 Radio equipment tray
58 Hydraulic reservoir
59 Welded steel-tube fuselage frame
60 Diagonal brace wires
61 Aerial mast
62 Plywood decking
63 Dorsal wooden formers
64 Stringers
65 Tail fin attachment bolts
66 Right tailplane
67 Right elevator

68 Tail fin structure
69 Rudder post
70 Rudder structure
71 Rudder trim tab
72 Elevator trim tab
73 Tailplane structure
74 Rudder control horn
75 Elevator control horn
76 Tailwheel oleo shock absorber
77 Non-retractable tailwheel
78 Wooden side stringers
79 Lifting tube
80 Elevator control cables
81 Ventral wooden formers
82 Radiator bath
83 Inset flap structure
84 Aileron control hinge
85 Aileron structue
86 Left wingtip/aileron profile
87 Navigation light
88 Wing skinning
89 Pitot tube
90 Leading-edge rib cut-outs
91 Forward wooden boxspar
92 Left outboard fuel tank
93 Fuel filler cap
94 Left wheel leg indicator
95 Mainwheel leg attachment plate
96 Landing light
97 Mainwheel leg fairing
98 Mainwheel door fairing
99 Left mainwheel
100 Axle fork
101 Torque links
102 Mainwheel oleo leg
103 Retraction/downlock strut
104 Pivot point
105 Retraction cylinder
106 Ventral radiator intake
107 Left inboard fuel tank
108 Inboard rib
109 Rib cut-outs
110 Mainwheel well
111 Engine bearer/fuselage forward frame attachment
112 Carburettor intake duct
113 Wing root carburettor air intake
114 RS-82 rocket fragmentation missiles (three per wing)

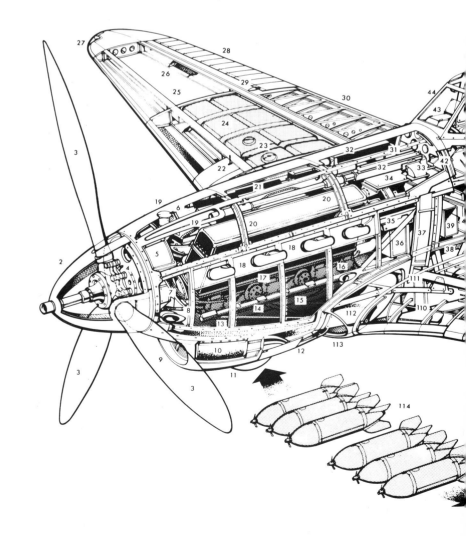

Left and far left: The Yak-1 was named *Krasavec* (beauty) and was so successful that its designer Alexander S Yakovlev was awarded the Order of Lenin, 100 000 roubles and a Zis car. The fabric-covered plywood skin was coated with a thick layer of polish to give a very smooth finish

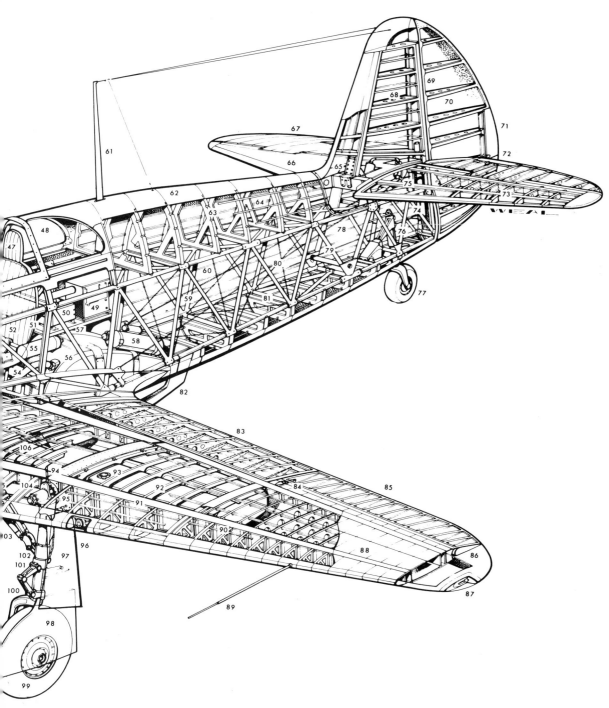

the second half of 1942 this was changed to Yak-9. Compared with its predecessor, the Yak-9 had increased range and a better rate of climb, though armament was reduced by the omission of one of the machine-guns.

The Yak-9 was to remain in production for five years, and the 16 769 examples completed in this period included a number of variants. These included the Yak-9PVO with night-flying equipment; the Yak-9D and -9DD with progressively increased fuel capacity; the Yak-9T and -9K, which entered production in 1943 with, respectively, 37-mm or 45-mm (1.77-in) anti-tank guns and wing racks for hollow-charge bombs; and the Yak-9B fighter-bomber of 1944, which carried an internal bombload of four 100-kg (220-lb) bombs. The final series began with the Yak-9U, which entered production in 1944 using the 1650-hp M-107A and had a top speed of 675 km/h (419.4 mph) at 5500 m (18 045 ft). The 3900 members of this series included the all-metal Yak-9UT and its -9UV two-seat trainer counterpart; the Yak-9T-45 with 45-mm cannon; and the postwar Yak-9P, which carried all-weather equipment and instruments.

Meanwhile, by the end of 1942 a Yak-1M had been adapted to take a new wing of reduced span and mixed construction, and with a 1300-hp M-105PF-2 engine and various aerodynamic improvements this demonstrated a speed of 680 km/h (422.5 mph) at 3700 m (12 139 ft). Production did not begin until late 1943, and a comparatively modest total of 4848 were completed in this series. However, the Yak-3, as the type was designated, proved an outstanding low-level fighter and was the vehicle for some remarkable achievements in combat. The M-107A-powered Yak-3U version was produced from late 1944 and although too late to see combat before the end of the war, it was often rated the best close-combat fighter of its type in the world. Small numbers were also built of the Yak-3T and the Yak-3P, with three 20-mm B-20 cannon in place of the standard armament of one 20-mm and two 12.7-mm weapons, while a postwar derivative was the Yak-11 basic trainer.

Although attempts to improve the high-altitude performance of the various wartime Yakovlev fighters met with repeated failure, this was outside the scope of the original design, testimony to whose soundness can be found in the variety of specialized roles for which it was adapted and the fantastic production total of over 36 000. The later models saw postwar service with the air forces of Soviet allies, many of which were still flying their Yaks in the late 1950s.

The Yak-9 was a second-generation fighter compared to earlier Yakovlev designs. It was one of the first Soviet fighters to be compared favourably with Western designs with its all-metal construction. The Yak-9U was fitted with additional navigational and radio equipment, and was recognizable by a transparent panel in the rear fuselage covering a direction-finding loop.

The Yak-9 remained in service with satellite air forces and many first line units of the Soviet Air Force into the early 1950s, as well as the French Groupe de Chasse GC 3 during World War II.

Above: A production line for Yak-7Bs, in a plant at Kuybishev to which the original factory was evacuated in late 1941. Only six weeks' output was lost in the giant move
Left: A Yak-3 of the Free French Normandie-Niemen Regiment. The French pilots preferred the Russian fighter to any other Allied type, being easier to fly, though with poor radio equipment and a rudimentary reflector sight

La-5, Lavochkin

FIRST FLIGHT 1942

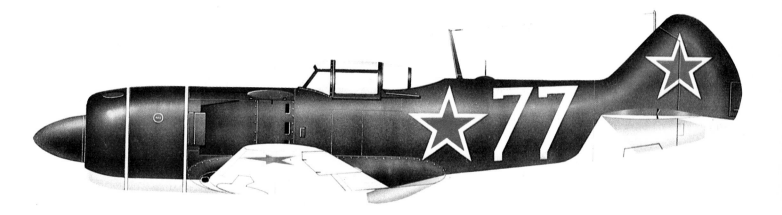

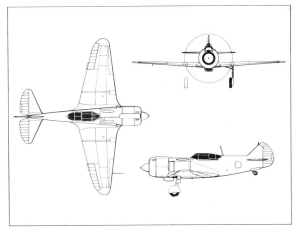

IN an attempt to improve the LaGG-3, the Lavochkin team took the drastic step of replacing the liquid-cooled engine with the 1600-hp Shvetsov M-82. Although the substitution of this shorter, wider and heavier radial involved numerous problems, the installation was outstanding, and very similar both to that of the Fw 190 and the Hawker Tempest II of two years later. The additional weight was compensated for by the extra power available and the elimination of the cooling system required for the original engine. However, the concentration of engine weight changed the centre of gravity to the extent that nose armament could be increased to two 20-mm (0.79-in) ShVAK cannon.

Tests of the prototype conversion began in March 1942, and the results, including substantially improved performance, were such that in July it was decided to convert all incomplete LaGG-3s to take the radial engine. Range was still short, and it took several months for major defects to be eradicated, but the LaGG-3's intractability had been replaced by outstanding manoeuvrability. By the end of the year production was in full swing. The designation was La-5.

Several modifications were made to the basic aircraft in the course of production. When old LaGG-3 airframes had been used up, an improved cockpit canopy was fitted, and the 1650-hp M-82F replaced the earlier model. In 1943 the fuel arrangement was changed to solve the problem of the unsatisfactory wing tanks, and power was further boosted by the use of the direct-injection M-82FN,

this model being designated La-5FN. Towards the end of the year, with the easing of the alloy shortages that had dictated its wooden construction, an La-5 was fitted with a new wing incorporating metal structural members. The reduced structural bulk allowed an increase in fuel capacity, and during 1944 the new wing was introduced on production La-5FNs.

At the same time, a more extensive modification of the design resulted in the new designation La-7. This used the new wing as well as a refined engine installation and various detail improvements which raised top speed to 680 km/h (423 mph) at 3000 m (9843 ft). From the spring of 1944 it supplanted the La-5FN in production. Developments included experimental rocket-boosted and

La-5FN

Type: fighter-bomber
Maker: State aircraft factories
Span: 9.68 m (31 ft 9 in)
Length: 8.7 m (28 ft 7 in)
Height: 2.54 m (8 ft 4 in)
Wing area: 17.51 m² (188.37 sq ft)
Weight: loaded 3360 kg (7400 lb); empty 2605 kg (5743 lb)
Powerplant: one 1850-hp ASh-82FN (M-82FN) 14-cylinder two-row radial
Performance: maximum speed 648 km/h (402 mph) at 5000 m (16 404 ft); range 765 km (475 miles); operational ceiling 10 000 m (32 808 ft)
Armament: two 20-mm (0.79-in) ShVAK cannon; six 82-mm (3.2-in) RS-82 rockets or 200 kg (441 lb) of bombs
Crew: 1
Production: approx 20 000 (all La-5 types)

Above: The La-5 was a popular aircraft with both pilots and groundcrews. The air-cooled engine was easy to maintain in sub-zero winter temperatures. The first aircraft to see action were flown by factory pilots at the Battle of Stalingrad in late 1942

Above: A Soviet pilot starts his pre-take-off checks in an La-5FN

Right: The La-5FN was so designated because of its *forsirovannii nyeposredstvenny* or boosted engine. It was powered by an ASh-82FN with direct fuel injection

Centre right: La-5FN fighters open up their engines on a rough strip on the Eastern Front. Groundcrew wait, ready to pull away the chocks. This fighter enjoyed immense popularity, and was flown by several aces from the summer of 1943

supercharged models, while some examples carried three lightweight B-20 20-mm cannon.

Towards the end of the war a major redesign resulted in the all-metal La-9, using the re-designated ASh-82FNV engine and armed with four 20-mm cannon. This remained in production after 1945, and was followed by the last of the line, the postwar La-11.

While the LaGG-3 had been at a severe disadvantage in aerial combat with the German Bf 109s, the appearance of its radial-engined successor enabled the Soviet pilots to turn the tables on both the Messerschmitt fighter and the Fw 190. Its limited range was slowly increased by augmenting the fuel capacity, and its manoeuvrability could not be equalled by any of its opponents. Other virtues shared by the La-5 and its successors included durability and ease of maintenance, vital attributes on the Eastern Front. All members of the series could carry RS-82 rockets or light bombs under the wings, and hollow-charge anti-tank bombs were often carried on close-support missions.

The La-9 was too late to see much combat during World War II, but both it and the La-11 which succeeded it saw widespread service with the air forces of the Soviet Union and its allies, receiving the respective NATO codenames Fritz and Fang. Two-seat trainer versions were produced of all members of the series, these being distinguished by the suffix UTI. Combined production of the La-5 and La-7 reached a total of some 26 000.

La-5FN

1 Hucks-type starter dog
2 Spinner
3 Propeller balance
4 Controllable frontal intake louvres
5 VISh-105V metal controllable-pitch three-blade propeller
6 Nose ring profile
7 intake centrebody
8 ShVAK cannon left
9 Supercharger air intake
10 Supercharger intake trunk fairing
11 Blast tube
12 Shvetsov M-82FN 14-cylinder two-row radial
13 Cowling ring
14 Cowling panel hinge line
15 Exhaust pipes
16 Exhaust outlet cluster (seven per side)
17 Outlet cover panel
18 Engine accessories
19 Mainspar/fuselage attachment
20 Ammunition tanks (200 rpg)
21 Link and cartridge ejection chutes
22 Engine bearer upper support bracket
23 Cannon breech fairing
24 Paired 20-mm (0.79-in) ShVAK cannon
25 Supercharger intake trunking
26 Stressed bakelite-ply skinning
27 Automatic leading-edge slat (obliquely-operated)
28 Pitot head
29 Right navigation light
30 Wingtip
31 Dural-framed fabric-covered aileron
32 Aileron trim tab
33 Armourglass windscreen
34 PBF-1a reflector gunsight
35 Cockpit air
36 Control column
37 Outlet louvres
38 Rudder pedal assembly
39 Underfloor control linkage
40 Rear spar/fuselage attachment
41 Rudder and elevator trim handwheels
42 Seat height adjustment
43 Boost controls
44 Seat harness

45 Pilot's seat
46 Throttle quadrant
47 Hydraulics main valve
48 Aft-sliding cockpit canopy
49 Fixed aft transparent cockpit fairing
50 Armourglass screen
51 Canopy track
52 RSI-4 HF R/T installation
53 Radio equipment shelf
54 Dural fuselage side panels
55 Control cables
56 Plywood-sheathed birch frames with triangular-section wooden stringers
57 Stressed bakelite-ply skinning
58 Accumulator
59 Accumulator access panel
60 Tailfin frontspar attachment
61 Aerial mast
62 Radio aerials
63 Right tailplane
64 Elevator hinge
65 Dural-framed fabric-covered elevator
66 Tailfin leading edge
67 Tailfin wooden structure (plywood skinning)
68 Aerial stub
69 Rudder balance
70 Rudder upper hinge
71 Dural-framed fabric-covered rudder
72 Rudder trim tab
73 Rear navigation light
74 Rudder centre hinge
75 Elevator control lever
76 Tailplane/fuselage attachment
77 Rudder control lever
78 Elevator trim tab
79 Dural-framed fabric-covered elevator
80 Wooden two-spar tailplane structure (plywood skinning)
81 Tailwheel doors
82 Aft-retracting tailwheel (usually locked in extended position)
83 Tailwheel leg
84 Tailwheel shock strut
85 Retraction mechanism
86 Stressed bakelite-ply skinning
87 Retractable access step
88 Wing root fillet
89 Dural-skinned flap construction
90 Aileron tab

91 Dural-framed fabric-covered aileron
92 Wingtip
93 Left navigation light
94 Leading-edge automatic slat (obliquely operated)
95 Outboard ribs
96 Automatic slat actuating mechanism
97 Rear boxspar
98 Forward boxspar
99 Leading-edge ribs
100 Fuel filler cap
101 Left fuel tank of three tank set
102 Mainwheel well
103 Oil cooler outlet flap
104 Engine oil cooler intake
105 Right mainwheel
106 Landing gear hydraulic jack and ram
107 Landing gear knuckle joint
108 Landing gear/front spar attachment
109 Mainwheel leg fairing plate
110 Mainwheel oleo leg
111 Left mainwheel
112 Mainwheel fairing plate
113 Torque links
114 Underwing stores shackles
115 50-kg (110-lb) bomb

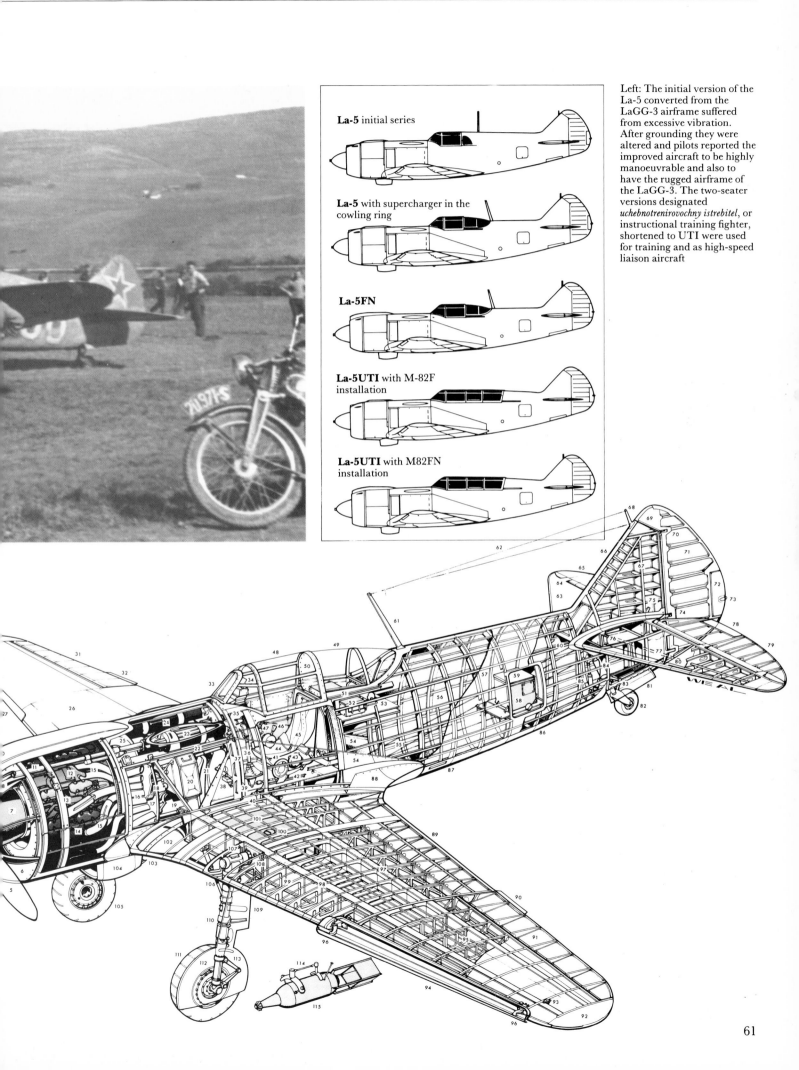

La-5 initial series

La-5 with supercharger in the cowling ring

La-5FN

La-5UTI with M-82F installation

La-5UTI with M82FN installation

Left: The initial version of the La-5 converted from the LaGG-3 airframe suffered from excessive vibration. After grounding they were altered and pilots reported the improved aircraft to be highly manoeuvrable and also to have the rugged airframe of the LaGG-3. The two-seater versions designated *uchebnotrenirovochny istrebitel*, or instructional training fighter, shortened to UTI were used for training and as high-speed liaison aircraft

P-39 Airacobra, Bell

FIRST FLIGHT 1938

Top: The P-39 combined a mid-mounted engine, car type doors and a nosewheel
Above: P-39Cs on patrol just before Pearl Harbor
Right: A line up of fire-power – the 37-mm (1.46-in) cannon mounted in the nose of the Airacobra. Together with machine-guns and a bomb it made it an effective attack aircraft

THE Airacobra was the Bell company's second fighter, a single-engined single-seater which introduced many novel features. Its configuration stemmed largely from the decision to use the new M4 37-mm (1.46-in) cannon positioned on the fuselage centreline; accordingly, the engine, a turbo-supercharged 1150-hp Allison V-1710-17, was sited behind the cockpit, on the centre of gravity. The propeller was driven through an extension shaft and reduction gearing, leaving the nose free for a heavy cannon firing through the propeller hub, a pair of 12.7-mm (0.5-in) machine-guns and the retracting front leg of a tricycle landing gear, then a novelty.

A single prototype was ordered in October 1938, which made its first flight in April 1938, demon-strating a speed of 627.6 km/h (390 mph), so that 13 service-test YP-39s were ordered in April 1939.

While the YP-39s were under construction the prototype was re-engined with a V-1710-39 without turbo-supercharger to become the XP-39B, and this and other changes, almost all reducing performance, were incorporated in the YP-39s. The first production order, for 80 P-39Cs, was placed in August 1939, but only 20 were completed. Two 7.62-mm (0.30-in) machine-guns which had been added to the original nose armament were replaced by a pair of similar weapons in each wing. Self-sealing fuel tanks were fitted. A total of 923 of the new model were delivered, with the designation P-39D.

In April 1940 the RAF had ordered 675 of a

Above: A wave from a USAAF pilot during night-flying training. The picture was certainly posed for propaganda purposes, since few pilots would welcome a searchlight shining at them as this would destroy their night vision. The crutch for the bomb or drop-tank can be seen under the fuselage

62

Right: One of the unusual features of the Airacobra was the cockpit access. Unlike most fighters which had a sliding or hinged canopy, the Airacobra was fitted with doors like a civilian sporting aircraft. Though this made entry easy, emergency exit was occasionally more difficult than in conventional designs

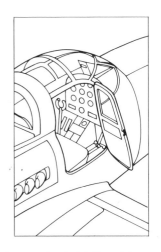

Left: The mid-mounted engine not only allowed heavy nose armament to be carried, but also gave the pilot protection from the rear
Below: A drop-tank equipped P-39 in service with the Soviet air force. The Russians liked the aircraft, flying it at low altitudes against ground targets where its heavy fire-power devastated German soft-skinned vehicles

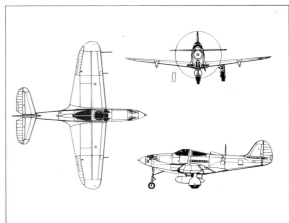

P-39N

Type: ground-attack fighter
Maker: Bell Aircraft Corporation
Span: 10.36 m (34 ft)
Length: 9.2 m (30 ft 2 in)
Height: 3.78 m (12 ft 5 in)
Wing area: 19.79 m² (213 sq ft)
Weight: maximum 3447 kg (7600 lb); empty 2903 kg (6400 lb)
Powerplant: one 1200-hp Allison V-1710-85 V-12 liquid-cooled engine
Performance: maximum speed 605 km/h (376 mph) at 4572 m (15 000 ft); range 1569 km (975 miles) with drop-tanks; operational ceiling 11 735 m (38 500 ft)
Armament: one 37-mm (1.46-in) M4 cannon; two 0.5-in (12.7-mm) and four 0.30-in (7.62-mm) Browning machine-guns; 227-kg (500-lb) bombload
Crew: 1
Production: 2095 (total 9558)

similar model, but with a 20-mm (0.79-in) His-pano-Suiza cannon. They were tried by 601 Sqn who rejected them. The US passed 212 to the USSR, and most of the remainder were taken over by the USAAF, given the designation P-400, and used with P-39Ds in the early stages of the Pacific war and subsequently in North Africa. A further 336 P-39D-1s, with 20-mm instead of 37-mm cannon, and 158 D-2s, with similar armament and 1325-hp V-1710-63 engines, were built for the Soviet Union.

The single XP-39E had experimental square-tipped laminar-flow wings, but an order for 4000 P-39Es was cancelled, and the next production version was the P-39F, 229 of which were built, differing from the D only in the make of propeller

used; the 25 P-39Js were similar but with V-1710-59 engines. A reversion to the V-1710-63 resulted in 210 P-39Ks and 250 P-39Ls, which were again distinguished by the propeller. These had originally been part of an order for 1800 P-39Gs, none of which was delivered as such, the series continuing with 240 P-39Ms, which used the 1200-hp V-1710-83.

A final engine change, to the 1200-hp V-1710-85, was made for the two largest series of Airacobras. These were the P-39N and Q, produced for the Soviet Union, which received almost half of all P-39s: the main difference between the 2095 Ns and 4905 Qs was the substitution in the latter of two 12.7-mm machine guns for the four 7.62-mm guns in the wings, and later Qs omitted the wing guns.

J22, FFVS

FIRST FLIGHT 1942

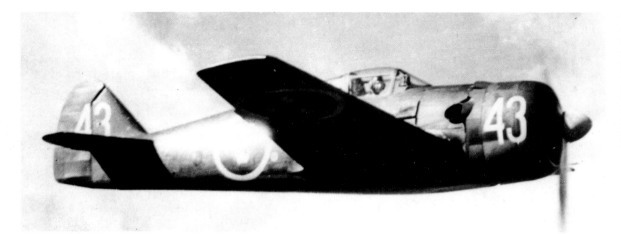

THE US Government's prohibition of aircraft exports in 1940 hit Sweden particularly hard. Plans to modernize her air force were heavily dependent on new fighters ordered from Vultee and Seversky, and the 60 Seversky EP-1s that were delivered before the embargo represented barely one-sixth of the total number ordered. Buying modern fighters elsewhere proved impossible, and semi-obsolescent Fiat CR.42s and Reggiane Re 2000s could only be considered as a stop-gap.

Faced with the lack of supplies from abroad, the Swedish air force took the bold step of asking a member of the control commission, which had been overseeing the work at the Seversky factory, to organize the design and construction of a Swedish fighter. The problems faced included shortages of everything from materials to manufacturing capacity, and a prime requirement was a suitable engine, for which manufacturing licences were as difficult to find as the aircraft.

The solution was to copy, by measurement and analysis, the Pratt & Whitney Twin Wasp engine – an extremely difficult operation – but by 1942 Svenska Flygmotor was ready to begin production of its version, designated STWc3.

Several hundred small contractors produced components which were assembled by the Flygförvaltningens Verkstad (government aircraft works), housed in a hangar at Bromma airport, near Stockholm and financed by the main Swedish airline ABA, and by air force workshops. The J22, as the new fighter was designated, had been made as light as possible: construction was a combina-

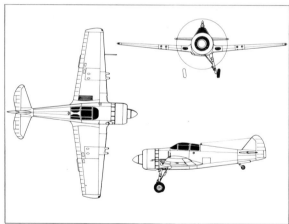

tion of steel-tube framework and load-bearing plywood covering. The two prototypes were followed by 141 production J22As, armed with two 13.2-mm (0.52-in) and two 8-mm (0.315-in) machine-guns in the wings. The first was delivered in October 1943, and production was completed by 57 J22Bs, which had four of the larger-calibre machine-guns.

In spite of the low power available, the J22 proved respectably fast and fully manoeuvrable. It formed the basis of Sweden's fighter defences from 1944, when it replaced the Italian fighters, until the early 1950s, when it was itself superseded by the jet-powered Saab J21R and the de Havilland Vampire. The only other role undertaken by the J22 was that of photographic reconnaissance.

J22B

Type: single-seat fighter
Maker: Flygförvaltningens Verkstad; Flygvåpnet workshops, Arboga
Span: 10 m (32 ft 9¾ in)
Length: 7.8 m (25 ft 7 in)
Height: 2.8 m (9 ft 2¼ in)
Wing area: 16.01 m² (172.33 sq ft)
Weight: loaded 2835 kg (6250 lb); empty 2020 kg (4453 lb)
Powerplant: one 1065-hp Svenska Flygmotor STWc3 (Pratt & Whitney R-1830 Twin Wasp) 14-cylinder air-cooled radial
Performance: maximum speed 575 km/h (357 mph) at 3500 m (11 483 ft); range 1270 km (2044 miles); operational ceiling 9300 m (30 512 ft)
Armament: four 13.2-mm (0.52-in) Madsen M-39A machine-guns
Crew: 1
Production: 57

Hawk 75, Curtiss

FIRST FLIGHT 1935

THE 1934 United States Army Air Corps specification for a 483-km/h (300-mph) all-metal, low-wing monoplane fighter brought submissions from a number of companies, among them Curtiss, whose Model 75, powered by a 775-hp Wright XR-1670, flew for the first time in April 1935. Problems with both this engine and the Pratt & Whitney R-1535 Twin Wasp Junior which was substituted in the Model 75A led to the use in the Model 75B of a Wright XR-1820 Cyclone. When the required speed still proved unattainable the army asked for three Y1P-36 development aircraft to be powered by the Pratt & Whitney R-1830 Twin Wasp. Flown in February 1937, the first Y1P-36 achieved 474 km/h (294.5 mph) in trials, leading to an order for 210.

The Curtiss Model 75 – the greatest design by Don R Berlin – in its various derivatives was to be one of the most widely used aircraft of World War II. At the same time as development of the USAAC fighter was proceeding, an export version with fixed landing gear and bomb racks was produced for export. Designated Model 75-H, or Hawk 75, it attracted orders from China, Argentina and Thailand for small batches which were delivered during 1938. The 30 Chinese Hawk 75-Ms had four 0.3-in (7.62-mm) machine-guns, the 30 Argentinian Hawk 75-0s had six similar weapons, and the 25 Thai Hawk 75-Ns had two 7.92-mm (0.312-in) machine-guns and two 23-mm (0.91-in) Madsen cannon; all were powered by the 840-hp GR-1820-G3 Cyclone, and licence pro-

Above: A P-36A of the 'A' Flight Leader of the 55th Pursuit Squadron which was part of the 20th Pursuit Group. It had a blue – previously white – band around the nose for quick recognition. The group designator (PT) is painted on the tail

duction of small numbers was also undertaken in China and Argentina.

Meanwhile, in April 1938 the first P-36s were delivered to the USAAC. Most were delivered as P-36As with the 1050-hp R-1830-17, while others were used as development aircraft for a variety of purposes. One was completed as the XP-37, with an early Allison V-1710 liquid-cooled engine of about 900 hp, and a more powerful Allison was fitted to another example to produce the XP-40. The P-36B and XP-42 used 1100-hp R-1830-25 and 1050-hp R-1830-31 engines, respectively. The 30 P-36Cs had two 0.3-in wing guns in addition to the original standard of one 0.5-in (12.7-mm) and one 0.3-in in the nose; the XP-36D had two nose 0.5-in and four wing 0.3-in weapons; the XP-36E had double the wing armament and only one 0.5-in machine-gun in the nose, and the XP-36F combined the original nose armament with a pair of wing-mounted 23-mm Madsens.

The P-36A was also produced in a series of export versions designated Hawk 75A-1 to A-6, the A-1, A-2, A-3 and A-6 having progressively more powerful versions of the Twin Wasp. The remainder used the 1200-hp Cyclone. The first customer for the export P-36As was France, which from 1938 ordered 100 A-1s, 100 A-2s, 135 A-3s and 285 A-4s. The bulk of the first three batches were delivered before May 1940, seeing considerable action against the Luftwaffe before the June 1940 armistice. The rest of the A-4s were diverted to Britain, where they were named Mohawks. These served with the South African Air Force and the RAF in

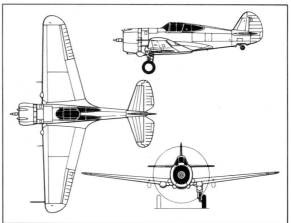

India, and 12 were supplied to Portugal. Norway was another early customer, ordering 24 A-6s and 36 A-8s.

The destruction of two Japanese aircraft by P-36As during the Pearl Harbor attack was the second leg of a unique double for the Hawk 75. French Hawk 75C-1s claimed the first aerial victories of the war, and the P-36A's Japanese victims were the first combat successes for the USAAF. Moreover, the use by Finland of French and Norwegian Hawks captured during the German invasions, and the use of Vichy French examples against Allied forces in North Africa and Syria, meant that the type served not only in virtually all theatres, but also on both sides, during the first years of the war.

P-36A

Type: single-seat fighter
Maker: Curtiss-Wright Corporation, Airplane Division
Span: 11.38 m (37 ft 4 in)
Length: 8.69 m (28 ft 6 in)
Height: 3.71 m (12 ft 2 in)
Wing area: 21.93 m² (236 sq ft)
Weight: normal 2563 kg (5650 lb); empty 2072 kg (4567 lb)
Powerplant: one 1050-hp Pratt & Whitney R-1830-17 Twin Wasp 14-cylinder air-cooled radial engine
Performance: maximum speed 504 km/h (313 mph) at 3048 m (10 000 ft); range 1328 km (825 miles); operational ceiling 10 272 m (33 700 ft)
Armament: one 0.5-in (12.7-mm) and one 0.3-in (7.62-mm) Browning machine gun
Crew: 1
Production: 177 (1424 all types)

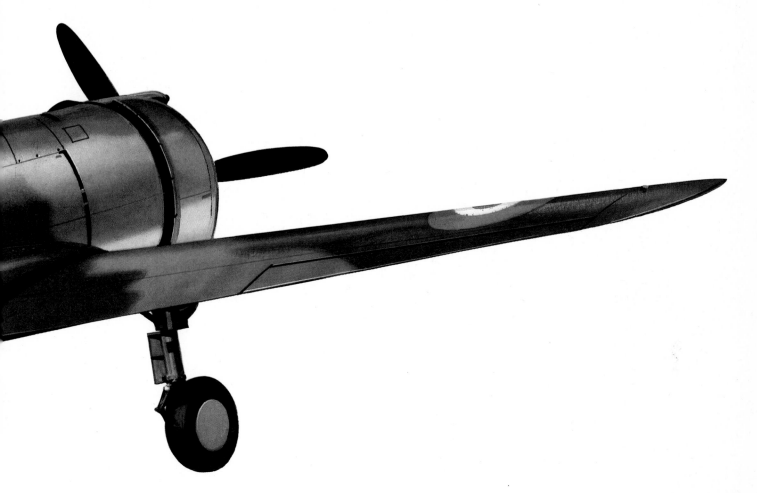

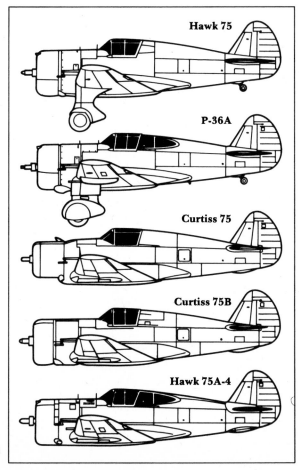

Hawk 75

P-36A

Curtiss 75

Curtiss 75B

Hawk 75A-4

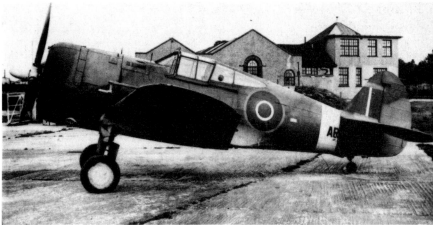

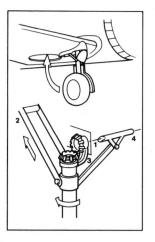

Top: A Curtiss Hawk of GC II/5 with the Cigogne (stork) emblem of the 2e Escadrille. This unit saw action against the US forces landing in Morocco in November 1942
Above: The Hawk 75A-4, with the GR-1820-G205A Cyclone 9 engine, was known as the Mohawk IV when they were used in RAF service.
Far left: Hawk 75 was the export version of the Curtiss 75, with fixed landing gear and bomb racks, and powered by the 840-hp GR-1820-63 Cyclone. Because the Curtiss 75 had problems with its 775-hp Wright XR-1670, the 75B adopted the XR-1820. The P-36A had even greater power with its 1050-hp R-1830-17, and had a 23-mm (0·91-cal) Madsen cannon in a fairing under each wing. The Hawk 75A-4 was an export version
Left: The early retractable gear of the P-36 which was effected not by 'bevel gears' but by a jack within the wing skin

1 Fixed quadrant in wing skin
2 Jack
3 Casting swinging around the centreline of fixed quadrant
4 Pivot

Hawk 81, Curtiss

FIRST FLIGHT 1938

WHEN the P-36A was being produced, several examples were tested with alternative power-plant and armament. A promising line of development was represented by the XP-40 conversion of a P-36A. The XP-40 flew for the first time in October 1938, powered by the higher-altitude V-1710-19 version of the Allison engine. Although initial performance was disappointing, the gradual elimination of drag-inducing features, most significantly the repositioning of the original ventral radiator under the nose, resulted in a speed of 587 km/h (365 mph). Consequently, in April 1939 a total of 524 production P-40s were ordered.

In October 1939 substantial French orders for Hawk 75s were supplemented by a new order for 230 Hawk 81As (the Curtiss Company designation for the P-40). Four 7.5-mm (0.295-in) machine-guns were to be mounted in the wings in addition to the P-40's standard pair of nose-mounted 0.5-in (12.7-mm) weapons. French equipment was to be fitted, but none had been delivered when France capitulated to Germany in 1940. Like the P-40, the French Hawk 81A-1 carried no combat protection, and when the order was taken over by Britain the last 90 were modified as Hawk 81A-2s, with armoured windscreens, cockpit protection and self-sealing fuel tanks. These entered RAF service as Tomahawk IIAs, while the first 140, named Tomahawk I, were issued to newly formed army co-operation squadrons for reconnaissance work.

Meanwhile, the USAAF cancelled its order after 200 of its P-40s had been delivered, replacing it with new orders for improved models. These comprised 131 P-40Bs, with similar protection to that carried by the Tomahawk IIA and two wing-mounted 0.3-in guns, as well as 193 P-40Cs, with a new fuel system, provision for a drop-tank and four wing guns. The first 20 of a new British order for 950 were Tomahawk IIAs, and the remainder were IIBs, replacing the IIA's 0.3-in wing guns with 0.303-in (7.7-mm) weapons.

Large numbers of the USAAF P-40s were destroyed in the early stages of the Pacific war, and these were soon replaced by improved models based on the Hawk 87 development, production of which began in mid 1941. The British Tomahawks saw extensive service with RAF and Commonwealth air force squadrons in North Africa in 1941–42, while a total of 195 were supplied to the USSR in 1941.

Perhaps the most famous of all the early P-40s were those supplied to the American Volunteer Group, formed in 1941 by former USAAC captain Claire Chennault. The AVG was supplied with 100 Hawk 81A-2s, originally part of the RAF order, and from late 1941 they defended the vital Burma Road. The AVG's garish tiger-shark markings led to their nickname of the Flying Tigers, and the combination of effective tactics (essentially, using the P-40's superior speed and firepower to inflict damage while avoiding prolonged dog-fighting with their more manoeuvrable Japanese opponents) and an efficient early warning system enabled the AVG to compile one of the best records of any fighter unit. When the AVG became the 23rd Pursuit Group, USAAF, in July 1942, it had destroyed 286 Japanese aircraft, with only 23 pilots lost.

Tomahawk IIB

1 Spinner
2 Propeller pitch-change mechanism
3 Propeller hub shaft
4 Spinner back-plate
5 Three-blade constant-speed Curtiss electric propeller
6 Supercharger air intake
7 Fuselage machine-gun barrel fairings
8 Supercharger intake duct
9 Fuselage machine-gun forward support bracket
10 Cowling frames
11 Propeller reduction gear casing
12 Radiator piping
13 Three-part intake
14 Quick-release radiator panel catch
15 Oil coolant radiator (centre)
16 Left glycol radiator
17 Right mainwheel
18 Radiator cooling gills
19 Wingroot fairing
20 Cowling frame
21 Engine bearer support strut
22 Main engine bearer assembly
23 Anti-vibration dampers
24 Exhaust stubs
25 Allison V-1710-C15 engine
26 Supercharger assembly
27 Right wing skinning
28 Right navigation light
29 Aileron
30 Aileron control ball and socket linkage
31 Aileron tab
32 Right split flap
33 Flap control push-rod rollers
34 Bead sight
35 Coolant expansion tank
36 Machine-gun blast tubes
37 Firewall bulkhead
38 Engine support bearer attachments
39 Gun cooling louvres
40 Ammunition tank
41 Ejection chute
42 Rudder pedal assembly
43 Control column
44 Instrument panel
45 Two 0·5-cal (12,7-mm) M-2 fuselage machine-guns
46 Windscreen hot air
47 Ring sight
48 Clear vision windscreen
49 Faired rear-view mirror
50 Aft-sliding Plexiglas canopy
51 Cockpit ventilation control
52 Throttle quadrant
53 Engine control rods
54 Pilot's seat
55 Control linkage
56 Harness
57 Seat support frame
58 Pilot's headrest
59 Rear-view vision cut-out
60 Fuselage fuel tank filler cap
61 Fuselage auxiliary fuel tank
62 Control cables
63 Hydraulics tank
64 Oil tank
65 Oil tank filler cap
66 Aerials
67 Dorsal (offset) identification light
68 Aerial lead-in
69 TR9D radio receiver/transmitter equipment
70 Fuselage stringers
71 Fuselage frame
72 Right tailplane

73 Right elevator
74 Tailfin structure
75 Tailfin navigation lights
76 Aerial attachment
77 Rudder upper (external) hinge bracket
78 Rudder structure
79 Rudder centre hinge
80 Rudder trim tab
81 Elevator tab
82 Left elevator
83 Tailplane structure
84 Rudder lower hinge
85 Tailwheel door
86 Retractable tailwheel
87 Tailwheel oleo leg
88 Access plates
89 Elevator control horn linkage
90 Tailplane attachments
91 Trim tab control chains
92 Tailwheel retraction mechanism
93 Elevator control cables
94 Lifting tube
95 Rudder control cables
96 Battery
97 Fuselage compartment access door

98 Oxygen cylinders
99 Hydraulics pump
100 Wingroot fillet
101 Left split flap
102 Left mainwheel well
103 Wing main (aft) fuel tank
104 Wing/fuselage attachment plates
105 Wing reserve (forward) fuel tank
106 Rotation bevel gears
107 Undercarriage leg fairing
108 Fairing doors
109 Brace strut
110 Brake cable
111 Mainwheel oleo pneumatic leg
112 Smooth contour tyre
113 Hub cover
114 Torque links
115 Retraction drag struts
116 Wing machine-gun barrels
117 Undercarriage retraction cylinder
118 Inboard wing gun ammunition box
119 Blast tubes
120 Outboard wing gun ammunition box
121 Two 0·3-cal (7,62-mm) Colt MG-40 wing machine-guns

Far left: A Curtiss P-40 of the USAAF; the red centre was painted out of the star insignia in the spring of 1942 in order to prevent confusion with the Japanese Hinomaru 'meat ball' marking
Left: Shark's teeth on a P-40B of the American Volunteer Group. This unit operated in China against the Japanese. The aircraft had RAF-style dark earth, dark green and sky camouflage. The AVG was the first American unit in World War II to display kill markings

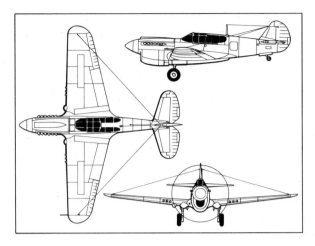

P-40C

Type: single-seat fighter
Maker: Curtiss-Wright Corporation, Airplane Division
Span: 11.37 m (37 ft 3½ in)
Length: 9.66 m (31 ft 8½ in)
Height: 3.23 m (10 ft 7 in)
Wing area: 21.93 m² (236 sq ft)
Weight: normal 3424 kg (7549 lb); empty 2636 kg (5812 lb)
Powerplant: one 1090-hp Allison V-1710-33 liquid-cooled V-12 engine
Performance: maximum speed 555 km/h (345 mph) at 4572 m (15 000 ft); range 1287 km (800 miles); operational ceiling 8992 m (29 500 ft)
Armament: two 0.5-in (12.7-mm) and four 0.3-in (7.62-mm) Browning machine-guns
Crew: 1
Production: 193 (13 740 all types)

122 Outboard wing structure
123 Aileron control link access
124 Aileron trim tab
125 Left aileron
126 Left wingtip structure
127 Aerial attachment
128 Left navigation light
129 Leading-edge ribs
130 Pitot tube

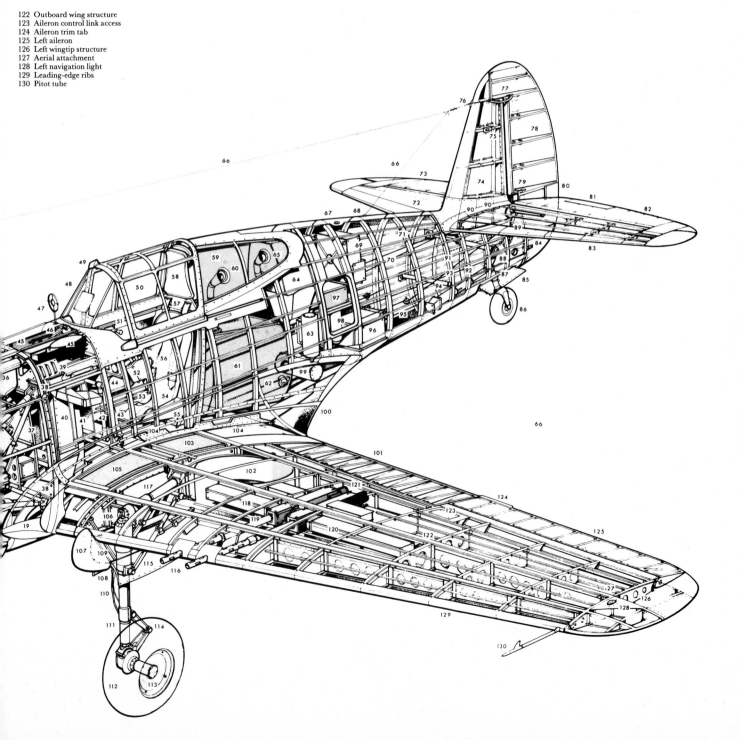

Hawk 87, Curtiss
FIRST FLIGHT 1939

CURTISS decided to adapt the P-40 in 1939 to take the new 1150-hp Allison V-1710-39 powerplant. This was achieved with the minimum of changes beyond a redesigned nose and concentrating all armament in the wings. The resulting Hawk 87 could carry a drop-tank or 227-kg (500-lb) bomb under the fuselage. Original armament was four 0.5-in (12.7-mm) machine-guns, but another two were soon added.

The first order for the H-87 came in May 1940 from Britain and consisted of 560 Kittyhawk Is, as the type was designated in British and Commonwealth service, all but the first 20 having six guns. The United States Army followed with an order for 1540 P-40Ds in June. The addition of the extra guns resulted in the designation changing to P-40E after only 22 four-gun Ds had been delivered. A total of 2320 P-40Es were built, 820 for the USAAF, which named the type Warhawk, and the rest for Lend-Lease supply to Britain.

In June 1941 the first flight was made of a new variant, the XP-40F, powered by a Packard-built Rolls-Royce Merlin. This engine offered improved altitude performance, and 1311 production P-40Fs were built with the 1300-hp Packard V-1650-1 version of the Merlin, incorporating increased fuel capacity as well as provision for a 45-kg (100-lb) bomb under each wing. Later batches of the P-40F used a slightly lengthened rear fuselage, and 249 became RAF Kittyhawk IIs.

The designation P-40G had been used for one of the original P-40s armed with six wing guns. The next production model was the P-40K, which

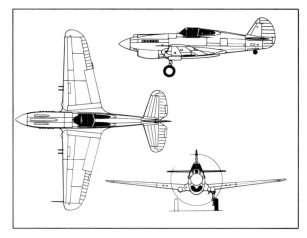

reverted to an Allison engine, the 1325-hp V-1710-73. Delivery of 1300 began in August 1942, 500 of them with the longer fuselage, and all were delivered by the end of the year. Other new models to appear in 1942 were the P-40L and M, powered by the Packard V-1650 and the 1200-hp Allison V-1710-81, respectively. The P-40L was designed as a lightweight version, all but the first 50 of 700 built having no wing fuel tanks and only four 0.5-in guns, though its maximum weight of 4423 kg (9750 lb) was only 113 kg (250 lb) less than that of the P-40K. The 600 P-40Ms produced were used mainly as Kittyhawk IIs.

The final production version of the Warhawk was the P-40N, maximum weight of which was reduced to 4014 kg (8850 lb) by the omission of

P-40N-1 Warhawk

Type: fighter-bomber
Maker: Curtiss-Wright Corporation, Airplane Division
Span: 11.36 m (37 ft 3½ in)
Length: 10.16 m (33 ft 4 in)
Height: 3.71 m (12 ft 2 in)
Wing area: 21.93 m² (236 sq ft)
Weight: normal 3357 kg (7400 lb); empty 2722 kg (6000 lb)
Powerplant: one 1200-hp Allison V-1710-81 V-12 liquid-cooled engine
Performance: maximum speed 552 km/h (343 mph) at 4572 m (15 000 ft); range 1207 km (750 miles); operational ceiling 9144 m (30 000 ft)
Armament: four 0.5-in (12.7-mm) Browning machine-guns; 680-kg (1500-lb) bombload
Crew: 1
Production: 400

wing tanks and two machine-guns, aided by the use of lighter components, with three 227-kg (500-lb) bombs to be carried. No fewer than 5215 P-40Ns were built before production ended in November 1944: the first 2577 used the V-1710-81 engine, and the armament reverted to six 0.5-in guns on the next 3022, with the V-1710-99, and the last 220, which used the V-1710-115. The XP-40Q was a K modified to take a 1425-hp V-1710-121 engine, bubble canopy and square-tipped wings, but no production was undertaken of this variant.

By the time the P-40N appeared the USAAF was using more modern fighters, and most Ns were supplied to the Allies under Lend-Lease, the RAF designation being Kittyhawk IV. They were used mainly as escorts and ground-attack fighters.

Above left: A P-40E with the red-bordered insignia which was used between July and August 1943. In RAF service the P-40E was designated Kittyhawk IA
Above: The personal aircraft of Major John S Chennault – son of the Flying Tigers commander – on the Aleutians in May 1943
Left: P-40K Warhawks assembled at Gura, East Africa
Below: A P-40 of 112 Squadron is taxied by its groundcrew. The man sitting on the wing is the usual look-out whose task is to warn of obstructions ahead

DH.98 Mosquito fighter, de Havilland

FIRST FLIGHT 1941

THE various requirements of Air Ministry Specification P.13/36 led to de Havilland proposing an unarmed wooden two-seater powered by two Rolls-Royce Merlins or Napier Sabres, on the grounds that the speed achieved by such an aircraft would render defensive armament unnecessary. The wooden construction would make it quicker and easier to build, while using skills and materials likely to be more readily available in wartime than those required for all-metal types. At the same time, long-range fighter and photographic-reconnaissance versions were considered, all under the company designation DH.98. The armament selected for the fighter version was four 20-mm (0.79-in) cannon in the nose.

De Havilland's proposal received little official encouragement until the end of 1939, when a single prototype was commissioned, though this order was increased to 50 bomber-reconnaissance DH.98s in March 1940. In July the order was amended to include a single prototype of a long-range and night-fighter, the armament of which was to comprise four 0.303-in (7.7-mm) machine-guns in the nose in addition to the four cannon. The first DH.98 was flown in November 1940, and the third, which was the first Mosquito Mk II fighter, followed in May 1941. Performance in trials included an outstanding 608 km/h (378 mph) at 6706 m (22 000 ft). Experiments with turret-armed models and bellows airbrakes were soon abandoned, and later trials with the Turbinlite searchlight, fitted to many of the RAF's Havoc night-fighters, proved similarly unrewarding. De-

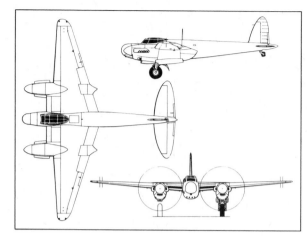

velopment of the type as a night-fighter involved the installation of AI. Mk IV or V airborne interception radar, the application of matt all-black finish and the fitting of glare-suppressing exhaust shrouds (which gave constant trouble).

The first Mosquito night-fighter squadron was formed in December 1941, becoming operational the following April, and by January 1943 eight squadrons were equipped with the type. The availability of the more effective AI. Mk VIII centimetric radar sets led to 97 of the 589 Mk IIs built being converted to NF. Mk XIIs from the beginning of 1943, with the new radar carried at the expense of the machine-guns. A further 99 became NF. XVIIs with AI. Mk X (US SCR-720) radar. Both of the newer radar systems used nose

Mosquito NF. 30

Type: two-seat night-fighter
Maker: de Havilland Aircraft Co Ltd
Span: 16.5 m (54 ft 2 in)
Length: 13.56 m (44 ft 6 in)
Height: 4.65 m (15 ft 3 in)
Wing area: 42.18 m² (454 sq ft)
Weight: normal 9072 kg (20 000 lb); empty 6985 kg (15 400 lb)
Powerplant: two 1650-hp Rolls-Royce Merlin 72 V-12 liquid-cooled engines
Performance: maximum speed 655 km/h (407 mph) at 8534 m (28 000 ft); range 2092 km (1300 miles); operational ceiling 11 887 m (39 000 ft)
Armament: four 20-mm (0.79-in) Hispano-Suiza cannon
Crew: 2
Production: 530 (7781 all types)

Left: A de Havilland
Mosquito II night-fighter in
its overall black camouflage.
The shrouded exhausts can
just be seen on the left engine.
This aircraft would have been
equipped with radar, but it
may have been painted out in
this wartime photograph, or
removed for intruder missions
over Europe
Below left: The different
cockpit and nose layouts of
the Mosquito bomber and
fighter. The B IV has
  1 2500-lb (1140-kg) bombs
  2 bomb-aimer's window
  3 small crew entry door
The NF. Mk II is equipped
with flat bullet-proof screen,
larger crew entry door (dotted
line), and radar, camera and
four Browning machine-guns
in the nose
Below: A Mosquito makes a
low pass. The wooden
construction was very tough
and gave the aircraft an
ability for quick front-line
repair. Home-based
Mosquito fighters defended
Britain for three years, and in
60 nights of action shot down
600 enemy raiders and 60
flying bombs

radomes rather than the arrow-head and exposed
dipole aerials of the earlier types, and the AI. Mk
X installation involved a redesigned 'bull nose'.
Another 25 Mk IIs, with the vital radar removed
(to avoid the possibility of capture), were used on
intruder raids over Europe from mid 1942.

Meanwhile, development of other Mosquito
variants was continuing, and by mid 1941 a new
wing, with provision for a drop-tank or a 113-kg
(250-lb) bomb, had been developed for the FB. VI
fighter-bomber. The combination of this wing with
the NF. XII fuselage resulted in the NF. XIII
night-fighter, 270 of which were built with the
1480-hp Merlin 21 or 1390-hp Merlin 23 engines,
as used on the earlier types. The substitution of
1640-hp Merlin 25s resulted in a further 280

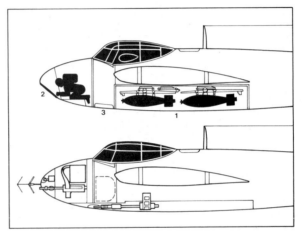

NF. XIXs, using either AI. Mk VIII or Mk X
radar in either universal or thimble radomes.

A high-altitude Mosquito, designated NF. XV,
was produced to counter the Luftwaffe's Ju 86P
high-level bombers which began operating over
Britain in mid 1942. Wing span was increased to
18.03 m (59 ft 2 in), a cabin pressurization system
was used and four 0.303-in machine-guns were
carried in a fairing under the forward fuselage. The
use of two-stage Merlin 61 engines driving four-
blade propellers enabled the prototype to reach
13 106 m (43 000 ft) on official trials. Another four
Mk IIs were converted to NF. XVs, but the Ju 86P
was withdrawn before any entered service.

In April 1944 another night-fighter version, a
converted Mk XIX designated NF. 30, was flown

Left: A British-built FB. VI
reassembled at Bankstown,
Australia, in 1945, in service
with the RAAF. The aircraft
is powered by either two
Packard-Merlin 31s or 33s.
Mosquito fighter-bombers
saw action against Japanese
communications and strong-
points in the Burmese jungle

NF Mk II

1 Rudder mass balance
2 Rudder post
3 Rudder upper hinge
4 Rudder frame
5 Rudder trim tab
6 Tab control link
7 Left elevator tab
8 Tail cone
9 Tail navigation light
10 Tail information light
11 Tab hinge fairing
12 Right elevator trim tab
13 Right elevator
14 Elevator mass balance
15 Tailplane structure
16 Aerial attachment
17 Retractable anti-shimmy tailwheel
18 Axle fork
19 Retraction mechanism unit
20 Rudder (internal) static balance
21 Elevator trim jack
22 Elevator torque tube
23 Rudder torque shaft
24 Fin structure
25 Front spar
26 Pitot head
27 TR.1143 aerial attachment
28 Left elevator
29 Tailplane
30 Fin/fuselage bulkhead attachment
31 Rudder control linkage
32 Bulkhead No 6
33 Elevator cables
34 Rudder cables
35 Ply/balsa/ply fuselage sandwich
   skinning
36 Flare chute
37 Bulkhead No 5
38 TR.1133 aerial
39 Beam (blind) approach aerial
40 External guttering strake
41 Aft fuselage entry/access
42 Trim tab controls
43 Aerial leads
44 Transmitter/receiver (No 2 set)
45 De-icing fluid tank
46 Transmitter/receiver (No 1 set)
47 Long-range fuel tank
48 Bulkhead No 4
49 Compressed air bottles
50 Hydraulic reservoir
51 Bulkhead No 3
52 Junction box/power unit
53 Wing fix brace aft attachment
54 Aerials
55 Aerial mast
56 Dinghy jettisonable panel
57 Aerial matching unit
58 Dinghy stowage
59 Aileron control linkage
60 Long-range fuel tank
61 Fuselage frame
62 Electrical leads
63 Wing fix attachment
64 Canopy aft section
65 Signal flare port
66 Left inboard tank
67 Dorsal identification light
68 Nacelle aft fairing
69 Left flap jack inspection panel
70 Fuel filler access
71 Nacelle fillet
72 Left outboard fuel tank
73 Left outboard fuel tank
74 Landing lamp
75 Flap outer section
76 Aileron trim tab
77 Outboard wing ribs

78 Left aileron
79 Hinge fairing
80 Rear spar
81 Resin lamp
82 AI Mk IV (airborne interception
   radar) left azimuth aerials
83 Left navigation light
84 Leading-edge ribs
85 Front spar
86 Three-blade de Havilland
   hydromatic propeller
87 Spinner
88 Propeller boss
89 Constant speed unit
90 Coolant header tank
91 Exhaust shroud intake
92 Auxiliary (cooling air) intake
93 Exhaust stubs
94 1460-hp Rolls-Royce Merlin 21
95 Coolant pipes
96 Radiator inspection panel section
97 Windscreen wiper
98 Gunsight
99 Flat bullet-proof windscreen
100 Control column
101 Seat harness
102 Jettisonable canopy section
103 Pilot's head/back armour
104 Front spar carry-through
105 Observer's back armour plate
106 IFF detonator switchbox
107 Instrument panel
108 Bulkhead
109 Parachute stowage
110 Ammunition boxes
111 Ammunition feed chutes
112 Four 0·303-cal (7,7-mm) Brownings
113 Camera gun
114 Gun barrels (blast tubes omitted)
115 Camera gun spout and port
116 AI Mk IV transmitter aerial
117 Machine-gun muzzles
118 Left mainwheel
119 Cartridge case and link panel
120 Spent case chute
121 Ventral cannon blast tubes
122 Gun heating
123 Underfloor 20-mm cannon (four)
124 Crew entry door
125 Cannon ammunition feed chutes
126 Ammunition boxes
127 Oil and coolant radiator housings
128 Radiator flap pneumatic ram
129 Wing inboard rib
130 Right inboard fuel tank
131 Right inboard fuel tank
132 Rear spar fixing
133 Right flap section
134 Flap jack and crank
135 Nacelle aft fairing
136 Flap outer section
137 Aileron tab chain drive
138 Aileron balance cables
139 Aileron trim tab
140 Right aileron
141 Wing stringers
142 AI Mk IV right azimuth aerials
143 Resin lamp
144 Right navigation light
145 Wing outer ribs
146 Leading-edge ribs
147 Front spar
148 AI Mk IV elevation aerials
149 Undercarriage retraction jack
150 Undercarriage radius rod/rear spar
151 Flap hydraulic actuator
152 Nacelle fillet
153 Control lines
154 Undercarriage jacking lug
155 Right oil tank

156 Engine bearer supports
157 Exhaust flame damper shroud
158 Spinner back plate
159 Right spinner
160 De Havilland hydromatic propeller
161 Right engine nacelle
162 Carburettor air intake
163 Intake fairing
164 Radius rod hinge
165 Undercarriage door elasticated
   cord and drum
166 Main undercarriage doors
167 Mudguards
168 Wheel door guides
169 Undercarriage compression legs
170 Rubber shock pads (cuffed)
171 Mainwheel axle
172 Right mainwheel

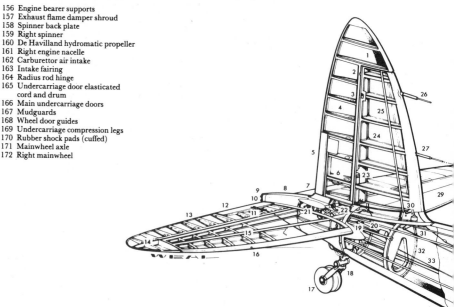

with two-stage Merlin 72 engines, and 70 of these were followed by a further 460 with the Merlin 113. The Merlin 113 also powered the NF. 36, first flown in May 1945, which used the AI. Mk X radar, while the postwar NF. 38 replaced this with the British AI. Mk IX and had Merlin 114A engines. A total of 163 NF. 36s and 82 NF. 38s were built, and the NF. 30 and 36 were the standard British home-based night-fighters until 1951-3, when they were replaced by night-fighter versions of the jet-propelled Gloster Meteor and de Havilland Vampire. The NF. 38, however, proved unsuitable for operational use, a particular fault allegedly being its inability to maintain the required height and speed on a single engine. Most served with the Yugoslav air force.

These Mosquitos represented only one line of a family that also included highly successful pathfinders, strategic bombers, light bombers, fighter-bombers, reconnaissance and anti-shipping aircraft. And as well as equipping the UK-based night-fighter squadrons, the successive NF models saw action in other roles. Malta-based Mk II and NF. XII intruders operated over Sicily before and during the Allied landings on the island, being joined subsequently by later marks in Italy. A few served briefly in the Pacific after the end of the war in Europe. The night-fighters were also used for experimental electronic countermeasures in support of bombing raids on Germany, and against V-1s. Hotted-up Mosquitos were responsible for the destruction of 623 flying bombs.

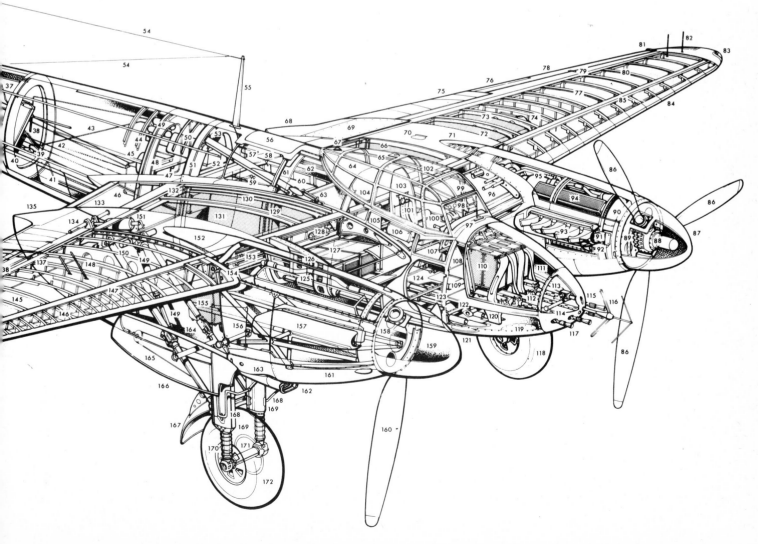

A6M Zero, Mitsubishi

FIRST FLIGHT 1939

THE Imperial Navy's 1937 specification for a carrier-based fighter to succeed its new A5M from Mitsubishi reflected the rapid growth in sophistication of Japanese aircraft. Manoeuvrability was still a prime requirement, but exceptional range and competitive speed were combined with an armament of two 20-mm (0.79-in) cannon and two 7.7-mm (0.303-in) machine-guns, plus a light bombload and a comprehensive radio outfit in a stringent formula.

Jiro Horikoshi, designer of the A5M, was given the task of producing its successor, and his first prototype, a low-wing all-metal monoplane designated A6M1, powered by a 780-hp Mitsubishi Zuisei 13 radial, flew for the first time on April 1, 1939. Its maximum speed of 489 km/h (304 mph) was slightly below that demanded, but the other requirements were met. After a second A6M1 had flown in October 1939, the installation of a 925-hp Nakajima NK1C Sakae 12 in the third prototype, designated A6M2, enabled it to reach a more than satisfactory 534 km/h (332 mph). Service evaluation of trials A6M2 aircraft during the first half of 1940 was followed by combat trials and the beginning of production, with the service designation Type 0 carrier Fighter Model 11. The Type 0 designation resulted in the unofficial name Reisen, a contraction of *Rei Sentoki* (Zero Fighter), and as the Zero it was to achieve an almost unparalleled reputation as a combat aircraft.

A year of combat in China, during which 99 Chinese aircraft were destroyed with the loss of only two Zeros, which were the victims of anti-aircraft fire from the ground, was accompanied by a series of modifications to the wings. The most significant of these was the introduction of folding wingtips on the Model 21 after 64 Model 11s had been delivered. A new powerplant, the 1130-hp NK1F Sakae 21, distinguished the next production model the A6M3, which flew for the first time in June 1941. The first of three variants of this version, designated Model 32, dispensed with the folding wingtips, thus reducing span to the 11 m (36 ft 1 in) required by the standard Japanese carrier elevator.

The Model 22 restored these in order to accommodate additional fuel tanks in the wings, with fuselage tankage reduced because of the greater dimensions of the Sakae powerplant, which also had a higher fuel consumption. Consequently range fell from the A6M2's 3103 km (1928 miles) to 2379 km (1478 miles), and a number of losses had been suffered in long over-water flights to the Guadalcanal beach-heads. Finally, the Model 22A, or A6M3a, introduced longer-barrelled cannon.

The A6M4 was a Model 21 conversion which was abandoned because of problems with its turbo-supercharged Sakae engine. The Zero's fortunes reflected those of Japan itself: superiority over Allied fighters, at the outset virtually absolute, was first eroded, then neutralized, and from 1943 the Mitsubishi designers could hope only to minimize its growing inferiority.

One area where improvement was both desirable and possible was diving speed. An A6M3 was given thicker-skinned wings with rounded, non-folding tips, and new exhaust stubs which provided

Above: The Mitsubishi A6M5c version had additional armament, armour, fuel tankage and bomb racks. The proposed new engine was never made available, so the aircraft was seriously underpowered. Though production stopped after 93 aircraft, later versions of the Zero retained the cannon and machine-gun armament
Left: An A6M5a with the surrender markings of a green cross on a white square. This insignia was adopted at the Allies' orders when Japanese aircraft flew to surrender points

A6M3 Model 22

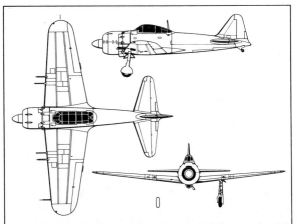

Type: carrier-borne fighter/fighter-bomber
Maker: Mitsubishi Jukogyo KK; Nakajima Hikoki KK
Span: 12 m (39 ft 4½ in)
Length: 9.06 m (29 ft 8¾ in)
Height: 3.51 m (11 ft 6¼ in)
Wing area: 22.44 m² (241.55 sq ft)
Weight: normal 2679 kg (5906 lb); empty 1863 kg (4107 lb)
Powerplant: one 1130-hp Nakajima NK1C Sakae 21 14-cylinder two-row radial engine
Performance: maximum speed 541 km/h (336 mph) at 6000 m (19 685 ft); cruising speed 354 km/h (220 mph)
Armament: two 20-mm (0.79-in) Type 99 cannon; two 7.7-mm (0.303-in) Type 97 machine-guns; two 60-kg (132-lb) bombs
Crew: 1
Production: approx 10 449 plus 515 trainers and 327 seaplanes (all types)

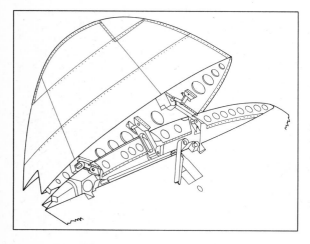

Above and right: The wing
fold on the A6M Zero – this
produced a modest saving on
span of 1 m (3 ft 3⅓ in).
However this manually folded
tip was lighter than the more
complex systems used by
Allied carrier aircraft. It was
designed to allow the Zero to
fit into the 11 m (36 ft 1 in)
deck elevators on Japanese
carriers. These tips were later
deleted and the span reduced.
This led to an increase in level
speed but with a small loss in
altitude performance and
manoeuvrability

some additional thrust, to become the prototype
A6M5, or Model 42. The modifications gave a
maximum diving speed of 660 km/h (410 mph) as
well as some improvement in level speed, and
production of the A6M5 began in the summer of
1943. From the spring of 1944 it was joined by the
A6M5a, or Model 52A, which had belt-fed Type 99
cannon in wings whose even thicker skins allowed a
further increase in diving speed to 740 km/h
(460 mph).

The A6M5b (Model 52B) introduced a new
armoured windshield and fuel-tank fire extin-
guishers to combat the Zero's tendency to burst
into flames when hit, and a 13-mm (0.512-in) Type
3 machine-gun replaced one of the 7.7-mm
weapons in the nose. Protection and firepower were

further increased in the A5M6 (Model 52C), which
carried armour plate, self-sealing tanks of increased capacity and three 13-mm guns in addition
to the two 20-mm cannon. However, the increased
weight with no extra power led to deterioration in
performance. Attempts to remedy this by installing
a water-methanol-boosted Sakae 31A towards the
end of 1944 produced the A6M6c (Model 53C),
but problems with the engine meant only a few
were built. The Model 63, or A6M7, replaced the
fuselage drop-tank with a carrier for a 500-kg
(1102-lb) or 250-kg (551-lb) bomb and carried two
smaller tanks under the wings, and in May 1945
this became the last Zero to enter production.

A further variant, the A6M8, would have used
the 1340-hp Mitsubishi Kinsei 62 engine and at

Left: A squadron leader's A6M2 of the 2nd Carrier Division. The top of the engine cowling is painted in black anti-glare finish
Below: An A6M2 captured intact in China during a test flight. It is fitted with a drop-tank. The good power-to-weight ratio, fuel economy of the pilots, and early use of drop-tanks gave Japanese aircraft a range that came as a great surprise to the Allies
Right: US Navy gunners fire point-blank into a Zero – codename Zeke – as it makes a kamikaze attack on their warship. The aircraft was

blown apart seconds after the picture was taken, and fell in the sea. Though kamikaze attacks scored few dramatic successes, one of their chief effects was to place US Navy AA gunners under intense strain, which resulted in numerous battle-fatigue casualties

Above: The A6M5 which entered service as the Type 0 Model 52. The Sakae 21 engine was given individual exhaust stacks to provide some thrust augmentation. More Zero-Sens of this variant were built than of any other model, with production being undertaken by Mitsubishi and Nakajima
Left: Groundcrew at work on an A6M2-N, the seaplane version first encountered at Guadalcanal. A total of 327 were built, but though it was virtually a copy of the Zero-Sen its floats caused a reduction in performance, and by the end of the war it was used only for training

573 km/h (356 mph) would have been the fastest of all Zeros, but although two A6M8c prototypes were flown in the early summer of 1945, large production orders came too late. Other variants of the Zero were A6M2-K and A6M5-K two-seat trainers and the Nakajima-built A6M2-N float-plane fighter. Codenamed Rufe by the Allies, the A6M2-N entered production towards the end of 1941 and many of the 327 built served as interceptors in the Solomon and Aleutian Islands, although the type was also used as a seaplane trainer.

In service from Pearl Harbor until the end of the war, the Zero at first appeared invincible, but gradual attrition of aircraft, their carriers and the experienced pilots was accompanied by the arrival of American fighters which were faster, more

heavily armed and better protected. First the Lightning, then the Hellcat that had been designed specifically to counter it, and the long-delayed Corsair, forced it to fight ever more on the defensive, and the qualities that had made it the finest Pacific fighter did not equip it for such a role.

The Zero found grim new work in October 1944 when it was used in kamikaze attacks at Leyte. Fitted with a 250-kg (551-lb) bomb in place of the ventral tank, A6M5s flown by volunteers from the 201st Kokutai sank the escort carrier *St Lo* and damaged the carriers *Kalinin Bay*, *Kitkun Bay* and *White Plains*. The wooden decks of the carriers were an easy target for the pilots even when they were under concentrated AA fire.

Ki-43 Hayabusa, Nakajima

FIRST FLIGHT 1939

THE Imperial Japanese Army Air Force asked Nakajima to design a successor to their Ki-27 towards the end of 1937, and the first of three Ki-43 prototypes was flown in January 1939. Powered by the 925-hp Nakajima Ha-25 radial, the prototypes were officially tested in the spring of 1939, with disappointing results. They only just met the modest performance requirements. Another deficiency was the feeble armament of two nose-mounted 7.7-mm (0.303-in) machine-guns. A further ten development aircraft incorporated various improvements, most significant of which were 'butterfly' flaps which produced a dramatic improvement in combat manoeuvrability.

Other changes tried on pre-production aircraft included substituting an 1100-hp Ha-105 engine and the installation of twin 12.7-mm (0.5-in) machine-guns. But when production of the Ki-43-I began in early 1941, the original engine and armament were used, though some were given one 7.7-mm and one 12.7-mm gun and designated Ki-43-Ib. As soon as sufficient guns were available two of the heavier weapons were fitted and the designation changed again to Ki-43-Ic.

During 1942 production began of the Ki-43-II. Powered by the Ha-105, the new model featured a number of improvements, including a new, stronger wing of slightly reduced span with attachment points for 250-kg (551-lb) bombs or drop-tanks to increase range, cockpit armour and rubber-encased fuel tanks to give a modicum of protection against fire. The Ki-43-II superseded its predecessor on the production line from November

Above: A Ki-43 Army Type 1 Hayabusa in Manchuria on skis
Left: A Ki-43-II receives field maintenance
Above right: A Ki-43-I, with a 'combat stripe' around the rear fuselage to identify it as serving in an operational area
Below: A Ki-43-II of the 25th Sentai, 2nd Chutai. It was not normal practice to paint the individual aircraft number in such a large size. The fighter shows the typical weathering around the cowling and spinner, as suffered in the tropics. The Allied codename was Oscar

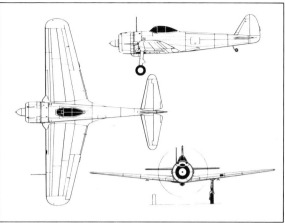

Ki-43-IIb Hayabusa

Type: single-seat fighter and fighter-bomber
Maker: Nakajima Hikoki KK; Tachikawa Hikoki KK
Span: 10.84 m (35 ft 6¾ in)
Length: 8.92 m (29 ft 3¼ in)
Height: 3.1 m (10 ft 2 in)
Wing area: 21.04 m² (230.35 sq ft)
Weight: normal 2218 kg (4890 lb); empty 1729 kg (3812 lb)
Powerplant: one 1100-hp Nakajima Ha-115 Army Type 1 14-cylinder two-row radial engine
Performance: maximum speed 530 km/h (329 mph) at 4000 m (13 123 ft); range 1620 km (1007 miles); operational ceiling 11 215 m (36 795 ft)
Armament: two 12.7-mm (0.5-in) Ho-103 machine-guns
Crew: 1
Production: 5919 (all types)

1942, the last of 716 Ki-43-Is being completed the following February; minor changes to the engine installation distinguished the Ki-43-IIb. The Ki-43-II Kai, which entered production in mid 1943, featured ejector exhaust stubs in place of the standard collector ring.

During 1944, after constructing ten Ki-43-III prototypes, Nakajima switched their efforts to building the Ki-84, and Tachikawa, which had been supplying Hayabusas since early 1943, became the sole producer. The Ki-43-III was distinguished by its 1230-hp Ha-115-III engine, giving better rate of climb and new top speed of 576 km/h (358 mph) at 6680 m (21 916 ft).

Although it was considered one of the most manoeuvrable of all fighters, the Hayabusa saw most service at a time when the emphasis in fighter design had switched to power. In fact, its only real strength was its manoeuvrability, and this advantage was nullified when Allied trials of a captured example enabled effective counter-tactics to be evolved in late 1943. The two-gun armament was patently inadequate, but no improvement was effected until mid 1945, when two Ki-43-IIIb prototypes were completed with two 20-mm (0.79-in) cannon.

Nevertheless, Tachikawa continued to produce the type until the end of the war, completing over 2000 in the last 16 months of the conflict, and bringing total production to 5919, with large numbers remaining in front-line service until fighting ceased in August 1945.

Fw 190, Focke-Wulf

FIRST FLIGHT 1939

THE search for a successor to the Bf 109 got under way in earnest in the spring of 1938, when Focke-Wulf submitted to the *Reichsluftfahrt-ministerium* (air ministry) design proposals for new fighters. One of these, in spite of the trend towards inline engines, was based on the new BMW 139 two-row radial, partly in expectation of greater power and partly because the Focke-Wulf technical director Kurt Tank foresaw heavy demand for the existing inline powerplants. These arguments proved conclusive, and the Fw 190 V1 prototype made its first flight on June 1, 1939, with a BMW engine in the nose and a roasting pilot just behind it!

The problem of cockpit overheating, and difficulties with the engine, caused the third and fourth prototypes to be abandoned, and the V5 began trials in April 1940 with another new radial, the BMW 801. Longer and heavier than the 139, the new engine allowed the cockpit to be further aft, which in turn provided space in the nose for armament, while, by way of compensation for the increased weight, wings of greater area were fitted.

Several of the pre-production A-0 series were used as development aircraft, while others were used for service evaluation from March 1941. The 1600-hp BMW 801C engine installation, with complex control and cooling systems, proved so troublesome that the whole programme was jeopardized. However, deliveries of 100 production A-1s began in June, supplemented from August by the first A-2s, which retained the A-1's pair of 7.92-mm (0.312-in) MG 17s in the nose but

replaced the two wing-mounted machine-guns with 20-mm (0.79-in) cannon. By the end of the year 142 A-2s had been delivered and II and III/JG 26 (II and III *Gruppen* of *Jagdgeschwader* [fighter group] 26) had equipped with Fw 190As, the majority of which were given an additional pair of wing-mounted 20-mm MG FF cannon.

Next model was the A-3, powered by a 1700-hp BMW 801D and standardizing the additional cannon; subsequent A-series sub-types included the A-4, with methanol-water booster; the A-5, produced from April 1943, with a new engine mounting; the A-6, produced from June 1943 for service on the Eastern Front, which carried two MG 17s plus four MG 151/20s in modified wings; and a small number of A-7s, which replaced the

Top: An Fw 190A-3 of 8/JG 2, with this famous unit's eagle emblem on the nose and fuselage sides
Above: An Fw 190D-9. The aircraft entered service in the winter of 1943–44 and proved popular with its methanol-water boosted engine.
Right: A line-up of Fw 190Gs of 1/S G, a ground-attack unit at Deblin-Irena in Poland. Some aircraft have the Micky Mouse unit insignia on the nose

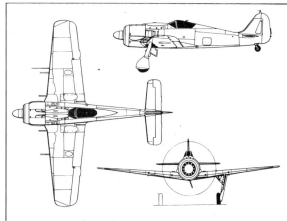

Fw 190A-8

Type: multirole fighter
Maker: Focke-Wulf
Flugzeugbau GmbH
Span: 10.5 m (34 ft 5½ in)
Length: 8.96 m (29 ft 4¾ in)
Height 3.96 m (13 ft)
Wing area: 18.3 m²
(197 sq ft)
Weight: maximum 4899 kg
(10 800 lb); empty 3471 kg
(7652 lb)
Powerplant: one 1700-hp
BMW 801D-2 14-cylinder air-
cooled radial engine
Performance: maximum
speed 657 km/h (408 mph) at
6300 m (20 699 ft); range
800 km (497 miles);

operational ceiling 10 300 m
(33 792 ft)
Armament: two 13-mm
(0.512-in) MG 131 machine-
guns; four 20-mm (0.79-in)
MG 151/20 machine-guns
Crew: 1
Production: approx 19 424
(all types)

Fw 190D-9

Specifications similar to Fw
190F-3 except in following:
Length: 10.2 m (33 ft 5½ in)
Height: 3.36 m (11 ft 0¼ in)
Wing area: 18.3 m²
(196.98 sq ft)
Weight: maximum 4840 kg

(10 670 lb); empty 3490 kg
(7694 lb)
Powerplant: one 2240-hp
Junkers Jumo 213A-1 liquid-
cooled radial engine
Performance: maximum
speed 685.5 km/h (426 mph)
at 6599 m (21 650 ft); range
837 km (520 miles);
operational ceiling 5639 m
(18 500 ft)
Armament: two 20-mm
(0.79-in) MG 151 cannon;
two 13-mm (0.51-in) MG 131
machine-guns; one 500-kg
(1102-lb) bomb
Production: minimum 650

Fw 190F-3

Specifications similar to the
Fw 190A-8 except in following
particulars:
Weight: maximum 4922 kg
(10 850 lb); empty 3324 kg
(7328 lb)
Performance: maximum
speed 634 km/h (394 mph) at
5500 m (18 045 ft); range
750 km (466 miles)
Armament: two 7.92-mm
(0.31-in) MG 17 machine-
guns; two 20-mm (0.79-in)
MG 151 cannon; racks for
bombs up to 250 kg (550 lb) or
two 30-mm (1.18-in) MK 103
cannon
Production: 550 (F type)

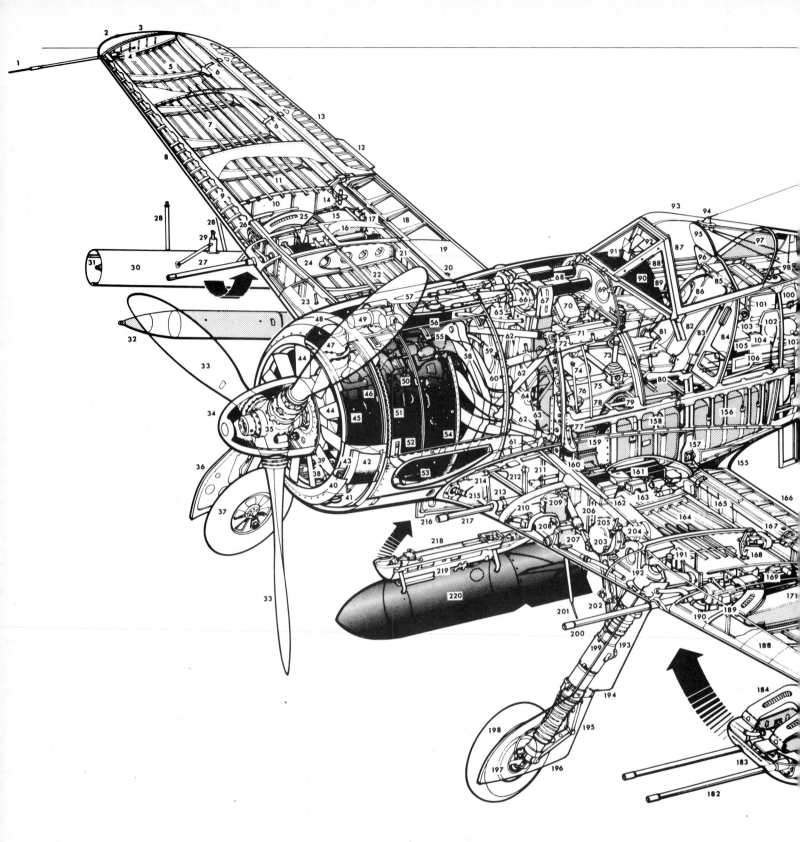

MG 17s with 13-mm (0.512-in) MG 131s. Finally, the A-8, with methanol-water booster, was the most numerous of the A series, most of which could conveniently be converted for a variety of specialized roles.

Fighter-bomber conversions carried bombloads of up to 1000 kg (2205 lb), sometimes with drop-tanks, while formation destroyers had additional MG 151/20s or 30-mm (1.18-in) MK 103 or 108 cannon under the wings, or used 21-cm (8.27-in) rocket launchers to break up bomber formations. A small number were given additional armour for use as rams, and reconnaissance-fighters carried cameras in the rear fuselage. In all but the flying rams it was usual to remove the MG FFs.

This adaptability led to specialized series of

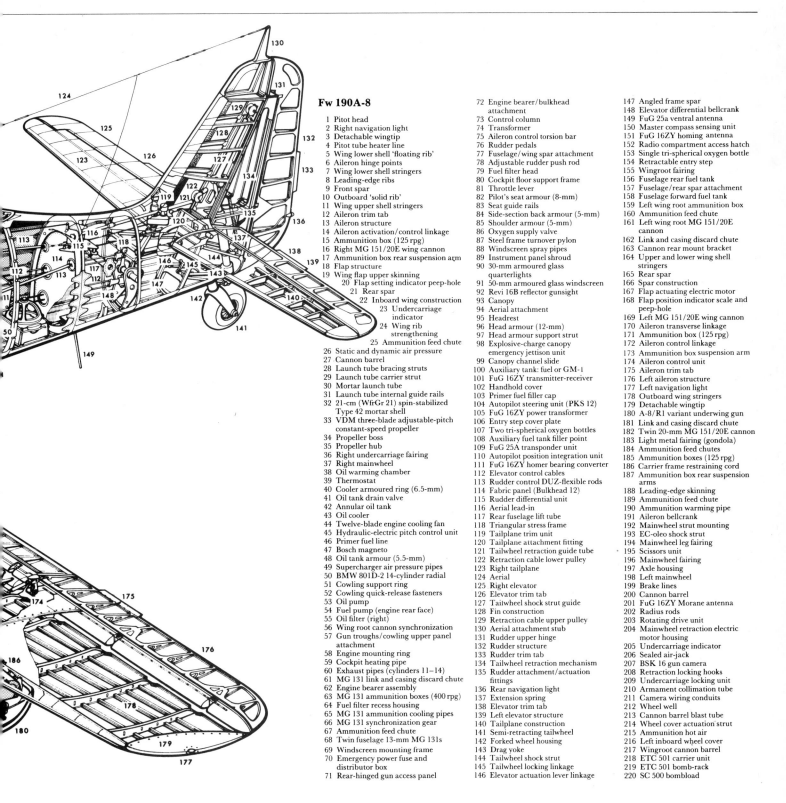

Fw 190A-8

1 Pitot head
2 Right navigation light
3 Detachable wingtip
4 Pitot tube heater line
5 Wing lower shell 'floating rib'
6 Aileron hinge points
7 Wing lower shell stringers
8 Leading-edge ribs
9 Front spar
10 Outboard 'solid rib'
11 Wing upper shell stringers
12 Aileron trim tab
13 Aileron structure
14 Aileron activation/control linkage
15 Ammunition box (125 rpg)
16 Right MG 151/20E wing cannon
17 Ammunition box rear suspension arm
18 Flap structure
19 Wing flap upper skinning
20 Flap setting indicator peep-hole
21 Rear spar
22 Inboard wing construction
23 Undercarriage indicator
24 Wing rib strengthening
25 Ammunition feed chute
26 Static and dynamic air pressure
27 Cannon barrel
28 Launch tube bracing struts
29 Launch tube carrier strut
30 Mortar launch tube
31 Launch tube internal guide rails
32 21-cm (WfrGr 21) spin-stabilized Type 42 mortar shell
33 VDM three-blade adjustable-pitch constant-speed propeller
34 Propeller boss
35 Propeller hub
36 Right undercarriage fairing
37 Right mainwheel
38 Oil warming chamber
39 Thermostat
40 Cooler armoured ring (6.5-mm)
41 Oil tank drain valve
42 Annular oil tank
43 Oil cooler
44 Twelve-blade engine cooling fan
45 Hydraulic-electric pitch control unit
46 Primer fuel line
47 Bosch magneto
48 Oil tank armour (5.5-mm)
49 Supercharger air pressure pipes
50 BMW 801D-2 14-cylinder radial
51 Cowling support ring
52 Cowling quick-release fasteners
53 Oil pump
54 Fuel pump (engine rear face)
55 Oil filter (right)
56 Wing root cannon synchronization
57 Gun troughs/cowling upper panel attachment
58 Engine mounting ring
59 Cockpit heating pipe
60 Exhaust pipes (cylinders 11–14)
61 MG 131 link and casing discard chute
62 Engine bearer assembly
63 MG 131 ammunition boxes (400 rpg)
64 Fuel filter recess housing
65 MG 131 ammunition cooling pipes
66 MG 131 synchronization gear
67 Ammunition feed chute
68 Twin fuselage 13-mm MG 131s
69 Windscreen mounting frame
70 Emergency power fuse and distributor box
71 Rear-hinged gun access panel

72 Engine bearer/bulkhead attachment
73 Control column
74 Transformer
75 Aileron control torsion bar
76 Rudder pedals
77 Fuselage/wing spar attachment
78 Adjustable rudder push rod
79 Fuel filter head
80 Cockpit floor support frame
81 Throttle lever
82 Pilot's seat armour (8-mm)
83 Seat guide rails
84 Side-section back armour (5-mm)
85 Shoulder armour (5-mm)
86 Oxygen supply valve
87 Steel frame turnover pylon
88 Windscreen spray pipes
89 Instrument panel shroud
90 30-mm armoured glass quarterlights
91 50-mm armoured glass windscreen
92 Revi 16B reflector gunsight
93 Canopy
94 Aerial attachment
95 Headrest
96 Head armour (12-mm)
97 Head armour support strut
98 Explosive-charge canopy emergency jettison unit
99 Canopy channel slide
100 Auxiliary tank: fuel or GM-1
101 FuG 16ZY transmitter-receiver
102 Handhold cover
103 Primer fuel filler cap
104 Autopilot steering unit (PKS 12)
105 FuG 16ZY power transformer
106 Entry step cover plate
107 Two tri-spherical oxygen bottles
108 Auxiliary fuel tank filler point
109 FuG 25A transponder
110 Autopilot position integration unit
111 FuG 16ZY homer bearing converter
112 Elevator control cables
113 Rudder control DUZ-flexible rods
114 Fabric panel (Bulkhead 12)
115 Rudder differential unit
116 Aerial lead-in
117 Rear fuselage lift tube
118 Triangular stress frame
119 Tailplane trim unit
120 Tailplane attachment fitting
121 Tailwheel retraction guide tube
122 Retraction cable lower pulley
123 Right tailplane
124 Aerial
125 Right elevator
126 Elevator trim tab
127 Tailwheel shock strut guide
128 Fin construction
129 Retraction cable upper pulley
130 Aerial attachment stub
131 Rudder upper hinge
132 Rudder structure
133 Rudder trim tab
134 Tailwheel retraction mechanism
135 Rudder attachment/actuation fittings
136 Rear navigation light
137 Extension spring
138 Elevator trim tab
139 Left elevator structure
140 Tailplane construction
141 Semi-retracting tailwheel
142 Forked wheel housing
143 Drag yoke
144 Tailwheel shock strut
145 Tailwheel locking linkage
146 Elevator actuation lever linkage

147 Angled frame spar
148 Elevator differential bellcrank
149 FuG 25a ventral antenna
150 Master compass sensing unit
151 FuG 16ZY homing antenna
152 Radio compartment access hatch
153 Single tri-spherical oxygen bottle
154 Retractable entry step
155 Wingroot fairing
156 Fuselage rear fuel tank
157 Fuselage/rear spar attachment
158 Fuselage forward fuel tank
159 Left wing root ammunition box
160 Ammunition feed chute
161 Left wing root MG 151/20E cannon
162 Link and casing discard chute
163 Cannon rear mount bracket
164 Upper and lower wing shell stringers
165 Rear spar
166 Spar construction
167 Flap actuating electric motor
168 Flap position indicator scale and peep-hole
169 Left MG 151/20E wing cannon
170 Aileron transverse linkage
171 Ammunition box (125 rpg)
172 Aileron control linkage
173 Ammunition box suspension arm
174 Aileron control unit
175 Aileron trim tab
176 Left aileron structure
177 Left navigation light
178 Outboard wing stringers
179 Detachable wingtip
180 A-8/R1 variant underwing gun
181 Link and casing discard chute
182 Twin 20-mm MG 151/20E cannon
183 Light metal fairing (gondola)
184 Ammunition feed chutes
185 Ammunition boxes (125 rpg)
186 Carrier frame restraining cord
187 Ammunition box rear suspension arms
188 Leading-edge skinning
189 Ammunition feed chute
190 Ammunition warming pipe
191 Aileron bellcrank
192 Mainwheel strut mounting
193 EC-oleo shock strut
194 Mainwheel leg fairing
195 Scissors unit
196 Mainwheel fairing
197 Axle housing
198 Left mainwheel
199 Brake lines
200 Cannon barrel
201 FuG 16ZY Morane antenna
202 Radius rods
203 Rotating drive unit
204 Mainwheel retraction electric motor housing
205 Undercarriage indicator
206 Sealed air-jack
207 BSK 16 gun camera
208 Retraction locking hooks
209 Undercarriage locking unit
210 Armament collimation tube
211 Camera wiring conduits
212 Wheel well
213 Cannon barrel blast tube
214 Wheel cover actuation strut
215 Ammunition hot air
216 Left inboard wheel cover
217 Wingroot cannon barrel
218 ETC 501 carrier unit
219 ETC 501 bomb-rack
220 SC 500 bombload

Fw 190s, the close-support Fs and long-range fighter-bomber Gs, though the proposed photo-reconnaissance E series was abandoned, conversions of the standard fighter proving adequate in this role. The A series of straight fighters was continued with the D series and, ultimately, the Ta 152. Meanwhile, attempts to improve altitude performance gave rise to the abortive Fw 190B and C series which unfortunately did not progress beyond the development stage.

The close-support and long-range fighter-bomber programmes proved more productive. The small number of Fw 190F-1s used for evaluation were based on the A-4, with the addition of racks for one 500-kg (1102-lb) or four 50-kg (110-lb) bombs under the fuselage and provision for a 250-

kg (551-lb) bomb under each wing, the MG FFs being removed.

The F-2 was a similar conversion of the A-5, while the F-3 was equivalent to the A-6. The F-5, F-6 and F-7 were dropped in favour of the G series towards the end of 1943, but the first two were revived the following year as the F-8 and F-9. The former was similar to the F-3, but had four underwing racks for 50-kg bombs and MG 131s replacing the nose MG 17s, while the F-9 was powered by a turbo-supercharged 2000-hp BMW 801TS.

The long-range G series, which began to replace Ju 87 dive-bombers in the second half of 1943, were also based on A-series sub-types, the G-1, G-2 and G-8 corresponding to the A-4, A-5 and A-8. The

Far left: An Fw 190A-4/R-6 fitted with 21-cm (8.26-in) WG 21 rocket tubes. These unguided weapons were very effective against daylight bombers and meant that they did not have to risk the full weight of accurate defensive fire from the bombers

85

G-3 was a modified version of the G-2 with auto-pilot and fuel injection. To enable a pair of 300-litre (66-Imp gal) wing tanks to be carried, both the nose machine-guns and MG FF cannon were removed, and racks for one 500-kg or 250-kg, or four 50-kg bombs or a drop-tank were fitted below the fuselage.

As regards interceptor development, the distinguishing feature of the D series, which continued numerical sequence of the As, was the use of a liquid-cooled V-12 engine, the 1770-hp Junkers Jumo 213A, in a lengthened nose. The rear fuselage was extended and control surfaces were increased in area as a consequence. Armament of the D-9 comprised two MG 131s in the nose and an MG 151/20 in each wing root, with provision for 500-kg bombs to be carried under fuselage and wings. The ground-attack D-12 replaced the nose machine-guns with an MK 108 firing through the propeller hub, and also substituted a 2060-hp Jumo 213F engine. Other proposed variants failed to achieve production.

Further development of the interceptor was aimed at improving altitude performance, and with a change of designation, the Ta 152H (*Höhenjäger* [altitude fighter]) was developed through a series of prototypes from mid 1943. Production Ta 152H-1s, some 150 of which were delivered from late 1944, featured considerably larger wings of 14.5 m (47 ft 7 in) span and an 1880-hp Jumo 213E engine with an MK 108 firing through the propeller hub. Meanwhile, the 152C-1 had entered production with a 2300-hp DB 603LA engine and an MK 108 and two MG 151s in the nose. It was to be followed by the C-3, with DB 603L engine and the longer-barrelled MK 103 in place of the MK 108, but Germany's defeat ended both this development and the planned Ta 152E photo-reconnaissance model.

In operational service, the Fw 190 rapidly established a formidable reputation with its combination of performance, manoeuvrability and firepower. Early service was in western Europe, where its impact was such that the Spitfire production programme suffered hasty re-arrangement: the Spitfire Mk V having proved inadequate against the new German fighter, the Mk IX was rushed into production as a temporary expedient, and eventually achieved one of the biggest production totals of any Spitfire variant.

The Fw 190 was to see service on every front where the Luftwaffe fought, and with a remarkable variety of weapons, including bombs of up to 1800 kg (3968 lb), torpedoes, rockets, wire-guided missiles and recoilless guns, many of which were developed for antitank strikes against the Soviet Union on the Eastern Front. Some 190s were even used as the manned components of Mistel assemblies.

Before the end of the war factories established throughout Europe had assembled some 20 000 of all models, and afterwards SNCAC in France continued to build A-8s as NC 900 fighter-bombers for the French Armée de l'Air, while some of the 75 A-3s supplied to Turkey in 1942 remained in Turkish service throughout the Second World War until 1948.

Above: An Fw 190 and Ju 88 'Mistel' combination. Captured by the US Army at the close of the war, these two aircraft constituted a 'guided missile', with the Ju 88 loaded with explosive and the Fw 190 flying it by remote control. Near the target it broke away and gave radio instructions to the bomber on its power dive
Right: An Fw 190A-8/U1 with its twin cockpit. The conversion was used for training and high-speed liaison work

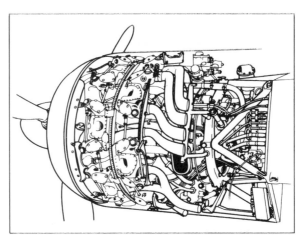

Far left: A long-range Fw 190G fighter-bomber with a 500-kg (1102-lb) bomb and two 300-litre (66-Imp/gal) drop-tanks. These aircraft were intended for both ground-attack roles and interception, and were powered by the BMW 801D
Left: The BMW 801D-2 radial engine. The prototype suffered from overheating and the engine was redesigned with a cooling fan. With MW50 boost giving 2100 hp, the emergency speed was raised to 670 km/h (416 mph)

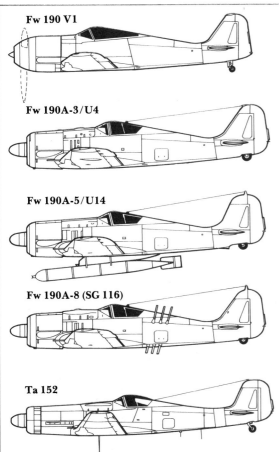

Fw 190 V1

Fw 190A-3/U4

Fw 190A-5/U14

Fw 190A-8 (SG 116)

Ta 152

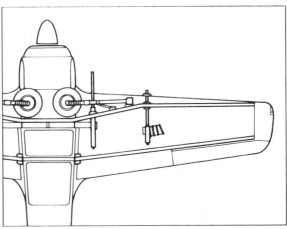

Above: An Fw 190F-8 fitted with an SC 250 bomb
Left: The interior of the Fw 190 cockpit, like all single-seat fighters, is compact and filled with controls
Far left: The changing shape of the Fw 190. It was fitted with various underwing and centreline loads including a torpedo which required an extended tailwheel on the fighter. The Fw 190A-8 (SG 116) was fitted with a photo-electric cell which triggered three single-shot cannon mounted in the fuselage. It was intended to operate the system by the shadow of a bomber as the fighter flew beneath it
Below left: The wing spar and landing gear of an Fw 190A-3 with its cannon armament. The wheels are fitted into a small area near the nose and the rear spar attached to the fuselage frame.

Boomerang, Commonwealth Aircraft Corporation

FIRST FLIGHT 1942

Far left: A CA-12 Boomerang fighter-bomber of No 5 Squadron RAAF
Left: A Boomerang of the CA-13 model at the CAC factory at Fishermen's Bend, Melbourne
Below: The Boomerang proved a very effective ground-attack aircraft; operating with a Forward Air Controller it was used to mark targets for medium-bomber formations

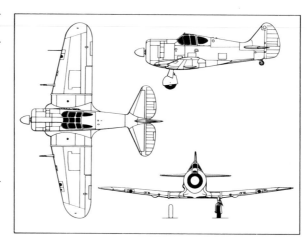

THE outbreak of war in the Pacific at the end of 1941 found the Royal Australian Air Force devoid of fighters except for two squadrons of Brewster Buffalos based in Malaya. Since neither Britain nor the United States could guarantee supplies of new fighters, an indigenous substitute seemed the only solution. Fortunately, the Commonwealth Aircraft Corporation had been formed in 1936, and since 1939 had been producing the Wirraway, a licence-built North American NA-33. Production had also begun of Pratt & Whitney R-1830 Twin Wasp engines for licence-built Bristol Beaufort torpedo bombers, and the CAC's chief designer, Wing Commander Wackett, had already considered using the Twin Wasp to power a fighter development of the Wirraway. A new forward fuselage to accommodate the Twin Wasp, a single-seat cockpit and a wing armament of two 20-mm (0.79-in) cannon and four 0.303-in (7.7-mm) machine-guns were the principal changes.

In February 1942 the proposal received official approval with an order for 105 examples, and three months later the first CA-12 Boomerang made its first flight. Although not particularly fast, the Boomerang proved to have an exceptional rate of climb and comparable manoeuvrability to that of the Kittyhawks and Airacobras which the RAAF had received in the meantime. Following completion of the first order in June 1943, a further 95 CA-13s were ordered with minor modifications, and the 49 CA-19s which completed production of the Boomerang by February 1945 again showed only detail changes. One CA-14 was produced with a turbo-supercharger in an effort to improve altitude performance, but although trials in mid 1944 showed an improved maximum speed of 560 km/h (348 mph) at 8535 m (28 000 ft), supplies of the much faster Spitfire VIII rendered further work on the CA-14 unnecessary.

Training of Boomerang pilots began in October 1942, and the type began operational service in New Guinea the following April. In fact, the Boomerang saw only limited service as a fighter, during which it failed to destroy a single enemy aircraft. But from mid 1943 until the end of the war in the Pacific, it gave tremendous service in a wide variety of roles with army co-operation squadrons, particularly in support of ground forces during the long jungle campaigns.

CA-12 Boomerang
Type: single-seat fighter
Maker: Commonwealth Aircraft Corporation
Span: 10.97 m (36 ft)
Length: 8.15 m (26 ft 9 in)
Height: 3.96 m (13 ft)
Wing area: 20.90 m² (225 sq ft)
Weight: normal 3492 kg (7699 lb); empty 2437 kg (5373 lb)
Powerplant: one 1200-hp CAC-built Pratt & Whitney R-1830 S3C4-G Twin Wasp 14-cylinder two-row radial engine
Performance: maximum speed 491 km/h (305 mph) at 4724 m (15 500 ft); range 1497 km (930 miles); operational ceiling 10 364 m (34 000 ft)
Armament: two 20-mm (0.79-in) Hispano-Suiza cannon; four 0.303-in (7.7-mm) Browning machine-guns
Crew: 1
Production: 105

P-38 Lightning, Lockheed

FIRST FLIGHT 1939

Left: A P-38L preserved by
enthusiasts in the United
States. The L (Model 422),
which was numerically the
most important Lightning,
had 1600-hp V-1710-111/113
engines but was similar to the
J. The number built was 3810
by Lockheed, with an
additional 113 by Vultee at
Nashville before a contract for
2000 was cancelled on VJ
Day. The L was the first
model to carry rocket
projectiles, in tiers under the
wing. On the P-38, the
radiators were unusually
positioned in the sides of the
tail booms, with the turbo
superchargers on top of the
booms

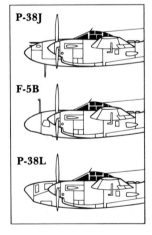

P-38J

F-5B

P-38L

Above: The P-38J's power-
plant comprised two 1425-hp
V-1710-89/91 engines, which
were used with a new cooling
system for the compressed air
from the superchargers,
which involved redesigned
engine nacelles. The P-38J
had a 20-mm (0.79-cal)
cannon and four 0.5-cal (12.7-
mm) machine-guns in the
nose. The F-5B was a photo-
reconnaissance version with
weapons removed. The P-38L
Droop Snoot, with 1475-hp
V-1710-111/113 engines
carried a navigator/bomb-
aimer in the transparent nose
cone.

WHEN the United States Army Air Corps issued a specification for a high-altitude interceptor in 1937, Lockheed were already aware of the qualities demanded by the more forward-looking theorists such as Claire Chennault: speed, ceiling and firepower were the prime requirements, and these, combined with the ability to carry enough fuel for acceptable range, added up to a basic requirement for power. Therefore, two of the new Allison V-1710 engines were chosen, and after examining every possible arrangement Lent of two engines the Lockheed designers settled on a twin-boom configuration, with pilot and armament in a central nacelle. Predicted performance was such that this design was eventually selected by the Air Corps and in June 1937 a prototype was ordered by

the United States Army Air Corps as the XP-38.

The XP-38 flew for the first time in January 1939, powered by two 960-hp V-1710s, but crashed on landing the following month after a record-breaking transcontinental flight. The 13 YP-38s that followed in 1940–41 used one each of the V-1710-27 and -29 1150-hp engines with turbo-superchargers, the different engine models being used to drive 'handed' propellers rotating in opposite directions. Armament was a 37-mm (1.46-in) M2 cannon plus four machine-guns, two each of 0.3-in (7.62-mm) and 0.5-in (12.7-mm) calibre. By mid 1940 Lockheed had received orders from France, Britain and the USAAC. The French order was taken over by Britain as a result of the invasion of France, and since the British insisted that their

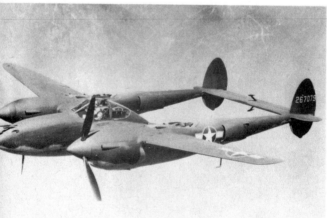

Lightning I should have lower-powered, non-supercharged engines and propellers rotating in the same direction, it proved unacceptable to the RAF.

All but three of the 140 Lightning Is were taken over by the USAAF and designated P-322s. The remaining 524 Lightning IIs had 1325-hp V-1710-49/53 or V-1710-51/55 turbo-supercharged engines and 'handed' propellers, but these too were taken over by the USAAF in 1942 and designated P-38F and P-38G.

Meanwhile, 30 production P-38s had been delivered to the USAAF from mid 1941. These had 1150-hp V-1710-27/29 engines and all four machine-guns were of 0.5-in calibre. However, the absence of combat protection led to the introduc-tion of the new designation P-38D for the remaining 36 originally ordered, these having self-sealing fuel tanks. The 210 P-38Es that followed replaced the 37-mm cannon with a 20-mm (0.79-in) weapon.

The Lightning remained in production until the end of the war, gaining steadily in performance and demonstrating remarkable versatility. The 527 P-38Fs produced from early 1942 introduced racks for two drop-tanks of up to 1136 litres (250 Imp gal) capacity or a pair of 454-kg (1000-lb) bombs, and later examples were the first to be fitted with Fowler flaps for improved combat manoeuvr-ability.

The last 200 of the 1082 P-38Gs built, and the 601 P-38Hs that followed, increased the bombload

Top left and left: The P-38J, which had larger air intakes under the propellers. It was in this type that the leading American fighter ace of World War II, Major Richard Bong, scored all 40 of his victories in the Pacific
Above: An F-5B photo-reconnaissance aircraft (foreground) with a P-38J Lightning behind. The reconnaissance version is painted with high-altitude blue camouflage

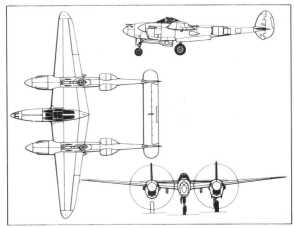

P-38L-1 Lightning

Type: single-seat multirole fighter
Maker: Lockheed Aircraft Corporation
Span: 15.85 m (52 ft)
Length: 11.53 m (37 ft 10 in)
Height: 3.91 m (12 ft 10 in)
Wing area: 30.43 m^2 (327.6 sq ft)
Weight: maximum 9798 kg (21 600 lb); empty 5806 kg (12 800 lb)
Powerplant: two 1475-hp Allison V-1710-111/113 V-12 liquid-cooled engines
Performance: maximum speed 666 km/h (414 mph) at 7620 m (25 000 ft); range 724 km (450 miles) without drop-tanks; operational ceiling 13 412 km (44 000 ft)
Armament: one 20-mm (0.79-in) AN-M2 cannon; four 0.5-in (12.7-mm) machine-guns; 1451-kg (3200-lb) bombload or rockets
Crew: 1
Production: 3923 (all P-38Ls); 9921 (all versions)

to 1451 kg (3200 lb), the latter variant being powered by 1425-hp V-1710-89/91 engines. The same
powerplant was used in the P-38J, but in conjunction with a new cooling system for the compressed
air from the superchargers involving redesigned
engine nacelles; this modification allowed the full
power of the engine to be utilized and maximum
speed to be raised to 666 km/h (414 mph). A total
of 2970 P-38Js were delivered from 1943, and
production was completed by 3923 P-38Ls, with
1475-hp V-1710-111/113 engines.

Lightnings entered service in 1941 and were
deployed in Europe, North Africa and the Pacific
during 1942. Much of the type's early service was
as a bomber escort, and later it was used extensively as a ground-attack aircraft carrying rockets or
bombs. The Droop Snoot modification, with a
navigator/bomb-aimer carried in the nose, and
later radar-equipped Lightnings operated as pathfinders with P-38 formations on bombing missions.
Towards the end of the war 75 P-38Ls in the
Pacific were modified as P-38M radar-equipped
night-fighters. The Lightning ended the war with
more Japanese aircraft to its credit than any other
type, among its victims being the aircraft carrying
the Japanese naval commander, Admiral
Yamamoto who was flying in a Mitsubishi G4 M1-
L2 Navy Type 1 over Bougainville, in April 1943.
Apart from many F-4 and F-5 photo-reconnaissance conversions, individual P-38s were modified
experimentally to act as glider tugs, torpedo carriers and smoke-layers.

Ki-44, Nakajima

FIRST FLIGHT 1940

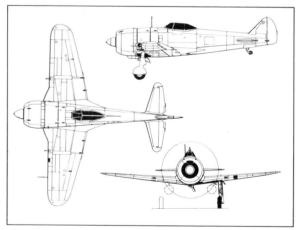

To counter the prevailing tide of Japanese fighter development, which tended to stress manoeuvrability, often at the expense of all other qualities, an Imperial Army specification for a new interceptor issued to Nakajima in 1939 included among its requirements the ability to climb to 5000 m (16 404 ft) in under five minutes, a speed of 600 km/h (373 mph) at 4000 m (13 123 ft) and an armament of four machine-guns. The 1250-hp Nakajima Ha-41 radial engine powered the three Ki-44 prototypes, the first of which was flown in August 1940, but performance was disappointing, the maximum speed achieved being only 550 km/h (342 mph). By September 1941, however, an acceptable design had been finalized, and a combat evaluation squadron was formed to assess the aircraft's capabilities.

While the first Ki-44s went into action in China and Malaya late in 1941, Nakajima initiated production of 40 Ki-44-Is, with two 7.7-mm (0.303-in) machine-guns in the nose and a 12.7-mm (0.5-in) weapon in each wing; Ki-44-Ias, with four of the larger-calibre guns; and Ki-44-Ibs, with minor changes to the landing gear and cooling system. This work was begun before the type was officially accepted for service, and in fact it was not until September 1942, by which time two Sentais were equipped, that the Ki-44-I was accorded the official designation Army Fighter Type 2 Model 1.

By then development had begun of a new version, the Model 2, or Ki-44-II, powered by the 1520-hp Ha-109 and incorporating protection for the pilot and fuel tanks and provision for drop-

tanks. The Ki-44-IIa reverted to the original armament, while the Ki-44-IIb had four 12.7-mm machine-guns, but the Ki-44-IIc introduced cannon in place of the wing machine-guns. Cannon of 20-mm, 37-mm (1.46-in) and 40-mm (1.57-in) calibre were used, most IIcs having the 37-mm weapon for use against American bombers, while the 40-mm Ho-301 was a short-range weapon carried on ground-attack missions.

An all-cannon armament, comprising either four 20-mm or two 20-mm and two 37-mm guns, characterized the final variant, designated Ki-44-IIIa or IIIb according to the armament. The Model 3 also featured a 2000-hp Nakajima Ha-145 18-cylinder radial, ejector exhausts and increased wing area. However, official trials of the

Ki-44-IIb

Type: single-seat interceptor
Maker: Nakajima Hikoki KK
Span: 9.45 m (31 ft)
Length: 8.84 m (29 ft)
Height: 3.25 m (10 ft 8 in)
Wing area: 15 m² (161.46 sq ft)
Weight: normal 2764 kg (6094 lb); empty 2106 kg (4643 lb)
Powerplant: one 1520-hp Nakajima Ha-109 Army Type 2 14-cylinder two-row radial engine
Performance: maximum speed 605 km/h (376 mph) at 5200 m (17 060 ft); range 1190 km (739 miles) with drop-tanks; operational ceiling 11 200 m (36 745 ft)
Armament: four 12.7-mm (0.5-in) Ho-103 machine-guns
Crew: 1
Production: 1225 (all types)

Ki-44-III during the second half of 1943 did not prove successful and the Model 2 continued to be built until the end of 1944. Of the total of 1225 Ki-44s delivered by the time production ended, the majority were of the Ki-44-II variant.

The Ki-44 had sacrificed a good deal of manoeuvrability in favour of speed, climb and firepower. It was, however, the most stable gun platform of any Japanese wartime fighter, and this fact, together with its exceptional rate of climb – 5000 m (16 404 ft) in only 4¼ min – and high diving speed, made it an excellent interceptor. The modest numbers built inevitably restricted its service, and the majority served as home-defence interceptors in Japan. Three Sentais were still equipped with the Ki-44 when the war ended.

Top: A Ki-44 of the 23rd Fighter Sentai. The symbol on the tail is an abstraction of the number 23. The white fuselage band indicates home defence
Above left: A Ki-44 of the 85th Sentai. This fighter is the personal aircraft of the leader of the 2nd Chutai
Above: Aircraft of the Akeno flying school in Japan
Left: The first Nakajima Ki-44, showing the engine cooling gills and rear air outlet louvres. The Allied codename was Tojo

Ki-45, Kawasaki

FIRST FLIGHT 1941

THE Imperial Japanese Army specification issued to Kawasaki in December 1938 outlined a requirement for a twin-engined, two-seat fighter with a speed of 540 km/h (335.5 mph) at 3500 m (11 483 ft). The specified 820-hp Nakajima Ha-20b (licence-built Bristol Mercury) engines were installed in the first prototype, which was completed in January 1939, but neither this nor another two prototypes could manage more than 480 km/h (298 mph). However, in April 1941, Kawasaki were instructed to try again using the more compact 1050-hp Nakajima Ha-25. The remaining six prototypes were fitted with this powerplant which resulted in a recorded speed of 520 km/h (323 mph).

Meanwhile, a thorough reworking of the design produced the Ki-45 Kai, the first prototype of which was flown in September 1941. Armament consisted of two 12.7-mm (0.5-in) machine-guns in the nose, a 20-mm (0.79-in) cannon in a ventral tunnel and a 7.92-mm (0.312-in) machine-gun on a retractable pillar mounting in the rear of the crew compartment. The Ki-45 Kai proved acceptable at last, and production began in early 1942, the first examples named Toryu entering service in August of that year.

Although designed as a long-range escort fighter, the Toryu was to serve in almost every role but escort. Since it was not particularly effective in air-to-air combat, it was used frequently as an anti-shipping and ground-attack aircraft, its slow-firing Ho-3 cannon proving more effective against surface targets. Accordingly, the Ki-45 Kai-b transferred the 20-mm weapon to the nose, omitting the machine-guns, and was equipped with a 37-mm (1.46-in) Type 98 cannon, mounted in the ventral tunnel and hand-loaded by the observer.

This was only the first of several variations in armament. When B-24 Liberators were switched to night attacks, some Toryus were used as night-fighters with field installations of twin 12.7-mm machine-guns firing obliquely forward. The success of this arrangement led to the production from March 1944 of the Ki-45 Kai-c, with no nose armament but two oblique-firing 20-mm cannon and a semi-automatic 37-mm Ho-203 belly cannon. This was produced in parallel with the Kai-d, a specialized anti-shipping variant which had two 20-mm Ho-5 nose cannon, the ventral 37-mm Ho-203 and provision for two 250-kg (551-lb) bombs. Later Kai-cs were powered by the heavier but more reliable 1080-hp Mitsubishi Ha-102 engines, and although they did not carry radar the Toryu night-fighters enjoyed some success against B-29 Superfortresses over Japan, one Sentai alone claiming over 150.

Further development of the Ki-45 was to have been based on the 1500-hp Mitsubishi Ha-112-II engine, but with the first prototype Ki-45-II almost complete it was decided to convert it to a single-seater with the new designation Ki-96. This decision was itself reversed by the time the first Ki-96 flew in September 1943, and the design was developed as the two-seat Ki-102, the first prototype of which flew in March 1944. Armament was a 57-mm (2.24-in) Ho-141 in the nose and two 20-mm Ho-5s in the lower fuselage.

Right: A Ki-45-Kai-c of the 53rd Fighter Sentai based at Matsudo, near Tokyo, in the spring of 1945. This type of machine was used to pioneer the oblique cannon installation later adopted by the Luftwaffe in their night-fighters. It allowed the aircraft to pass beneath an enemy bomber and fire at its unprotected belly. Some Ki-45-Kai-c aircraft were fitted with a nose-mounted searchlight

Ki-45

1 Rudder
2 Rudder hinge
3 Rudder trim tab
4 Fin construction
5 Rear navigation light
6 Elevator tab
7 Right elevator
8 Tailplane
9 Tailwheel position retracted
10 Semi-retractable tailwheel
11 Tailwheel retraction/shock strut
12 Lift point
13 Fuselage construction
14 Control cables
15 Type 99-KAI-Hei radio pack
16 Hand-held 7.92-mm Type 98 machine-gun (deleted from late-production aircraft)
17 Aerial
18 Hinged rear canopy section
19 Unprotected radio operator/gunner's seat
20 Ho-203 37-mm cannon
21 Oxygen bottles
22 Main fuselage fuel tank
23 Ammunition feed chute for obliquely-mounted 20-mm Ho-5 cannon
24 Twin obliquely-mounted 20-mm Ho-5 cannon
25 Aerial mast
26 Shrouded cannon muzzles
27 Pilot's head armour
28 Pilot's armoured seat
29 Sideways-hinging canopy
30 Curved windscreen (with bullet-resistant glass insert)
31 Type 100 reflector gunsight
32 Instrument panel
33 Left fuel tank
34 Left leading-edge unprotected fuel tank
35 Unprotected oil tank
36 Wing construction
37 Landing light
38 Pitot tube
39 Starter dog
40 Nose cone
41 Mainwheel leg strut
42 Rudder pedal
43 Ventral cannon tunnel
44 Sumitomo-Hamilton constant-speed propeller
45 Cannon cooling louvres
46 Ha-102 (Army Type 1) 14-cylinder radial engine
47 Ejector exhausts
48 Right mainwheel
49 Undercarriage door
50 Ho-203 37-mm cannon
51 Flaps
52 Mainspar
53 Flap actuating mechanism
54 Aileron trim tab
55 Right aileron
56 Wing skinning
57 Right navigation light

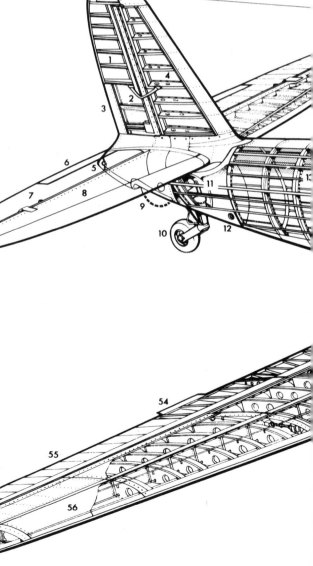

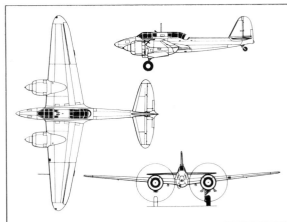

Ki-45 Kai-c

Type: two-seat multirole fighter
Maker: Kawasaki Kokuki Kogyo KK
Span: 15.02 m (49 ft 3¼ in)
Length: 11 m (36 ft 1 in)
Height: 3.7 m (12 ft 1¾ in)
Wing area: 32 m² (344.46 sq ft)
Weight: normal 5500 kg (12 125 lb); empty 4000 kg (8818 lb)
Powerplant: two 1080-hp Mitsubishi Ha-102 Army Type 101 14-cylinder two-row radial engines
Performance: maximum speed 547 km/h (340 mph) at 6500 m (21 325 ft); range 2000 km (1243 miles); operational ceiling 10 000 m (32 808 ft)
Armament: one 37-mm (1.46-in) Ho-203 and two 20-mm (0.79-in) Type 98 cannon
Crew: 2
Production: 477 (1701 all versions)

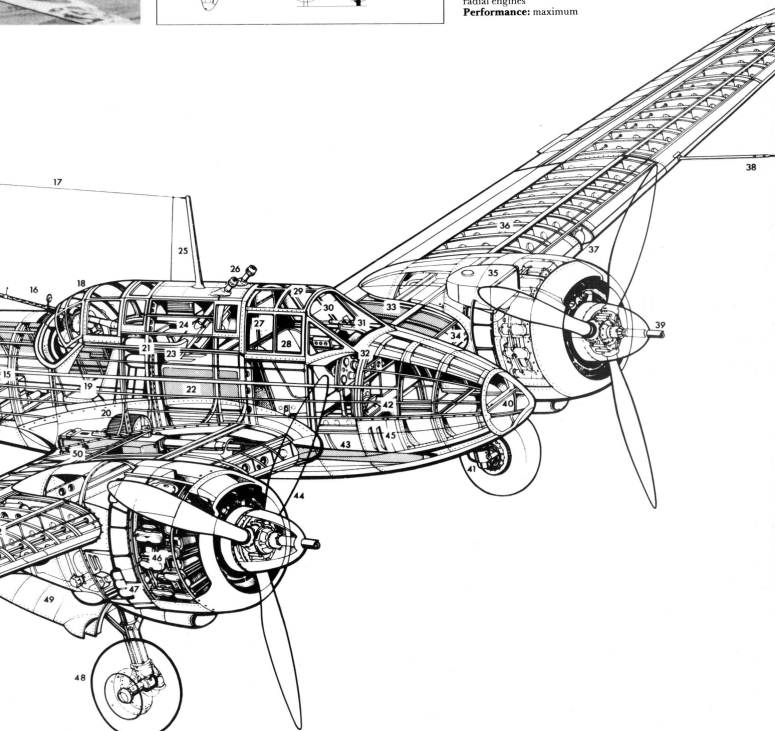

Ki-61, Kawasaki

FIRST FLIGHT 1941

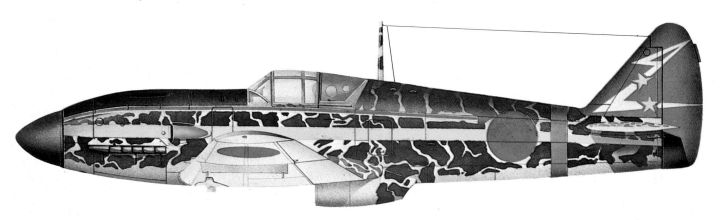

THE acquisition by Kawasaki of blueprints and examples of the German Daimler-Benz DB 601A engine in 1940 led to orders from the Imperial Japanese Army Air Force in February of that year for prototypes of two new interceptors based on this powerplant, the heavyweight Ki-60 and the lighter Ki-61. Work on the latter was postponed until the end of the year, initial efforts being concentrated on the ultimately unsuccessful Ki-60, but by December 1941 the first prototype Ki-61 was complete and an assembly line had been prepared. Trials revealed a top speed of 590 km/h (367 mph) at 6000 m (19 685 ft), and while not quite as manoeuvrable as some of its contemporaries, the Ki-61 had the relatively heavy armament of two 12.7-mm (0.5-in) and two 7.7-mm (0.303-in) machine-guns, with self-sealing fuel tanks, cockpit armour, and high diving speed.

Production began during 1942 of two initial versions, the Ki-61-Ia, with the original armament, and the Ki-61-Ib with 12.7-mm instead of 7.7-mm guns in the wings. These entered service in early 1943 as the Type 3 Army fighter, and during that year 388 examples were given a pair of 20-mm (0.79-in) Mauser MG 151 cannon in place of the wing machine-guns. Minor modifications and further changes in armament in 1944 produced the Ki-61-I Kai-c, with two 20-mm Ho-5 cannon in the nose and 12.7-mm guns in the wings, and a small number of the Kai-d, with 30-mm (1.18-in) wing cannon and 12.7-mm nose guns.

By this time prototypes had been tested of the Ki-61-II, using the uprated Ha-140 version of the

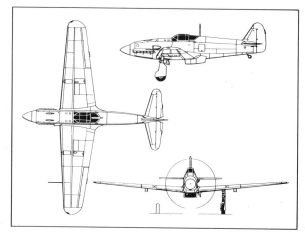

engine, and a new wing; but production examples, designated Ki-61-II Kai, reverted to the original wing. In January 1945, with 374 airframes completed, the engine factory was destroyed by bombing, leaving 275 Ki-61-II Kai airframes without engines. The only suitable alternative to the Ha-140 was the 1500-hp Mitsubishi Ha-112 radial, and in the remarkably short time of less than three months a suitable installation had been evolved, the remaining Ki-61-II airframes being fitted with the radial to become Ki-100s. Not only were 275 Ki-100-Ia conversions produced, but another 118 were built from scratch as the Ki-100-Ib, with a new cockpit canopy. The Ki-100 proved an even better fighter than the Ki-61, being both more manoeuvrable and more reliable.

Ki-61-I Kai-c

Type: single-seat interceptor
Maker: Kawasaki Kokuki Kogyo KK
Span: 12 m (39 ft 4½ in)
Length: 8.94 m (29 ft 4 in)
Height: 3.7 m (12 ft 1¾ in)
Wing area: 20 m² (215.28 sq ft)
Weight: normal 3470 kg (7650 lb); empty 2630 kg (5798 lb)
Powerplant: one 1100-hp Ha-40 Army Type 2 Model 22 (DB 601A) liquid-cooled V-12 engine
Performance: maximum speed 590 km/h (367 mph) at 4260 m (13 976 ft); range 1800 km (1118 miles); operational ceiling 10 000 m (32 808 ft)
Armament: two 20-mm (0.79-in) Ho-5 cannon; two 12.7-mm (0.5-in) Type 1 machine-guns; 500-kg (1102-lb) bombload
Crew: 1
Production: 3078 (all types)

J1N, Nakajima

FIRST FLIGHT 1941

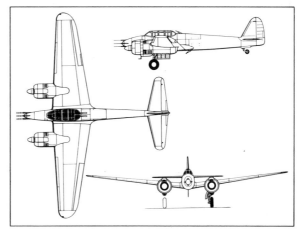

THE development of a twin-engined long-range escort fighter was begun by Nakajima in mid 1938 in response to an Imperial Japanese Navy specification which stipulated a maximum range of 3704 km (2303 miles) with a somewhat unrealistic demand for manoeuvrability comparable to that of enemy single-seaters. The prototype J1N1, which was flown for the first time in May 1941, employed a complex arrangement of wing control surfaces which greatly enhanced manoeuvrability, but suffered from aileron buffeting and consequent severe vibration.

The armament, which included a 20-mm (0.79-in) cannon and two 7.7-mm (0.303-in) machine-guns in the nose, as well as four rearward-firing 7.7-mm guns in two remotely-controlled barbettes on top of the rear fuselage, was another problem. These barbettes proved over-complicated and were removed, while the control problems led to the abandonment of plans to use the J1N1 as a fighter. But gradual improvement in handling was achieved and in July 1942 the J1N1-C was ordered into production as the Navy Type 2 Model 11 reconnaissance aircraft, entering service in this role in 1943.

Meanwhile, new armament schemes had been devised for the type. The J1N1-F had a single 20-mm cannon in a dorsal turret, while the J1N1-C Kai, a field conversion, mounted four 20-mm cannon in pairs to fire obliquely upwards and downwards at an angle of 30°. Small numbers of these were operated as night-fighters during 1943, and the J1N1-C Kai proved sufficiently successful

for production of a purpose-built night-fighter, the J1N1-S Gekko, to begin in August 1943.

The Gekko reduced the crew from three to two, and used a similar armament arrangement in a lighter, streamlined fuselage; airborne interception radar was provided and performance was improved. The majority of the 470 J1N1s built were completed as Gekkos, though there appears to have been no attempt to improve performance further by fitting more powerful engines. Considerable early success was followed by diminishing effectiveness as the type was withdrawn from the Pacific and used against B-29 Superfortresses over Japan. The B-29 flew too high and fast for the Gekko, which was otherwise the most successful of Japan's night-fighters.

J1N1-S Gekko

Type: two-seat night-fighter
Maker: Nakajima Hikoki KK
Span: 16.98 m (55 ft 8½ in)
Length: 12.18 m (39 ft 11½ in)
Height: 4.56 m (14 ft 11½ in)
Wing area: 40 m² (430.57 sq ft)
Weight: normal 6900 kg (15 212 lb); empty 4850 kg (10 692 lb)
Powerplant: two 1130-hp Nakajima NK1C Sakae 21 14-cylinder two-row radial engines
Performance: maximum speed 507 km/h (315 mph) at 5840 m (19 160 ft); range 2550 km (1585 miles); operational ceiling 9320 m (30 577 ft)
Armament: four 20-mm (0.79-in) Type 99-II cannon
Crew: 2
Production: approx 400

Top: The first prototype of the Nakajima J1N1-C Gekko in its reconnaissance role. Later, as a night-fighter, it proved effective against the B-24, but could seldom manage a firing pass at a B-29. The Allied codename was Irving

N1K1, Kawanishi

FIRST FLIGHT 1942

THE first fighter built under the N1K designation was the N1K1 Kyofu, a single-float fighter seaplane built in response to an Imperial Navy specification of September 1940 and flown for the first time in May 1942. Powered by a 1460-hp Mitsubishi Kasei 14 radial, the first Kyofu used a pair of two-blade contra-rotating propellers, but another seven prototypes and the 89 production N1K1s delivered between December 1942 and March 1944 used a single three-blade propeller driven by either a 1460-hp Kasei 13 or a 1530-hp Kasei 15. Armament was two 7.7-mm (0.303-in) machine-guns in the nose and a 20-mm (0.79-in) cannon in each wing.

Meanwhile, Kawanishi had produced a land-plane development of the Kyofu. With the minimum of structural modification, an 1820-hp Nakajima Homare 11 engine was installed in a Kyofu airframe, though the floatplane's mid-wing configuration required the main land gears to have unusually long legs which were retracted telescopically. The first N1K1-J Shiden, as the landplane was designated, flew in December 1942, and production began the following August. The 1007 Shidens built included four models: the N1K1-J Shiden 11, with a similar armament to that of the Kyofu plus a second 20-mm cannon in a gondola under each wing; the N1K1-Ja Model 11A, with four 20-mm cannon in the wings and no machine-guns; the N1K1-Jb, with squared-off vertical tail and provision for a 250-kg (551-lb) bomb under each wing; and the N1K1-Jc Shiden 11C fighter-bomber, which could carry four 250-kg bombs. All were powered by the 1990-hp Homare 21 engine, and some were modified as N1K1-J Kais to accommodate a solid rocket under the fuselage.

During 1943 the totally redesigned low-wing N1K2-J Shiden-Kai was produced, with half as many parts and easy to make in large numbers. The first flew in December 1943. Armament was similar to that of the N1K1-Jb, but with four 250-kg bombs the designation became N1K2-Ja. The 428 built also included a few two-seat trainers, a carrier version, re-engined models and two N1K3-J Shiden 31s, with a longer fuselage and two nose-mounted 13.3-mm (0.52-in) machine-guns. The Shiden Kai combined the excellent manoeuvrability of the original floatplane with a powerful armament and good performance.

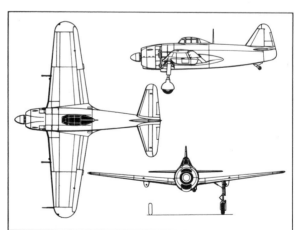

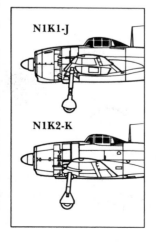

N1K1-J

N1K2-K

Left: The early N1K1-J with its large engine scoop and the N1K2-K Shiden-Rensen two-seat dual-control trainer with improved cowling design

N1K2-J

Type: single-seat fighter
Maker: Kawanishi Kokuki KK; Mitsubishi Jukogyo KK; Omura Kaigun Kokusho and others
Span: 11.97 m (39 ft 3¼ in)
Length: 9.35 m (30 ft 8 in)
Height: 3.96 m (13 ft)
Wing area: 23.5 m² (252.96 sq ft)
Weight: normal 4000 kg (8818 lb); empty 2655 kg (5853 lb)
Powerplant: one 1990-hp Nakajima Homare 21 18-cylinder two-row radial engine
Performance: maximum speed 594 km/h (369 mph) at 5600 m (18 373 ft); range 1720 km (1069 miles); operational ceiling 10 760 m (35 302 ft)
Armament: four 20-mm (0.79-in) Type 99-II cannon; two 250-kg (551-lb) bombs
Crew: 1
Production: 428 (all types)

J2M Raiden, Mitsubishi
FIRST FLIGHT 1942

THE design of the Imperial Navy's first interceptor was begun by Mitsubishi in 1940, with Jiro Horikoshi, whose previous credits included the A5M and A6M Zero, in charge. The extremely compact J2M1 prototype which flew for the first time in March 1942 was powered by a 1460-hp Mitsubishi MK4C Kasei 13. But despite the fuselage being so streamlined that an extension shaft was needed to connect the propeller to the engine in its elongated cowling, and the minimal height of the cockpit canopy, the 575 km/h (357 mph) top speed did not achieve the required performance. Accordingly, a new prototype, designated J2M2, was given an 1820-hp Kasei 23a engine with ejector exhausts and a four-blade propeller in place of the J2M1's three-blade type. Also, there was a provision for a cockpit canopy of much more reasonable size.

Performance of the new model was judged adequate, and the J2M2 was accepted for service as the Raiden Model 11 in October 1941. The engine installation gave constant trouble, with the extension shaft prone to severe vibration. A number of early J2M2s unfortunately broke up in mid-air, with the result that it was not until December 1943 that the first operational unit began conversion to the type.

Only 159 J2M2s were built, and by the end of 1943 production had switched to the J2M3 Raiden Model 21, which replaced its predecessor's armament of two nose-mounted 7.7-mm (0.303-in) machine-guns and two 20-mm (0.79-in) wing cannon with four 20-mm cannon, all in the wings.

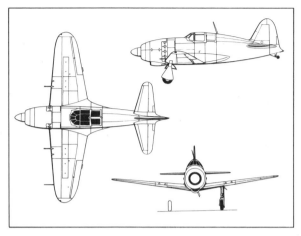

Initially these comprised two each of the Type 99-I and Type 99-II cannon, but the J2M3a (Model 21A) standardized four of the faster-firing Type 99-IIs.

A similar variation in armament differentiated the J2M6 and J2M6a (Models 31 and 31A), whose principal distinguishing feature was the adoption of a still larger cockpit canopy. Further development was aimed at improving altitude performance, and the first J2M4 Model 32 flew in August 1944 with a turbo-supercharged engine and an additional pair of 20-mm cannon in the nose. The turbo-charging system did not prove satisfactory, however, and only two J2M4s were built, a more promising line of development being offered by the J2M5.

J2M3 Raiden Model 21

Type: single-seat interceptor
Maker: Mitsubishi Jukogyo KK; Koza Kaigun Kokusho
Span: 10.8 m (35 ft 5¼ in)
Length: 9.7 m (31 ft 10 in)
Height: 3.81 m (12 ft 6 in)
Wing area: 20.05 m² (215.82 sq ft)
Weight: normal 3435 kg (7573 lb); empty 2460 kg (5423 lb)
Powerplant: one 1820-hp Mitsubishi Kasei 23a 14-cylinder two-row radial engine
Performance: maximum speed 612 km/h (380 mph) at 6000 m (19 685 ft); range 1055 km (656 miles); operational ceiling 11 700 m (38 386 ft)
Armament: two 20-mm (0.79-in) Type 99-I and two 20-mm Type 99-II cannon
Crew: 1
Production: 476

Below: A Mitsubishi J2M3a Raiden of the 302nd Air Corps. This aircraft has four wing-mounted Type 99-II cannon. Later machines, designated J2M6a, had a domed canopy to give better visibility

First flown in May 1944, the J2M5 used a gear-driven supercharger in conjunction with an 1820-hp Kasei 26a engine and was armed with only two 20-mm cannon. The J2M5 enjoyed a substantially better climb rate, and was capable of 610 km/h (379 mph) at 6500 m (21 325 ft), allowing it to compete with the B-29 Superfortress, but the American bombing raids had wrought such havoc by late 1944 that hardly any Kasei 26a engines were available. Consequently, only three dozen or so J2M5 Raiden 33s were built, and a plan to re-engine earlier models with the Kasei 26a under the designation J2M7 Raiden Model 23 was similarly frustrated by shortages of the powerplant. Consequently, only 40 Raidens of all marks had been completed by the end of the war, compared with an original production target of 3600 during 1944 alone.

Like the other more powerful, less manoeuvrable fighters introduced into Japanese service during World War II, the Raiden was the object of initial hostility from its pilots. However, it was to prove its worth as an interceptor during the closing stages of the war, after seeing its first combat during the Battle of the Marianas in September 1944. Evaluation by Allied pilots of two examples captured in January 1945 showed it to be capable of climbing more steeply than any Allied fighter and to be exceptionally responsive to controls except at speeds in excess of 525 km/h (326 mph). The total of Mitsubishi-built J2Ms was 476, not including a batch of J2M5s built by Koza.

Above: A captured Mitsubishi J2M3 Raiden under evaluation. It was an effective bomber destroyer with powerful armament and adequate protection
Right: A turbo-supercharger in an experimental J2M4, installed to give the aircraft sufficient power to reach the high-flying B-29 bombers. The installation suffered teething troubles and only two were built

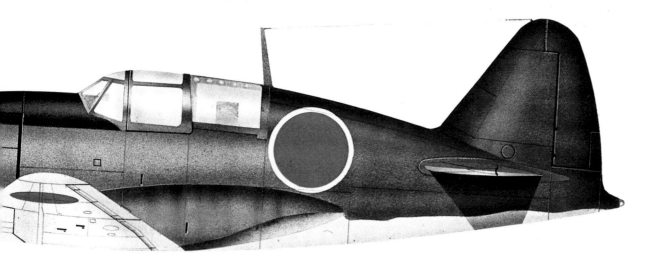

Top: Mitsubishi J2M3; though built in conjunction with the J2M2 it supplanted this aircraft principally because of its heavier armament
Left: A slightly battered Raiden captured by US forces. Most of the aircraft operated from the Japanese homeland, but some saw action in the Philippines
Above: The Mitsubishi MK4R-A Kasei installation in a J2M3 Raiden (Thunderbolt). The types went through four different powerplants, some with turbo-superchargers to enable them to reach USAAF bombers

P-51 Mustang, North American

FIRST FLIGHT 1940

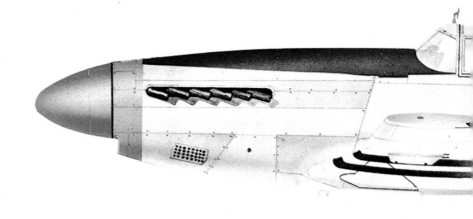

THE origins of one of the finest American fighters of World War II were the discussions between the British Purchasing Commission and North American Aviation in January 1940.

Requirements included an inline engine, eight guns and performance superior to that of the Curtiss P-40, which the commission originally wanted North American to build under licence. Although the company had little previous experience of fighter construction, NAA president James Kindelberger had visited British and German aircraft manufacturers two years earlier, and the company-funded NA-73 which was rolled out, minus engine, inside the deadline, featured the most advanced laminar-flow wing yet seen and a radiator position which almost eliminated drag.

Allison finally delivered the V-1710-F3R engine, and the prototype's first flight in October 1940 coincided with the beginning of production for the Royal Air Force. Although the engine performed poorly at altitude, low-level speeds were exceptional, and camera-equipped Mustang Is began operations in the tactical reconnaissance role with RAF Army Cooperation Command in May 1942. The Mk I was armed with two nose 0.5-in (12.7-mm) machine-guns plus one 0.5-in and two 0.3-in (7.62-mm) machine-guns in each wing.

Meanwhile, the United States Army Air Force had tested two early production aircraft with the designation XP-51. Unimpressed, they nevertheless ordered 150 P-51's for supply to the RAF under Lend-Lease as Mk IAs, with self-sealing fuel tanks and four 20-mm (0.79-in) M2 cannons in the wings. In the event, a number of P-51s were retained by the USAAF, and 57 were later converted to P-51-1s (originally F-6A) photographic machines. The next to serve with the USAAF were A-36A dive-bomber versions, 500 were delivered between September 1942 and March 1943, with six 0.5-in guns, divebrakes and racks for a 227-kg (500-lb) bomb under each wing.

Some improvement in altitude performance was achieved by fitting the 1200-hp V-1710-81 version of the Allison engine, and 310 P-51As with this powerplant and four 0.5-in guns were built for the USAAF, another 50 going to the RAF as Mustang IIs. A more significant improvement was achieved in Britain, where four Mustang Is were given Rolls-Royce Merlin 60-series engines. The experiment was repeated in the United States, where two P-51s became XP-78s (later XP-51Bs) when fitted with Packard-built Merlins. Speeds of 708 km/h (440 mph) at 7620 m (25 000 ft) led to orders for 1990 P-51Bs, with 1380-hp Packard V-1650-3 (Merlin 61) engines, new ailerons, four 0.5-in guns and racks for 454-kg (1000-lb) bombs or drop-tanks. A further 1750 similar P-51Cs were built by a new North American factory at Dallas, Texas, and later aircraft had 1490-hp V-1650-7 engines.

Of the B and C models, 910 went to the RAF as Mustang IIIs, and 281 of the 875 Mk IVs also supplied were equivalent to the P-51D, the most prolific of all Mustangs. The most distinctive features of the D were the new bubble canopy (later fitted to many of the earlier machines) and re-aligned rear fuselage to give all-round pilot vision, but the more powerful V-1650-7 also improved climb rate

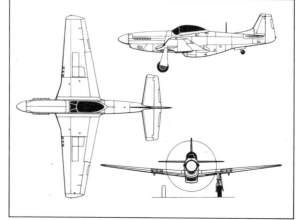

P-51 Mustang

Type: multirole fighter
Maker: North American Aviation Inc
Span: 11.28 m (37 ft)
Length: 9.83 m (32 ft 3 in)
Height: 3.7 m (12 ft 2 in)
Wing area: 21.65 m² (233 sq ft)
Weight: maximum 3991.6 kg (8800 lb); empty 2971 kg (6550 lb)
Powerplant: one 1150-hp Allison 1710-39 V-12 liquid-cooled engine
Performance: maximum speed 622.7 km/h (387 mph) at 4570 m (15 000 ft); range 563 km (350 miles);

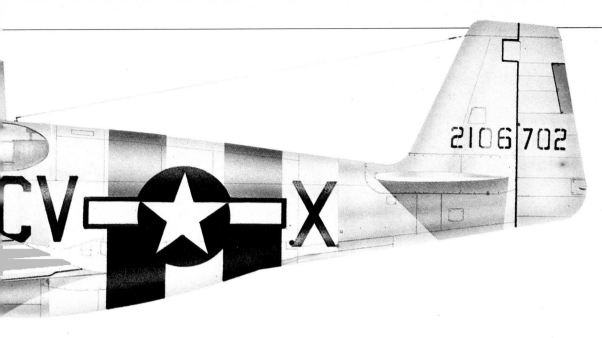

Left: A P-51B Mustang with a Packard-Merlin V-1650-7 1790-hp engine. It is painted with D-Day stripes and an olive drab anti-glare panel on the nose. With drop-tanks they could manage the round trip from their UK bases to Berlin, much to the surprise of the Luftwaffe

Below: Nose of the NA-73X prototype Mustang. In production versions the nose armament installation was refined; in the Merlin-engine version all guns were in the wings

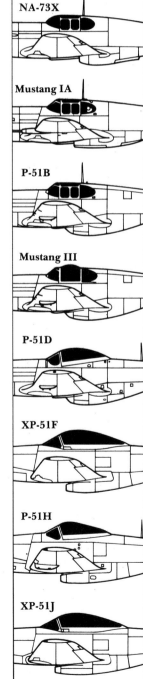

NA-73X

Mustang IA

P-51B

Mustang III

P-51D

XP-51F

P-51H

XP-51J

Far left: A P-51D with its bubble canopy and three infantry-type Bazookas under each wing for ground-straffing. The Mustang was later adapted to take four 5-in (127-mm) rockets on zero-length rails under each wing

Left: The changing shape of the Mustang. The Mustang III incorporated a Malcolm hood. The basic development of engine, canopy and armament led in 1944 to the lightened F, H and J, among the fastest of all piston-engined aircraft

operational ceiling 9555 m (31 350 ft)
Armament: four 20-mm (0.79-in) cannon
Crew: 1
Production: 310

P-51B

Specifications similar to the P-51 except in the following particulars:
Weight: maximum 5352.4 kg (11 800 lb); empty 3168.3 kg (6985 lb)
Powerplant: one 1380-hp Packard Merlin V-1650-3 V-12 liquid-cooled engine

Performance: maximum speed 708 km/h (440 mph) at 9144 m (30 000 ft); range 644 km (400 miles); ceiling 12 740 m (41 800 ft)
Armament: four 12.7-mm (0.5-in) machine-guns; two 454-kg (1000-lb) bombs
Production: 1988

P-51D

Specifications similar to the P-51 except in the following particulars:
Weight: maximum 5262 kg (11 600 lb); empty 3232 kg (7125 lb)

Powerplant: one 1490-hp Packard V-1650-7 Merlin V-12 liquid-cooled engine
Performance: maximum speed 703 km/h (437 mph) at 7620 m (25 000 ft); range 1529 km (950 miles) with internal fuel only or 3700 km (2300 miles) with two 416-litre (91.6-Imp gal) drop-tanks; operational ceiling 12 772 m (41 900 ft)
Armament: six 0.5-in (12.7-mm) Browning machine-guns; two 454-kg (1000-lb) bombs
Crew: 1
Production: 7965 (15 576 ll types)

and an extra pair of 0.5-in machine-guns were fitted as standard. A total of 7965 were built, and these were followed by 1337 P-51Ks with different propellers, of which 594 became RAF Mk IVs. Ten TP-51D two-seat trainers were also built, with earlier models converted to TPs.

Gun armament was reduced again to four 0.5-in in the three XP-51Fs and two XP-51Gs – there was no E model – which were designed for lightness as pure fighters and had loaded weights of only 4110 kg (9060 lb) and 4028 kg (8880 lb) respectively. These formed the basis for 555 P-51H production aircraft, which reverted to six guns and a gross weight of 4990 kg (11 000 lb), and whose 1380-hp V-1650-9 engines gave them a top speed of 532 km/h (487 mph). The two XP-51Js were

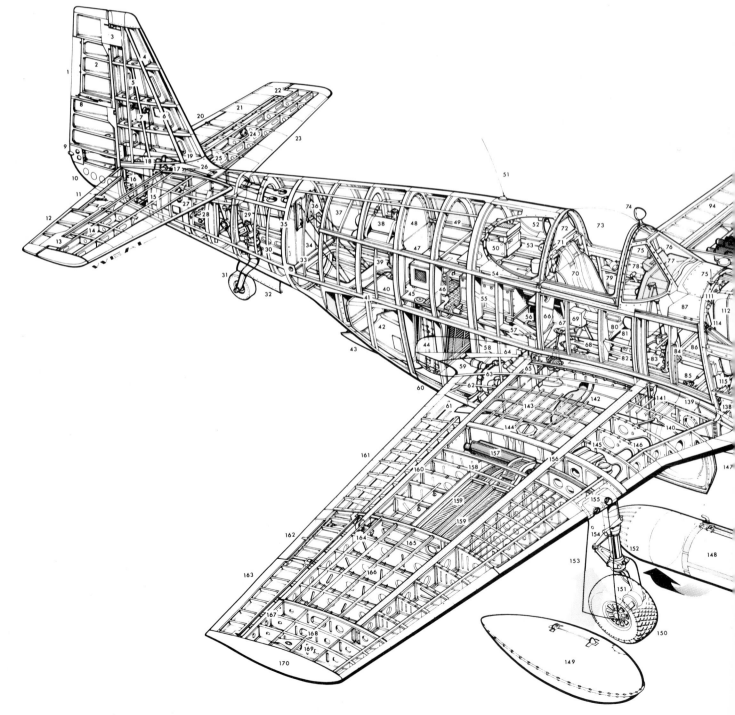

P-51Fs with new propellers, and the single P-51M was a Dallas-built P-51H with 1400-hp V-1650-9A engine: 1629 were cancelled when the war ended.

Mustangs made their mark in every theatre during World War II: as ground-attack aircraft in Europe, the Far East and the Pacific, often carrying four of the US 127-mm (5-in) or British 27-kg (60-lb) rockets under each wing; escorting bombers over Germany and Japan, for which their great range, especially when carrying drop-tanks, made them invaluable; as interceptors, in which role they proved adept at dealing with V-1 flying bombs, and capable of holding their own against the jet-powered Me 262; and as photographic reconnaissance machines, a total of 425 P-51B, C, D and Ks being converted as F-6B, C, D and K for the

purpose. Some of these were later redesignated RF-51D and K. RAF service ended in 1947, and USAF P-51Bs and Ks were retired in 1949–51, but many F-51Ds and Hs were sent to Korea with Air National Guard units in 1951.

Mustangs saw extensive postwar service with many other air forces, including that of Australia, where Commonwealth Aircraft built 300 under licence as the CA-17 and CA-18, and also equipped many of the world's smaller air forces until the 1960s. Surplus Mustangs have enjoyed a considerable vogue as sporting aircraft, and in the late 1960s a number were rebuilt by Cavalier for the US Military Assistance Program. In 1971 the USAF tested Lycoming T55 Piper Enforcer P-51 derivatives in the counter-insurgency role.

Far left: A preserved P-51D with its tally of victories painted by the cockpit. The Mustang continued in service after World War II, and when Air National Guard Wings were activated for the Korean war it was once more in action. In 1980 the US considered using the Piper Enforcer version against tanks in the European theatre!

P-51B

1 Rudder trim tab, plastics construction
2 Rudder frame (fabric covered)
3 Rudder balance
4 Fin front spar
5 Fin structure
6 Access panel
7 Rudder trim tab actuating drum
8 Rudder trim tab control link
9 Rear navigation light
10 Rudder metal bottom section
11 Elevator plywood trim tab
12 Right elevator frame
13 Elevator balance weight
14 Right tailplane structure
15 Reinforced bracket (rear steering stresses)
16 Rudder operating horn forging
17 Elevator operating horns
18 Tab control turnbuckles
19 Fin front spar/fuselage attachment
20 Left elevator tab
21 Fabric-covered elevator
22 Elevator balance weight
23 Left tailplane
24 Tab control drum
25 Fin root fairing
26 Elevator cables
27 Tab control access panels
28 Tailwheel steering mechanism
29 Tailwheel retraction mechanism
30 Tailwheel leg assembly
31 Forward-retracting steerable tailwheel
32 Tailwheel doors
33 Lifting tube
34 Fuselage aft bulkhead/breakpoint
35 Fuselage breakpoint
36 Control cable pulley brackets
37 Fuselage frames
38 Oxygen bottles
39 Cooling air exit flap actuating mechanism
40 Rudder cables
41 Fuselage lower longeron
42 Rear tunnel
43 Cooling air exit flap
44 Coolant radiator assembly
45 Radio and equipment shelf
46 Power and supply pack
47 Fuselage upper longeron
48 Radio bay aft bulkhead (plywood)
49 Fuselage stringers
50 SCR-695 radio transmitter-receiver (on upper sliding shelf)
51 Whip aerial
52 Junction box
53 Cockpit aft glazing
54 Canopy track
55 SCR-522 radio transmitter-receiver
56 Battery installation
57 Radiator/supercharger coolant pipes
58 Radiator forward air duct
59 Coolant header tank/radiator pipe
60 Coolant radiator ventral access cover
61 Oil cooler air inlet door
62 Oil radiator
63 Oil pipes
64 Flap control linkage
65 Wing rear spar/fuselage attachment bracket
66 Crash pylon structure
67 Aileron control linkage
68 Hydraulic hand pump
69 Radio control boxes
70 Pilot's seat
71 Seat suspension frame
72 Pilot's head/back armour
73 Rearward-sliding clear-vision canopy
74 External rear-view mirror
75 Ring and bead gunsight

76 Bullet-proof windshield
77 Gyroscopic gunsight
78 Engine controls
79 Signal pistol discharge tube
80 Circuit-breaker panel
81 Oxygen regulator
82 Pilot's foot-rest and seat mounting bracket
83 Control linkage
84 Rudder pedal
85 Tailwheel lock control
86 Wing centre-section
87 Hydraulic reservoir
88 Left wing fuel tank filler point
89 Left 0.5-in (12.7-mm) machine-guns
90 Ammunition feed chutes
91 Gun bay access door (raised)
92 Ammunition box troughs
93 Aileron control cables
94 Flap lower skin (Alclad)
95 Aileron profile (internal aerodynamic balance diaphragm)
96 Aileron control drum and mounting bracket
97 Aileron trim tab control drum
98 Aileron trim tab, plastics (phenol fibre) construction
99 Left aileron assembly
100 Wing skinning
101 Outer section sub-assembly
102 Left navigation light
103 Left wingtip
104 Leading-edge skin
105 Landing lamp
106 Weapons/stores pylon
107 454-kg (1000-lb) bomb
108 Gun ports
109 Machine-gun barrels
110 Detachable cowling panels
111 Firewall/integral armour
112 Oil tank
113 Oil pipes
114 Upper longeron/engine mount attachment
115 Oil tank metal retaining straps
116 Carburettor
117 Engine bearer assembly
118 Cowling panel frames
119 Engine aftercooler
120 Engine leads
121 Packard (Rolls-Royce Merlin) V-1650 engine
122 Exhaust fairing panel
123 Stub exhausts
124 Magneto
125 Coolant pipes
126 Cowling forward frame
127 Coolant header tanks
128 Armour plate
129 Propeller hub
130 Spinner
131 Four-blade Hamilton Standard Hydromatic propeller
132 Carburettor air intake, integral with 133
133 Engine mount front frame assembly
134 Intake trunking
135 Engine mount reinforcing tie
136 Hand crank
137 Carburettor/trunking vibration-absorbing connection
138 Wing centre-section front bulkhead
139 Wing centre-section end rib
140 Right mainwheel well
141 Wing front spar/fuselage attachment bracket
142 Ventral air intake (radiator and oil cooler assemblies)
143 Right wing fuel tank
144 Fuel filler point

145 Mainwheel leg mount/pivot
146 Mainwheel leg rib cut-outs
147 Main gear fairing doors
148 Auxiliary fuel tank
149 Auxiliary fuel tank
150 68.6-cm (27-in) smooth-contour mainwheel
151 Axle fork
152 Towing lugs
153 Landing gear fairing
154 Main gear shock strut
155 Blast tubes
156 Wing front spar
157 Gun bay
158 Ammunition feed chutes
159 Ammunition boxes
160 Wing rear spar
161 Flap structure
162 Right aileron tab
163 Right aileron
164 Right aileron tab adjustment mechanism (ground setting)
165 Wing rib strengthening
166 Outboard section structure
167 Outer section single spar
168 Wingtip sub-assembly
169 Right navigation light
170 Detachable wingtip

P-47 Thunderbolt, Republic

FIRST FLIGHT 1941

THE bulky outlines of the Thunderbolt were largely dictated by the big radial engine and supercharger intake in the nose. The designations XP-47 and XP-47A covered projected developments of the Republic AP-10 design for a high-speed, light-weight fighter to be powered by a liquid-cooled Allison V-1710 engine. Ordered in January 1940, these prototypes were later cancelled and the designation XP-47B was applied to a new project for a large and heavily-armed fighter designed around the 2000-hp Pratt & Whitney R-2800 Double Wasp and carrying no fewer than eight 0.5-in (12.7-mm) machine-guns in the wings. The XP-47B's first flight in May 1941 was followed by a long test programme before the first production order, for 773 machines, was placed in September 1941.

The first 171 production Thunderbolts were P-47Bs, which were delivered in 1942 and taken to Europe by the USAAF's 56th and 78th Fighter Groups in early 1943. Service trials with the 56th were marked by a number of engine failures and crashes, and revealed deficiencies in climb, manoeuvrability and fuel capacity, though top speed with the R-2800-21 engine was an impressive 690 km/h (429 mph). The 602 P-47Cs which made up the next order had the engine 33 cm (13 in) further forward, for improved manoeuvrability, and had provision for a 757-litre (167-Imp gal) drop-tank or 227-kg (500-lb) bomb on the centreline. Other changes enabled 2100-hp R-2800-59 or -63 engines to be fitted.

After the P-47C's operational debut in Europe in

Top: A P-47N of the 437th FS with zero-length rocket installations and a 454-kg (1000-lb) M65 bomb inboard. Wing-mounted ordnance was more popular than belly-mounted since there was slightly less danger with a wheels-up landing or landing-gear collapse
Above left: A P-47D assigned to escort duties for USAAF twin-engined bombers
Above: A P-47D-26-RA in 1944. The canopy gave better vision
Above right: A major field overhaul for Thunderbolts of the 7th AAF

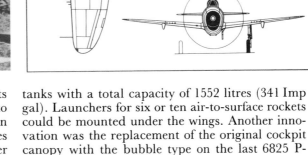

P-47N Thunderbolt

Type: single-seat fighter and fighter-bomber
Maker: Republic Aviation Corporation
Span: 12.98 m (42 ft 7 in)
Length: 11.07 m (36 ft 4 in)
Height: 4.47 m (14 ft 8 in)
Wing area: 30.86 m² (332.2 sq ft)
Weight: normal 9389 kg (20 699 lb); empty 4987 kg (10 994 lb)
Powerplant: one 2800-hp Pratt & Whitney R-2800-57, -73 or -77 18-cylinder two-row radial engine
Performance: maximum speed 752 km/h (467 mph) at 9754 m (32 000 ft); range 3492 km (2170 miles) with drop-tanks; operational ceiling 13 107 m (43 000 ft)
Armament: eight 0.5-in (12.7-mm) Browning machine-guns; ten 5-in (127-mm) HVAR air-to-surface rockets; 1134 kg (2500 lb) of bombs
Crew: 1
Production: 1816 (15 660 all types)

March 1943, new VHF radio was fitted and its introduction in the Pacific in mid-summer led to new requests for additional fuel. These were met in the P-47D by provision for an extra 275 litres (60 Imp gal) of fuel, while the addition of water injection gave a further boost to performance. An eventual total of 12 602 P-47Ds was built, 6509 by the original Republic factory at Farmingdale, New York, and 6093 by a new factory at Evansville, Indiana. Progressive improvements made to P-47Ds of later production batches included increases in bombload in stages from a single 227-kg (500-lb) bomb under the fuselage to another under each wing and finally a 454-kg (1000-lb) bomb on each wing in addition to the ventral 500-lb weapon. The bomb racks could also accommodate drop-

tanks with a total capacity of 1552 litres (341 Imp gal). Launchers for six or ten air-to-surface rockets could be mounted under the wings. Another innovation was the replacement of the original cockpit canopy with the bubble type on the last 6825 P-47Ds.

No other single model of a US fighter was built in such quantities. The XP-47E and F were experimental conversions of single P-47Bs with pressurized cabin and laminar-flow wings respectively, while the 354 P-47Gs built by Curtiss corresponded to the D variant. The single Curtiss-built XP-47H was a modified P-47D with a 2300-hp Chrysler XIV-2220 engine which achieved a top speed of 790 km/h (491 mph), and the XP-47J reached 811 km/h (504 mph), a record for a piston-

Left: The P-47N was a long-range version of the Thunderbolt designed for use in the Pacific. Pairs of interconnected fuel cells were installed in the long-span wings. On August 8, 1945, 151 P-47Ns escorting 400 B-29 bombers in a raid on Yawata on Kyushu made contact with 60 enemy fighters. In a fast-moving action the Japanese lost 13 aircraft and five Thunderbolts were shot down. Four of the US pilots were recovered from the sea. Five days later only one P-47N was lost when 20 Japanese were downed in 30 minutes action

Republic P-47D-10

1 Rudder upper hinge
2 Aerial attachment
3 Fin flanged ribs
4 Rudder post/fin aft spar
5 Fin front spar
6 Rudder trim tab worm and screw actuating mechanism
7 Rudder centre hinge
8 Rudder trim tab
9 Rudder structure
10 Tail navigation light
11 Elevator fixed tab
12 Elevator trim tab
13 Right elevator structure
14 Elevator outboard hinge
15 Elevator torque tube
16 Elevator trim tab worm and screw actuating mechanism
17 Chain drive
18 Right tailplane
19 Tail jacking point
20 Rudder control cables
21 Elevator control rod and linkage
22 Fin spar/fuselage attachment points
23 Left elevator
24 Aerial
25 Left tailplane structure (two spars and flanged ribs)
26 Tailwheel retraction worm gear
27 Tailwheel anti-shimmy damper
28 Tailwheel oleo
29 Tailwheel doors
30 Retractable and steerable tailwheel
31 Tailwheel fork
32 Tailwheel mount and pivot
33 Rudder cables
34 Rudder and elevator trim control cables
35 Lifting tube
36 Elevator rod linkage
37 Semi-monocoque all-metal fuselage construction
38 Fuselage dorsal 'razorback' profile
39 Aerial lead-in
40 Fuselage stringers
41 Supercharger air filter
42 Supercharger
43 Turbine casing
44 Turbo-supercharger compartment air vent
45 Turbo-supercharger exhaust hood fairing (stainless steel)
46 Outlet louvres
47 Intercooler exhaust doors (left and right)
48 Exhaust pipes
49 Cooling air ducts
50 Intercooler unit (cooling and supercharged air)
51 Radio transmitter and receiver packs (Detrola)
52 Canopy track
53 Elevator rod linkage
54 Aerial mast
55 Formation light
56 Rearward-vision frame cutout and glazing
57 Oxygen bottles
58 Supercharged and cooling air pipe (supercharger to carburettor) left
59 Elevator linkage
60 Supercharged and cooling air pipe (supercharger to carburettor) right
61 Central duct (to intercooler unit)
62 Wingroot air louvres
63 Wingroot fillet
64 Auxiliary fuel tank
65 Auxiliary fuel filler point
66 Rudder cable turnbuckle
67 Cockpit floor support
68 Seat adjustment lever
69 Pilot's seat
70 Canopy emergency release (left and right)
71 Trim tab controls
72 Back and head armour
73 Headrest
74 Rearward-sliding canopy
75 Rear-view mirror fairing
76 'Vee' windshields with central pillar
77 Internal bulletproof glass screen
78 Gunsight
79 Engine control quadrant (cockpit left wall)
80 Control column
81 Rudder pedals
82 Oxygen regulator
83 Underfloor elevator control quadrant
84 Rudder cable linkage
85 Wing rear spar/fuselage attachment (tapered bolts/bushings)
86 Wing supporting lower bulkhead section
87 Main fuel tank
88 Fuselage forward structure
89 Stainless steel/Alclad firewall bulkhead
90 Cowl flap valve
91 Main fuel filler point
92 Anti-freeze fluid tank
93 Hydraulic reservoir
94 Aileron control rod
95 Aileron trim tab control cables
96 Aileron hinge access panels
97 Aileron and tab control linkage
98 Aileron trim tab (left wing only)
99 Frise-type aileron
100 Wing rear (No 2) spar
101 Left navigation light
102 Pitot head
103 Wing front (No 1) spar
104 Wing stressed skin
105 Four-gun ammunition troughs (individual bays)
106 Staggered gun barrels
107 Removable panel
108 Inter-spar gun bay access panel
109 Forward gunsight bead
110 Oil feed pipes
111 Oil tank
112 Hydraulic pressure line
113 Engine upper bearers
114 Engine control correlating cam
115 Eclipse pump (anti-icing)
116 Fuel level transmitter
117 Generator
118 Battery junction box
119 Storage battery
120 Exhaust collector ring
121 Cowl flap actuating cylinder
122 Exhaust outlets to collector ring
123 Cowl flaps
124 Supercharged and cooling air ducts to carburettor (left and right)
125 Exhaust upper outlets
126 Cowling frame
127 Pratt & Whitney R-2800-59 18-cylinder twin-row engine
128 Cowling nose panel
129 Magnetos
130 Propeller governor
131 Propeller hub
132 Reduction gear casing
133 Spinner
134 Propeller cuffs
135 Four-blade Curtiss constant-speed electric propeller
136 Oil cooler intakes (left and right)
137 Supercharger intercooler (central) air intake
138 Ducting
139 Oil cooler feed pipes
140 Right oil cooler
141 Engine lower bearers
142 Oil cooler exhaust variable shutter
143 Fixed deflector
144 Excess exhaust gas gate
145 Belly stores/weapons shackles
146 Metal auxiliary drop-tank
147 Inboard mainwheel well door
148 Mainwheel well door actuating cylinder
149 Camera gun left
150 Cabin air-conditioning intake (right wing only)
151 Wingroot fairing
152 Wing front spar/fuselage attachment/tapered bolts/bushings)
153 Wing inboard rib mainwheel well recess
154 Wing front (No 1) spar
155 Undercarriage pivot point
156 Hydraulic retraction cylinder
157 Auxiliary (undercarriage mounting) wing spar
158 Gun bay warm air flexible duct
159 Wing rear (No 2) spar
160 Landing flap inboard hinge
161 Auxiliary (No 3) wing spar inboard section (flap mounting)
162 NACA slotted trailing-edge landing flaps
163 Landing flap centre hinge
164 Landing flap hydraulic cylinder
165 Four 0·5-cal (12,7-mm) Browning machine-guns
166 Inter-spar gun bay inboard rib
167 Ammunition feed chutes
168 Individual ammunition troughs
169 Underwing stores/weapons pylon
170 Landing flap outboard hinge
171 Flap door
172 Landing flap profile
173 Aileron fixed tab (right wing only)
174 Frise-type aileron structure
175 Aileron hinge/steel forging spar attachments
176 Auxiliary (No 3) wing spar outboard section (aileron mounting)
177 Multi-cellular wing construction
178 Wing outboard ribs
179 Wingtip structure
180 Right navigation light
181 Leading-edge rib sections
182 Bomb shackles
183 227-kg (500-lb) M-43 demolition bomb
184 Undercarriage leg fairing (overlapping upper section)
185 Mainwheel fairing (lower section)
186 Wheel fork
187 Right mainwheel
188 Brake lines
189 Landing-gear air-oil shock strut
190 Machine-gun barrel blast tubes
191 Staggered gun barrels
192 Rocket-launcher slide bar
193 Centre strap
194 Front mount (attached below front spar between inboard pair of guns)
195 Deflector arms
196 Triple-tube 4·5-cal (11,5-cm) rocket-launcher (Type M10)
197 Front retaining band
198 4·5-cal (11,5-cm) M8 rocket

engined aircraft, with an R-2800-57 in a redesigned installation. The designation XP-47K covered the test machine for the bubble canopy used on later Ds, the XP-47L was another modified D with increased fuel capacity, and three YP-47Ms were Ds fitted with 2800-hp R-2800-57 engines.

The last Thunderbolt was the ultra-long-range P-47N, powered by the 2800-hp R-2800-77 and grossing a massive 9389 kg (20 700 lb). The new wing with span increased by 28 cm (11 in) accommodated 423 litres (93 Imp gal) of fuel in the root. First tested on the XP-47K, this wing was then fitted to the 1816 production P-47Ns.

In wartime service, the Thunderbolt equipped USAAF units in both Europe and the Pacific, while 830 P-47Ds were supplied to the RAF as Thunderbolt Mks I and II, the latter having the bubble canopy; another 196 went to the Soviet Union under Lend-Lease. Although range limitations hampered bomber escort work in Europe, and performance below 4572 m (15 000 ft) was poor, the Thunderbolt came into its own at higher altitudes, where its exceptional speed, resilience and firepower combined with a terminal dive velocity of 885 km/h (550 mph) to make it the equal of any enemy fighter. Before, during and after the Allied invasion of Europe, the P-47D was used extensively against ground targets and as an escort in daylight bombing raids on Germany. RAF Thunderbolts were used exclusively in the Far East. Other air forces to use the Thunderbolt during World War II included those of Brazil, which received 88 in 1944–45, and France, to which 446 were supplied

in the last year of the war in Europe. The Brazilian 1st fighter group joined the US 12th Air Force in Italy in October 1944 after being equipped with P-47Ds. Although the P-47N did not reach Europe until April 1944 it was introduced in the Pacific in January of that year, where its range of over 3219 km (2000 miles) enabled it to escort B-29s on raids over Japan, though it was more commonly employed for ground attacks.

After the war, P-47Ds and Ns remained in USAF service until 1949 and thereafter equipped Air National Guard units until 1953. Foreign service was less extensive than that of the Mustang, but several South American and other air forces used P-47Ds, and occasionally P-47Ns, during the 1950s, some surviving into the next decade.

Above: A P-47D-25 or D-30 with bubble canopy. The size of the cockpit in the Thunderbolt was a source of constant surprise to new pilots. One joker suggested that if you had to take evasive action in an air fight it was easier to undo your straps and run round the cockpit. However the heavy firepower was also impressive, and a Polish pilot reported enemy aircraft exploded when they were hit by the eight 'point-fifties'

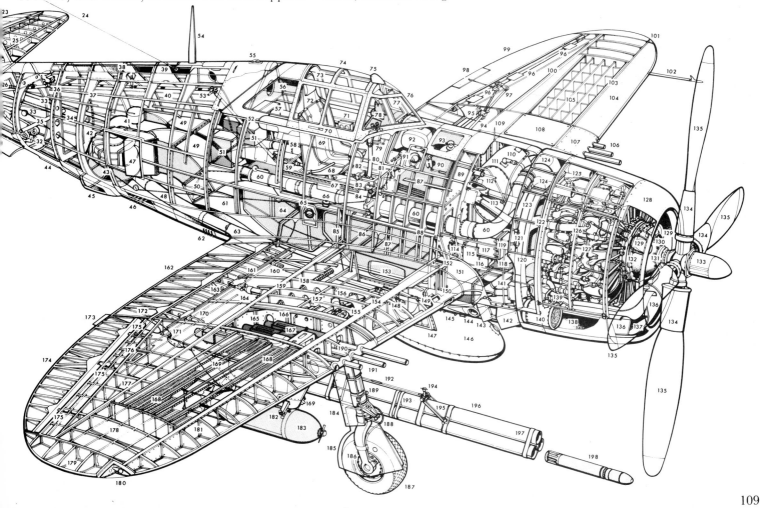

Ju 88G, Junkers
FIRST FLIGHT 1943

BY mid 1939, with production of Ju 88A bomb-ers under way, attention was being given to the utilization of the Junkers design's excellent per-formance in other roles. One of these was that of Zerstörer heavy fighter. The B series prototypes had served to develop the installation of BMW 801 radials in place of the original Jumo engines. After the abandonment of a heavy fighter conversion of the Ju 88 V7, one of the A series pre-production aircraft, a new model was proposed using BMW 801 MA engines in conjunction with a modified A-1 airframe and designated Ju 88C-1.

This too was abandoned when BMW 801 sup-plies were earmarked for the Fw 190, but some A-1s, retaining their 1200-hp Junkers Jumo 211B-1 engines, the rearward-firing dorsal and ventral machine-guns and the aft bomb bay, were given a redesigned nose housing three 7.92-mm (0.312-in) MG 17 machine-guns and a 20-mm (0.79-in) MG FF cannon to become Ju 88C-2s. These were pressed into service as night-fighters.

The Ju 88C-3 and C-5 were experimental radial-engined conversions of the C-2, but from late 1941 the C-2 was joined by the purpose-built C-4, based on the A-4 bomber, but with two more MG FF cannon in the gondola under the nose as well as attachment points under the wings for two pods, each containing six 7.92-mm MG 81s. Production began in 1942 of the more heavily armoured C-6, with 1350-hp Jumo 211J engines, and while most early C series aircraft were used in the destroyer role in the Mediterranean, by the end of 1942 the first Ju 88 fighters were being equipped with radar. The addition of Lichtenstein equipment gave rise to the designation C-6b. Early in 1943 the C-6b was joined by the similarly armed and equipped Ju 88R-1 and R-2, distinguished only by their powerplant of BMW 801MA or 801D radials. By the beginning of the following year, the Ju 88C-6c was being fitted with the higher-frequency Lich-tenstein SN-2. Another innovation introduced by the C-6c was the 'Schräge Musik' arrangement of two 20-mm cannon mounted in the fuselage.

The Ju 88C-7a, C-7b and C-7c were further destroyer versions, but during 1943 an R-2 was modified to form the prototype of a more effective night-fighter. This entered service in the spring of 1944 as the G-1, retaining the BMW 801D engine but using the larger tail unit of the Ju 188 and with a revised armament of four 20-mm MG 151s in a ventral tray plus a manually-aimed 13-mm (0.512-in) MG 131 in the rear of the crew compartment. Additional avionics equipment required a fourth crew member. This was made standard on the G-4, while the G-6a, with BMW 801G engines, incorpo-rated the oblique-firing MG 151s and a second, rearward-facing Lichtenstein set. The G-6b added a Naxos set for intercepting Allied bombers' H$_2$S radar signals, and the G-6c was powered by the 1750-hp Jumo 213A.

The last series of Ju 88 night-fighters, introduced in late 1944, comprised the G-7a, with Jumo 213E engines; the G-7b, with Neptun radar; and the G-7c, with centimetric Berlin radar. By the closing stages of the war, night-fighters were at a low priority, and only about 750 of these extremely capable G-series night-fighters were built.

Junkers Ju 88G-1

1 Right navigation light
2 Wingtip profile
3 FuG 227 'Flensburg' radar receiver antenna
4 Right aileron
5 Aileron control runs
6 Right flaps
7 Flap-fairing strip
8 Wing ribs
9 Right outer fuel tank
10 Fuel filler cap
11 Leading-edge structure
12 Annular exhaust slot
13 Cylinder head fairings
14 Adjustable nacelle nose ring
15 Twelve-blade cooling fan
16 Propeller boss
17 Variable-pitch VS 111 wooden propeller
18 Leading-edge radar array
19 FuG 220 'Lichtenstein' SN-2 intercept radar array
20 Nose cone
21 Forward armoured bulkhead
22 Gyro compass
23 Instrument panel
24 Armour-glass windscreen
25 Folding seat
26 Control column
27 Rudder pedal/brake cylinder
28 Control runs
29 Pilot's armoured seat
30 Sliding window section
31 Headrest
32 Jettisonable canopy roof section
33 Gun restraint
34 Wireless operator/gunner's seat
35 Rheinmetall Borsig MG 131 machine-gun (13-mm)
36 Radio equipment (FuG 10P HF, FuG 16ZY VHF, FuG 25 IFF)
37 Ammunition box (500 rounds of 13-mm)
38 FuG 220 'Lichtenstein' SN-2 indicator box
39 FuG 227 'Flensburg' indicator box
40 Control linkage
41 Bulkhead
42 Armoured gun mount
43 Aerial post traverse check
44 Fuel filler cap
45 Whip aerial
46 Forward fuselage fuel tank
47 Fuselage horizontal construction joint
48 Bulkhead
49 Fuel filler cap
50 Aft fuselage fuel tank
51 Access hatch
52 Bulkhead
53 Control linkage access plate
54 Fuselage stringers
55 Upper longeron
56 Maintenance walkway
57 Control linkage
58 Horizontal construction joint
59 Z-section fuselage frames
60 Dinghy stowage
61 Fuel vent pipe
62 Master compass
63 Spherical oxygen bottles
64 Accumulator
65 Tailplane centre-section carry-through
66 Right tailplane
67 Elevator balance
68 Aerial
69 Right elevator
70 Elevator tab
71 Tailfin forward spar/fuselage attachment
72 Tailfin structure
73 Rudder actuator
74 Rudder post
75 Rudder mass balance
76 Rudder upper hinge
77 Rudder tab (upper section)
78 Inspection/maintenance handhold
79 Rudder structure
80 Tailfin aft spar/fuselage attachment
81 Rudder tab (lower section)
82 Rear navigation light
83 Elevator tab
84 Left elevator
85 Elevator balance
86 Elevator tab actuator
87 Heated leading edge
88 Tail bumper/fuel vent outlet
89 Taiwheel doors
90 Tailwheel retraction mechanism
91 Shock absorber leg
92 Mudguard
93 Tailwheel
94 Access hatch
95 Fixed antenna
96 D/F loop
97 Lower longeron
98 Nacelle/flap fairing
99 Left flap
100 Wing centre/outer section attachment point
101 Aileron controls
102 Aileron tab (left only)
103 Aileron hinges
104 Rear spar
105 Left aileron
106 Left navigation light
107 FuG 101a radio altimeter antenna
108 Wing structure
109 Leading-edge radar array
110 Forward spar
111 Pitot head
112 Landing lamp
113 Mainwheel well rear bulkhead
114 Left outer fuel tank location
115 Ventral gun pack (offset to the left)
116 Ball-and-socket fuselage-wing

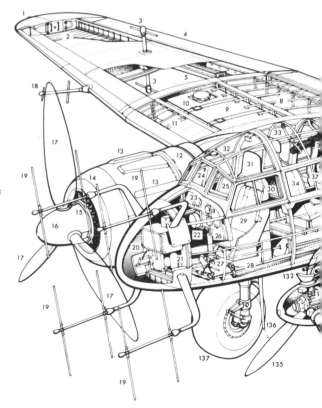

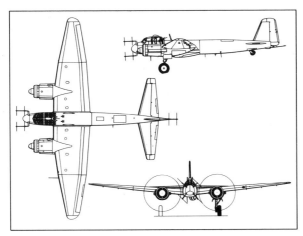

Ju 88G-7b

Type: four-seat night-fighter
Maker: Junkers Flugzeug und Motorenwerke
Span: 20 m (65 ft 7½ in)
Length: 14.55 m (47 ft 8¾ in) without antennae
Height: 4.85 m (15 ft 11 in)
Wing area: 54.5 m² (586.65 sq ft)
Weight: normal 13 100 kg (28 881 lb); maximum 14 670 kg (32 350 lb)
Powerplant: two 1725-hp Junkers Jumo 213E V-12 engines
Performance: maximum speed 645 km/h (401 mph) at 8800 m (28 870 ft); range 2250 km (1398 miles); operational ceiling 8800 m (28 870 ft)
Armament: six 20-mm (0.79-in) MG 151/20 cannon; one 13-mm (0.512-in) MG 131 machine-gun
Crew: 4
Production: approximately 750 (all G models); over 5000 (all fighter types)

attachment points
117 Left inner fuel tank location
118 Ammunition boxes for MG 151 cannon (200 rpg)
119 Mauser MG 151/20 cannon (four) of 20-mm calibre
120 Mainwheel leg retraction yoke
121 Leg pivot member
122 Mainwheel door actuating jack
123 Mainwheel door (rear section)
124 Mainwheel door (forward section)
125 Leg support strut
126 Left mainwheel
127 Mainwheel leg
128 Annular exhaust slot
129 Exhaust stubs (internal)
130 BMW 801D air-cooled radial
131 Annular oil tank
132 Cannon muzzles (depressed 5°)
133 Twelve-blade cooling fan
134 Propeller mechansim
135 Variable-pitch wooden VS 111 propeller
136 FuG 16ZY antenna
137 Right mainwheel

Above left: The Ju 88G-6b which had BMW 801G air-cooled radial engines. It also mounted the 'Schräge Musik' MG 151 cannon firing obliquely upwards, which enabled the fighter to fly under enemy bombers and make a long firing pass at the wing spars

F6F Hellcat, Grumman

FIRST FLIGHT 1942

THE two prototypes, XF6F-1 and XF6F-2, of a new Grumman fighter ordered at the end of June 1941, were intended to be F4F Wildcats modified to use the 1600-hp Wright R-2600-10 and turbo-supercharged R-2600-16 Cyclone engines respectively. The F6F Hellcat that eventually entered production was a completely new design, powered by the R-2800 Double Wasp.

The XF6F-1 flew in June 1942 with the Cyclone engine, but when the second prototype flew the following month it was as the XF6F-3 with an R-2800-10. At the same time, a low-mounted wing had replaced the Wildcat's mid-wing configuration and the whole airframe had become considerably bigger and heavier, with better armour protection, main gears retracting rearwards into the inner wings, six 0.5-in (12.7-mm) machine-guns and more than double the F4F's fuel capacity. The first production order was placed in May 1942, before either prototype had flown, and with very few changes required the first flight of a production F6F-3 was made in October. Squadron deliveries began in January 1943.

Meanwhile, the original XF6F-1 was given an R-2800-27 engine and flown as the XF6F-4 in October 1942, but the only other production model of the Hellcat was the F6F-5, introduced in 1944. The F6F-5 used the same R-2800-10W with water boost that had been introduced on later F6F-3s, allied to a number of small aerodynamic and equipment improvements, including the provision of attachment points for three 454-kg (1000-lb)

Above: A Hellcat lands on the escort flat-top USS *Matanikau*. Its markings of RR indicate that it is from the USS *Yorktown* and its damaged tail suggests that this is an emergency landing. The arrester hook has just caught on No 3 barrier
Above right: One of the F6F-3s built by Grumman. This aircraft has the red border to its insignia. It is probably a production machine which has just received a test flight but has not yet been assigned to a unit
Right: A Hellcat preserved by the Confederate Air Force.

The F6F destroyed a claimed 4947 enemy aircraft in air-to-air combat and 209 on the ground during the war with Japan. During the Korean war drone versions were used in a guided-missile role against targets in North Korea. The first was launched on August 28, 1952, with a Douglas AD as a controller

bombs under the fuselage and the wings inboard of the folding point, plus six 5-in (127-mm) rockets under the outer wings. Some later F6F-5s also mounted two 20-mm (0.79-in) cannon in place of two of the machine-guns. The last of 4402 USN F6F-3s was completed in April 1944; the last of 7870 F6F-5s was delivered in November 1945.

Although there were only two basic models of the Hellcat, a number of variants were produced. In July 1943 an F6F-3 became the prototype XF6F-3N night-fighter, with an outerwing radome for the APS-6 radar set, and 149 F6F-3Ns were built, as well as 18 F6F-3Es with APS-4 radar. APS-6 was also fitted to 1434 F6F-5Ns, while the F6F-3P and -5P were high-altitude photographic reconnaissance versions. Postwar conversion included a number of F6F-5K target drones and -5D drone directors. In the two years from its combat debut in August 1943, combined victories of the Hellcat in the hands of shore- and carrier-based navy and marine corps squadrons amounted to a total of 5156, and the overall ratio of victories to losses was better than 19:1. The Hellcat's superior speed, protection and firepower gave it an overwhelming advantage over the A6M Zero.

The type was also used by the Royal Navy, 252 F6F-3s operated as Hellcat Is by the Fleet Air Arm, and 930 F6F-5s becoming Hellcat IIs in British service, which were the standard fighters aboard RN escort carriers in the Far East, and another three FAA squadrons used the F6F-5N, of which 80 were supplied to Britain in 1945.

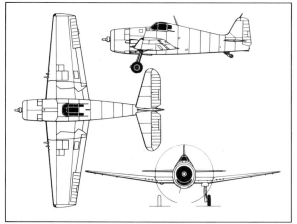

F6F-5 Hellcat

Type: carrier-based fighter
Maker: Grumman Aircraft Engineering Corporation
Span: 13.06 m (42 ft 10 in)
Length: 10.24 m (33 ft 7 in)
Height: 3.99 m (13 ft 1 in)
Wing area: 31.03 m² (334 sq ft)
Weight: normal 6991 kg (15 413 lb); empty 4190 kg (9238 lb)
Powerplant: one 2000-hp Pratt & Whitney R-2800-10W Double Wasp 18-cylinder two-row radial engine
Performance: maximum speed 612 km/h (380 mph) at 7133 m (23 400 ft); range 1521 km (945 miles); operational ceiling 11 369 m (37 300 ft)
Armament: six 0.5-in (12.7-mm) Browning machine-guns; 1361-kg (3000-lb) bombload; six 5-in (127-mm) rockets
Crew: 1
Production: 7870

F4U Corsair, Vought

FIRST FLIGHT 1939

THE most significant feature of a new fighter design submitted by Vought, ordered in prototype form as the XF4U-1 by the US Navy in June 1938, was the new 2000-hp Pratt & Whitney Double Wasp engine. The use of this engine, whose greater power necessitated the largest propeller of any contemporary fighter, dictated the adoption of an inverted gull wing in order to keep the main landing gear legs reasonably short, while allowing adequate ground clearance for the airscrew. Flight testing of the prototype began in May 1939 and revealed handling difficulties and problems with the engine still under development. Official trials began in October 1940.

In spite of various setbacks, the XF4U-1 demonstrated outstanding performance, including a speed of 650 km/h (404 mph) – then a record for a military aircraft – and a production order for 584 F4U-1s was placed in June 1941.

Modifications included an increase in armament from a 0.5-in (12.7-mm) and a 0.3-in (7.62-mm) machine-gun in the nose and one of the heavier weapons in each wing, to six wing-mounted 0.5-in guns, which involved the elimination of wing fuel tanks and moving the cockpit aft to accommodate an enormous fuel cell in the mid fuselage. The first F4U-1s were delivered in July 1942, by which time Goodyear and Brewster were preparing to build the type under the respective designations FG-1 and F3A-1, their first Corsairs being completed in early 1943.

The difficulty of landing the Corsair, com-

Above: An F4U-1A, which besides operating as a fighter was a highly efficient close-support aircraft armed with bombs, HE and AP rockets and napalm
Below left: F4U-2s aboard USS *Intrepid* await take-off orders
Bottom left: An F4U-1 under construction at Stratford, Connecticut, in 1942
Below: A privately owned Corsair of today. During World War II and in Korea most flew in the US Navy Midnight Blue. French naval units flew Corsairs in Indo-China, Algeria and Suez

pounded by the rear cockpit position, delayed the type's acceptance for carrier flying (except for the clipped-wing Fleet Air Arm Corsairs), and first deliveries were made to shore-based US Marine Corps squadrons while further changes were made. During production of 2814 F4U-1s, 1694 non-folding FG-1s and 738 F3A-1s, the main gears were modified, a raised cockpit canopy was introduced and the water-injected R-2800-8W was used. In addition, 200 F4U-1Cs had an armament of four 20-mm (0.79-in) cannon, and 1685 F4U-1Ds and 2303 FG-1Ds introduced attachment points on each inner wing either for a drop-tank or for 454-kg (1000-lb) or 726-kg (1600-lb) bombs, later augmented by rocket launchers outboard.

Meanwhile, by the end of 1942 an F4U-1 had been converted to an F4U-2 night-fighter with a wingtip radome for the APS-6 radar. A further 33 were similarly converted. The turbo-supercharged F4U-3 was abandoned, but the installation of the 2100-hp R-2800-18W engine driving a four-blade propeller resulted in the F4U-4, which remained in production until 1947, the 2344 built including 297 F4U-4Cs, with four 20-mm cannon, nine photo-reconnaissance F4U-4Ps and an F4U-4N night-fighter. Orders for Goodyear FG-4s were cancelled at the end of the war.

A number of postwar developments kept the Corsair in production until 1952. The F4U-5, first flown in April 1946, which used the 2300-hp R-2800-32W engine and had four 20-mm cannon; the 567 examples produced from 1947–51 included 314 F4U-5N and -5NL night-fighters, the latter

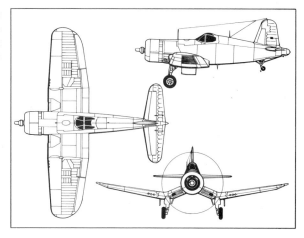

F4U-4 Corsair

Type: carrier-based fighter-bomber
Maker: Vought-Sikorsky Division of United Aircraft Corporation
Span: 12.49 m (40 ft 11¾ in)
Length: 10.27 m (33 ft 8¼ in)
Height: 4.5 m (14 ft 9 in)
Wing area: 29.17 m² (314 sq ft)
Weight: normal 6500 kg (14 330 lb); empty 4235 kg (9336 lb)
Powerplant: one 2100-hp Pratt & Whitney R-2800-18W Double Wasp 18-cylinder two-row radial engine
Performance: maximum speed 718 km/h (446 mph) at 7986 m (26 200 ft); range 1802 km (1120 miles); operational ceiling 12 650 m (41 500 ft)
Armament: six 0.5-in (12.7-mm) Browning machine-guns; 1905-kg (4200-lb) bombload
Crew: 1
Production: 2344 (12 571 all types)

being winterized versions, and 30 photo-reconnaissance F4U-5Ps. The F4U-6, subsequently re-designated AU-1, was a heavily armoured ground-attack version, of which 110 were built in 1952; and 94 F4U-7s, a specialized ground-attack version of the F4U-4, were built in 1952 for service with the French in Indo-China.

The Corsair's protracted development was thus matched by an even longer production run, and after achieving an outstanding reputation during World War II, when 2000 were used by the Fleet Air Arm and 425 by the Royal New Zealand Air Force, the type received a new lease of life during the Korean war when many Corsairs were recalled from the reserves to see extensive service in the ground-attack role.

Far left: The prototype of the AU-1 attack version which was adopted by the US Marine Corps in Korea. It was heavily armoured and could carry either 10 HVARs (rockets) or 10 45.4-kg (100-lb) bombs
Left: An F4U-5 which flew just after World War II. It was armed with four 20-mm (0.79-in) cannon and could carry rockets or bombs. Like earlier Corsairs it had folding wings and an arrester hook
Below left: An F4U-1A with a 454-kg (1000-lb) bomb on a Brewster adaptor rack. With this installation Corsairs could be used as dive-bombers
Below right: The F4U-1C, which was the first cannon-armed version. It had a similar powerplant to the F4U-1A, and went into action in April 1945

Typhoon, Hawker

FIRST FLIGHT 1940

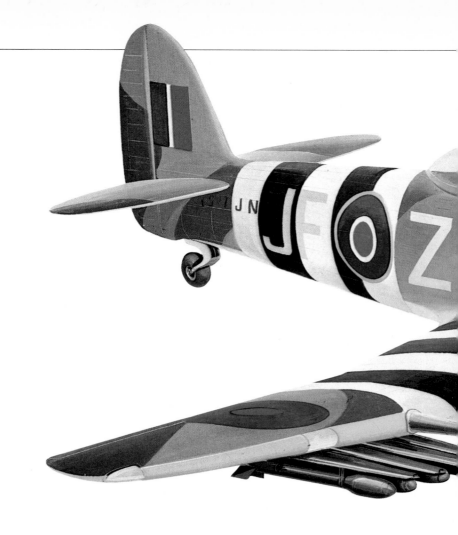

HAWKER produced two designs to the F.18/37 specification for a 644-km/h (400-mph) 12-gun fighter, both of which received production orders. The first of these was the Tornado, the original prototype of which flew in October 1939 powered by a 1760-hp Rolls-Royce Vulture II engine, but the second prototype was unfortunately delayed by the priority given to the Hurricane production until December 1940. Ultimately, the Vulture engine was abandoned, and only one of 500 production Tornados ordered from Avro was completed, this and a third prototype serving thereafter as testbeds for the Bristol Centaurus engine.

The second design's prototype, named Typhoon, flew in February 1940, but assembly was undertaken by Gloster, and the first production Typhoon was flown in May 1941. Like the Tornado, the Typhoon suffered from having an unreliable new engine, the H-type Napier Sabre I rated at 2100 hp. Vibration problems were particularly severe, and at one stage of flight testing the aft fuselage collapsed. Problems with the engine were gradually overcome with the progressive substitution of the 2180-hp Sabre IIA, 2200-hp Sabre IIB and 2260-hp Sabre IIC. The Typhoon IA was armed with 12 0.303-in (7.7-mm) machine-guns, but this was soon replaced by the Mk IB with four 20-mm (0.79-in) cannon.

Although altitude performance and rate of climb proved disappointing, the Typhoon was introduced into RAF service in mid 1941. By the end of the year two squadrons were operational with the type, which was the only RAF fighter with the speed to intercept low-flying Fw 190A intruders. Unfortunately, a high rate of structural and engine failure during the early part of its career resulted in many accidental losses, though the aft fuselage was later strengthened. During 1941 a revised design, powered by the Sabre IV engine, was produced as the Typhoon II, though with further work this became the Tempest.

Although a failure as an interceptor, the Typhoon achieved considerable success as a ground-attack aircraft. From 1942 work was concentrated on adapting it for this role. Strengthening of the wings allowed a progressive increase in bombload from two 113-kg (250-lb) to two 454-kg (1000-lb) bombs, but the most significant development was the provision of rocket armament. During 1943 the low-drag, single-rail Mk III launcher was produced for the 3-in (76.2-mm) rocket, which had a 27-kg (60-lb) armour-piercing warhead, and Typhoons were fitted with eight of these. That year also saw the beginning of cross-Channel bombing raids on targets in occupied Europe, and train-busting Typhoons were soon claiming the destruction of up to 150 locomotives per month.

In 1944, with the build-up to the Operation Overlord invasion of France, 26 RAF squadrons were equipped with the type. These were used in preliminary attacks for the D-Day landings, including two radar stations. During and after the landings they were employed in close-support work, destroying huge numbers of German tanks in the process, and although production ended in 1944 Typhoons were heavily engaged until the end of the war in Europe.

Left: A Hawker Typhoon IB of the 2nd Tactical Air Force in its D-Day stripes. The rocket armament was used to great effect against German armour; earlier it had devastated the coastal radar stations on June 2 and 5, 1944. During the fighting in France and north-east Europe Typhoons were on call for ground forces in what became known as a 'cab rank' system. On July 17, 1944, Wing Commander J Baldwin leading Typhoons of No 193 Squadron made a cannon attack on the staff car carrying Field Marshal Rommel, wounding him so badly that he withdrew from the Normandy fighting. Cannon were an effective way of aiming rockets, for once the pilot had observed strikes on the target he would then fire his rockets. A full salvo gave him the firepower of the broadside from an 8-in (203-mm) cruiser

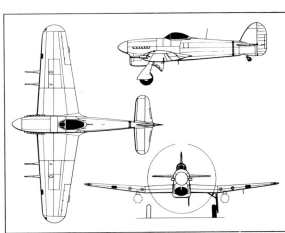

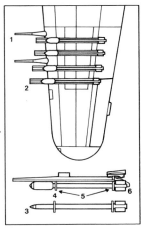

Far left: The main flying instruments such as the artificial horizon, altimeter, air-speed indicator and direction indicator are grouped in the central panel
Centre left: A Typhoon IB with the late production blister canopy and whip aerial
Left: Rocket installation
  1 4 20-mm (0.79-cla) Hispano-Suiza cannon
  2 8 27-kg (60-lb) HE rockets, 4 each wing
  3 Thin-bodied rocket
  4 Stotted rails carrying HE rockets
  5 Pair of hanging brackets
  6 Electrical firing cable

Typhoon IB

Type: single-seat fighter-bomber
Maker: Hawker Aircraft Ltd; Gloster Aircraft Ltd
Span: 12.68 m (41 ft 7 in)
Length: 9.72 m (31 ft 10¾ in)
Height: 4.52 m (14 ft 10 in)
Wing area: 25.92 m² (279 sq ft)
Weight: normal 5171 kg (11 400 lb); empty 4010 kg (8840 lb)
Powerplant: one 2200-hp Napier Sabre IIB H-24 liquid-cooled engine
Performance: maximum speed 685 km/h (409 mph) at 3048 m (10 000 ft); range 1465 km (910 miles) with drop-tanks; operational ceiling 10 363 km (34 000 ft)
Armament: four 20-mm (0.79-in) Hispano-Suiza cannon; 907-kg (2000-lb) bombload or eight rockets
Crew: 1
Production: 3345 (all types), 3330 by Gloster

Tempest, Hawker

FIRST FLIGHT 1942

Left: A Tempest V Series 2 in 1944. This mark was an effective interceptor against V-1 flying bombs, destroying 638, and also in 'Rat Scrambles' in which they bounced Me 262 jet-fighters as they were coming in to land
Below left: The 2520-hp Bristol Centaurus engine of a Mk II
Below: A Mk II streams contrails from its wingtips as it pulls round in a tight turn

IN November 1941 two prototypes were ordered of the Typhoon II, which combined a lengthened fuselage with a new elliptical wing and the 2240-hp Napier Sabre IV engine. By June 1942 the name had been changed to Tempest, and a whole family of designs with different powerplants had been proposed, though prototypes of only three were built: the Mk I, powered by the Sabre IV; the Mk II, with the 2520-hp Bristol Centaurus V or VI; and the Mk V, with the Sabre II.

The last of these was the first to fly, in September 1942, by which time production had been ordered, and the Tempest V entered RAF service in April 1944. Sabre IIA, IIB or IIC engines were used, and armament consisted of four 20-mm (0.79-in) cannon, with provision for two 454-kg (1000-lb) bombs or eight rockets. A total of 705 were built, a number of modifications being introduced after the completion of the first 100, and these were used for ground-attack during the advance across occupied Europe in 1944–45 and against V-1s, destroying 638 flying bombs as well as 20 of the German Me 262 jet fighters.

Although the prototype Mk I had flown in February 1943, difficulties with the Sabre V engine caused planned production to be cancelled. By June 1943 the radial-engined Mk II had been flown, this model being intended for service in the Pacific and having the impressive range of 2639 km (1640 miles). Much quieter and smoother, and slightly faster than the Mk V, its production was delayed by the Mk V and by a switch of manufacture to the Bristol Aeroplane Co, and deliveries did

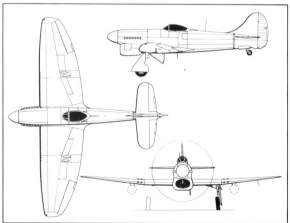

not begin until October 1944. The 472 built saw extensive overseas service in the postwar years, including action against guerillas in Malaya for five years after withdrawal of other marks.

The final version of the Tempest was the Mk VI, which was powered by the 2340-hp Sabre V with the oil coolers in the wing roots. The prototype flew in May 1944, and deliveries of production Tempest VIs in 1945–47 totalled 142. After being retired from front-line service in 1947 many Tempest Vs and VIs were converted as target tugs. In 1947 89 Mk IIs were transferred to India and another 24 were supplied to Pakistan the following year. Those remaining in RAF service were the force's last fighter-bombers, powered by a single piston engine.

Tempest V Series I

Type: interceptor and fighter-bomber
Maker: Hawker Aircraft Ltd
Span: 12.19 m (40 ft)
Length: 10.26 m (33 ft 8 in)
Height: 4.9 m (16 ft 1 in)
Wing area: 28.06 m² (302 sq ft)
Weight: normal 5216 kg (11 500 lb); empty 4196 kg (9250 lb)
Powerplant: one 2180-hp Napier Sabre IIA H-24 liquid-cooled engine
Performance: maximum speed 702 km/h (436 mph) at 5639 m (18 500 ft); range 1191 km (740 miles); operational ceiling 11 125 m (36 500 ft)
Armament: four 20-mm (0.79-in) Hispano-Suiza cannon; 907-kg (2000-lb) bombload or eight rockets
Crew: 1
Production: 100

P-59A Airacomet, Bell

FIRST FLIGHT 1942

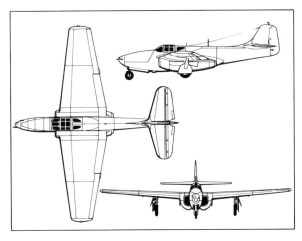

Above: The second
production P-59A-1-BE
Airacomet. Though the
Airacomet is of interest as the
first jet aircraft to be built in
the United States, it did not
enjoy a memorable service
record
Left: One of the prototype
XP-59As. The aircraft were
built by Bell, partly because
its plant was near the General
Electric factory which was
building the turbojets based
on the Whittle patents

WHILE the German jet-propelled He 178 had been flown in August 1939, little progress with gas-turbine propulsion had been made in the United States by April 1941, when General H H Arnold was given a demonstration of the British Whittle turbojet and the Gloster E.28/39 it was shortly to power on its first flight. Consequently, General Arnold instigated the acquisition of a licence for the Whittle W.2B engine and the development of an American jet fighter. General Electric were to develop the powerplant, and in September 1941 Bell Aircraft were asked to design an airframe to accommodate it. For security reasons, the designation XP-59A was allocated to the new fighter. The basic design, for a mid-wing aircraft with tricycle landing gear and one engine below each wing root, was evolved quite quickly and construction of the three XP-59A prototypes ordered began in January 1942.

The first prototype was completed in September 1942 and made its first flight at Muroc, California (now Edwards AFB), on October 1. Prolonged testing and modification of the first prototype, which was joined by the second and third the following spring, revealed numerous problems with the engine, which was designated GE Type I-A and developed 590 kg (1300 lb) st. This was less than had been estimated and performance was not impressive, though some improvement was obtained when the YP-59A, 13 of which were delivered from mid 1943, was fitted with the 748-kg (1650-lb) st I-16 (later designated J31). The USAAF's trials culminated in comparative evalua-

tion with the P-47D Thunderbolt and P-38J Lightning in early 1944. These revealed the YP-59A to be distinctly inferior as a combat aircraft, and a June 1943 order for 100 production P-59A Airacomets was reduced to 50, of which 30 had increased fuel capacity and the designation P-59B.

A number of these were subjected to further tests and experiments, but 14 As and 19 Bs were used to equip the USAAF's first jet-fighter unit, the 412th Fighter Group. The 412th had been formed in 1943 for training rather than operational service, and although the Airacomet was nominally the USAAF's first jet fighter, its main function was as a research aircraft and familiarization trainer. The 412th's P-59s were replaced by P-80 Shooting Stars in 1946.

P-59A Airacomet

Type: experimental fighter
Maker: Bell Aircraft Corporation
Span: 13.87 m (45 ft 6 in)
Length: 11.62 m (38 ft 1½ in)
Height: 3.66 m (12 ft)
Wing area: 35.86 m² (386 sq ft)
Weight: normal 4936 kg (10 882 lb); empty 3606 kg (7950 lb)
Powerplant: two 748-kg (1650-lb) st General Electric J31-GE-3 turbojets
Performance: maximum speed 658 km/h (409 mph) at 10 668 m (35 000 ft); range 386 km (240 miles); operational ceiling 14 082 m (46 201 ft)
Armament: one 37-mm (1.46-in) M4 cannon; three 0.5-in (12.7-mm) machine-guns
Crew: 1
Production: 20

Ki-84 Hayate, Nakajima

FIRST FLIGHT 1943

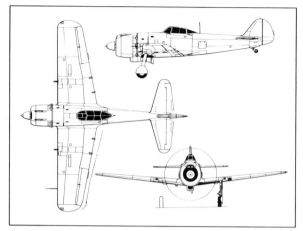

IN 1942 Nakajima began work on a successor to the Ki-43, the official requirement for the new type stipulating a speed of over 640 km/h (398 mph), long range, good manoeuvrability and an armament of two 20-mm (0.79-in) cannon and two 12.7-mm (0.5-in) machine-guns. Powerplant was to be the 1800-hp Nakajima Ha-45. The first prototype was flown in April 1943 and although it just failed to meet the required speed, it was followed by a second prototype and a total of 125 pre-production aircraft. By the end of the year preparations for production had begun. Unfortunately, production of the engines, which had proved troublesome in tests, was slower than the airframes, and it was not until mid 1944 that substantial deliveries could begin. Nevertheless, the first Ki-84 Sentai was formed in April 1944 to serve in China, and by the end of the year 16 Sentais were equipped with the type.

As well as the initial model, Ki-84-Ia, the total of 3382 production Hayates included numbers of the Ki-84-Ib, with two 20-mm cannon replacing the machine-guns in the nose; the Ki-84-Ic, with 30-mm (1.18-in) cannon in place of the original 20-mm wing guns; and a few of the Ki-84-II, whose rear fuselage and wingtips were made of wood in order to save aluminium. In addition, there were a number of derivatives. One prototype of the all-wood Ki-106 was flown in July 1945, the same month as the first flight of the Ki-116, which was a Ki-84 adapted by Mansyu to take a 1550-hp Mitsubishi Ha-112-II engine. The Nakajima-designed Ki-113, using steel construction, was not completed, while the projected Ki-84R, with turbo-supercharger, and the Ki-84N and Ki-84P, planned to use the 2500-hp Ha-44 engine, were never even started.

Competitive performance, effective armament and good protection for pilot and fuel tanks made the Ki-84 at least the equal of any Allied fighter during the battle for the Philippines in the second half of 1944, and later over Okinawa and the home islands. As well as proving an exceptional fighter, the Hayate was used for ground-attack and dive-bombing missions, carrying two bombs of up to 250 kg (551 lb). The effects of Allied bombing were such as to cause serious reductions in production quantities and quality, but the Ki-84 remained an important Japanese fighter until 1945.

Ki-84-Ia

Type: single-seat fighter
Maker: Nakajima Hikoki KK; Mansyu Hikoki Seizo KK
Span: 11.24 m (36 ft 10½ in)
Length: 9.92 m (32 ft 6½ in)
Height: 3.38 m (11 ft 1 in)
Wing area: 21 m² (226.05 sq ft)
Weight: normal 3716 kg (8192 lb); empty 2660 kg (5864 lb)
Powerplant: one 2000-hp Nakajima Ha-45-21 18-cylinder two-row radial engine
Performance: maximum speed 624 km/h (388 mph) at 6500 m (21 325 ft); range 1650 km (1025 miles); operational ceiling 11 000 m (36 089 ft)
Armament: two 20-mm (0.79-in) Ho-5 cannon; two 12.7-mm (0.5-in) Ho-103 machine-guns; 500-kg (1102-lb) bombload
Crew: 1
Production: 3382 (all types)

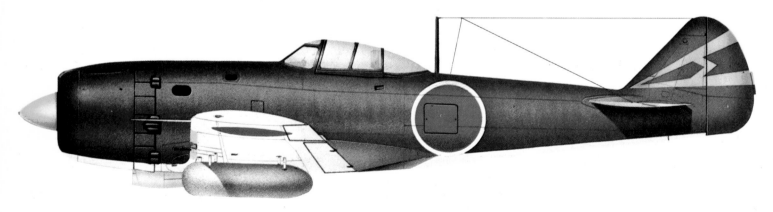

Left: An Army Nakajima Ki-84 Hayate of the 11th Sentai. The Ki-84 was slightly slower than the Mustang and Thunderbolt, but could out-climb and out-manoeuvre them

Below: The Hayate (Gale) had the Allied reporting name of Frank. The aircraft illustrated is from the 52nd Sentai which saw action over Leyte and the Philippines. It carries a drop-tank on the left wing, with a bomb on the right

Firefly, Fairey

FIRST FLIGHT 1941

Left: The Fairey Firefly first saw action in the attack on the *Tirpitz* in July 1944. It was the first Fleet Air Arm aircraft over Japan in July 1944, saw intense action throughout what is today Indonesia, and then dropped supplies to Japanese PoW camps
Below left: The wing-fold on the Firefly gave it a particularly compact shape for easy loading onto the elevator of a carrier
Below: The trainer version of the Firefly which at the time of its introduction was one of the world's fastest trainers, capable of speeds above 485 km/h (300 mph)

THE first prototype Firefly I was flown in December 1941, designed to meet a 1940 specification for a two-seat naval fighter and powered by a 1730-hp Rolls-Royce Griffon IIB engine. It was armed with four 20-mm (0.79-in) wing-mounted cannon. A further three prototypes followed during 1942, and in March 1943 deliveries began of the Firefly F.I. The large observer's cabin made the type suitable for the installation of radar equipment. In addition to 429 F.Is built, 376 FR.I reconnaissance fighters were completed, with underwing radomes for the ASH surface-search radar; later examples were powered by the 1990-hp Griffon XII. Produced concurrently with the F.I were 37 NF.II night-fighters, which had a lengthened forward fuselage to balance the weight of the additional equipment in the rear cabin and radomes for the AI. Mk X airborne interception radar in wing fairings. But these were superseded by NF.I conversions, which used the APS-6 radar with a ventral radome. Other F.Is, designated FR.IA, carried ASH equipment.

Meanwhile, an F.I had been given a 2035-hp Griffon 61 engine, and designated Firefly F.III proved capable of 562 km/h (349 mph), but the Mk III was abandoned in favour of a more thorough redesign. The resulting Mk IV used the 2250-hp Griffon 74 engine with a four-blade propeller; the radiator was moved from the nose to the wing roots; the wingtips were clipped, reducing overall span to 12.55 m (41 ft 2 in), and the wings had pods for fuel and radar as well as racks for 907 kg (2000 lb) of bombs, 16 rockets or more fuel tanks.

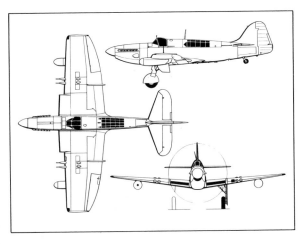

The first of 160 production FR.IVs flew in May 1945, and this model was followed by 352 Mk Vs, with improved equipment and hydraulic wing folding, production including examples of the anti-submarine AS.5, the NF.5 night-fighter and the FR.5 reconnaissance-fighter. Subsequent models, produced in the early 1950s, were designed exclusively for anti-submarine work and comprised 133 AS.6s and 151 AS.7s, the latter being a three-seater incorporating major structural changes. In addition, many earlier Fireflies were converted as trainers, target tugs and radio-controlled drones.

Exports included 40 FR.IVs to Holland, batches of Mk Vs to Australia and New Zealand and target tugs to Sweden. Numerous British and Commonwealth Fireflies saw action during the Korean war.

Firefly FR.I

Type: two-seat reconnaissance-fighter
Maker: Fairey Aviation Co; General Aircraft Ltd
Span: 13.56 m (44 ft 6 in)
Length: 11.46 m (37 ft 7¼ in)
Height: 4.14 m (13 ft 7 in)
Wing area: 30.47 m² (328 sq ft)
Weight: normal 6359 kg (14 020 lb); empty 4423 kg (9750 lb)
Powerplant: one 1730-hp Rolls-Royce Griffon IIB V-12 liquid-cooled engine
Performance: maximum speed 509 km/h (316 mph) at 4267 m (14 000 ft); range 1722 km (1070 miles) with drop-tanks; operational ceiling 8535 m (28 000 ft)
Armament: four 20-mm (0.79-in) Hispano-Suiza cannon; 907-kg (2000-lb) bombload or eight rockets
Crew: 2
Production: 376

P-61 Black Widow, Northrop

FIRST FLIGHT 1942

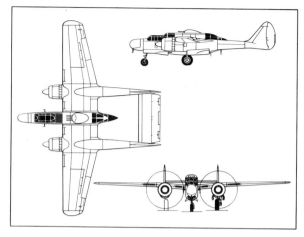

WHILST workable British airborne interception radar had been developed by mid 1940, the RAF lacked suitable aircraft to carry it, so Northrop was asked to develop a specialized night-fighter giving space for the radar equipment and operator, and long endurance. The project was taken over by the US Army Air Corps, and by March 1941 two XP-61 prototypes and 15 YP-61 development aircraft had been ordered.

The original armament scheme of four cannon in the wings plus four-gun dorsal and two-gun ventral barbettes was modified to comprise four 20-mm (0.79-in) cannon in the lower fuselage and a remotely-controlled dorsal barbette with four 0.5-in (12.7-mm) machine-guns. The R-2800 engines were carried on twin booms which supported the tailplane, leaving the fuselage free for the SCR-720 radar, armament, part-fuel and three-man crew. Control of such a necessarily big and heavy fighter was a problem, and various arrangements of sophisticated wing control surfaces were tried, the final configuration combining double-slotted flaps, roll control spoilers and small ailerons.

The first XP-61 flew in May 1942, but although production orders had been placed by then it was mid 1943 before the prototypes were accepted by the USAAF and October of that year before the first of 200 production P-61As was completed. Most P-61As omitted the dorsal barbette and both the R-2800-10 and R-2800-65 engines were used. The 450 P-61Bs which followed featured numerous minor modifications, and later batches of both types introduced provision for four large drop-tanks or bombs to be carried under the wings. A further 511 P-61Cs were ordered with turbo-supercharged 2800-hp R-2800-73 engines, but only 41 of these had been completed by August 1945, when the remainder were cancelled. Two XP-61Ds and two XP-61Es were produced by converting earlier models, but the former's R-2800-14 engines proved unreliable and the latter was developed as the photo-reconnaissance F-15.

Although it had been planned to supply Black Widows to Britain, Beaufighter and Mosquito night-fighters made this unnecessary. P-61s, usually finished in glossy black, were used by USAAF squadrons in Europe and the Pacific from early 1944, often flying with a two-man crew on night-intruder and ground-attack missions.

P-61B Black Widow

Type: three-seat night-fighter
Maker: Northrop Aircraft Inc
Span: 20.14 m (66 ft 0¾ in)
Length: 15.11 m (49 ft 7 in)
Height: 4.47 m (14 ft 8 in)
Wing area: 61.54 m² (662.36 sq ft)
Weight: normal 13 472 kg (29 700 lb); empty 10 637 kg (23 450 lb)
Powerplant: two 2000-hp Pratt & Whitney R-2800-65 Double Wasp 18-cylinder two-row radial engines
Performance: maximum speed 589 km/h (366 mph) at 6096 m (20 000 ft); range 982 km (610 miles); operational ceiling 10 089 m (33 100 ft)
Armament: four 20-mm (0.79-in) M2 cannon; four 0.5-in (12.7-mm) Browning machine-guns; 2903-kg (6400-lb) bombload
Crew: 3
Production: 450

Left: A P-61B-10-NO which had turbocharged R-2800-73 engines which gave a marked improvement in performance
Above: The four 20-mm cannon of the Black Widow. Besides these belly guns most examples had a turret with four 0.5-in machine-guns above and behind the cockpit. With this heavy firepower they had a high first-burst kill probability, and pilots reported that enemy aircraft 'shuddered and went down' after strikes from the eight heavy guns

He 219, Heinkel

FIRST FLIGHT 1942

THE Luftwaffe's urgent requirement for an effective night-fighter in 1941 led to the revival of Heinkel's Projekt 1060, a 1940 design study for an advanced multirole combat aircraft, under the designation He 219. The V1 first prototype made its first flight in November 1942, powered by two 1750-hp Daimler-Benz DB 603A engines, and a number of armament options, including remotely controlled barbettes, were tested on this and subsequent prototype and pre-production aircraft. Political resistance to the type was to some extent overcome by the first operational flight of a pre-production A-0, which resulted in the destruction of five Lancaster bombers, and the fact that six Mosquitos – previously almost immune – were among 20 more aircraft quickly downed.

It had been planned to install more powerful DB 603E or 603G engines in the production He 219A-1 Uhu (Owl). Shortages made this impossible, and the DB 603A was retained in the first production model, the A-2, whose armament comprised a 20-mm (0.79-in) MG 151 cannon in each wing root, two 20-mm or 30-mm (1.18-in) cannon in a ventral tray and two oblique-firing 30-mm MK 108s in the central fuselage. The 40 A-2s completed by early 1944 were followed by the A-5, which used DB 603A, 603Aa, 603E or 603G engines and added a third crew member to man the observer's gun. The A-6, intended as a counter to the Mosquito night-fighters, was a lightened version without the oblique cannon and powered by turbo-supercharged DB 603L engines. The A-7 featured a heavily armoured pressurized cabin with ejector seats for

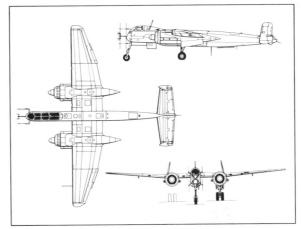

the crew, comprehensive avionics and an armament of up to four 30-mm and two 20-mm cannon in the wing roots and ventral tray in addition to the oblique-firing pair of MK 108s.

Unfortunately for the Luftwaffe, official opposition and Allied bombing combined to prevent more than 268 production A-series aircraft being delivered before the end of the war, and only one night-fighter gruppe, I/NJG 1, was equipped with the type, which proved to be one of the most effective night-fighters of the war. A few B-2s were built, similar to the A-6 but with increased span, and prototypes were completed of the entirely redesigned C-1 night-fighter and C-2 fighter-bomber, but the undoubted potential of the design had been largely wasted.

He 219A-7

Type: two-seat night-fighter
Maker: Ernst Heinkel AG
Span: 18.5 m (60 ft 8¼ in)
Length: 15.55 m (51 ft 0¼ in)
Height: 4.1 m (13 ft 5½ in)
Wing area: 44.5 m² (479 sq ft)
Weight: normal 15 300 kg (33 730 lb); empty 11 200 kg (24 691 lb)
Powerplant: two 1900-hp Daimler-Benz DB 603G V-12 liquid-cooled engines
Performance: maximum speed 670 km/h (416 mph) at 7000 m (22 966 ft); range 2000 km (1243 miles); operational ceiling 12 700 m (41 667 ft)
Armament: (typically) four 30-mm (1.18-in) MK 108 and four 20-mm (0.79-in) MG 151 cannon
Crew: 2
Production: 268 (all A types)

Top: The He 219V16 – the 16th prototype – was initially configured as an He 219A-0/R6 and subsequently as an A-5/R2. It is seen with SN-2 airborne radar for night-fighter work. In this role it was particularly popular for its interception of Mosquito Pathfinders and nuisance bombers

Me 163, Messerschmitt
FIRST FLIGHT 1941

Left: An Me 163B in flight with the skid retracted
Below left: A Komet on its launching dolly with the landing skid deployed
Below: The basic Me 163 airframe showing the thrust chamber of the Walter bi-fuel rocket. The T-stoff fuel (hydrogen-peroxide and water) was a very unstable liquid which would self-combust with any organic matter. When it mixed with the other liquid, Z-stoff (calcium permanganate solution), they produced a violent reaction in the thrust chamber

THE world's first operational rocket-propelled fighter began life before the war when Dr Alexander Lippisch was asked to design a tailless aircraft to be powered by a Walter R I-203 400-kg (882-lb) thrust rocket. A wooden test aircraft was begun under the designation DFS 194, but construction of the metal fuselage, considered necessary for the highly reactive rocket fuel, proved beyond the institute's resources, so in January 1939 Lippisch's team joined Messerschmitt and the design became the Me 163.

Delays to the programme resulted in the wooden DFS 194 being fitted with the rocket, and when flight trials produced speeds of up to 550 km/h (342 mph) Messerschmitt was instructed to produce six Me 163A prototypes as a prelude to production Me 163Bs with much more powerful motors. When fitted with a 750-kg (1653-lb) thrust R II-203b it was found that the maximum speed of the Me 163A, at over 850 km/h (528 mph), was still restricted by the limited amount of fuel that could be carried in the diminutive airframe.

Construction of the prototype and production Me 163B airframes proceeded, but the new engines were late. It was July 1943 before the intended engine was installed in one of the prototypes, and May 1944 before the first production B-1a Komet entered Luftwaffe service: by July 1944 only 16 were operational. In any case, although escorting fighters had little chance of intercepting the rockets, except on their unpowered return flight, the latter, attacking at over 900 km/h (559 mph), had hardly any more chance of getting in an effective

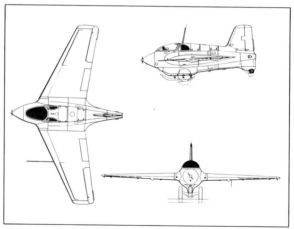

burst from their slow-firing MK 108s. Some promise of success was offered by the Jagdfaust, a battery of 50-mm (1.97-in) shells fired automatically by an optical sensor reacting to a bomber's shadow, but the war was over before it could be installed on a large scale. The introduction of an auxiliary combustion chamber for cruising flight on the prototype C-1 was another promising line of development, but production was never begun. The two-seat, unpowered Me 163S trainer might also have reduced the number of accidents resulting from the heavy demands made on pilot skill by taking off from a jettisonable dolly and landing on a retractable skid, but the whole programme had suffered too many delays for the Me 163 to become an effective weapon in the time available.

Me 163B-1a

Type: single-seat rocket-powered interceptor
Maker: Messerschmitt AG
Span: 9.32 m (30 ft 7 in)
Length: 5.69 m (18 ft 8 in)
Height: 2.74 m (8 ft 11¾ in)
Wing area: 18.5 m² (199.14 sq ft)
Weight: normal 4310 kg (9502 lb); empty 1905 kg (4200 lb)
Powerplant: one 1700-kg (3748-lb) thrust Walter HWK 109-509A-1 liquid-fuelled rocket
Performance: maximum speed 960 km/h (597 mph) at 9000 m (29 528 ft); range 80 km (50 miles); operational ceiling 12 000 m (39 370 ft)
Armament: two 30-mm (1.18-in) MK 108 or 20-mm (0.79-in) MG 151 cannon
Crew: 1
Production: 279

Meteor I, Gloster

FIRST FLIGHT 1943

THE ideas of Frank Whittle, who had patented an aircraft gas-turbine engine in 1930, received little official encouragement until 1939, when the Air Ministry ordered an engine from his firm, Power Jets, and asked Gloster to design an aircraft to use the new powerplant. The first E.28/39, a designation stemming from that of the official specification, was flown in May 1941 powered by a single 386-kg (850-lb) st Whittle W.1. Although this was chiefly an engine testbed, Gloster had already begun work on a twin-engined F.9/40 fighter.

Basic design features of the aircraft included mid-wing nacelles for the engines, tricycle landing gear, high-set tailplane, pressurized cabin and armament of four 20-mm (0.79-in) cannon in the sides of the nose. Eight G.41 prototypes were fitted with various engines, most derived from the Power Jets W.1. The first flew on March 5, 1943 with a 1043-kg (2300-lb) st de Havilland-built Halford H.1, but the final choice was the Whittle W.2B/23 built by Rolls-Royce as the Welland I and delivering 771 kg (1700 lb) thrust.

An initial production batch of 20 Meteor Is was ordered, the first of these flying in January 1944. In July squadron deliveries began, 616 Squadron RAF becoming the world's first operational jet fighter unit with 16 of the Mk Is. A second series of Meteors was planned to have the more powerful 1225-kg (2700-lb) st de Havilland Goblin (Halford H.1) used by the first prototype but de Havilland's own Vampire was in production by this stage and Goblin supplies were reserved for the company's

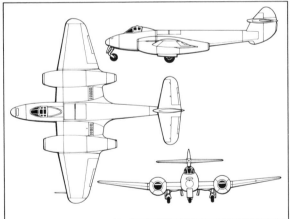

own Vampire. The Mk II, therefore, was cancelled. After one prototype had been built and the majority of the 210 F. IIIs that followed used 907-kg (2000-lb) st Rolls-Royce Derwent I engines in a refined airframe, though the first 15 retained the Welland and were delivered to 616 Squadron from December 1944.

The only Allied jet fighter to become operational during World War II, the Meteor proved useful in shooting down V-1 flying bombs in the summer of 1944; from early 1945 616 Squadron was based on the continent, where its Meteors were used mainly for ground attacks. The Mks I and III were only the first of a series of Meteors that were to remain in production and service long after World War II ended.

Meteor I

Type: single-seat jet fighter
Maker: Gloster Aircraft Co
Span: 13.11 m (43 ft)
Length: 12.57 m (41 ft 3 in)
Height: 3.96 m (13 ft)
Wing area: 34.75 m² (374 sq ft)
Weight: normal 6257 kg (13 795 lb); empty 3692 kg (8140 lb)
Powerplant: two 771-kg (1700-lb) st Rolls-Royce W.2B/23C Welland I turbojets
Performance: maximum speed 668 km/h (415 mph) at 3048 m (10 000 ft); operational ceiling 12 192 m (40 000 ft)
Armament: four 20-mm (0.79-in) Hispano-Suiza cannon
Crew: 1
Production: 38 (3545 all types)

Top: The fifth Meteor prototype became the first aircraft to fly using Halford H.I (Goblin) turbojets in place of the less-powerful Rover-built W.2B engines

Me 262, Messerschmitt

FIRST FLIGHT 1942

EXPECTATIONS that the axial-flow BMW 003 turbojet would reach a workable stage by the end of 1939 resulted in Messerschmitt being asked to design an aircraft to use it. By August 1940 work had begun on three prototypes. The Me 262, as the design was designated, was developed as a prospective fighter, and featured slightly-swept wings and a triangular-section fuselage, the original tailwheel landing gear being changed subsequently to a tricycle type in order to overcome difficulties in taking off. These were caused by the elevators failing to work effectively in the aerodynamic shadow of the deep fuselage. It was November 1941, however, before the first supposedly airworthy BMW 003s were ready for installation. By this time the Me 262 V1 first prototype had undergone flight trials with a nose-mounted piston engine, and fortunately this was retained for the first flight with the turbojets installed, in March 1942. Both jets suffered broken compressor blades within seconds of take-off, and the aircraft just managed to fly a circuit on its propeller.

It was to be nearly two more years before a redesigned BMW engine was completed, and in the meantime a pair of 850-kg (1874-lb) thrust Jumo 004A engines were fitted to the third prototype, the Me 262 V3 making a successful take-off and first flight with these engines in July 1942.

It was the end of 1943, however, before any of the prototypes was fitted with armament, and by then there was an additional requirement – from Hitler personally – for the type to carry bombs. But the Me 262 was now a top-priority programme and in July 1944, the first production Me 262s were delivered to a special Luftwaffe test unit.

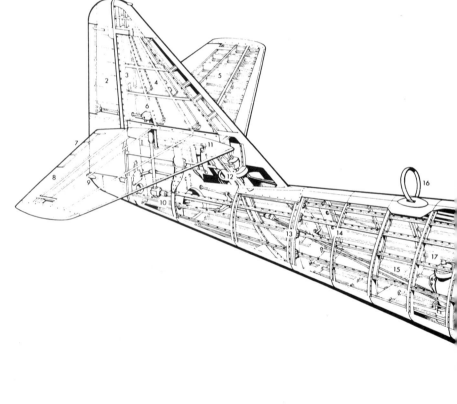

The first production model was the Me 262A-1a Schwalbe interceptor, with a nose armament of four 30-mm (1.18-in) MK 108 cannon. The poor performance of these weapons led to a number of alternative armament schemes being tested, including the use of cannon up to 55-mm (2.17-in) calibre. The use of wire-guided X-4 missiles was also proposed, but underwing racks for 12 spin-stablized R4M rockets on each side, introduced on the A-1b, proved the most immediately effective solution. Other production variants in the A series included small numbers of the A-2a Sturmvogel fighter-bomber, which carried two 250-kg (551-lb) or one 500-kg (1102-lb) bombs, one example being modified to accommodate a bomb-aimer in the nose, and the photo-reconnaissance A-5a, with only two MK 108s.

By the end of 1944 the Me 262B-1a two-seat trainer had appeared, but only 15 were completed as such, a few more being given Neptun V radar to become B-1a/U1 night-fighters, and only one example of the definitive B-2a night-fighter, which was to have had Berlin radar, was flown during the war. Also, shortly before Germany's capitulation, two A-1as were fitted with rocket boosters to become the fast-climbing C-1a and C-2a.

Shortages of time and resources prevented the Me 262s achieving service in sufficient numbers to have a significant effect on the course of the war. After 1945 some Me 262s were rebuilt in Czechoslovakia and entered Czech air force service as S-92s.

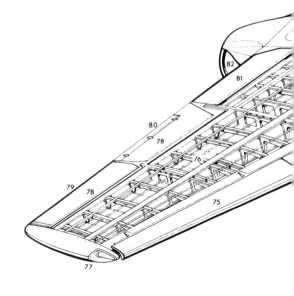

Left: An Me 262A-1a of JG 7 Kommando Novotny in 1945. Known as the Schwalbe (swallow), the Me 262A-1a fighter gave Luftwaffe pilots an experience of jet flight which one described as 'like angels pushing'. However there was a high accident rate, since there was a general belief that no specialized conversion training was necessary. Bombing and Hitler's intervention delayed introduction of the 262, and its employment as a bomber made it slow enough for conventional fighters to intercept

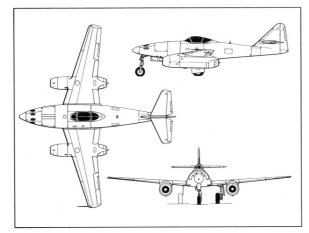

Me 262A-1a

Type: jet interceptor
Maker: Messerschmitt AG
Span: 12.48 m (40 ft 11¼ in)
Length: 10.6 m (34 ft 9¼ in)
Height: 3.84 m (12 ft 7¼ in)
Wing area: 21.75 m² (234.12 sq ft)
Weight: normal 6396 kg (14 101 lb); empty 3652 kg (8051 lb)
Powerplant: two 900-kg (1984-lb) st Junkers Jumo 004B turbojets
Performance: maximum speed 870 km/h (541 mph) at 6000 m (19 685 ft); range 1050 km (652 miles);

operational ceiling 11 450 m (37 566 ft)
Armament: four 30-mm (1.18-in) MK 108 cannon
Crew: 1
Production: 1433 (all types)

Me 262A-1a

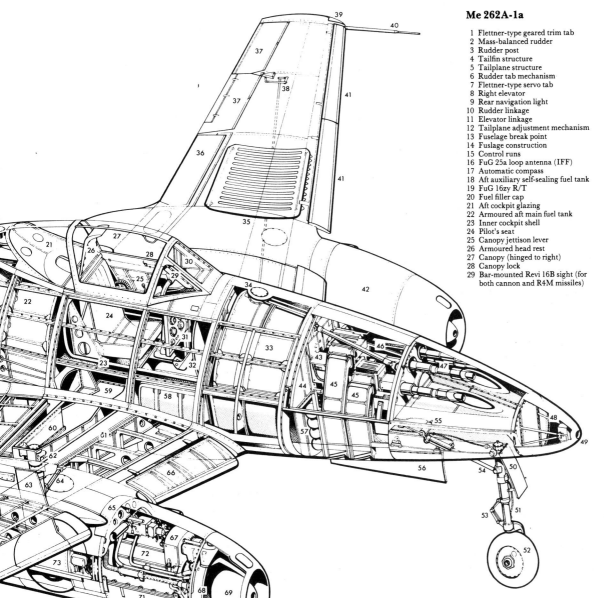

1 Flettner-type geared trim tab
2 Mass-balanced rudder
3 Rudder post
4 Tailfin structure
5 Tailplane structure
6 Rudder tab mechanism
7 Flettner-type servo tab
8 Right elevator
9 Rear navigation light
10 Rudder linkage
11 Elevator linkage
12 Tailplane adjustment mechanism
13 Fuselage break point
14 Fuselage construction
15 Control runs
16 FuG 25a loop antenna (IFF)
17 Automatic compass
18 Aft auxiliary self-sealing fuel tank
19 FuG 16zy R/T
20 Fuel filler cap
21 Aft cockpit glazing
22 Armoured aft main fuel tank
23 Inner cockpit shell
24 Pilot's seat
25 Canopy jettison lever
26 Armoured head rest
27 Canopy (hinged to right)
28 Canopy lock
29 Bar-mounted Revi 16B sight (for both cannon and R4M missiles)
30 Armourglass windscreen
31 Instrument panel
32 Rudder pedal
33 Armoured forward main fuel tank
34 Fuel filler cap
35 Underwing wooden rack for 12 R4M 55-mm rockets
36 Left outer flap section
37 Frise-type aileron
38 Aileron control linkage
39 Left navigation light
40 Pitot head
41 Automatic leading-edge slats
42 Left engine cowling
43 Electrical firing mechanism
44 Firewall
45 Spent cartridge ejector chutes
46 Four 30-mm Rheinmetall Borsig MK 108 cannon
47 Cannon muzzles
48 Combat camera
49 Camera aperture
50 Nosewheel fairing
51 Nosewheel leg
52 Nosewheel
53 Torque scissors
54 Retraction jack
55 Hydraulic lines
56 Main nosewheel door (right)
57 Compressed air bottles
58 Forward auxiliary fuel tank
59 Mainwheel well
60 Torque box
61 Main spar
62 Mainwheel leg pivot point
63 Mainwheel door
64 Mainwheel retraction rod
65 Engine support arch
66 Leading-edged slat structure
67 Auxiliaries gearbox
68 Annular oil tank
69 Riedel starter motor housing
70 Engine air intake
71 Hinged cowling section
72 Junkers Jumo 004B-2 axial-flow turbojet
73 Right mainwheel
74 Wing structure
75 Automatic leading-edge slats
76 Mainspar
77 Right navigation light
78 Frise-type ailerons
79 Trim tab
80 Flettner-type geared tab
81 Right outer flap section
82 Engine exhaust orifice
83 Engine support bearer
84 Right inner flap structure
85 Faired wing root

He 162, Heinkel

FIRST FLIGHT 1944

Above and left: The He 162 Salamander was built from wood, duralumin, steel and plastics, with a one-piece wing with anhedral tips to reduce the effective dihedral angle. The centre of gravity was moved forward by the simple expedient of placing a weight in the nose. On December 10, 1944, a prototype broke up in the air during a demonstration flight in front of senior Nazi party and service officers. The He 162 was in large-scale production when the European war ended, and a few examples are preserved

THE remarkable story of the He 162 began with a specification issued to Heinkel, among other firms, in September 1944, to which preliminary designs were required in a matter of days. The specification covered a BMW 003-powered *Volksjäger* (people's fighter), suitable for rapid production by semi-skilled personnel and combining the basic requirements of a successful interceptor. Heinkel already had some experience of the BMW 003, and had been working on a lightweight jet-propelled interceptor. With the benefit of this head start the company submitted a proposal on September 14 and began construction of a prototype only ten days later. By the end of the month the only other serious contender, from Blohm und Voss, was eliminated and Heinkel was instructed to plan for production of 1000 He 162s per month by April 1945. On December 6 the first prototype was flown, reaching a speed of 840 km/h (552 mph). By this time production had already begun.

Ease of production was the overriding requirement of the specification, and the He 162 was of the simplest possible configuration. The BMW 003 was mounted on top of the metal monocoque fuselage, twin vertical tails avoided the jet efflux, and two MG 151 cannon were in the lower fuselage. The aircraft was provided with an ejector seat for the pilot, it being sometimes preferable to dispose of the machine rather than the pilot. Several prototypes had been completed before the first production He 162A-1s appeared with two 30-mm (1.18-in) MK 108 cannon, but these guns proved to have too violent an action for the

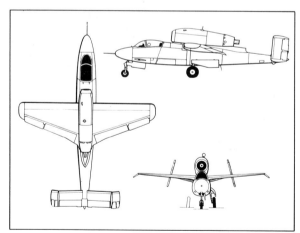

airframe, and this model was quickly replaced by the A-2, the first examples of which appeared in the last week of January 1945. A whole series of further type numbers was allocated for proposed versions with different armament, alternative powerplant and other changes, but the A-2 remained the only production model, with the name Salamander.

The 150 or so He 162s which actually entered service, further examples being completed but not flown, were too late to see combat, though a number of units had begun converting to the type when the war in Europe ended. Many hundreds were more or less completed. The He 162 is remembered more for the speed of its construction – exactly three months from specification to first flight – than for its contribution to aerial warfare.

He 162A-2

Type: jet-powered interceptor
Maker: Ernst Heinkel AG
Span: 7.2 m (23 ft 7½ in)
Length: 9.05 m (29 ft 8¼ in)
Height: 2.6 m (8 ft 6¼ in)
Wing area: 11.22 m² (120.56 sq ft)
Weight: normal 2805 kg (6184 lb); empty 1700 kg (3748 lb)
Powerplant: one 800-kg (1764-lb) st BMW 003E turbojet
Performance: maximum speed 905 km/h (562 mph) at 6000 m (19 685 ft); range 975 km (606 miles); operational ceiling 12 000 m (39 370 ft)
Armament: two 20-mm (0.79-in) MG 151 cannon
Crew: 1
Production: approx 270

F7F Tigercat, Grumman

FIRST FLIGHT 1943

WITH the advent of the large *Midway*-class carrier, the United States Navy became interested in the development of twin-engined fighters for shipboard operations. On June 30, 1939, an order was placed with Grumman for a prototype fighter designated XF5F-1.

The initial flight test results were available in mid 1941, and although the XF5F-1 had problem areas it proved useful for the development of a bigger aircraft ordered on June 30, 1941. This new naval fighter was designated XF7F-1 and was the first twin to be built in quantities for the navy.

The F7F-1 carried heavy armament: four 20-mm (0.79-in) cannon mounted in the wing roots; four 12.7-mm (0.5-in) guns in the nose; wing strong-points which could carry 454-kg (1000-lb) bombs; and a torpedo to be carried under the fuselage.

The first prototype flew in December 1943, at a time when the need for fighters was at its peak in the Pacific theatre of operations. This led to an order for 500 aircraft, the majority of which were destined for the US Marine Corps squadrons. Aircraft began coming off the production line in April 1944, by which time changing requirements and operational problems resulted in the production programme slowing down. When 34 single-seater Tigercats (as the F7F-1 was called by the US Navy) had been delivered, production was switched to a two-seater night fighter version designated F7F-2N with APS-6 and SCR-720 radar displacing the nose guns. Grumman built 65 two-seaters before reverting to single-seater production of 189 F7F-3 aircraft, virtually the same as the original model but re-engined with Pratt & Whitney R-2800-34Ws, not -22Ws.

After this, the original contract was cancelled, but further orders kept the Tigercat in production until late 1946 with two further versions, designated F7F-3N and -4N. Both were two-seat night fighters, with radar replacing the nose guns. Altogether 60 -3Ns and 13 -4Ns were delivered. Two more variants were produced by post-delivery modifications, the specially equipped F7F-3Es and the photographic reconnaissance F7F-3Ps.

The Tigercat was among the last of the piston-engined fighters, and was too late for combat in World War II, though several squadrons were operational on Pacific islands, and by VJ-Day some were moving into China where they were active alongside army P-51s.

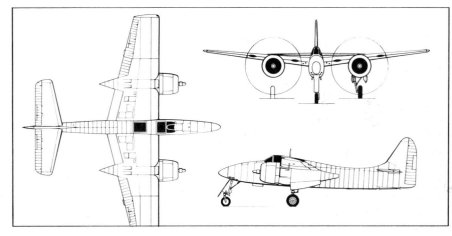

Top: The Grumman F7F-3 was the principal version of the Tigercat
Above: The Tigercat had a heavy armament which was intended for its role as a fighter. When it was redeployed for ground attack, this combination of cannon and machine-guns was supplemented with rockets and bombs
Left: The folding wings and centreline tank of a F7F-3N night-fighter Tigercat, which had nose radar in place of the 12.7-mm (0.5-in) guns

F7F-3

Type: single-seat naval fighter-bomber
Maker: Grumman Aircraft Engineering Corporation
Span: 15.7 m (51 ft 6 in)
Length: 13.8 m (45 ft 4 in)
Height: 5.05 m (16 ft 7 in)
Wing area: 42.27 m² (455 sq ft)
Weight: maximum 11 667 kg (25 720 lb); empty 7380 kg (16 270 lb)
Powerplant: two 2100-hp Pratt & Whitney R-2800-34W Double Wasp engines
Performance: maximum speed 700 km/h (435 mph) at 6706 m (22 000 ft); range 1931 km (1200 miles); service ceiling 12 405 km (40 700 ft)
Armament: four 20-mm (0.79-in) guns; four 12.7-mm (0.5-in) guns; two 454-kg (1000-lb) bombs, rockets or single torpedo
Crew: 1
Production: 189

F8F Bearcat, Grumman
FIRST FLIGHT 1944

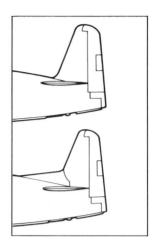

THE F8F was Grumman's last production in a line of piston-engined fighters which began with the FF-1 when the company was set up in 1931.

The company designated the project G-58 and development started in 1943. The requirement was for a high-performance aircraft capable of operation from even the smallest carrier. The G-58 was dimensionally smaller, but had a similar configuration to that of the F6F.

Grumman received an order from the US Navy on November 27, 1943, for two prototypes which were given the designation XF8F-1. One of the initial design features, and a most unusual one, was the provision of break points in the wings, along with explosive bolts. The purpose of these was to overcome a potentially dangerous situation if the

aircraft was handled too vigorously: the tips would fail at selected known points, but balance would hopefully be restored. However, this provision was abandoned at a later stage in the development programme, though the wings folded only at the tips. Unlike the Hellcat, the landing gear of the Bearcat retracted inwards.

The engine chosen to power the Bearcat was the Pratt & Whitney R-2800 Double Wasp which had also powered the Hellcat. Unlike most new 'developments' the Bearcat was a smaller aircraft than the Hellcat and significantly lighter which gave it an outstanding power-to-weight ratio.

The Bearcat's range was average at 1778 km (1105 miles), but its excellent climb capability of 1393 m (4570 ft)/min more than made up for this.

Above left: A Grumman F8F Bearcat with wings folded for stowage. The US Navy was operating 24 squadrons of F8F-1 and F8F-2 by May 1949

Above: The tail surfaces of the XF8F-1 and F8F-1 showing the small dorsal fin which was added to production aircraft

Above: F8F-1s in flight; each aircraft carries a centreline drop-tank
Right: An F8F-1 taxies on a US Navy air station in the Pacific

F8F-1

1 Four-blade Aeroproducts constant speed propellor
2 Propeller hub pitch change mechanism
3 Propeller fixing bolts
4 Engine cowling ring
5 Cowling ring fasteners
6 Reduction gear casing
7 Engine magnetoes
8 Detachable engine cowlings
9 Cowling frames
10 2100-hp Pratt & Whitney R-2800-34W Double Wasp radial
11 Exhaust collector
12 Oil cooler
13 Stainless steel fireproof bulkhead
14 Cowling air flap
15 Right 12.7-mm (0.5-in) machine-guns
16 Ammunition feed chutes
17 Ammunition tanks
18 Machine-gun barrels
19 Blast suppressing muzzles
20 Mk 9 HVAR, 127-mm (5-in) rocket projectiles
21 Aileron hinge control mechanism
22 Wing fold hinge joint
23 Wing folding bar socket fitting
24 Right navigation light
25 Right aileron
26 Formation light
27 Outer wing panel folded position
28 Aileron tab
29 Right flap
30 Oil tank
31 Induction air duct
32 Water injection tank
33 Hydraulic distribution unit
34 Engine bearer struts
35 Armoured cockpit bulkhead
36 Engine control runs
37 Access plate
38 Instrument panel
39 Rudder pedals
40 Fuel feed pipe
41 Trim controls
42 Pilot's side console panel
43 Engine throttle and propeller controls
44 Control column
45 Oxygen regulator
46 MK 8 reflector gunsight
47 Windscreen panels
48 Rearward sliding cockpit canopy cover
49 Headrest
50 Head armour
51 Safety harness
52 Canopy sliding rail
53 Pilot's seat
54 Back armour
55 Cockpit rear bulkhead
56 Bag type main fuel tank
57 Fire extinguisher
58 Radio transmitter
59 Dynamotor
60 Radio equipment racks
61 Battery
62 Roll-over crash support arch
63 Fuselage skin plating
64 Handhold
65 Tailplane control cables
66 Whip aerials
67 Formation light
68 Fin root fillet fairing
69 Right tailplane
70 Right elevator
71 Elevator tab
72 Torque shaft trim tab control
73 Fin front spar attachment
74 Rudder trim control
75 Tailfin construction
76 Sternpost
77 Aerial cable
78 Fin tip fairing
79 Rudder balance
80 Rudder construction
81 Rudder tab
82 Arrestor hook shock absorber
83 Arrestor hook guide rails
84 Elevator tab
85 Deck arresting hook
86 Elevator construction
87 Tailplane construction
88 Elevator control horns
89 Tailplane attachment joints
90 Tailwheel bay
91 Retractable tailwheel
92 Tailwheel lag fairings
93 Shock absorber strut
94 Retraction jack
95 Rear fuselage bulkhead
96 Fuselage frame and stringer construction
97 Remote compass transmitter
98 Whip aerial
99 Ventral access door
100 Footstep
101 Left flap construction
102 Wing root strengthened walkway
103 Wing rib construction
104 Hydraulic flap jack
105 Left gun bay
106 Twin 12.7-mm (0.5-in) machine-guns
107 Ammunition feed chutes
108 Ammunition tanks
109 Sloping rear spar
110 Wing fold hinge joint
111 Aileron trim tab
112 Left formation light
113 Aileron construction
114 Aileron hinges
115 Wingtip fairing
116 Left navigation light
117 Outer wing panel rib construction
118 Auxiliary drop-tank
119 Mk 9 HVAR, 127-mm (5-in) rocket projectiles
120 Rocket pylons
121 Pitot tube
122 Manual wing folding bar socket fitting
123 Wing folding hinges
124 Locking mechanism
125 Wing main spar
126 Approach light
127 454-kg (1000-lb) bomb
128 Left wing pylon
129 Machine-gun barrels
130 Blast suppressing muzzles
131 Landing gear leg fairing door
132 Left mainwheel
133 Landing gear scissor links
134 Landing gear air-oil shock strut
135 Landing gear trunion
136 Hydraulic retraction jack
137 Gun camera
138 Landing gear trunion pivot fixing
139 Induction air duct
140 Oil cooler air duct
141 Ram air intakes
142 Landing gear wheel door
143 Oil cooler air flap
144 Fuselage drop-tank
145 Hydraulic brake unit
146 Right mainwheel

The first of the two prototypes made its maiden flight on August 21, 1944, with an R-2800-22W engine. It was an excellent first flight. The aircraft proved its high performance capability with a 1463 m (4800 ft)/min rate-of-climb and a maximum speed of 682 km/h (424 mph).

Armament consisted of four 12.7-mm (0.5-in) machine-guns, mounted in the wings, and two 454-kg (1000-lb) bombs or four 12.7-cm (5-in) rockets could be carried on inner-wing racks, or two drop-tanks.

The navy came up with a production contract on October 6, 1944. Grumman was to supply 2023 F8F-1 aircraft. A few months later, on February 5, 1945, Eastern Aircraft (General Motors) was contracted to produce 1876 Bearcats with the designation F3M-1. Grumman started deliveries in February 1945, and the aircraft were assigned to US Navy Squadron VF-19 which began to equip in May of that year.

World War II ended without the Bearcat having seen operational service. The navy reduced its contracts to 770 aircraft but added an order for 126 F8F-1B Bearcats, with four 20-mm (0.79-in) cannon. Of the original order, 15 aircraft were revised as night fighters, with the designation F8F-2N, with APS-6 radar. Navy squadrons continued to re-equip with the Bearcat and by 1948, the type was in service with 24 units.

Another version, the F8F-2, appeared in 1948 armed with 20-mm (0.79-mm) cannon. There were 293 of these built, as well as 12 night fighters, designated F8F-2N. Other changes included a

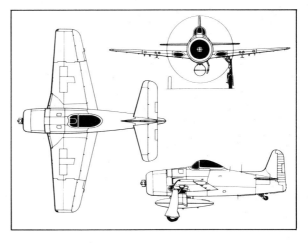

taller fin and rudder, and the engine cowling was revised. Grumman also produced 60 F8F-2P photographic aircraft.

Production ended in May 1949. At this time, 12 navy squadrons operated the F8F-1 and 12 the F8F-2. By the end of 1952, the type was completely out of service.

The Bearcat's operational life with the US Navy was relatively short, but surplus aircraft were sold to the French Armée de l'Air and the Royal Thai Air Force, and the Bearcat gave an excellent account of itself in the Indo-Chinese war, fought between France and the communist Viet-Minh.

Compared with modern jet combat aircraft, the Bearcat was a bulky, ungainly construction, but it was one of the best USN fighters.

F8F-1

Type: single-seat naval fighter
Maker: Grumman Aircraft Engineering Corporation
Span: 10.92 m (35 ft 10 in)
Length: 8.61 m (28 ft 3 in)
Height: 4.22 m (13 ft 10 in)
Wing area: 22.67 m² (244 sq ft)
Weight: maximum 5873 kg (12 947 lb); empty 3207 kg (7070 lb)
Powerplant: one 2100-hp Pratt & Whitney R-2800-34W 18-cylinder air-cooled radial engine
Performance: maximum speed 677 km/h (421 mph) at 6004 m (19 700 ft); range 1778 km (1105 miles); service ceiling 11795 m (38 700 ft)
Armament: four 12.7-mm (0.5-in) machine-guns
Crew: 1
Production: 1155 (all types)

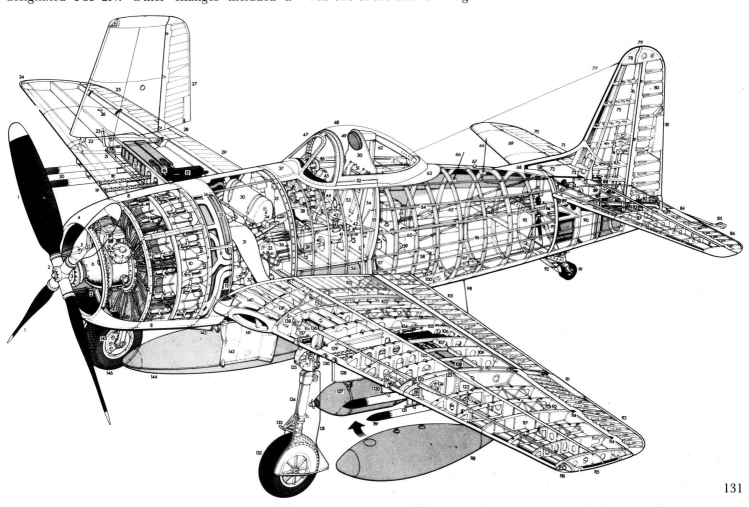

D H. 100 Vampire, de Havilland

FIRST FLIGHT 1943

THE prototype Vampire single-seat fighter LZ548/G was flown for the first time by Geoffrey de Havilland Jnr on September 29, 1943. It was an all-metal aircraft, except for the short fuselage nacelle, which was a plywood and balsa construction derived from the Mosquito. The powerplant was a 1224-kg (2700-lb) st Goblin I turbojet made by the de Havilland Engine company, fitted behind the pilot and fed by wing root inlets, the tail was mounted on twin booms and the tailplane set high and clear of the jet efflux.

On May 13, 1944, a contract was placed for 120 Vampire F.1s to be built in the Preston works of the English Electric company. The first production aircraft to come off the line was first flown at Samlesbury on April 20, 1945. The first batch of 40 were used mainly for test purposes, including squadron evaluation, RAE tests, engine and armament development, and aerodynamic tests using tip-mounted cameras. The 41st F.1 and subsequent aircraft were powered by the 1406-kg (3100-lb) Goblin 2 and fitted with Mosquito slipper tanks. Cockpits were pressurized from the 51st aircraft onwards and were equipped with one-piece canopies from January 1946.

From 1946–51, Vampires were in service with the Second Tactical Air Force in Germany. In 1948 they replaced the Mosquitos of No 605 (County of Warwick) Squadron at Honiley and became the first jet aircraft to serve with the Royal Auxiliary Air Force.

Three of the early production Vampires were fitted with Rolls-Royce Nene I engines, and could

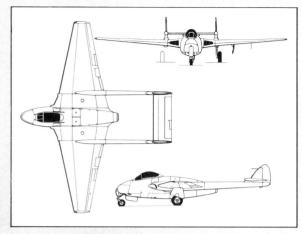

be identified by 'elephant ear' intakes on top of the nacelle. Designated Vampire II, they were used for performance and engine trials.

The third production aircraft, TG278, first flew on May 8, 1947, as a testbed for the de Havilland Ghost turbojet. It had a 1.2-m (4-ft) extension to each wingtip and a special canopy. During high altitude trials, John Cunningham established a new world record of 18 119 m (59 446 ft) on March 23, 1948. This aircraft was later fitted with a Mk 3 tailplane during the development of a Ghost-engined production version which was at first designated Vampire Mk 8, but was eventually built as the DH.112 Venom. One Vampire F.1 was supplied to the Royal Canadian Air Force and another went to Canada for winterization trials.

FB.5

Type: single-seat jet fighter-bomber
Maker: de Havilland Aircraft Co Ltd
Span: 11.58 m (38 ft)
Length: 9.37 m (30 ft 9 in)
Height: 2.69 m (8 ft 10 in)
Wing area: 24.34 m² (262 sq ft)
Weight: maximum 5620 kg (12 390 lb); empty 3290 kg (7253 lb)
Powerplant: one 1520-kg (3350-lb) st de Havilland Goblin 2 turbojet
Performance: maximum speed 914 km/h (568 mph); range 1931 km (1200 miles); service ceiling 12 192 m (44 000 ft)
Armament: four 20-mm (0.79-in) cannon; 907-kg (2000-lb) bombs or rockets
Crew: 1
Production: 2464 (all single-seat marks)

Instability problems were cured by reducing the height of the tailplane and a long-range wing increased internal tankage. This configuration was designated as Vampire F.3 when put into production, and it replaced the Mk 1 both in Germany and the United Kingdom. Six aircraft of No 54 Squadron became the first jet fighters to fly the Atlantic under their own power and reach Goose Bay on July 14, 1948, routeing through Iceland and Greenland.

A Vampire variant comprising a Vampire 3 airframe was developed in Australia as the FB.30, 80 of which were built by de Havilland Pty Ltd. Powered by Australian-made R-R Nene 2-VH engines, it first flew on June 29, 1948.

The Vampire FB.5 was a ground-attack variant, with strengthened and clipped wings for the carriage of bombs or rockets, and a long-stroke undercarriage. It first flew on June 23, 1948, and saw operational service in Malaya. One was sent to Australia where 29 Mk 30s were reworked to FB.5 wing standard. The Mk 5 was sold to France, Italy and Sweden. The Mk 52 export version, based on this model was supplied to Egypt, Finland, Iraq, Lebanon, Norway and Venezuela. Standard Mk 5s went to India and the South African Air Force. SNCASE built 250 FB.53s of French design with large wing-root inlets and with French-built Hispano-Suiza Nenes.

Vampires saw service in many different roles, including a naval version, and the aircraft had the distinction of being the first pure jet ever to operate from a carrier on December 3, 1945.

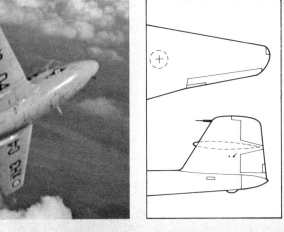

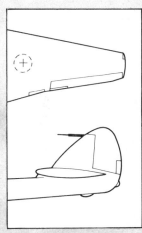

Top left: A de Havilland Vampire T.11 of the RAF Historic Flight, which is now the last Vampire to remain airworthy with the Royal Air Force
Above left: A two-seat Sea Vampire T.22 at the Imperial War Museum, Duxford airfield
Left: An early production Vampire fitted with a Rolls-Royce Nene I engine – with its characteristic 'elephant ear' intakes. The French SNCASE Mistral had enlarged main intakes instead
Top: The larger pointed wings and angular tail of the earlier Vampire F.1
Above: The clipped wing and pointed tail unit of the Vampire FB.5. The wings were strengthened to take bombs

DH.103 Hornet, de Havilland

FIRST FLIGHT 1944

THE requirement for a long-range fighter led de Havilland to consider, as early as 1940, a scaled-down single-seat Mosquito variant, to be called the Hornet. High speed and long range were both dependent on having the minimum possible drag, and to achieve this, Rolls-Royce developed a special Merlin engine of the least possible frontal area. This effected an extremely clean installation, which was demonstrated on the mock-up shown to the Ministry of Aircraft Production in 1943.

Although the Hornet was similar to the Mosquito in general configuration, it was structurally an entirely new design, except for the very slender fuselage, which was constructed in the same way as the earlier aircraft. The two-spar wing was made in one piece with a laminar flow aerofoil and comprised a composite wood and metal internal structure with a stressed birch-ply double upper skin and an undersurface of reinforced Alclad.

The Hornet was the first aircraft with a wood-bonded-to-metal construction, which was made possible by using Redux adhesive. It was powered by two Rolls-Royce Merlins, a 130 on one side and a 131 on the other, which were contra-rotating to avoid swing on take-off. Armament comprised four 20-mm (0.79-in) Hispano cannons, situated in the nose under the pilot.

The first prototype, RR915, was flown on July 28, 1944, only 13 months after detail design started. The performance was even better than that predicted. A second prototype was fitted with two 909-litre (200-Imp gal) drop-tanks.

Production of the Hornet began at Hatfield in

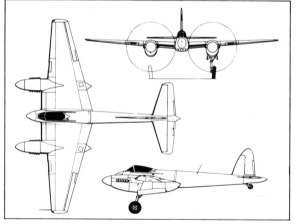

late 1944, and the first production aircraft went to Boscombe Down on February 28, 1945. An alternative role for the Hornet was photographic reconnaissance, and three prototypes and five others were built before that order was cancelled. Wider tailplanes with larger horn balances on the elevators, and two 909-litre drop-tanks were features of the Mk 3 Hornet: two 454-kg (1000-lb) bombs could be fitted in place of the drop-tanks.

Hornet production was switched to Chester towards the end of 1948, and when the contract ended in June 1952 a total of 211 aircraft had been delivered to the Royal Air Force. Most of the Mk 3s went to Malaya for anti-terrorist duties, and were the last piston-engined RAF fighters to see active service.

Hornet F.3

Type: single-seat fighter-bomber
Maker: de Havilland Aircraft Co Ltd
Span: 13.72 m (45 ft)
Length: 11.17 m (36 ft 8 in)
Height: 4.32 m (14 ft 2 in)
Wing area: 33.53 m² (361 sq ft)
Weight: maximum 9480 kg (20 900 lb); empty 5842 kg (12 880 lb)
Powerplant: two 2030-hp Rolls-Royce Merlin 133 or 134 V-12 liquid-cooled engines
Performance: maximum speed 760 km/h (472 mph); range 4828 km (3000 miles); service ceiling 10 668 m (35 000 ft)
Armament: four 20-mm (0.79-in) Hispano cannon; underwing provision for two 454-kg (1000-lb) bombs
Crew: 1
Production: 211

Top: Groundcrew check two Hornet F.3s. In operations in the 1950s in Malaya they became the last piston-driven fighters to see active service in the RAF

DH.103 Sea Hornet, de Havilland

FIRST FLIGHT 1945

THE possibility of a naval version of the Hornet was considered early in the project stage of the aircraft. Accordingly, opposite-handed engines and high-drag flaps had been specified in the design. In late 1944, three early production Hornet F.1s were selected for modification to naval standards, to Specification N5/44. Heston Aircraft was selected to do the design work, which comprised a folding wing actuated by a Lockheed hydraulic jack, an arrester hook on a flush-fitting external V frame, accelerator pick-up points, and mountings for ASH radar and naval radio equipment. Airdraulic undercarriage legs were supplied by de Havilland to absorb the high rate of descent entailed in deck landings.

The first prototype flew on April 19, 1945, without the folding wing. The third prototype was the first to fly with full naval modifications, and carrier trials began on August 10, 1945. A production order resulted, the aircraft being designated Sea Hornet F.20.

The Sea Hornet's armament consisted of four 20-mm (0.79-in) Hispanos in the nose, with provision for two 454-kg (1000-lb) bombs or eight 27-kg (60-lb) rockets under the mainplane. Optional reconnaissance capability was provided by built-in camera windows in the rear fuselage. The first squadron to be equipped with Sea Hornets was No 801, which was re-formed at Ford on June 1, 1947, and after a period at Arbroath, embarked on HMS *Implacable* in 1949. Three aircraft were attached to No 806 Squadron, to form part of a composite naval group which embarked in HMCS *Magnificent*

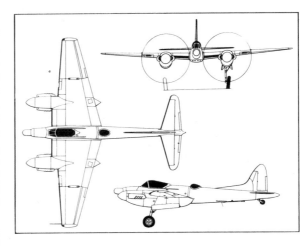

in May 1948, to take part in the International Air Exposition held in New York from July 31 to August 8 that year.

The F.20 was converted into a radar-equipped two-seater, to meet an urgent naval requirement for a high-performance night fighter. Heston Aircraft had the design responsibility and carried out the modifications to Specification N21/45. The aircraft first flew on July 9, 1946, equipped with Merlin 133/34 powerplants, increased tailplane span, heated radar-navigator's cockpit in the rear fuselage, with one-piece canopy, ASH radar and flame-damping exhaust manifolds. Designated Sea Hornet NF.21, 79 were built. Total of all variants of Sea Hornets was 198 machines, when production ended in 1951.

Sea Hornet NF.21

Type: two-seat naval night fighter
Maker: de Havilland Aircraft Co Ltd
Span: 13.72 m (45 ft)
Length: 11.28 m (37 ft)
Height: 3.96 m (13 ft)
Wing area: 33.53 m² (361 sq ft)
Weight: maximum 8858 kg (19 530 lb); empty 6454 kg (14 230 lb)
Powerplant: two 2030-hp Rolls-Royce Merlin 133 or 134 engines
Performance: maximum speed 692 km/h (430 mph); range 2414 km (1500 miles); service ceiling 10 972 m (36 000 ft)
Armament: four 20-mm (0.79-in) Hispano nose-mounted cannon; two 454-kg (1000-lb) bombs under mainplane, or alternative provision for eight 27-kg (60-lb) rocket projectiles
Crew: 2
Production: 79

Left: A Sea Hornet F.20. The camera port can be seen just forward of the roundel on the fuselage. This gave the aircraft an optional reconnaissance capability. Production of the F.20 ended in 1951
Above: The wingfold on the first fully navalized version of the Sea Hornet, PX219

Saab 21

FIRST FLIGHT 1943

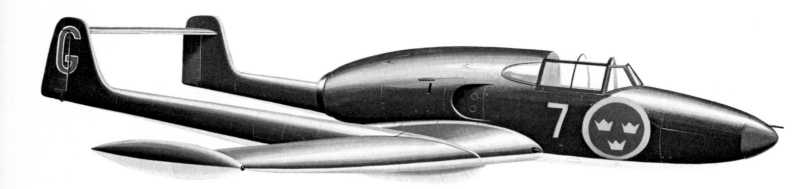

Above: A J-21R of F7 Wing
Far left and left: The piston-engined ground-attack J-21A, serving with wings F8 and F9

THE Saab J-21 has the distinction of being the only production combat aircraft to enter service in both piston-engine and jet-powered versions. Design was begun in 1941, and a twin-boom pusher configuration with a high-speed aerofoil section was adopted.

The initial planned powerplant was to have been a Pratt & Whitney Twin Wasp radial engine of 1200 hp, but when the 1475-hp Daimler-Benz DB605B became available this was adopted in preference. The J-21 prototype (initially designated L-21) first flew on July 30, 1943.

The first production aircraft, designated J-21A-1, were armed with a single 0.79-in (20-mm) Hispano cannon and a pair of 0.52-in (13.2-mm) Browning machine-guns in the nose. All except the first few aircraft were powered by a licence-built version of the DB605 from Svenska Flygmotor.

The similarly armed J-21A-2 version was followed by the J-21A-3, fitted with underwing racks for bombs or rockets, wingtip fuel tanks and provision for a ventral gun pack containing eight 13.2-mm (0.52-in) machine-guns. Most of the A-2/A-3 versions were adopted for attack duties, armed with air-to-surface weapons, and redesignated A-21A. Production was complete by 1948.

Although in 1945 there were plans to develop a J-21B, powered by a 2000-hp Rolls-Royce Griffon, these were abandoned in favour of the J-21R. Four J-21As were converted to J-21R configuration, which produced more problems than originally anticipated. The wings and tail unit had to be restressed, and because of the lower thrust-line the

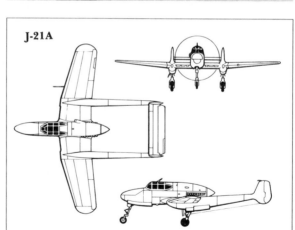

J-21A

undercarriage had to be modified. The air intakes, mounted above the wing, aft of the cockpit, were found to be of low efficiency. The first prototype flew from Norrköping on March 10, 1947.

Throughout this time, a much superior aircraft, the J-29 Tunnen, was on the drawing board, and as a result, the original order for 120 J-21Rs was halved, and Saab built only 30 J-21RAs, and 30 J-21RBs. The J-21R was armed with a single 0.79-in (20-mm) Bofors cannon and four 0.52-in (13.2-mm) Bofors machine-guns in the nose in the fighter role.

When later modified for attack duties, as the A-21R, the ventral gun pack of the J-21A-3 was installed with provision for bombs and rockets. It was withdrawn from service in 1956.

J-21RB

Type: single-seat attack fighter
Maker: Svenska Aeroplan A B (Saab)
Span: 11.38 m (37 ft 4 in)
Length: 10.13 m (34 ft 3 in)
Height: 2.94 m (9 ft 8 in)
Wing area: 22.2 m² (239 sq ft)
Weight: maximum 4990 kg (11 000 lb); empty 3200 kg (7055 lb)
Powerplant: one 1500-kg (3300-lb) st de Havilland Goblin 3 turbojet
Performance: maximum speed 800 km/h (497 mph) at 8000 m (26 247 ft); range at 8000 m (26 247 ft) 719 km (447 miles); service ceiling 12 000 m (39 370 ft)
Armament: one 20-mm (0.79 in) Bofors cannon; four 13.2-mm (0.52-in) Bofors machine-guns in the nose; provision for a belly gun pack of eight 13.2-mm (0.52-in) Bofors machine-guns; either ten 10-cm (3.94-in) or five 18-cm (7.09-in) Bofors rocket projectiles, or ten 8-cm (3.15-in) British anti-tank rockets
Crew: 1
Production: 361 (all types)

Meteor NF.11-14, Armstrong Whitworth

FIRST FLIGHT 1950

IT was not until January 1947 that the Air Ministry issued Specification F.44/46, which called for a two-seat twin-engined jet all-weather fighter to replace the Mosquito. Several manufacturers, including Hawker and Gloster, submitted proposals, but none fulfilled the requirements. The advent of jet bombers emphasized the urgency of the problem, and as an interim measure Gloster suggested that a modified Meteor could be used. The two-seat T.7 was already in service, and conversion to a night-fighter configuration would be relatively simple.

The new variant required a 1.5-m (5-ft) extension to the front fuselage to accommodate the radar, the wings were to be of unclipped Meteor 3 planform, and fuel capacity the same as the Mk 4 and Mk 7. This proposal was accepted, somewhat to the embarrassment of Gloster, whose design team was already overloaded. However, Armstrong Whitworth, who were also in the Hawker Siddeley Group, were already involved in Meteor production, and in 1949 it was decided that they should assume responsibility for the development and production of the Meteor night fighter.

Flight testing of the aerodynamic configuration began in October 1949 with a modified production T.7. Important modifications introduced by AWA included repositioning the four 20-mm (0.79-in) cannon in the outer wings, and the introduction of a pressurized cockpit, which provided the crew with a 7315-m (24 000-ft) cabin pressure at 12 192 m (40 000 ft).

WA546, the first true NF.11 prototype, flew on

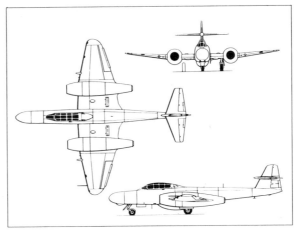

May 31, 1950, from Baginton. Production was soon under way, with a total of 341 NF.11s, including the prototypes, being built.

The NF.12 was a development of the earlier variants with a 432-mm (17-in) longer nose to house the American-built Westinghouse APS-21 AI radar, and with Derwent 9 engines. Deliveries started in late 1953 and the total built was 100 aircraft. Only 40 tropicalized NF.11s designated NF.13 were built.

The final and best version was the NF.14, a development of the NF.12, with a longer nose, APS-43 radar, a two-piece sliding blown canopy, yaw dampers, larger fin and other minor changes. There were 100 built, the last being delivered on May 26, 1955.

NF Mk 11

Type: two-seat night fighter
Maker: Sir W G Armstrong Whitworth Aircraft Ltd
Span: 13.1 m (43 ft)
Length: 15.2 m (49 ft 11¼ in)
Height: 4.2 m (13 ft 11 in)
Wing area: 34.74 m²
(374 sq ft)
Weight: maximum 9626 kg (21 200 lb); empty 5724 kg (12 620 lb)
Powerplant: two 1588-kg (3500-lb) st Rolls-Royce Derwent 8 turbojets
Performance: maximum speed 940 km/h (585 mph); range not available; service ceiling 12 192 m (40 000 ft)
Armament: four 20-mm (0.79-in) cannon
Crew: 2
Production: 100 (592 all NF types)

Above: Meteor NF.14s take off from the maker's airfield at Baginton, Coventry
Far left: The NF.11 retained the same hinged, framed canopy as the T.7
Left: The NF.14 had a rearward-sliding frameless canopy, as well as a larger fin, longer nose, and an autostabilizer which improved directional stability for accurate gun aiming

Meteor F.4, Gloster

FIRST FLIGHT 1945

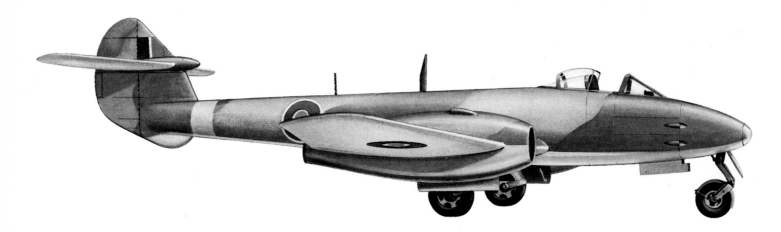

THE Meteor F.4 followed the combat-tested F.1 and F.3 Meteors which had seen action in the closing months of World War II. It was fitted with a scaled-down version of the Rolls-Royce Nene turbojet which was named the Derwent 5 and made its first flight in May 1945.

It was similar to the F.3, but the more powerful engines had larger nacelles and there was provision beneath the fuselage for the ventral fuel tank. The most notable feature was the clipped wing, which was introduced to improve the rate of roll. This improved version had a rate of roll of more than 80° per second, but paid the penalty of increased take-off and landing speeds.

The Royal Air Force High Speed Flight used F.3 Meteors which had been brought up to F.4 stan-dard in an attempt at the world speed record, which they broke in November 1945 at Herne Bay, with a speed of 975 km/h (606 mph). A year later at Tangmere an F.4 nudged this up to 991 km/h (616 mph). In February 1948 Gloster Aircraft made their own record-breaking flight when a test pilot flew at 872 km/h (542 mph) over a 100-km (62-mile) closed-circuit.

Gloster realized they had an aircraft with considerable sales potential, and therefore they took an F.4 on a promotional tour in Europe in 1947. Sadly this tour was cut short when a Belgian pilot crashed the aircraft (G-AIDC), whilst landing at Brussels.

Following some further development, which included the T.7 tandem trainer version, Gloster

Above: The Meteor F.4 was a successful aircraft which set several speed records and enjoyed some export success
Below: The RAF's last operational Meteor F8 on a sortie from RAF Brawdy in June 1978

produced the F.8. This was to be the main single-seat day interceptor for the RAF between 1950 and 1955. The first prototype, a modified F.4, flew on October 12, 1948. The most notable change from earlier versions was the tail which had been developed at RAE Farnborough. It was also fitted to the two prototype E.1/44 fighters with single Nene engines.

Built in larger numbers than any other model, the F.8 was also used for a variety of trials. These included airborne radar for Fireflash missiles, air-to-air refuelling and powerplant trials, including fitting an Armstrong Siddeley Screamer rocket engine under the fuselage. The Martin-Baker ejector seat was standard on all aircraft.

On August 31, 1951, R B Prickett established a time-to-height record of 12 000 m (39 370 ft) in 3 min 9½ sec from Moreton Valence in England, in an F.8 with Armstrong Siddeley Sapphire 2 engines.

In 1952 Armstrong Whitworth received a contract to develop a two-seat version with one pilot in the nose, lying on his front on an inclined couch, and a pilot in the conventional position. The theory was that the prone pilot could stand the g forces better. This testbed flew in February 1954 from Baginton. The aircraft was successful, but in the end the anti-g suit proved an easier solution.

The most successful feature of the F.8 however, was its foreign sales. Egypt ordered 19 aircraft in 1949, though a government ban on arms sales to the Middle East produced a series of delays. Belgium and Holland were not only good customers, but also built the F.8 under licence. N V Koninklijke Ñederlandse Vliegtuigenfabriek Fokker, the most prolific, built 155 F.8s between 1951 and 1954, some of which were supplied to the Belgians.

The Danes bought 19 F.8s which were delivered in 1951. That year an embargo on arms sales halted the production of 12 aircraft for Syria, but these were later completed in 1956. An order from Brazil for 70 aircraft was paid for with 15 000 tons of raw cotton.

The Israeli and Australian aircraft saw action at Suez and in the Korean war respectively. The Australian aircraft destroyed three MiG-15s, and heavily damaged ground installations and other targets.

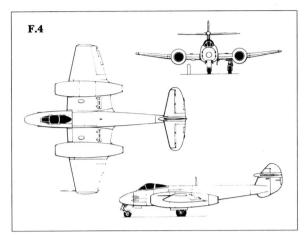

F.4

Meteor F.8

Type: single-seat fighter-bomber
Maker: Gloster Aircraft Co Ltd
Span: 11.3 m (37 ft 2 in)
Length: 13.5 m (44 ft 7 in)
Height: 3.96 m (13 ft)
Wing area: 32.51 m² (350 sq ft)
Weight: maximum 8664 kg (19 100 lb); empty 4846 kg (10 684 lb)
Powerplant: two 1587-kg (3500-lb) st Rolls-Royce Derwent 8 turbojets
Performance: maximum speed 962 km/h (598 mph) at 3048 m (10 000 ft); range 1577 km (980 miles); service ceiling 13 106 m (43 000 ft)
Armament: four fixed British Hispano 20-mm (0.79-in) cannon mounted in front fuselage sides, two 454-kg (1000-lb) bombs or 16 rockets
Crew: 1
Production: 1570

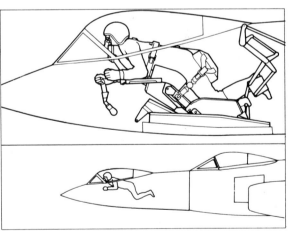

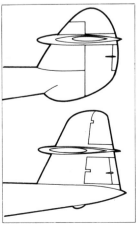

Above: The Armstrong Whitworth trial aircraft with a pilot on an inclined couch. Controls like the pedals had to be redesigned and considerable thought went into an escape system for emergencies
Left above: The rounded tail unit of the Meteor F.4
Left below: The F.8 had an angular tail developed after wind tunnel trials at the Royal Aircraft Establishment, Farnborough. It was greatly superior to that of the F.4

FR-1 Fireball, Ryan

FIRST FLIGHT 1944

THE Ryan Aeronautical Corporation, of San Diego, California, was one of nine manufacturers invited, in 1942, to submit designs to the United States Navy for a naval jet fighter.

The Ryan design was selected as showing the greatest promise, although the company had no experience in the manufacture of naval aircraft. In February 1943, Ryan was asked to build three prototypes, one of which made a first flight on June 25, 1944.

The prototype, XFR-1, was powered by a 1350-hp Wright R-1820-72W Cyclone radial engine in the nose, and a General Electric J31 turbojet mounted in the rear fuselage, fed by wing-root inlets.

It was a low-wing monoplane with a blister cockpit. Armament consisted of four fixed forward-firing 12.7-mm (0.5-in) guns and there was provision for a drop-tank on the right wing. Its stubby profile and unstreamlined wings and tail gave it an appearance somewhat similar to a Republic Thunderbolt. The wings could be folded for carrier stowing. The main units of the tricycle landing gear retracted outwards and gave a particularly stable landing platform.

The FR-1 had a laminar-flow wing-section with a flush-riveted skin and metal-covered control surfaces. The prototypes had double-slotted flaps, but after the first 14 aircraft, single-slotted flaps were planned for production machines.

The initial production contract, placed on December 2, 1943, was for 100 Fireball FR-1 aircraft. Then at the end of January 1945, the navy

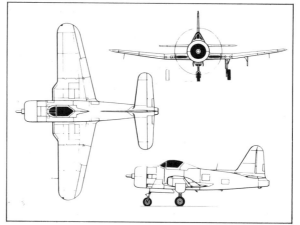

ordered 600 more. However, on V-J Day, 634 aircraft were cancelled, leaving 66 remaining.

Deliveries to US Navy Squadron VF-66, which had been formed specifically to operate FR-1 aircraft, were begun in January 1945 and were completed in November of that year. Three FR-1s underwent carrier trials on board USS *Ranger* on May 1, 1945. The following October, VF-66 was disbanded. It had never seen service at sea.

The FR-1 aircraft, along with the personnel of the defunct squadron, were sent to Navy Squadron VF-41. They took part in exercises onboard USS *Wake Island*, USS *Bairoko*, and USS *Badoeng Strait*, between November 1945 and June 1947, soon after which the FR-1 Fireball was finally withdrawn from naval service.

FR-1

Type: single-seat naval fighter
Maker: Ryan Aeronautical Corporation
Span: 12.19 m (40 ft)
Length: 9.85 m (32 ft 4 in)
Height: 4.24 m (13 ft 11 in)
Wing area: 25.55 m² (275 sq ft)
Weight: maximum 5286 kg (11 652 lb); empty 3487 kg (7689 lb)
Powerplant: one 1350-hp Wright R-1820-72W Cyclone radial and one 726-kg (1600-lb) st General Electric J31 turbojet
Performance: maximum speed 650 km/h (404 mph) at 5245 m (17 800 ft); range 2607 km (1620 miles); service ceiling 13 137 m (43 100 ft)
Armament: four 12.7-mm (0.5-in) guns
Crew: 1
Production: 66

Top: The Ryan FR Fireball in US Navy service. It was a novel design combining jet and piston propulsion in one aircraft

FH-1 Phantom, McDonnell

FIRST FLIGHT 1945

MCDONNELL Aircraft Corporation found themselves in the fortunate position of having design capacity to spare, and adequate manufacturing facilities available, in 1942 when the US Navy Bureau of Aeronautics. The Bureau of Aeronautics instructed McDonnell to design and produce an interceptor fighter for defensive combat patrol. It was to be the first jet fighter to operate from a carrier and fly at 4572 m (15 000 ft) but speed, duration and armament were not specified. A Letter of Intent was issued on January 7, 1943 and was followed by an order for two prototypes, designated XFD-1.

The design team was led by Kendall Perkins, who decided that the aircraft was to be designed on as conservative a basis as possible, and that design simplicity was to be emphasized to ease production and maintenance. The powerplant installation presented an unusual number of options, as Westinghouse had proposed a series of paper 'designs'. Comparison was made between designs having ten, eight, six, four or two engines. The twin-engined configuration was found to be the best, resulting in a lighter airframe, with simpler controls and instrumentation. After considering positioning the engines in wing nacelles or in the fuselage, they were finally installed in the wing root fillets.

Construction started in January 1944, and a year later the first Phantom was ready for flight testing. After successful manufacturer's trials the prototype was evaluated by the US Navy at Patuxent River, and on July 21, 1946, it underwent carrier trials

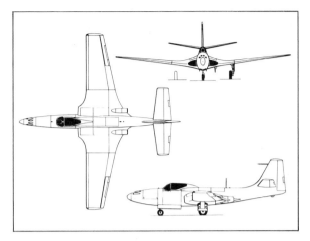

aboard the USS *Franklin D Roosevelt*, the first American jet aircraft to do so.

A production line of 100 FD-1s began on March 7, 1945, but only 60 aircraft had been produced when the war ended. Production aircraft were delivered under the FH-1 designation to avoid confusion with Douglas. Powered by two J30-WE-20 turbojets of 726 kg (1600 lb) thrust, and armed with four 12.7-mm (0.5-in) guns in the nose, the FH-1 had a slightly longer fuselage than the prototype, larger fin and rudder, and greater fuel capacity. It was first flown on October 28, 1946, and was delivered in January 1947. Although the service life of the Phantom was relatively short, it had the distinction of equipping the first shipborne jet-fighter squadron in the world.

FH-1

Type: single-seat naval fighter
Maker: McDonnell Aircraft Corporation
Span: 12.42 m (40 ft 9 in)
Length: 11.81 m (38 ft 9 in)
Height: 4.32 m (14 ft 2 in)
Wing area: 25.64 m² (276 sq ft)
Weight: maximum 5459 kg (12 035 lb); empty 3031 kg (6683 lb)
Powerplant: two 726-kg (1600-lb) thrust Westinghouse J30-WE-20 turbojets
Performance: maximum speed 771 km/h (479 mph) at sea level; range 1115 km (695 miles); service ceiling 12 525 m (41 100 ft)
Armament: four 12.7-mm (0.5-in) nose-mounted machine-guns; underwing provision for eight zero-length rocket-launchers
Crew: 1
Production: 60

Above: A McDonnell FD-1 Phantom; it became the first jet operational with the US Marine Corps
Left: An FD-1; a contract for 100 was reduced to 60 at the end of World War II

MiG-9, Mikoyan

FIRST FLIGHT 1946

T HE Soviet authorities issued a requirement in February 1945, for a single-seat jet fighter. The Mikoyan-Gurevich design bureau was one of several organizations to produce prototypes to this requirement. Under the designation I-300, the bureau began work on its first jet fighter which was an all-metal, mid-wing monoplane with a tricycle undercarriage.

Although designed around a pair of Soviet jet engines (the Lyulka RD-1, sometimes known as the S-18), which had been bench-tested in 1944, the MiG bureau installed two German BMW 109-003A turbojets, each of 800 kg (1760 lb) thrust, later put into production as the RD-20. They were less powerful than the Russian engines, but were readily available, and the engine bay was fitted in the lower fuselage ahead of the wing. They were mounted side-by-side, and exhausted under the rear fuselage, beneath the trailing edge of the wing. The nose inlet was bifurcated and a separate duct fed each engine.

The prototype I-300 made its maiden flight on April 24, 1946, beating its rival, the Yak-15, by one hour and becoming the Soviet Union's first jet-powered aircraft to fly. By this time the I-300 had become the MiG-9.

Unlike the Yak-15, which was basically the Yak-3 airframe modified to accommodate a single RD-10 turbojet, the MiG-9 was a completely new design, and exhibited excellent flying characteristics. During test flights, it recorded a maximum speed of 911 km/h (566 mph), some 85.3 km/h (53 mph) faster than its rival.

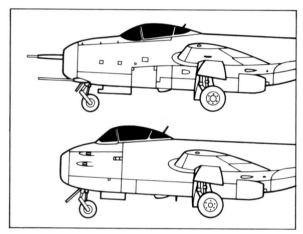

Above: The MiG-9 with tip-tanks and three cannon mounted around the nose air intake

Left: The MiG-9 showing the position of the cannon and cockpit and (below) the MiG-9FR with its pressurized cockpit, ejection seat and cannon repositioned so that they did not intrude in the cockpit

Below: The MiG-9 which received the NATO reporting name Fargo in 1954

The MiG-9's development was hastened by political pressure, for Stalin demanded 15 aircraft to be ready to take part in a fly-past on November 7, 1946.

The unswept wing, originally developed for the I-250N, had a 9% laminar-flow section, and was fitted with spring-tab split ailerons. The main landing gears were hinged on the fuselage, and folded outwards into the wings. A conventional tail unit, with rather low fin-mounted fixed tailplane was fitted. With four bag tanks in the fuselage, and three in each wing, giving a total fuel capacity of 1596 litres (351 Imp gal), the range was good.

The armament consisted of a single 37-mm (1.46-in) Nudelmann N-37 cannon, mounted in the partition between the bifurcated air intakes, with 40 rounds of ammunition, and a pair of 23-mm (0.9-in) Nudelmann-Suranov NS-23 cannon mounted in the lower forward fuselage, projecting forward of the intakes, with 80 rounds each. Later the N-37's ammunition capacity was increased to 90 rounds, and the NS-23s' to 150 rounds each.

The aircraft had plenty of teething problems. Test pilot Alexei Nikolaevich Grinchik, who took the MiG-9 on its maiden flight, was killed when his aircraft crashed out of a dive during a low altitude flight at high speed. Subsequent flights with Mark Gallai as pilot established that careless construction was to blame for the tragedy, the elevator trimmer circuit leads having been soldered to the wrong terminals.

A two-seat training variant was developed as the MiG-9U, while the MiG-9F was re-engined with

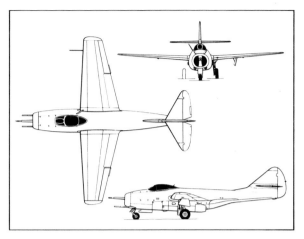

more powerful RD-21 turbojets, incorporating many Soviet developments, and rated at 1000 kg (2210 lb) st. The MiG-9FR featured a pressurized cockpit with an ejection seat, together with a re-profiled nose, similar to the F-86 Sabre. The N-37 cannon was moved to the right side of the nose, and the pair of NS-23 cannon moved to the left side. This version entered production in 1948, and drop-tanks, fitted under the wing just inboard of the tips, became a standard fit.

One of the first Soviet jet fighters to enter large-scale production and service, the MiG-9 was reckoned a fair comparison with contemporary western designs. NATO had given it the codename Fargo, but by 1950, however, it was being replaced in front-line service by the MiG-15.

MiG-9

Type: single-seat day fighter
Maker: Mikoyan-Gurevich Design Bureau
Span: 10.36 m (34 ft)
Length: 9.98 m (32 ft 9 in)
Height: 2.98 m (9 ft 8½ in)
Wing area: 18.2 m² (196 sq ft)
Weight: maximum 5070 kg (11 180 lb); empty 3570 kg (7870 lb)
Powerplant: two 800-kg (1765-lb) st RD-20 (BMW 109-003A) turbojets
Performance: maximum speed 900 km/h (559.2 mph) at 5000 m (16 404 ft); service ceiling 13 000 m (42 651 ft)
Armament: one 37-mm (1.46-in) N-37 and two 23-mm (0.9-in) NS-23 cannon
Crew: 1
Production: approx 550

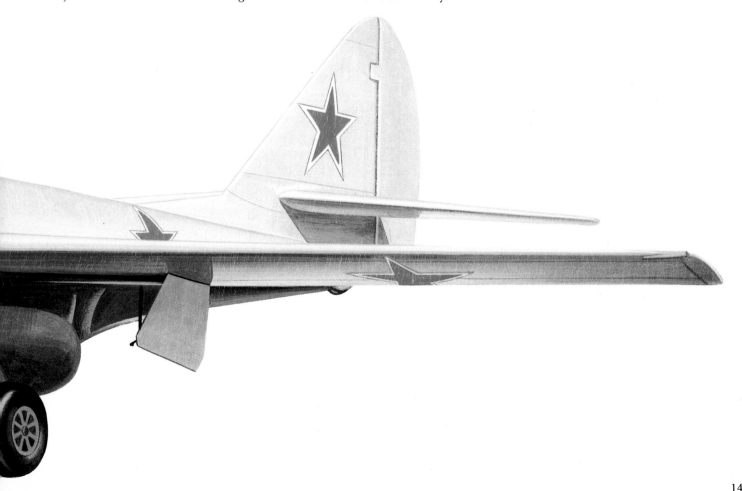

La-11, Lavochkin
FIRST FLIGHT 1947

THE last of the line of Lavochkin piston-engined fighters, the La-11, was first flown in 1947. It was developed from the La-9, and with a view to improving the effectiveness of the type as an escort fighter, the Soviet authorities issued an official requirement for a single-seater of greater range. Of all-metal stressed-skin construction, the La-11 was built in large numbers.

Externally, the La-11 differed from the La-9 by moving the oil coolant radiator, originally positioned under the centre fuselage about level with the wing trailing edge, to an internal duct to reduce drag, fed by a small intake in the lower part of the engine cowling. The fuel capacity was increased by 277.4 litres (61 Imp gal) to 1100 litres (242 Imp gal). With drop-tanks, the range of the La-11 was extended to 2550 km (1585 miles).

During La-9 production, the new 23-mm (0.9-in) Nudelmann-Suranov cannon, a harder-hitting weapon than previous guns, was fitted in the upper decking of the forward fuselage, firing through the propeller arc. To compensate for the increased weight of the La-11's fuel, the armament was reduced to three NS-23 cannon, one on the right-hand side and two to the left.

The La-11 (NATO codename – Fang) was supplied in large numbers to all Communist air forces, including China and North Korea, and served throughout the period 1948–58. Several La-11s were shot down during the Korean war.

Some La-11s were fitted with various camera configurations in the centre fuselage and used as fighter-reconnaissance aircraft.

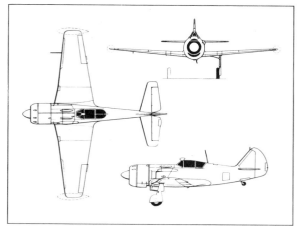

La-11

Type: single-seat escort fighter
Maker: Sergei Lavochkin Design Bureau
Span: 9.8 m (32 ft 2 in)
Length: 8.625 m (28 ft 3½ in)
Height: not available
Wing area: 17.71 m² (190 sq ft)
Weight: maximum 3996 kg (8809 lb); empty 2770 kg (6107 lb)
Powerplant: one 1850-hp 18-cylinder two-row ASh-82FNV radial engine
Performance: maximum speed 674 km/h (419 mph); combat range 750 km (466 miles); service ceiling 10 800 m (33 433 ft)
Armament: three 23-mm (0.9-in) NS-23 cannon
Crew: 1
Production: minimum 2500

Top: A factory-fresh Lavochkin La-11 awaits delivery to a Red Air Force unit
Above: The La-11 was outwardly very similar to the La-9
Far left and left: The La-11 in action in Korea. Like all Soviet machines it was good as a ground-attack aircraft, but was too slow for the more modern types that were operating with the UN Forces

Yak-15, Yakovlev
FIRST FLIGHT 1946

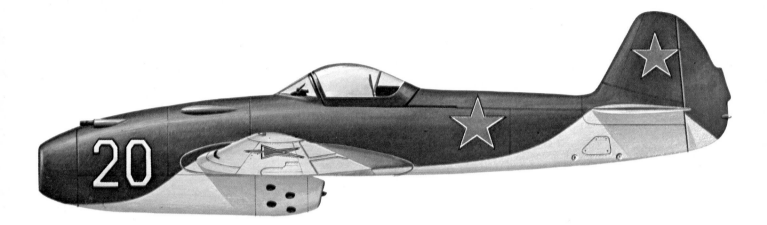

Above: The Yak-15 had a lower fuselage sheathed in steel to protect it from the hot fumes of the jet exhaust
Far left: An early version of the Yak-15 with a tail-mounted wheel
Left: A late production Yak-15 on patrol over a wintery landscape

FOLLOWING the Soviet requirement for a single-seat jet fighter, it was proposed that the Yakovlev bureau should put the German Me 262 into production. However, it was considered that as the Yak-3 had been developed to carry a liquid rocket engine, a jet-powered version was a distinct possibility.

The prototype Yak-15, as the type was designated, retained the cockpit, wings, tail and landing gear of the Yak-3, with the modifications being confined to the forward fuselage. This housed the German Junkers Jumo 004 rated at 898 kg (1980 lb) st. As the jet efflux was below the cockpit, the lower fuselage was sheathed in metal. On production aircraft, stainless steel was used, while the tailwheel was all-metal.

The first prototype flew on April 24, 1946, making its public debut at Tushino in August 1946. Production aircraft, which were powered by the Russian-built Jumo 004, redesignated RD-10, and armed with two 23-mm (0.9-in) NS-23 cannon mounted in the nose above the air intake, entered service in 1947. The Yak-15 was the first Soviet jet fighter to enter squadron service.

Yakovlev adapted the Yak-15 for two more of his fighter designs and Lavochkin may have modelled his La-152 upon it. Its loaded weight of only 2640 kg (5820 lb) made it the lightest-ever turbojet fighter. About 400 were produced between October 1946 and March 1948.

The type served with several Communist countries, including North Korea. As might be expected, the Yak-15's design was refined as a result of feedback from the service. A tricycle landing gear replaced the tailwheel configuration, the fin and rudder were enlarged and the more powerful RD-10A, rated at 1000 kg (2205 lb), installed. This version, designated Yak-17 (NATO codename Feather) superseded the Yak-15 on the production line in 1947.

A two-seat trainer version, the Yak-17UTI Magnet became the Soviet Union's first jet trainer, remaining in service until replaced by the MiG-15UTI Midget. It featured a lengthened fuselage and cockpit, and although usually unarmed, was sometimes fitted with a single 12.7-mm (0.5-in) Beresin machine-gun. Apart from seeing Soviet service, they were used also by Czechoslovakia and Poland.

Yak-15

Type: single-seat day fighter
Maker: A S Yakovlev Design Bureau
Span: 9.58 m (31 ft 5½ in)
Length: 8.78 m (28 ft 9½ in)
Height: 2.08 m (6 ft 10 in)
Wing area: 4.85 m² (159.8 sq ft)
Weight: maximum 2742 kg (6044 lb); empty 2345 kg (5170 lb)
Powerplant: one 898-kg (1980-lb) st Junkers Jumo 004 turbojet
Performance: maximum speed 797 km/h (495 mph) at 3048 m (10 000 ft); range 740 km (460 miles); service ceiling 11 582 m (38 000 ft)
Armament: two 23-mm (0.9-in) NS-23 cannon
Crew: 1
Production: not available

Yak-23, Yakovlev

FIRST FLIGHT 1947

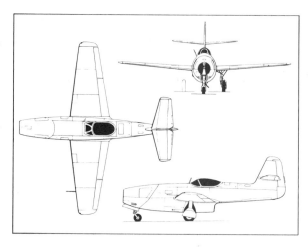

FOLLOWING on the Yak-15 and 17, of which it was an all-metal development, the Yak-23 was produced as an insurance against the failure of the more advanced MiG-15, which had NATO codename of Fagot. The improvements adopted included a redesigned wing, the tailplane mounted on the fin, a completely retractable tricycle undercarriage and a bifurcated air intake for an uprated powerplant – the RD-500 turbojet, a Soviet copy of the Rolls-Royce Derwent, rated at 1600 kg (3527 lb) st.

The Yak-23 had cleaner lines, and looked less like a jet adaption of a piston-engined fighter. In the light fighter class, with the NATO codename Flora, it was the first Soviet fighter to be equipped with an ejection seat. However, by western standards this was rudimentary to the degree of being crude, lacking a face blind, thigh guards, hood breaker or even a stabilizing drogue.

It was armed with a pair of 23-mm (0.9-in) Nudelmann-Suranov NS-23 cannon fitted in the lower forward fuselage on each side of the air intake. There was provision for two tip tanks of 190 litres (41.7 Imp gal) which increased the range from 925 km (575 miles) to 1200 km (746 miles) at 539 km/h (335 mph). The Yak-23 was also used for early trials with engine afterburners.

With the success of the MiG-15, it was decided to put the Yak-23 into limited production for the Soviet satellite air forces, including Albania, Bulgaria, Rumania and Hungary. It saw service in Czechoslovakia under the designation S101.

In 1957 a Polish pilot Andrzei Ablamowicz set two new international rate-of-climb records when he climbed to 3000 m (9840 ft) in 1 min 59 sec and to 6000 m (19 685 ft) in 3 min 17 sec. With its outstanding climb rate the Yak-23 combined exceptional manoeuvrability. These features made it a popular aircraft with satellite air forces, and it was useful in introducing Warsaw Pact pilots to their first essential jet fighter experience. Despite this, only one tandem two-seat Yak-23UTI aircraft was built.

The Yak-23 was later rearmed with Nudelmann-Richter cannon and had provision for carrying bombs or rockets up to 1000 kg (2205 lb). Like many Warsaw Pact types, it was redeployed for ground-attack work before being phased out of front-line service.

Yak-23

Type: single-seat interceptor fighter
Maker: A S Yakovlev Design Bureau
Span: 8.69 m (28 ft 6 in)
Length: 8.16 m (26 ft 9½ in)
Height: 2.99 m (9 ft 9¾ in)
Wing area: 13.6 m² (146.4 sq ft)
Weight: maximum 3384 kg (7460 lb); empty 1980 kg (4365 lb)
Powerplant: one 1600-kg (3527-lb) st RD-500 centrifugal-flow turbojet
Performance: maximum speed 883.5 km/h (549 mph); range 920 km (572 miles); service ceiling 14 800 m (48 555 ft)
Armament: two 23-mm (0.9-in) NS-23 cannon
Crew: 1
Production: 310

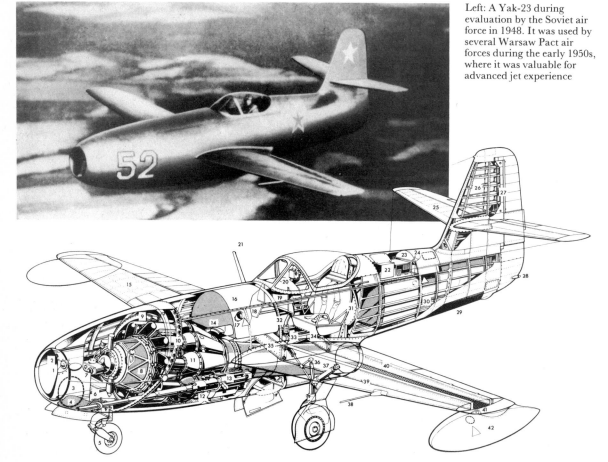

Left: A Yak-23 during evaluation by the Soviet air force in 1948. It was used by several Warsaw Pact air forces during the early 1950s, where it was valuable for advanced jet experience

Yak-23

1 Landing light
2 S-13 gun camera
3 Position of nosewheel retracted
4 Muzzle blast protection panel
5 Pneumatically-operated forward-retracting nosewheel
6 Nosewheel retraction mechanism
7 Auxiliary gearbox drives
8 Engine air intake surfaces
9 Forward engine bearer
10 Nose section attachment
11 Combustion chambers of angled RD-500 turbojet
12 Ammunition box
13 Breech of 23-mm cannon
14 Aft engine bearer
15 Dural skinning
16 Fuel tank
17 Fuel filler cap
18 Right control console
19 Instrument panel
20 Fixed gyro gunsight
21 Aerials
22 Battery
23 Radio compartment
24 Fuel filler cap
25 Dihedral (5°) tailplane
26 Fin structure
27 Rudder post
28 Rear navigation lamp
29 Tailplane blast protection panel
30 Control rods
31 Pilot's back armour
32 Control column
33 Rudder pedal
34 Aft spar carry-over
35 Forward spar carry-over
36 Mainwheel mechanism
37 Cranked mainwheel leg
38 Pitot head
39 Forward wing spar
40 Aft wing spar
41 Left navigation lamp
42 Auxiliary tank

P-80 Shooting Star,Lockheed

FIRST FLIGHT 1944

THE Shooting Star was the United States' first operational jet fighter and its first aircraft to achieve level flight speeds greater than 805 km/h (500 mph).

Lulu-Belle, as the XP-80 prototype was affectionately known, was the conception of Lockheed's chief research engineer, Clarence L 'Kelly' Johnson. It was not until 1943 that the corporation was invited by the USAAF to submit a design for a combat aircraft. It was to be built around the de Havilland Halford H-I engine. Lockheed subsequently submitted its Model L-140 design.

The powerplant was the DH H-1B with a 1225 kg (2700 lb) thrust rating that was not realized in practice. Armament consisted of six 12.7-mm (0.5-in) nose-mounted guns. The lightweight design incorporated a wing specially developed for outstanding high-speed performance.

On November 13, 1943, *Lulu-Belle* was taken to Muroc Army Air Base in California's Mojave Desert for ground and flight tests. Ground tests were completed by November 16 and the scene was set for a test flight. Unfortunately, the inlet ducts collapsed and wrecked the compressor.

A replacement engine taken out of the second prototype Vampire had to be ordered from England and on January 8, 1944 the XP-80, piloted by Milo Burcham, made its first flight. Burcham gave *Lulu-Belle* her head, in an incredible aerobatic display of unprecedented power and speed.

A wing fillet was added to correct the aircraft's tendency to roll sharply, and manoeuvring on the ground was always difficult.

The Shooting Star was redesigned and made longer, sleeker and significantly heavier. Other improvements included cabin pressurization and night-flying capability. Range was extended and fuel capacity was increased.

The first of three I-40 prototypes, designated XP-80A, made its first flight on June 10, 1944. Thirteen service test aircraft had been ordered and delivery of these began in October. Three of these were sent to Italy, but saw only limited operations and never faced enemy aircraft.

The war ended before the Shooting Star reached any combat units. Production orders were greatly reduced with 3083 cancelled out of 4000 being built by Lockheed, and North American's contract terminated.

The first of 676 production P-80As were powered by the 1746-kg (3850-lb) thrust J33-GE-9, an early I-40 production model which was replaced first by the 1814-kg (4000-lb) thrust GE-11, then the J33-A-17 (handed over to Allison to build) and finally the J33-A-21. The last batch was redesignated P-80B. The original XP-80B became the XP-80R racer powered by a J33-23 engine. Piloted by Colonel Albert Boyd, it broke the world speed record at 1004 km/h (623.8 mph) on June 19, 1947.

The US Air Force was formed in 1947 and the P-80 became the F-80. The F-80C was the final version of the Shooting Star, 798 of which equipped Air Force and Air National Guard Units.

The F-80 flew in Korea where it encountered the Russian MiG-15 for which it was no match. By the time the Korean war ended in 1953, the Shooting Star was obsolete.

Left: The cockpit interior of the RF-80 reconnaissance version of the Shooting Star. The camera control panel is in the centre and shows the switches for the cameras in three bays
Below: The F-80C saw action in Korea against Soviet MiG-15s

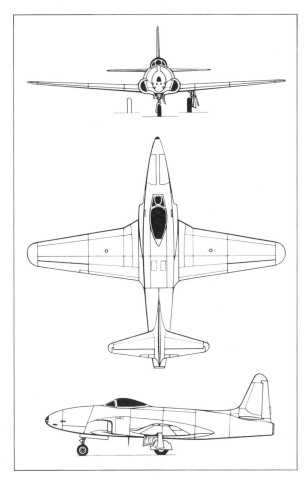

F-80C

Type: single-seat fighter-bomber
Maker: Lockheed Aircraft Corporation
Span: 11.85 m (38 ft 10½ in)
Length: 10.51 m (34 ft 6 in)
Height: 3.45 m (11 ft 4 in)
Wing area: 22 m² (237 sq ft)
Weight: maximum 7646 kg (16 856 lb); empty 3738 kg (8240 lb)
Powerplant: one 2086-kg (25 000-lb) st Allison J33-A-23 turbojet
Performance: maximum speed 933 km/h (580 mph) at 7620 m (25 000 ft); range 2220 km (1380 miles); service ceiling 13 440 m (44 100 ft)
Armament: six 12.7-mm (0.5-in) forward-firing nose-mounted machine guns; provision for two 454-kg (1000-lb) bombs on wing shackles
Crew: 1
Production: 798

F-94 Starfire, Lockheed

FIRST FLIGHT 1949

THE conversion of the original P-80 Shooting Star jet fighter into a two-seat all-weather radar-equipped fighter began in 1949. The work was simplified by that already done in the development of the basic design into the well-known T-33 two-seat jet trainer.

The first prototype YF-94 had originally been an F-80 before it was converted to the prototype T-33, and it made its first flight as a YF-94 on July 1, 1949. Modifications made included the installation of Hughes E-1 radar in the nose, provision for a radar operator in the rear seat and a 2722-kg (6000-lb) thrust afterburning J33-A-33 engine. Only four 12.7-mm (0.5-in) M-3 machine-guns, mounted in the front fuselage, comprised the armament. This variant was designated the F-94A and went into production in 1949, deliveries to the US 319th All-Weather Fighter Squadron beginning in June 1950. The total built was 110.

Lockheed maintained their policy of keeping costs as low as possible by taking the 19th F-94A and converting it to the YF-94B prototype in 1950, with larger tip tanks centred on the wings, modified hydraulics and a Sperry Zero Reader in the cockpit. F-94B production began in 1951 and the total build of the F-94B was 357. A few 94Bs were modified by having a longer nose with three 12.7-mm (0.5-in) guns above the radar.

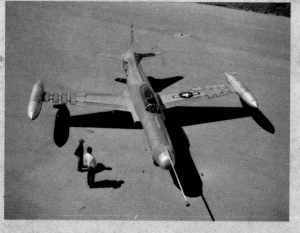

With the initial designation of F-97A, the F-94C represented a more fundamental redesign than the two previous versions. The Pratt & Whitney J48-P-5 engine (derived from the Rolls-Royce Tay) of 3765 kg (8300 lb) thrust with afterburner, was

installed and the wing was virtually a new design, with a thickness/chord ratio of 10%, compared with the previous 13%. Twenty four 69-mm (2.75-in) Mighty Mouse air rockets were mounted in a ring around the Hughes E-5 collision-course radar, and faired in by a retractable shield. A pod carrying 12 more of the missiles could be carried on each wing. The tailplane was swept back, and there was an increase from 0.80 to 0.85 in critical Mach number. The gross weight was also heavier, going up from 7484 kg (16 500 lb) to 9072 kg (20 000 lb).

Following in the original F-80 tradition, two F-94Bs were converted to provide two YF-94C prototypes, the first of which was first flown with a B type nose and revised wingtip tanks. The production run of the C went to a total of 387.

The Starfire saw extensive service in Korea. Many were employed in the defence of the United States and served with the US Air Defense Command squadrons as the first all-weather jet interceptors. Units equipped included some stationed in Japan, Alaska and other areas. Later Starfires were issued to Air National Guard squadrons. Some F-94s were also used in weapon trials and were involved in the development of the Hughes F-98 (GAR-1) Falcon missile.

Lockheed proposed a single-seat ground-support and long-range escort version of the F-94C during the Korean war, but only one prototype was produced by the conversion of a C type in 1951, and a production order for 112 F-94Ds failed to materialize.

F-94C

Type: two-seat all-weather fighter
Maker: Lockheed Aircraft Corporation
Span: 11.38 m (37 ft 4 in)
Length: 13.57 m (44 ft 6 in)
Height: 4.54 m (14 ft 11 in)
Wing area: 31.4 m² (338 sq ft)
Weight: maximum 10 977 kg (24 200 lb); empty 5760 kg (12 700 lb)
Powerplant: one 2840-kg (6250-lb) (3765-kg [8300-lb] with afterburner) thrust Pratt & Whitney J48-P-5 or P-5A turbojet
Performance: maximum speed 941 km/h (585 mph) at 9144 m (30 000 ft); range 1931 km (1200 miles); service ceiling 15 666 m (51 400 ft)
Armament: 24 69-mm (2.75-in) folding-fin air rockets in nose and 12 each in two wing-pods
Crew: 2
Production: 387

Top and above left: The F-94C had 48 69-mm (2.75-in) Mighty Mouse folding-fin rockets in a ring around the nose radome and in wingtip-mounted pods. The nose-mounted rockets were protected by a retracting shield, while the wing pods had jettisonable covers Far left and left: Two views of an F-94C with airspeed-measuring instruments and colourful wing and fuselage panels, probably for use in stall and spin evaluation. The F-94 was also used for weapons trials including the Hughes F-98 (GAR-1) Falcon missile

P-82 Twin Mustang, North American

FIRST FLIGHT 1945

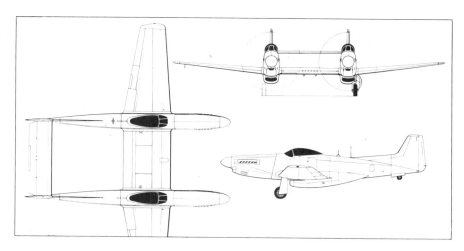

THE unusual configuration of the Twin Mustang was the result of a United States Army Air Force requirement in 1944 for a truly long-range escort fighter, mainly needed for operations in the Pacific area. The quick answer to the required formula of twin engines, two crew and a large amount of fuel was a Siamese-twin arrangement, whereby two Mustang P-51 fuselages were joined together by a new centre wing and tailplane, each fuselage having a standard P-51 outboard wing.

In detail though, the Twin Mustang differed extensively from the P-51. The fuselages were lengthened by extra sections with integral dorsal fins inserted ahead of the new tailplane, the outer-wing panels were redesigned to eliminate the wheel wells, while the systems and equipment were substantially amended.

North American Aviation received an order for two prototypes, designated XP-82. The power-plants were to be Packard Merlin V-1650-23/25 engines with counter-rotating propellers. A third prototype with two Allison V-1710-119 engines, with common rotation, was also ordered and designated the XP-82A.

An order for 500 P-82Bs, similar to the XP-82, was made by the USAAF, but only 20 of these were built. In 1946, the 10th and 11th P-82Bs were converted to the P-82C and P-82D versions respectively, as night fighters. Radar was fitted in a large nacelle under the centre section, and the right-hand cockpit was converted to take the radar operator. The P-82C had the big SCR-720 and the P-82D the 3-cm (1.18-in) waveband APS-4.

The US Air Force procurement in 1946 included a batch of 250 Twin Mustangs, 100 P-82E escort fighters, 100 P-82F night fighters with APS-4, and 50 P-82G with SCR-720. All three variants were powered by 1600-bhp Allison V-1710-143/145 engines with handed propellers. All versions from B to G were redesignated as F-82s in June 1948.

The major operator of the Twin Mustang was Air Defense Command, which had 225 on strength at the end of 1948. In 1950, F-82s went overseas to Japan as part of the 5th Air Force and were among the first USAF aircraft to operate over Korea.

When retired from the Far East Air Force, 14 Twin Mustangs were sent to Alaska and redesignated F-82H after winterization.

F-82E

Type: two-seat escort fighter
Maker: North American Aviation Inc
Span: 15.62 m (51 ft 3 in)
Length: 11.89 m (39 ft)
Height: 4.16 m (13 ft 8 in)
Wing area: 37.9 m² (408 sq ft)
Weight: maximum 11 278 kg (24 864 lb); empty 6509 kg (14 350 lb)
Powerplant: two 1600-hp Allison V-1710-143/145 V-12 liquid-cooled engines
Performance: maximum speed 748 km/h (465 mph); range 4025 km (2500 miles); service ceiling 12 192 m (40 000 ft)
Armament: six 12.7-mm (0.5-in) guns; four 454-kg (1000-lb) bombs
Crew: 2
Production: 100

Above left: A North American P-82B with four drop-tanks – armament was in the centre wing section
Far left: The night-fighter versions were equipped with APS-4 or SCR-720 radar in a centreline pod. The radar operator was housed in the right cockpit
Left: The XP-82, one of two prototypes armed with a pod containing a mix of six 12.7-mm (0.5-in) machine-guns and cannon

F-84 Thunderjet, Republic

FIRST FLIGHT 1946

IN 1944 the Republic Aviation Corporation were looking for a replacement for the Thunderbolt, which had been a very successful escort fighter and fighter-bomber. After studying 'jet Thunderbolts' a new design was created, a straight-wing single-seater of conventional design and construction, powered by a General Electric J35.

The first prototype XP-84 made its maiden flight from Lake Muroc on February 28, 1946, and the second followed in August 1946. Both these aircraft had General Electric J35-GE-7 turbojets of 1701 kg (3750 lb) st as powerplants, and it was with this engine that the second prototype raised the US national speed record to 983 km/h (611 mph) a month after it first flew. The Allison-built J35-A-15 of 1814 kg (4000 lb) st was installed in the initial

production aircraft. The first 15 of these were given the designation YP-84A, and were used for the service trials. This batch were similar to the prototypes except for the armament of six 12.7-mm (0.5-in) M2 machine-guns, four mounted in the upper front fuselage and the other two in the wings. They also had provision for wingtip fuel tanks.

The first operational variant was the P-84B, which had the M3 machine-guns fitted with a higher rate of fire, and, after 85 machines had been built, additional firepower was provided by the installation of eight retractable rocket launchers under the wing. This version had an ejection seat for the pilot: the engine was an Allison J35-A-15C of 1814 kg (4000 lb) st and gross weight was 6350 kg (14 000 lb). Deliveries began in the

Above: The F-84F was a private venture by Republic which extended the life of the F-84 by modernizing its design

Above: An RF-84K on the trapeze installed in the bomb bay of a GRB-36. This F-84 was a direct swept conversion of the original J35-powered aircraft
Right: An F-84F takes off using JATO (jet-assisted take-off) rockets during a 1954 demonstration at the US Air Force base, RAF Bentwaters, near Ipswich

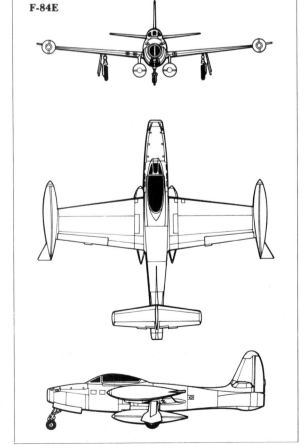

F-84E

F-84G

Type: single-seat fighter-bomber
Maker: Republic Aviation Corporation
Span: 11.4 m (37 ft 5 in)
Length: 11.6 m (38 ft)
Height: 3.9 m (12 ft 10 in)
Wing area: 24.15 m² (260 sq ft)
Weight: maximum 10 670 kg (23 523 lb); empty 5032 kg (11 093 lb)
Powerplant: one 2540-kg (5600-lb) st Allison J35-A-29 turbojet
Performance: maximum speed 1000 km/h (620 mph) at sea level; range 3100 km (1925 miles); service ceiling 12 350 m (40 518 ft)
Armament: six 12.7-mm (0.5-in) guns; two 454-kg (1000-lb) bombs or 16 HVARs, or other loads; maximum 1800 kg (3968 lb)
Crew: 1
Production: 3025

summer of 1947 and the designation was changed to F-84B in June 1948. Republic built a total of 224 of this version.

The second production variant was the P-84C (later F-84C), powered by the J35-A-13C of 1814 kg (4000 lb) st, and it also had a new electrical system. The total produced was 191. The gross weight had gone up to 7303 kg (16 100 lb).

The third production version, F-84D, had more significant modifications, with a thicker wing skin and a winterized fuel system suitable for the use of JP4. The gross weight was 7620 kg (16 800 lb), and it was powered by a J35-A-17D engine of 2268 kg (5000 lb) thrust. A total of 154 were produced.

The Thunderjet F-84D saw operational service in Korea from December 1950 onwards. It was followed by the F-84E variant, with a radar gunsight, a 305-mm (12-in) fuselage extension to increase pilot comfort, and improved wingtip tanks. A fuel system modification allowed two 871-litre (192-Imp gal) tanks to be carried under the inner wings. At first the F-84s were used on escort duties to the B-29 bombers, but later became involved more and more in ground-attack operations. A total of 843 F-84Es were built.

Towards the end of 1950 the US Air Force Tactical Air Command began to develop the F-84 to carry nuclear bombs for tactical warfare and by spring 1952 the Thunderjet was the first single-seat fighter-bomber to carry a nuclear weapon. Deliveries of this version began in 1951 with the designation F-84G. Powered by a 2540-kg (5600-

Above: An F-84F in the colours of the Thunderbirds aerobatic team. The Thunderstreak was widely used by NATO air forces, which received 1301, while a further 386 RF-84F Thunderflashes were purchased for Mutual Defence programmes

lb) st J35-A-29 engine, it could carry up to 1814 kg (4000 lb) of external stores and provision was made for flight refuelling. The gross weight was increased to 9979 kg (22 000 lb) for the F-84E. With nuclear capability, the G was used by both TAC and SAC (Strategic Air Command) units, and, with the latter, made a series of long-range refuelled flights. The production total of the F-84G was 3025, making the grand total of straight-wing Thunderjets 4457; 1936 of the G version went straight to various NATO air forces.

At the end of 1949, Republic began work on a swept-wing version of the Thunderjet. They kept costs down by using 60% of the tooling for the Thunderjet and a standard F-84E fuselage. The first prototype flew on June 3, 1950 powered by a

2359-kg (5200-lb) st Allison XJ35-A-25 engine. When more funds became available after the Korean war the aircraft designated F-84F, and now powered by a Wright YJ65-W-1, flew on February 14, 1951. It proved to be a highly successful design with production totalling 2711, of which 237 were by General Motors and 1301 were for NATO air forces.

A reconnaissance version, the RF-84F, carried cameras in the nose and intakes located in the wing roots. Republic built 718 of this version. An interesting development from the RF-84F was the FICON (Fighter Conveyor) project. A B-36 and Thunderjet were adapted so that the bomber could carry the fighter in its bomb bay and, using a hook and trapeze, recover the fighter.

Attacker, Supermarine

FIRST FLIGHT 1946

THE Attacker came from the same stable as the Spitfire, and like that fighter, its greatest rival was an aircraft from Hawker, in this case the Sea Hawk.

Joe Smith, who became chief designer of the Supermarine Aviation Works (Vickers) after the premature death in 1937 of Reginald Mitchell, had designed a completely new fighter to Specification F.1/43, named the Spiteful. The wing, with a span of 10.8 m (35 ft 6 in), had a compound straight taper and laminar aerofoil, with a main landing gear that retracted inwards, giving almost twice the track of the Spitfire.

Faced with the requirements of Specification E.10/44, which was really written around the Nene, Smith saw that, with only minor modifications, he could base his design on the Spiteful wing and landing gear and need only produce a new fuselage and tail. This would virtually cut the design work by half. Another bonus was the armament comprising four 20-mm (0.79-in) Hispano Mk 5 cannon mounted in the wing, well away from the engine inlets.

The fuselage shape of the Supermarine Type 392 was dictated by the Nene engine which was housed in the mid section, with a straight jetpipe going to the tail. The inlets were on the side of the fuselage forward of the wing, then a new location, with the front fuselage tailored to the width of the cockpit.

The first prototype TS409 was flown from Boscombe Down on July 27, 1946, by Jeffrey Quill, and though a very basic aircraft the performance was promising. The Attacker was unusual among jet aircraft in having a tailwheel (in fact twin tailwheels), and this caused erosion problems. This was partially solved by extending the jetpipe with a diagonal cut-off, which tilted the efflux slightly upwards without affecting the trim.

When a requirement was issued for a deck-landing version, it was decided to build the second and third prototypes to meet this standard. A naval variant of the Spiteful had already been produced, as the Seafang, and this simplified the work in regard to the folding wing and widened main undercarriage, which was modified to cope with the high rate of descent of deck landings.

The second prototype TS413 first flew on June 17, 1947, piloted by Mike Lithgow. Although still without folding wings, it was fitted with a Martin-

Above: A Royal Navy Attacker with the 1136.5-litre (250-Imp gal) belly tank for long-range missions
Below: The first prototype built to an RAF Specification E.10/44. After evaluation at Boscombe Down, it was rejected by the RAF but adopted by the Royal Navy after it had been adapted for carrier operations

Left: The Supermarine
Attacker was unusual among
jet fighters for its tail wheel.
Among the features which
distinguished it from its land-
based prototype was a
pronounced dorsal fin. It was
armed with four 20-mm (0.79-
in) cannon

Baker ejection seat, and also had small-lift spoilers above the wing to assist flight-path control on the approach. It also had plain flaps, catapult hooks in the mainwheel wells, fittings for RATOG (rocket assisted take-off gear), and lashing points. In October 1947, the TS413 was used for flight-deck trials aboard HMS *Illustrious* and, although it was the fastest aircraft embarked at that time, the trials were a great success. In spite of this, a decision on a production order was delayed for a further two years.

The third prototype had its wing moved back 343 mm (13.5 in), enlarged air intakes with better boundary layer bleeds and other minor improvements. TS409 was also brought up to the latest standard, and on February 27, 1948, Mike Lithgow

broke the world 100-km (62-mile) closed-circuit record, flying at 909 km/h (565 mph).

In November 1949, the first production order for 60 aircraft was received. Much of the delay had been caused by trivial modifications. The first production F.1 flew on April 4, 1950, powered by the Nene 3 of 2313 kg (5100 lb) thrust.

The only export order came from the Royal Pakistan Air Force which ordered 36 of a land-based variant of the F.1 with fixed wings and racks for underwing stores.

Other versions were the FB.1, distinguished from the F.1 by its underwing hardpoints for bombs or rockets, and the FB.2 with extended dorsal fin and a metal-framed canopy. Altogether 145 Attackers were built for the navy.

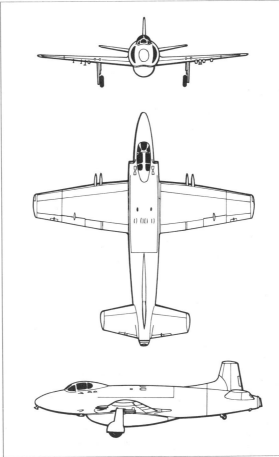

FB.2

Type: single-seat naval
fighter-bomber
Maker: Supermarine
Aviation Works (Vickers) Ltd
Span: 11.25 m (36 ft 11 in)
Length: 11.43 m (37 ft 6 in)
Height: 3.02 m (9 ft 11 in)
Wing area: 21 m² (226 sq ft)
Weight: maximum 5579 kg
(12 300 lb); empty 4495 kg
(9910 lb)
Powerplant: one 2315-kg
(5100-lb) st Rolls-Royce Nene
102 turbojet
Performance: maximum
speed 944 km/h (590 mph) at
sea level; maximum range
1915 km (1190 miles); service
ceiling 13 725 m (45 000 ft)
Armament: four 20-mm
(0.79-in) Mk 5 cannon; two
454-kg (1000-lb) bombs or 27-
kg (60-lb) rockets
Crew: 1
Production: 181 (all types)

F-86 Sabre, North American
FIRST FLIGHT 1947

IN 1944 North American Aviation was working on the NA-134 naval jet fighter, which became the XFJ-1, in the project stage, when the United States Army Air Force responded to a company proposal by ordering three prototypes of a longer and heavier land-based fighter. Two were for flight trials and the other for static ground tests, in the autumn of 1944. Given the USAAF designation XP-86, it was of conventional design. The estimated performance with General Electric TG-180 (J35) (later called Allison J35) turbojet was a speed of 937 km/h (582 mph), ceiling of 14 175 m (46 500 ft) and range of 1207 km (750 miles).

In 1945 NAA took the bold decision to delay the whole programme by about a year, to incorporate German research on high-speed aerodynamics. In particular, it was decided to incorporate wing sweepback of 35°. The fuselage was lengthened, with the pressurized cockpit well forward of the wing and above the engine air duct. Other advanced features of the design included power-boosted ailerons and full-span automatic leading-edge slats.

The first prototype made its maiden flight on October 1, 1947, with a Chevrolet-built J35-C-3 turbojet of only 1701 kg (3750 lb) st. A similar engine was also used for the second prototype. In the spring of 1948 the first prototype exceeded Mach 1 in a shallow dive. This made it the first important United States fighter to go supersonic. A production order for 221 P-86As had already been received from the USAF on December 28, 1947,

Above: A North American F-86A-5 of the USAF 116th Squadron. It is fitted with two 454-litre (100-Imp gal) combat tanks
Above right: The F-86D-20 with its plastic radome over the nose-mounted AN-APG-36 search radar. This gave it an all-weather capability; and (below) the F-86E-10/ Canadair Mk 4, a Canadian built version
Below: With its ammunition bays open, an F-86F-30 stands on a rain washed airfield in the USA. The doors to the ammunition bays were a useful step up to the cockpit

Above: The nosewheel of an F-86; during the Korean War Sabres operated from crude airstrips which placed considerable stress on the landing gear
Right: A rear view of an F-86F during routine servicing

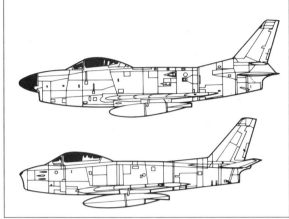

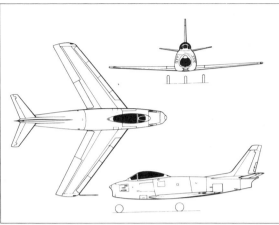

F-86F

Type: single-seat fighter-bomber
Maker: North American Aviation Inc
Span: 11.91 m (39 ft 1 in)
Length: 11.44 m (37 ft 6½ in)
Height: 4.46 m (14 ft 8 in)
Wing area: 26.75 m² (288 sq ft)
Weight: maximum 9349 kg (20 610 lb); empty 5046 kg (11 125 lb)
Powerplant: one 2710-kg (5970-lb) st General Electric J47-GE-27 turbojet
Performance: maximum speed 1091 km/h (678 mph) at sea level; range 2010 km (1250 miles); service ceiling 15 240 m (50 000 ft)
Armament: six M3 12.7-mm (0.5-in) guns; two Sidewinder missiles, two 454-kg (1000-lb) bombs, one 545-kg (1202-lb) Mk 6 20-KT Special (nuclear) store or eight rockets under wings
Crew: 1
Production: 1840

and for these production aircraft the General Electric J47-GE-1 of 2200 kg (4850 lb) st had been chosen. The first P-86A, with the J47 engine, flew on May 18, 1948. Four months later, on September 15, an F-86A (the designation having been changed just after the first production machine flew) established a world speed record at 1079.809 km/h (670.981 mph). Once production was in full swing deliveries were rapid, and by the end of 1949 two full fighter groups had been equipped, and another was converting. A total of 554 F-86As were built by North American, with successive batches being powered by the 2359-kg (5200-lb) J47-GE-3, -7, -9, and -13 engines.

The F-86C underwent considerable modification and the P-86B was cancelled: the nose intake was replaced by flush side intakes designed by NACA, twin mainwheels were fitted, the wing span was increased to 11.8 m (38 ft 9 in), and the length increased to 13.4 m (44 ft 1 in). The Pratt & Whitney J48-P-6 of 2835 kg (6250 lb) thrust, with afterburner, was fitted. The designation was changed to F-93. The first prototype YF-93A flew on January 25, 1950, but this version did not go into production.

A new day fighter version, the F-86E with the J47-GE-13 turbojet, went into production in December 1950. As a result of research experience with the Bell X-1 and XP-86, the control system had been modified to incorporate an all-flying tail with linked elevators, power boosted and with artificial feel. North American delivered 333 F-

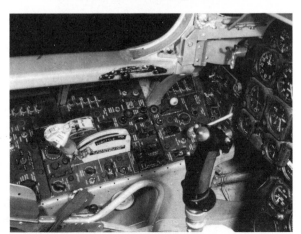

Above left: A pilot sits ready in his F-86F-30; he is wearing a 'bone dome' helmet, anti-glare visor and oxygen mask
Above: Nose of an F-86E showing the left group of six M3 12.7-mm (0.50-in) machine-guns which gave a tight group in air-to-air combat
Left: Part of the left side of the cockpit of an F-86H showing the external stores instruments, radio, throttle, cockpit heating and control column

Above left: 49-1131 was used by Air Training Command to test the use of 127-mm (5-inch) rockets
Above: The gun 'doors' on a F-86A-1

86Es between March 1951 and April 1952. A further 60 were bought from the first licensee, Canadair of Montreal, for the USAF, and another 60 for the Mutual Defense Aid Program. Canadair went on to build 1815 F-86s, most of them as improved and much more powerful versions with the Orenda engine; 445 with the J47 were sold to the RAF and later models went to the Luftwaffe.

F-86A units saw operational service in Korea. They went into action immediately after their arrival in December 1950 to counter the threat of the MiG-15, which had a performance superior to that of the F-80 and the F-84. The F-86 soon made its mark, and the first recorded swept-wing combat occurred on December 17, 1950, when four MiGs were shot down by the 4th Fighter-Interceptor Wing. The MiG was marginally better than the F-86 in a dogfight but this was more than offset by the well-trained and highly skilled American pilots, who thus gained ascendancy.

The Korean war was responsible for the opening of a second Sabre production line by North American at Columbus. The first Columbus version was the F-86F, which, to improve high-altitude manoeuvrability at the expense of greater field length, had a new wing leading edge with a 152-mm (6-in) extension at the root and 76-mm (3-in) at the tip; the slats were eliminated and small boundary layer fences were fitted. It was powered by a 2708-kg (5970-lb) st J47-GE-27 engine which gave a small increase in performance. The first flight was made at Los Angeles on March 19, 1952, and deliveries

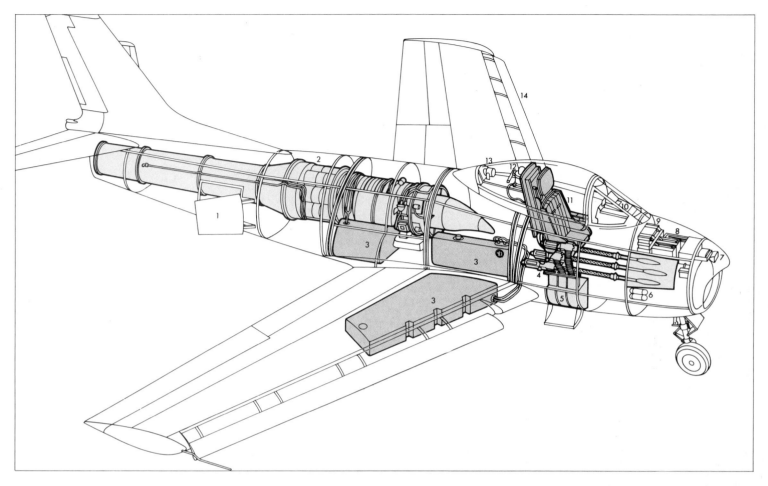

from Columbus were made in the same year. Production of the F-86F ended in 1956, by which time 1840 had been built at Los Angeles, and 700 at Columbus. Many were rebuilt with extended wing leading edges and tips.

The F-86H variant with a 4218-kg (9300-lb) General Electric J73-GE-3 was the final production model. Wing span was increased by 0.61 m (2 ft), fuselage length by 356 mm (14 in), and there was a larger tailplane, stronger undercarriage, and four 20-mm (0.79-in) M-39 revolver cannon in place of the six machine-guns in the nose. It was produced at Columbus and first flew on September 4, 1953. The total built was 473.

A completely redesigned all-weather interceptor variant was designated F-86D. Almost all of the

airframe and systems were redesigned to contain the Hughes E-4 fire-control system (APG-36 radar) for collision-course attacks. The engine was a 3470-kg (7650-lb) J47-GE-17 with afterburner. Armament comprised a retractable tray carrying 24 69-mm (2.75-in) rockets. Deliveries of 2504, the largest run of one version, began in March 1951.

A new world air speed record of 1124.104 km/h (698.505 mph) was established on November 19, 1952, by an F-86D.

The F-86L was an updated version of the F-86D, using the new wing of the rebuilt F-86F. The F-86K was a simplified version with four 20-mm (0.79-in) cannon instead of rockets and the Hughes fire-control system for traditional attack from astern, and was designed for NATO forces.

Above left: A 454-litre (100-Imp gal) drop-tank and napalm cannister on a Sabre
Above: An F-86A with its range of underwing stores including drop and ferry tanks, bombs, rockets, and the machine-guns with their ammunition in front

FJ Fury, North American

FIRST FLIGHT 1946

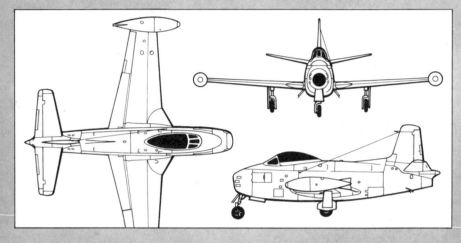

NORTH American received a contract for their first jet fighter from the US Navy on January 1, 1945. Known by the company designation NA-134, it was a conventional straight-wing design, powered by a General Electric J35 axial turbojet. It had an air intake in the nose, with the cockpit mounted above the intake duct. Officially designated the XFJ-1, the company received a production order for 100 on May 28, 1945. With a J35-GE-2 of 1733 kg (3820 lb) st as powerplant, the first prototype flew on November 27, 1946. An armament of six 12.7-mm (0.5-in) machine-guns were mounted in the side walls of the air intake.

The production FJ-1 was fitted with the Allison J35-A-2 and the first deliveries were made in March, 1948. As more advanced aircraft were then under development the contract was cut to 30 machines. Only one naval squadron was equipped with the Fury, and the FJ-1 became the first jet fighter in operational service at sea.

North American had had plans for a naval F-86 early in 1951, and the US Navy ordered three prototypes in March 1951. Two of the prototypes were basically F-86Es with arrester hooks, catapult points and a lengthened nosewheel leg to increase the angle of attack and to reduce the speed during carrier take-offs and landings. The third prototype XFJ-2B had four 20-mm (0.79-in) cannon fitted instead of the machine-guns, and was the first of the trio to fly on December 27, 1951. Carrier trials were carried out in December 1952 for the two XFJ-2s, using the USS *Coral Sea*.

A production order for 300 FJ-2s was received on February 10, 1951, and this work went to the North American Columbus plant, which was engaged already in the production of F-86s. The production FJ-2 had several major modifications for their naval role, which included folding wings, AN/APG-30 radar, increased wheel track and the 2722-kg (6000-lb) st J47-GE-2 powerplant. Although the first FJ-2 Fury was completed in the autumn of 1952, the programme was slowed by the requirements of the F-86 production and only 25 Furies had been built by the end of 1953. The contract was cut to 200 after the end of the Korean war. All FJ-2s went to Marine units, the deliveries beginning in January 1954.

Development of a new variant of the FJ-2 began in March 1952 with a Wright J65-W-2 engine of 3538 kg (7800 lb) st. A contract was placed on April 18, 1952, for 389 machines with the designation FJ-3. A trial installation was made in an FJ-2 which flew on July 3, 1953. The production FJ-3 had an enlarged inlet and air duct to feed the J65-W-4 engine of 3470 kg (7650 lb) st. The first FJ-3 flew on December 11, 1953, and deliveries to the navy began in September 1954. A further contract for 214 aircraft, which was reduced to 149, brought the total FJ-3 order to 538, the second batch being fitted with the J65-W-4D. A total of 21 squadrons flew the type, the delivery of which was completed in August 1956.

During the production run several major modifications were made, some of which were retrofits. The original leading-edge slats were replaced by extended leading edges with fences and extra fuel in the wing. All aircraft had two underwing store stations, and two more were added, with provision for carrying the Sidewinder missile. A total of 80 Sidewinder-equipped Furies, designated FJ-3M were produced, entering service in 1956.

The final variant of the Fury had a 50% increase in internal fuel capacity, which meant an extensive redesign of the fuselage. It also had a new thinner wing with mid-span ailerons and inboard high-lift flaps, wider-track landing gear and thinner tail surfaces. Production FJ-4s appeared in February 1955 with the 3493-kg (7700-lb) st J65-W-16A.

The FJ-4B version which followed was an attack fighter with a stiffened wing, with six pylons and a LABS (low-altitude bombing system) to deliver a tactical nuclear weapon. Production of the 222 ordered ended in May 1958.

FJ-1

Type: single-seat naval fighter
Maker: North American Aviation Inc
Span: 11.63 m (38 ft 2 in)
Length: 10.49 m (34 ft 5 in)
Height: 4.52 m (14 ft 10 in)
Wing area: 20.53 m² (221 sq ft)
Weight: maximum 7076 kg (15 600 lb); empty 4011 kg (8843 lb)
Powerplant: one 1815-kg (4000-lb) st Allison J35-A-2 turbojet
Performance: maximum speed 880 km/h (547 mph) at 2743 m (9000 ft); range 1900 km (1180 miles); service ceiling 9753 m (32 000 ft)
Armament: six 12.7-mm (0.5-in) guns
Crew: 1
Production: 30

Above: An FJ-4B, the attack
version of the Fury which
could carry a tactical nuclear
weapon. It is seen here armed
with napalm
Left: The cockpit interior of
an FJ Fury; panels to the left
and right have additional
controls

Above: The FJ-1 which
became the first jet fighter to
serve at sea under operational
conditions
Far left: The lengthened
nosewheel which increased
the angle of attack and
reduced speed during carrier
landings and take-offs
Left: An FJ-3 with its wings
folded and arrester hook and
airbrakes deployed

F9F Panther, Grumman

FIRST FLIGHT 1947

IN the early days of jet-engine development aircraft designers had a difficult task. Many of the powerplants on offer were low on thrust. When Grumman's first jet fighter was on the drawing board, in the closing days of the war, one of the engines available was the 680-kg (1500-lb) st Westinghouse J30, of which four were needed.

On April 22, 1946, a contract was issued for the XF9F-1, as the design was designated, but the Grumman design team became unhappy about the installation of four engines in the wing. They decided to use a single engine with a conventional fuselage installation, and chose the Rolls-Royce Nene. The new single-engine design was for a day fighter, designated XF9F-2.

The first of two prototypes made its first flight on

November 24, 1947. A third prototype XF9F-3 flew on August 16, 1948: this variant had an alternative engine, the 2087-kg (4600-lb) st Allison J33-A-8. Initial production contracts were placed for 47 F9F-2 and 54 F9F-3s with J33-A-8 engines. Production of the two Panther variants was simultaneous and both flew in November 1948, but the J42 version proved superior and its production proceeded on schedule, while the F9F-3s were converted to 2s and further contracts brought the total on order to 437. All production aircraft were fitted with permanent wingtip tanks. Deliveries to operational units commenced in May 1949.

It was planned to use the Allison J33-A-C6 in 73 F9F-4s, but these machines were absorbed in contracts for a total of 655 F9F-5s with the 2835-kg

Above: The F9F-8 shown in QF-9J (RPV, remotely-piloted drone) configuration
Below: An F9F-6P the swept-wing photo-reconnaissance version equipped with nose-mounted cameras
Below right: Seconds after landing an F9F-2 Cougar receives marshalling instructions from a crewman aboard a US Navy carrier. The pilot has begun to fold the wings to assist parking on the flight-deck

(6250-lb) st J48-P-2, J48-P-4 or J48-P-6A engines. The F9F-5 had a 0.61-cm (2-ft) extension of the fuselage and a taller fin. This batch was first flown on December 21, 1949, and included some camera-equipped F9F-5Ps.

The F9F-2 Panthers became the first US Navy jets to be used in combat when they went into action over Korea on July 3, 1950, and in November that year claimed their first victory over an enemy jet aircraft, a MiG-15.

The Panthers were succeeded by a swept-wing version and were adapted for special duties, one of which was the F9F-5KD, modified for use as a target drone or drone controller.

About a year after the Panther entered service, proposals were made for the development of a swept-wing version and a contract was received from the navy on March 2, 1951. Designated the XF9F-6, this variant comprised the fuselage and tail unit of the Panther with a J48-P-8 of 3289 kg (7250 lb) st, and a completely new, broader wing swept back 35°. The new wing had enlarged trailing-edge flaps and leading-edge slats, wing fences and spoilers for roll control. Tip tanks were not fitted, but the warload was unchanged.

The maiden flight of the XF9F-6 was made on September 20, 1951. Although the same designation series was used for both straight and swept-wing versions, Grumman continued their cat nomenclature and called their new machine the Cougar. Evaluation by the navy was completed during 1952 and they began to take delivery of the F9F-6s in November of that year. The total pro-

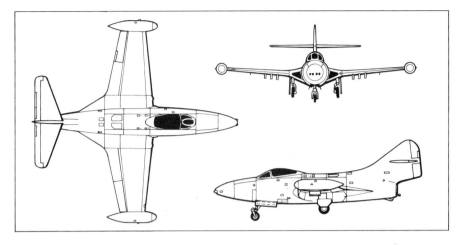

duction of the F9F-6 was 706, and the F9F-7 with Allison J33-A-16A engines totalled 168. A few Cougars were camera-equipped with the designation F9F-6P; later some surplus aircraft with the designation F9F-6K and F9F-6K2 were used as target drones, and drone directors were F9F-6Ds.

The F9F-8 was the final single-seat variant of the Cougar which had a 23-mm (8-in) fuselage extension and wing modifications to increase the chord by 15%. Among the 712 built were reconnaissance and attack versions.

The last version of the Cougar was a two-seat trainer with an 86.4-cm (34-in) longer fuselage to accommodate the tandem seats, and it had the designation F9F-8T. It first flew on April 4, 1956, and 399 were built.

F9F-5

Type: single-seat naval fighter
Maker: Grumman Aircraft Engineering Corporation
Span: 11.6 m (38 ft)
Length: 11.83 m (38 ft 10 in)
Height: 3.73 m (12 ft 3 in)
Wing area: 23.23 m² (250 sq ft)
Weight: maximum 8492 kg (18 721 lb); empty 4603 lb (10 147 lb)
Powerplant: one 2835-kg (6250-lb) st Pratt & Whitney J48-P-6A turbojet
Performance: maximum speed 1005 km/h (625 mph); range 2090 km (1300 miles); service ceiling over 13 000 m (42 650 ft)
Armament: four fixed forward-firing 20-mm (0.79-in) guns; up to 907-kg (2000-lb) bombs or rockets
Crew: 1
Production: 1385 (all types)

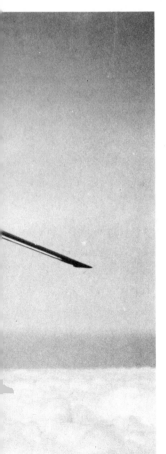

F2H Banshee, McDonnell

FIRST FLIGHT 1947

THE McDonnell FH-1 Phantom was the first jet fighter to operate from US Navy carriers and as such it was a success, but it was slow compared with other jet fighters of that era. The US Navy Bureau of Aeronautics invited the manufacturer to design a successor to the FH-1 and a Letter of Intent was issued on March 22, 1945, to cover the design and construction of three XF2D-1s.

The design team, headed by Herman D Barkley, produced a design very similar to the Phantom, to be powered by two 1361-kg (3000-lb) thrust Westinghouse axial turbojets mounted in the wingroot fillets. A longer fuselage provided room for greater internal fuel capacity. The location of the four 20-mm (0.79-in) cannon was changed from the top of the nose to the bottom, to shield the pilot from the glare during night firing. Mock-up inspection during April 1945 cleared this configuration and other major internal details. Despite this, construction of the prototypes did not begin until the end of January 1946, due to the postwar slowdown. The Phantom FH-1 had given McDonnell the reputation of being among the leaders in the manufacture of advanced naval fighters and the XF2D-1 Banshee was to endorse this opinion.

The first prototype, redesignated XF2H-1, made its maiden flight on January 11, 1947, with Robert M Eldholm as pilot. It was powered by two 1361-kg thrust Westinghouse J34-WE-22 turbojets. Flight trials resulted in a decision to fit a tailplane without dihedral on the production aircraft.

Except for the tail modification, the first production version of the F2H-1 was identical to the prototype. A batch of 56 were ordered and were delivered between August 1948 and August 1949. The F2H-2 version had a slightly elongated fuselage to house more fuel and had 757-litre (167-Imp gal) wingtip tanks fitted. Uprated J34-WE-34 engines of 1474 kg (3250 lb) thrust were installed. Ordered in May 1948, the first F2H-2 flew on August 18, 1949, and a total of 308 were built.

Three derivatives of the F2H-2 Banshee were the F2H-2B fighter-bomber fitted with wing racks for two 227-kg (500-lb) bombs (25 built), the F2H-2N which was the first single-seat, carrier-borne US Navy jet night fighter, with a slightly longer nose to house the Westinghouse APQ-41 radar (14 built), and the F2H-2P unarmed reconnaissance version with a longer nose to house six cameras (89 built).

The F2H-3 was an all-weather fighter with a fuselage 2.4 m (8 ft) longer than the -2, allowing the internal fuel capacity to be doubled and fitted with APQ-41 radar. Wing racks for two 227-kg (500-lb) or eight 113-kg (250-lb) bombs were fitted. The tail was redesigned, with the tailplane again having dihedral. The first production F2H-3, ordered in July 1950, made its first flight on March 29, 1952, and the last of the 250 built was delivered on September 24, 1953.

The last variant was the F2H-4, which differed from the -3 in having 1633-kg (3600-lb) thrust J34-WE-38 engines as powerplants and a APG-37 radar, 150 of which were built. Their tailplanes had triangular root extensions.

The Banshee saw operational service in Korea, where its good high-altitude performance led to use as an escort fighter. Five naval squadrons flew the F2H-2s from carriers of Task Force 77, while a marine unit flew the reconnaissance version (2P) from Pohang airfield. After Korea the -2s began to be phased out of first-line service, but the 2Ps remained in service for many years.

From mid 1952 until the autumn of 1959 the F2H-3 and F2H-4 Banshees were the standard all-weather carrier fighters of the US Navy, and they continued to be used by reserve units until the mid 1960s, redesignated F-2C and -2D, with Sidewinder missiles.

In the late 1950s the Banshee F2H-3 (F-2C) became the first operational jet of the Royal Canadian Navy, which had received 39, and was deployed on HMCS *Bonaventure* until September, 1962.

Top: A Banshee in the midnight blue of the US Navy. It saw action in Korea operating from carriers and airfields. The Banshee was the first operational jet with the Royal Canadian Navy when it served aboard the carrier *Bonaventure*
Above: A McDonnell F2H-2 Banshee. Its longer fuselage and tip-tanks were just the first step in giving the Banshee much greater fuel capacity

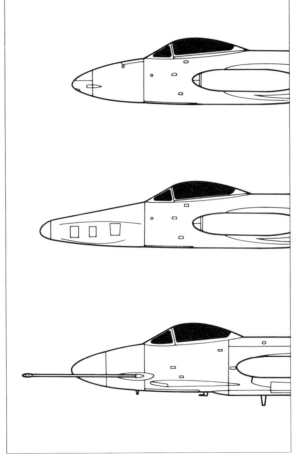

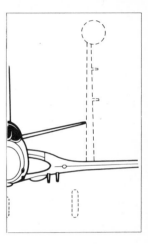

Top: A pilot taxies his F2H-2 Banshee off the hardstand before taking off from a US Navy Air Station in 1950
Left: (top to bottom) The nose of the F2H-2; the lengthened nose of the F2H-2P which contained three reconnaissance cameras; the completely redesigned F2H-4, which had much greater fuel capacity and an inflight refuelling probe
Above: The wing-fold on the F2H-4 which reduced the span so that the aircraft could be fitted onto the elevator on a carrier

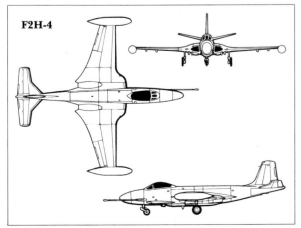

F2H-4

F2H-2

Type: single-seat naval fighter
Maker: McDonnell Aircraft Company
Span: 13.66 m (44 ft 10 in)
Length: 12.24 m (40 ft 2 in)
Height: 4.39 m (14 ft 5 in)
Wing area: 27.31 m² (294 sq ft)
Weight: maximum 10 120 kg (22 312 lb); empty 4442 kg (9794 lb)
Powerplant: two 1474-kg (3250-lb) st Westinghouse J34-WE-34 turbojets
Performance: maximum speed 945 km/h (587 miles) at sea level; range 2375 km (1475 miles); service ceiling 14 785 m (48 500 ft)
Armament: four 20-mm (0.79-in) cannon mounted in lower nose
Crew: 1
Production: 364

MiG-15, Mikoyan

FIRST FLIGHT 1947

THE MiG-15 was built following a requirement for a single-seat fighter with a maximum speed of Mach 0.9, good rate-of-climb to 10 000 m (32 800 ft), a minimum duration of 1 hour and large-calibre cannon armament.

The powerplant was a Rolls-Royce Nene engine, still four years away from British service, handed over in conjunction with the 1946 Anglo-Soviet Trade Agreement. A German-derived engine intended to develop 2000 kg (4409 lb) was to have been used, but development had hardly begun when the Mikoyan-Gurevich design bureau was offered the amazing windfall of the British engine. The fuselage had to be enlarged to accommodate the centrifugal Nene.

The first flight is believed to have been made on July 2, 1947. Following the failure of the prototype, designated S-1310, during low-speed tests, boundary-layer fences were added to the wing and anhedral replaced dihedral. Other modifications included shortening of the rear fuselage, a reduction in the length of the tailpipe from 3.8 m (12 ft 5½ in) to 2 m (6 ft 6¾ in), lowering of the horizontal tail and sweep-back of fin and rudder.

The modified prototype was designated S-01 and first flew on December 30, 1947. A major problem was the tendency of the aircraft to move out of a tight turn into a spin, but this was overcome temporarily by the use of anti-spin rockets.

The MiG-15 was put into production and the initial aircraft were delivered to the Russian air force in the latter part of 1948. This was six years

Below left: A MiG-15*bis* which was flown to Kimpo airfield by a North Korean pilot, Lieutenant Ro Kun Suk. It was evaluated by USAF pilots at Wright Patterson Air Force Base
Below right: A crewman doubles away from an East German MiG-15P as it taxies onto the runway

MiG-15*bis*

1 Bifurcated engine air intake
2 Landing light (moved to left wing root on later production aircraft)
3 Combat camera fairing
4 Accumulator
5 Radio transmitter
6 Radio receiver
7 Armour-glass windscreen
8 Gyro gunsight
9 Right electrics control panel
10 Ejector seat
11 Aft-sliding canopy (open position)
12 VHF blade antenna
13 Wing fence
14 Slipper-type drop-tank
15 Pitot pressure head
16 Compass unit
17 Right navigation light
18 Right aileron
19 Main fuel tank
20 Rear fuselage attachment joint
21 Engine bearers
22 Klimov VK-1 turbojet
23 Control rods
24 Rear fuselage frames
25 Fin mainspar
26 Rudder balance weight
27 Rudder (upper section)
28 Tail navigation light
29 Elevator trim tab
30 Left elevator
31 Single-spar tailplane
32 Jetpipe fairing
33 Air brake (partly extended)
34 Walkway (rubber coated)
35 Split landing flap
36 Trim operating mechanism
37 Aileron operating rods
38 Trim tab
39 Left aileron
40 Left rear spar
41 Left navigation light
42 Main spar
43 Rib
44 Attachment for slipper tank
45 Inward-retracting main undercarriage member
46 Mainspar branch
47 Twin air channel
48 Wing centre section
49 Fuel tank
50 Canopy jettison knob
51 Control column
52 Radio altimeter
53 Left air duct
54 Gun pack (shown cable-lowered for servicing)
55 Ammunition tank
56 Twin 23-mm NS-23 cannon
57 Single 37-mm N-37 cannon
58 Forward-retracting nosewheel
59 Nosewheel doors
60 Blast protection panel

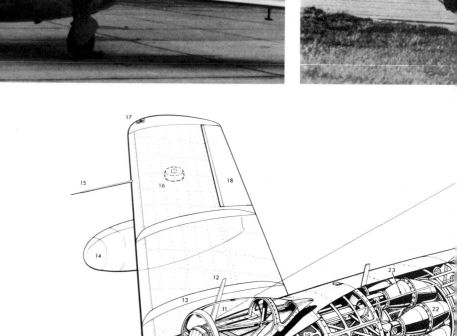

before any British swept-wing fighter entered service.

The powerplant for early production aircraft was the RD-45F engine, based closely on the Nene and made without obtaining a licence. A later version, the MiG-15*bis* (MiG-15SD) was powered by V K Klimov's later development of the Nene, the VK-1, which developed 3000 kg (6614 lb) with water injection.

Initial armament of the MiG-15 consisted of two nose-mounted 23-mm (0.9-in) NS-23 cannon. This later became one 37-mm (1.46-in) N-37 cannon situated on the right-hand side, and two 23-mm (0.9-in) NS-23 cannon on the left-hand side. There was underwing provision for drop-tanks, rockets or bombs. MiG-15*bis* production aircraft later had 23-mm (0.9-in) NR-23 revolver cannon instead of the NS-23 cannon.

Several other versions were produced: a trainer, the MiG-15UTI, MiG-15T, MiG-15*bis*T; a two-seat all-weather fighter designated SP-5, the MiG-15SB, and a Polish version of the MiG-15*bis*, designated SBLim-2.

The MiG-15 or MiG-15*bis* were used by the air forces of Albania, Algeria, Bulgaria, Cambodia, Czechoslovakia, China, Cuba, Finland, East Germany, Hungary, Iraq, North Korea, Morocco, Poland, Romania, Somalia, Syria, Tanganyika and the United Arab Emirates. More than 5000 fighters were built and an even greater number of trainers. Many of the latter may be rebuilt fighters, and several thousand UTIs are still used.

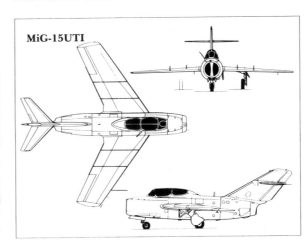

MiG-15UTI

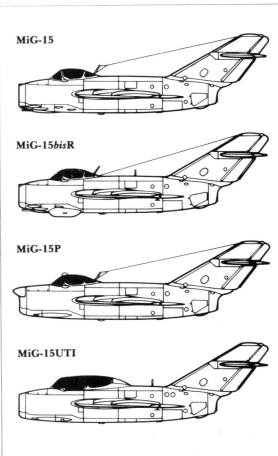

MiG-15

MiG-15*bis*R

MiG-15P

MiG-15UTI

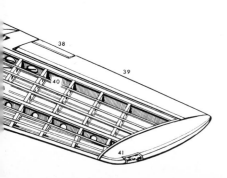

MiG-15

Type: single-seat jet fighter
Maker: Mikoyan-Gurevich Design Bureau
Span: 10.1 m (33 ft 1½ in)
Length: 11.1 m (36 ft 5 in)
Height: 3.4 m (11 ft 2 in)
Wing area: 23.7 m² (255 sq ft)
Weight: maximum 5120 kg (11 270 lb); empty 3780 kg (8335 lb)
Powerplant: one 2725-kg (6000-lb) st RD-45F centrifugal-flow turbojet
Performance: maximum speed 1072 km/h (670 mph); range 1920 km (1193 miles) at 380 km/h (236 mph); service ceiling 15 550 m (51 000 ft)
Armament: two Nudelmann-Suranov 23-mm (0.91-in) nose-mounted cannon (left-hand side) and one 37-mm (1.46-in) Nudelmann cannon nose-mounted on the right-hand side; underwing provision for rockets or two 454-kg (1000-lb) bombs.
Crew: 1
Production: not available

Left: MiG-15 variations. The MiG-15*bis*R fighter-reconnaissance aircraft was equipped with camera pack below the cannon magazines; the MiG-15P all-weather interceptor had twin 23-mm (0.91-in) cannon and Izumrud AI radar; the two seat MiG-15UTI trainer was normally fitted with underwing tanks

167

MiG-17, Mikoyan

FIRST FLIGHT 1949

FOLLOWING the success of the MiG-15, the MiG bureau began to refine the design, with the aim of improving the all-round performance of the aircraft, especially in the area of transonic performance. The fuselage was lengthened and a new wing of thinner section and greater sweep, reaching a maximum of 45°, was designed, improving the compressibility characteristics.

Powered by a Klimov VK-1 turbojet, the prototype aircraft, initially designated SI, flew in January 1949, some nine months after the MiG-15 entered service. As a result of experience in the Korean war, the armament was modified and several other changes were incorporated, including a fixed-incidence tailplane with a greater sweepback. The refined design is claimed to have exceeded the speed of sound in level flight in February 1950.

The new aircraft, now designated MiG-17 and codenamed Fresco-A by NATO, entered service with the Soviet air force in 1952, in preference to the Yak-50. The Klimov VK-1 turbojet, rated at 2700 kg (5952 lb) st, was retained and the armament consisted of one 37-mm (1.46-in) N-37 and two 23-mm (0.9-in) NR-23 cannons (as on the MiG-15SD or MiG-15*bis*), plus four underwing hardpoints – rockets or bombs on the inner pylons and drop-tanks on the outer ones.

The MiG-17P was fitted with Izumrud (Emerald) S-band radar, and codenamed Scan Fix by NATO. The main antenna was positioned on the splitter plate on the air intake, with the ranging element mounted on top of the intake. This model

was codenamed Fresco-B, and featured a further fuselage lengthening of 127 mm (5 in), additional cockpit glazing and the fuselage dive-brakes mounted further forward.

In 1954, the MiG-17F Fresco-C was put on the production line. The original engine was replaced by the VK-1F turbojet, rated at 3380 kg (7451 lb) with reheat. The rear fuselage was cut-back to expose the afterburner nozzle, and the armament was modified to three NR-23 cannon, each with 100 rounds of ammunition. This version was built in large numbers and supplied to Afghanistan, Albania, Bulgaria, Cuba, Egypt, Hungary, Indonesia, Iraq, Morocco, North Korea, North Vietnam, Romania and Syria. It was licence-built in Czechoslovakia as the S104, in Poland as the LIM-

Below: Pilots board their MiG-17PFUs in rather antique flying overalls and helmets. Their aircraft had a powerful armament of four AA-1 (Alkali) AAMs, which were beam riding on I/J-band radar

MiG-17PFU

1 Rudder upper hinge/balance
2 Rudder (upper section)
3 Passive tail-warning radar unit
4 Rear navigation light
5 Fixed incidence tailplane
6 Elevator control linkage
7 Control lines
8 Tailfin construction
9 Transformer
10 Gyro compass
11 Magnetic amplifier for gyro
12 Tail-warning master unit
13 Rudder (lower section)
14 Rudder trim tab
15 Tailpipe shroud
16 Afterburner nozzle
17 Right airbrake
18 Tail skid
19 Ventral strake
20 Airbrake hydraulic activator
21 Control linkage assembly
22 Rear fuselage structure
23 Afterburner pipe
24 Aft fuselage fuel tank
25 Afterburner outer casing
26 Klimov VK-1F turbojet
27 Inspection panel
28 IFF antenna
29 Engine intake grille
30 Inspection panel
31 Engine auxiliaries
32 Aft/forward fuselage breakpoint
33 Main fuselage fuel tank
34 Intake trunking
35 VHF antenna
36 Canopy track
37 Bulkhead
38 Ejector seat
39 Left control console (throttle quadrant)
40 Pilot's headrest
41 Canopy heating web
42 Rear-view mirror
43 Rocket-sight
44 Radar-scope shroud

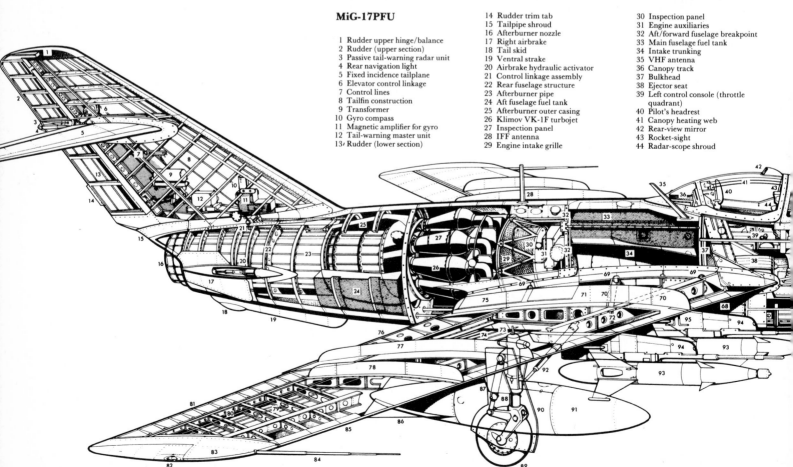

5P and in Communist China as the Shenyang F-4. It has been flown in action in the Middle East (against Israel), in North Vietnam and in Nigeria (during the civil war against Biafra).

The next variant was the MiG-17PF Fresco-D, entering service from 1955 as an all-weather fighter with improved Izumrud Scan Fix radar operating in both the S-band and X-band. The MiG-17PFU Fresco-E was similar to the -D, but with the gun armament replaced by four underwing AA-1 Alkali beam-riding air-to-air missiles, projecting forward of the wing leading edge, and the afterburner deleted.

Initially used as an interceptor, the MiG-17 was gradually switched to ground-attack as the MiG-19 Farmer entered service. Some MiG-17s were fitted with cameras in the forward fuselage, with one gun deleted, and used for reconnaissance.

Many of the Polish LIM-5P Fresco-C models had additional fuel tanks, twin-wheel main undercarriage with low-pressure tyres (which retracted into a larger centre section of reinforced plastic) fitted, being redesignated LIM-5M. The LIM-6 had additional stores pylons, rocket-assisted take-off packs, and brake parachutes installed; and those with modified ordnance racks were known as LIM-6*bis*. The Polish reconnaissance model was the LIM-6R. These remained in Polish service until replaced by Sukhoi Su-20 Fitter-Cs.

Production of the MiG-17 Fresco series was completed in 1958, and although withdrawn from Soviet service in the late 1960s, it still remains in worldwide service as a ground-attack fighter.

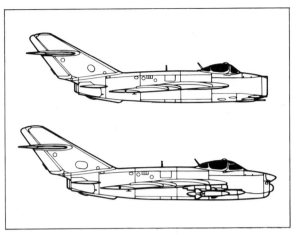

Left: The initial production MiG-17 (Fresco-A) which had the same engine as the MiG-15; and (below) the MiG-17PFU (Fresco-E) with nose radar and AAMs in place of cannon
Below: MiG-17F fighters on a winter patrol

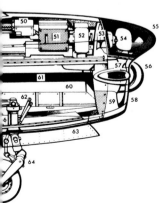

45 Enlarged cockpit quarter-light
46 Instrument panel
47 Control column
48 Rudder pedals
49 Windscreen
50 RDF ranging unit
51 VHF transmitter/receiver
52 Accumulator
53 Radar ranging unit
54 Radar scanner
55 Extended upper intake lip
56 AI scanner in central intake bullet
57 Combat camera housing
58 Bifurcated intake
59 Intake centre-body
60 Centre-section nosewheel well

61 Intake trunking
62 Nosewheel retraction radii
63 Nosewheel doors
64 Nosewheel fork
65 Forward-retracting nosewheel
66 Nosewheel strut
67 Forward fuselage members
68 Inboard-section wing leading edge
69 Three wing/fuselage attachment points
70 'Y'-section inner main spar
71 Inboard wing fence
72 Forward main spar
73 Undercarriage indicator spigot
74 Inner wing skinning
75 Split landing flap (inner section)
76 Split landing flap (structure outer section)
77 Centre wing fence
78 Outboard wing fence
79 Wing construction
80 Rear spar
81 Aileron construction
82 Right navigation light
83 Wingtip
84 Right pitot head
85 Outboard-section wing leading edge
86 Auxiliary-tank fin assembly
87 Triple-strut auxiliary-tank bracing
88 Mainwheel leg
89 Right mainwheel
90 Mainwheel door
91 Auxiliary tank
92 Mainwheel retraction rod
93 Alkali-type beam-riding air-to-air missiles
94 Weapon pylons
95 Altimeter radio dipole (left outboard/right inboard)

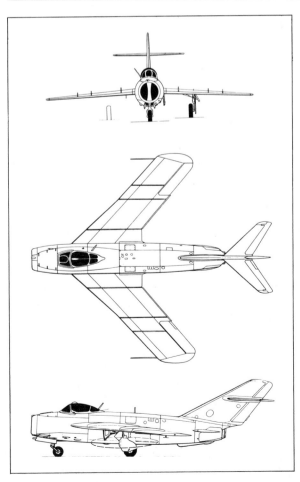

MiG-17F

Type: single-seat interceptor and ground-attack fighter
Maker: Mikoyan-Gurevich Design Bureau
Span: 9.63 m (31 ft 7¼ in)
Length: 11.09 m (36 ft 4½ in)
Height: 3.35 m (11 ft)
Wing area: 22.6 m² (243 sq ft)
Weight: maximum 6075 kg (13 393 lb); empty 3930 kg (8664 lb)
Powerplant: one Klimov VK-1F turbojet, rated at 2600 kg (5732 lb) st (dry) and 3380 kg (7452 lb) with reheat
Performance: maximum speed 1145 km/h (711 mph) at 3000 m (9840 ft); range (internal fuel) at 5000 m (16 400 ft), 680 km (422 miles); service ceiling 16 600 m (54 460 ft)
Armament three 23-mm (0.9-in) NR-23 cannon; two 250-kg (551-lb) bombs; four UV-16-57 rocket pods or four S-24 unguided rockets
Crew: 1
Production: minimum 9000

DH. 112 Venom, de Havilland

FIRST FLIGHT 1949

THE DH.112, or Vampire Mk 8 as it was known, differed from previous marks, having a thinner wing with a new aerofoil section and a thickness/chord ratio of 10%. The wing was slightly enlarged and had hardpoints to carry loads of up to 907 kg (2000 lb) on each wing. Drop-tanks on the wingtips contained 355 litres (78 Imp gal).

The Vampire Mk 8 was later renamed the Venom because its new powerplant gave it a performance superior to all previous Vampire marks, and also to the Gloster Meteor F.8. The Ghost engine was a little larger than the Goblin, but had 50% more thrust.

The maiden flight by the first prototype was made at Hatfield on September 2, 1949. Deliveries to the RAF began in August 1952. Some 363 Venom FB.1s were produced for the RAF. The FB.4 which followed included improved controls, and an export version, the FB.50, was built under licence in Switzerland.

The prototype Sea Venom made its maiden flight in April 1951. It featured a strengthened undercarriage, arrester hook, catapult spools and folding wings. Designated FAW.20, it was a two-seat aircraft with airborne interception radar mounted in the nose.

The first production Sea Venom FAW.20 flew in March 1953 and the type entered service with 890 Sqn a year later. The two other units to receive FAW.20s were 890 and 891 Sqns, but after problems with hook mountings the type was withdrawn from front-line service in September 1955.

The first production version of the FAW.21 flew in April 1954. It had Martin-Baker Mk 4 ejection seats, improved American APS-57 AI radar, power-operated controls and the Ghost 104 turbojet operated to 2245 kg (4950 lb) st. The tailplane extensions outboard of the fins were deleted and a blown canopy replaced the framed one of the FAW.20.

In May 1955, 809 Sqn became the first Sea Venom FAW.21 unit and a further six squadrons were equipped with the type. It was during the Anglo-French operations against the Egyptians in 1956 that Sea Venoms saw their first action. Number 809 Sqn aboard HMS *Albion* and 892 and 893 Sqns on HMS *Eagle* were deployed against ground targets around the Suez Canal. Using rockets and bombs they attacked a variety of targets including vehicle concentrations, barracks and communications.

The final production variant of the Sea Venom was the FAW.22, which had a Ghost 105 turbojet with 2404 kg (5400 lb) st. The first FAW.22 unit was 894 Sqn and three years later, in 1960, the last operational Sea Venom unit, 891 Sqn, saw action against Yemeni rebels north of Aden.

The Royal Australian Navy bought export versions. The French produced the Sea Venom under licence as the Aquilon (North Wind) and made extensive use of this versatile aircraft. Three major versions the Mk 20, 202 and 203 were built by SNCASE. Operated by land-based Aéronavale squadrons they flew ground-attack missions in Algeria from 1955 until the end of the war. They were withdrawn from French service in 1965.

Right: The family of French-built Sea Venoms, developed and constructed by SNCASE, were named Aquilon (North Wind). Some served with Aéronavale squadrons at Suez and in Algeria
Below: An early Sea Venom FAW.20 gets the 'cut' signal from the batsman during carrier qualification in late 1951

Above: From 1952 the most important RAF contracts concerned the two-seat NF.2 and NF.3 night fighters; this NF.3 served until 1958
Right: The Sea Venom arrester hook which was stowed above the jet nozzle

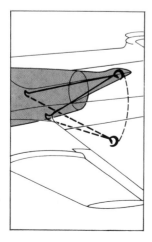

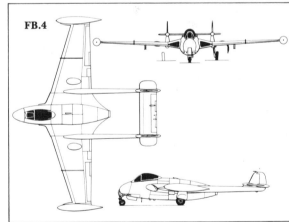

FB.4

FAW.22

Type: two-seat carrier-borne all-weather strike fighter
Maker: de Havilland Aircraft Co Ltd
Span: 13.05 m (42 ft 10 in)
Length: 11.17 m (36 ft 8 in)
Height: 2.59 m (8 ft 6¼ in)
Wing area: 26 m² (279.8 sq ft)
Weight: maximum 7167 kg (15 800 lb); empty not available
Powerplant: one 2404-kg (5300-lb) st de Havilland Ghost 105 turbojet
Performance: maximum speed 925 km/h (575 mph) at sea level; range (with tip tanks) 1529 km (950 miles); service ceiling 15 240 m (50 000 ft)
Armament: four 20-mm (0.79-in) Hispano Mk 5 cannon in lower forward fuselage, plus either two Firestreak missiles, two 454-kg (1000-lb) bombs or eight 27-kg (60-lb) rocket projectiles under each wing
Crew: 2
Production: 368

F3D Skyknight, Douglas

FIRST FLIGHT 1948

THE United States Navy requirement for a jet-engined carrier-borne night fighter was being discussed late in 1945. The aircraft was to be equipped with radar capable of detecting an enemy aircraft at a distance of 201 km (125 miles), flying at 805 km/h (500 mph) and at a height of 12 192 m (40 000 ft). The manufacturers involved were Douglas, Grumman, Curtiss and Fleetwings. In the event Douglas was awarded a contract for three prototype XF3D-1s.

A team led by Ed Heinemann designed the XF3D-1 at the El Segundo Division of Douglas. It was a mid-wing design with two Westinghouse J34-WE-24 turbojet engines of 1361 kg (3000 lb) thrust installed in semi-external nacelles under the fuselage centre section. Side-by-side seating was adopted for the crew, and to save weight a ventral tunnel was provided for emergency escape. Four 20-mm (0.79-in) cannon comprised the armament, and a large Westinghouse APQ-35 search and target-acquisition radar was housed in the nose of the aircraft.

Russel Thaw made the first flight on March 23, 1948, at El Segundo. Flight trials were continued there until October, when the three prototypes were taken to Edwards AFB for service trials. An order for 28 F3D-1 Skyknights was received in June 1948 and the first production aircraft first flew on February 13, 1950. Internal modifications and additional electronic equipment, including ECM and a tail-warning radar increased the gross weight by over 2268 kg (5000 lb).

A second production version of the Skyknight

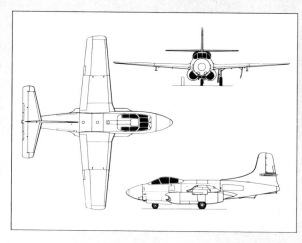

was ordered in August 1949, and it first flew on February 14, 1951. It was powered by two J34-WE-36 engines of 1542 kg (3400 lb) thrust, and was fitted with an automatic pilot, wing spoilers and included other improvements. A total of 237 F3D-2s were built.

The Skyknight saw operational service in Korea with the US Marines. It made history when on the night of November 2, 1952, it shot down a MiG-15, the first successful night interception by a non-German jet. After Korea the Skyknights remained operational with the marines until the mid 1960s, but were rapidly relegated to naval training and other duties. They were redesignated F-10, and in the Vietnam war were gradually restored to operational status in many vital roles.

F3D-2 (F-10B)

Type: two-seat carrier-based night fighter
Maker: Douglas Aircraft Co
Span: 15.25 m (50 ft)
Length: 13.84 m (45 ft 5 in)
Height: 4.9 m (16 ft 1 in)
Wing area: 37.16 m² (400 sq ft)
Weight: maximum 12 180 kg (26 850 lb); empty 8237 kg (18 160 lb)
Powerplant: two 1635-kg (3600-lb) st Westinghouse J34-WE-38 axial-flow turbojets
Performance: maximum speed 909 km/h (565 mph) at 6095 m (20 000 ft); range 1931 km (1200 miles); service ceiling 11 645 m (38 200 ft)
Armament: four 20-mm (0.79-in) cannon; underwing provision for bombs, rockets and other armament stores
Crew: 2
Production: 237

Below left: A clear view of the simple unstreamlined wing and tail design
Below: The US Navy F3D-2T2 Skyknight was an intensively used radar trainer
Bottom: A US Navy F3D-1 Skyknight. Many F3Ds were successful in Korea

F7U Cutlass, Vought

FIRST FLIGHT 1948

Left: An F7U-3 with wings folded is readied for take-off from a carrier deck
Below: An F7U-3 with underwing stores. It could carry missiles, rockets, or cameras in the F7U-3P reconnaissance version

IN postwar Europe, special teams visited all the major German aircraft firms and research institutions. Among the wealth of material found were details of work on tailless designs carried out by the Arado company. This work interested Chance Vought because of the company's long history of research into stubby tailless fighters. After further refinement, Chance Vought produced a wing with very low aspect ratio (3), sweepback of 38°, and almost parallel chord. Elevons were used for control in pitch and roll, and directional control was ensured by fins and rudders mounted on the wing trailing edge.

This layout seemed particularly attractive for a carrier-based fighter, for it offered a high rate of climb and top speed, combined with compactness when the outer wings were folded. Three XF7U-1 prototypes were ordered by the US Navy on June 25, 1946, to be powered by Westinghouse J34-WE-32 engines with afterburners. The maiden flight was made on September 29, 1948, by which time a production order for 14 F7U-1s had been placed, as well as development of the F7U-2 with J34-WE-42 engines and the F7U-3 with J46-WE-8As.

The first production F7U-1 flew on March 1, 1950, and all the 14 aircraft were sent to the Advanced Training Command at Corpus Christi Naval Air Station during 1952. The F7U-2 was cancelled before completion, as Westinghouse had run into trouble with its engines. In the meantime early experience with the F7U-1 airframe led to an extensive redesign for the F7U-3 aircraft. It made its maiden flight on December 20, 1951. The -3 had a new nose shape, redesigned fins and included other changes.

After long delays it was powered by the Allison J35, a larger engine than the J34 or J46. Four squadrons were equippped and production of this definitive version totalled 180.

The F7U-3 had basic armament which comprised four 20-mm (0.79-in) cannon in the upper lips of the intake fairings, with provision for underwing rocket pods or various other stores. Later, provision was made for the Cutlass to carry four Sperry Sparrow I beam-riding missiles in the F7U-3M version, of which 98 were built, and 12 examples of a camera-equipped variant, the F7U-3P, also went into service. Production ended in December 1955, when 290 F7U-3 Cutlass variants had been delivered. They had great performance and were extremely strong, but suffered a higher than average accident rate.

F7U-3

Type: single-seat naval fighter
Maker: Chance Vought Division of United Aircraft Corporation
Span: 11.78 m (38 ft 8 in)
Length: 13.48 m (44 ft 3 in)
Height: 4.45 m (14 ft 7½ in)
Wing area: 46.07 m² (496 sq ft)
Weight: maximum 14 352 kg (31 642 lb); empty 8260 kg (18 210 lb)
Powerplant: two 2086-kg (4600-lb) st Westinghouse J46-WE-8A afterburning turbojets
Performance: maximum speed 1094 km/h (680 mph) at 3048 m (10 000 ft); range 1062 km (660 miles); service ceiling 12 192 m (40 000 ft)
Armament: four 20-mm (0.79-in) guns; provision for four Sparrow I AAMs
Crew: 1
Production: 290

Ouragan, Dassault

FIRST FLIGHT 1949

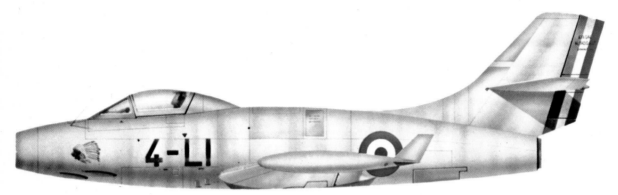

Left: A Dassault MD 450 Ouragan with the insignia of EC 2/4 La Fayette, one of the most famous fighter units of the French air force
Below: An Ouragan of EC 1/12 Cambresis, a squadron formed in April 1952

FOLLOWING his return from German deportation, the French aircraft designer Marcel Bloch changed his name to Dassault, and founded the Societé des Avions Marcel Dassault. The MD 450, initially a private venture, was to become Armée de l'Air's first jet fighter ordered in bulk.

Construction of the first aircraft began in April 1948, two months before the order for three prototypes was received. The MD 450 Ouragan was a low-wing monoplane of all-metal construction, powered by a Rolls-Royce Nene turbojet, built under licence by Hispano-Suiza, with a pressurized cockpit and retractable tricycle undercarriage produced by Messier. The prototype made its maiden flight on February 28, 1949.

The MD 450 Ouragan was armed with four 20-mm (0.79-in) cannon in the lower part of the nose, and had provision for two 454-kg (1000-lb) bombs or 16 rockets under the wings. Wingtip fuel tanks were fitted as standard.

The first of 350 Ouragans for Armée de l'Air entered service with 2ᵉ Escadre de Chasse at Dijon and the 4ᵉ EC at Bremgarten in Germany in 1952. Two other wings were equipped with the type. They were operational for six years until replaced by Mystère IVs.

India ordered the type in 1953, and received some 104 aircraft in all, 71 being new-build aircraft. The first Toofanis, as the Ouragan was known in Indian service, were handed over in June 1953. The Toofani was powered by the Nene 105A, rated at 2135 kg (4707 lb) st. It was replaced in front-line service in 1958 by the Mystère IV.

In 1955, the Israeli air force received 12 new-build aircraft, and went on to take delivery of a further 63 ex-Armée de l'Air Ouragans. These aircraft saw action in the Arab-Israeli war of 1956, and although outclassed by the MiG-15, they could absorb battle damage. They were also used again in 1967. El Salvador was supplied with 18 ex-Israeli Ouragans in 1975.

In France, India and Israel the Ouragan continued to serve in the operational training role long after they had been replaced as front-line fighters. Several of the French pre-production aircraft were used as testbeds for various trials, including an afterburning Nene 102A, rated at 3084 kg (6800 lb) st, twin-wheel undercarriage, parachute-braking, lateral air intakes and twin 30-mm (1.18-in) DEFA cannon installations.

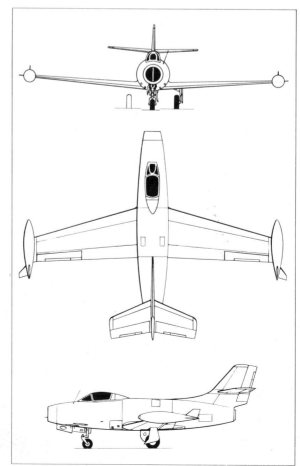

MD 450

Type: single-seat ground-attack fighter
Maker: Avions Marcel Dassault
Span: 13.16 m (43 ft 2 in) (over tip tanks)
Length: 10.73 m (35 ft 2½ in)
Height: 4.14 m (13 ft 7 in)
Wing area: 23.4 m² (252 sq ft)
Weight: maximum 6800 kg (14 991 lb); empty 4142 kg (9131 lb)
Powerplant: one 2300-kg (5070-lb) st Hispano-Suiza (Rolls-Royce) Nene 104B turbojet
Performance: maximum speed 941 km/h (585 mph) at sea level; range 966 km (660 miles); service ceiling 14 935 m (49 000 ft)
Armament: four 20-mm (0.79-in) Hispano Type 404 cannon; 998 kg (2200 lb) of underwing bombs or rockets
Crew: 1
Production: 448

Mystère II, Dassault

FIRST FLIGHT 1951

THE MD 452 Mystère was a continuation of the MD 450 Ouragan design, with a 30° swept-wing. The first prototype Mystère I, powered by an Hispano-Suiza Nene 104B turbojet, first flew from Istres on February 23, 1951, with test pilot Constantin Rozanoff at the controls. The second and third prototypes were powered by licence-built Rolls-Royce Tay 250 turbojets, rated at 2850 kg (6283 lb), again licence-built by Hispano-Suiza.

A further six prototypes, designated Mystère IIA with four 20-mm (0.79-in) cannon (two aircraft) and IIB with two 30-mm (1.18-in) DEFA 551 cannon (four aircraft), were flown – all powered by the Tay 250 turbojet. The SNECMA Atar 101 axial engine powered the 11 pre-production Mystère IICs which followed on, the last two examples being fitted with afterburning Atar 101F engines.

It was a pre-series Tay-powered Mystère IIA which became the first French aircraft to exceed the speed of sound, on October 28, 1952.

In April 1953, 150 Mystère IICs were ordered for Armée de l'Air, powered by Atar 101D turbojets. The first production aircraft flew in June 1954, and Armée de l'Air took delivery of its first Mystère IIC in October that year. As an operational fighter, its career was somewhat brief, the type being supplanted from early 1955 by the Mystère IV. It did continue in the operational training role until 1963, serving with 10ᵉ Escadre de Chasse based at Creil, and also with 5ᵉ EC based at Orange in the south of France.

Some 24 aircraft were produced for Israel, but as

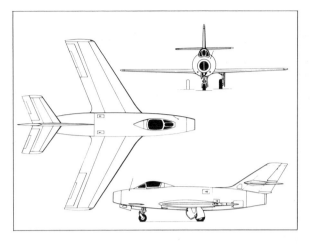

a result of the Mystère II's poor service record (structural failure being the cause of some early aircraft losses) they were not delivered, and Mystère IVs were selected instead.

A single prototype of the MD 453 Mystère III two-seat all-weather interceptor flew on July 18, 1952. It was intended to be the first of a series of all-weather interceptors with the Tay 250 turbojet. The makers dubbed it the Mystère de Nuit which described the night interception role for which it was equipped with nose-mounted radar. To accommodate the radar the air intakes were moved to the side. No production machines followed, since funds were reallocated to the more advanced Mystère IVN; however the III was used for research into ejector seats.

MD 452

Type: single-seat fighter-bomber
Maker: Avions Marcel Dassault
Span: 13.05 m (42 ft 9 in) (over tip tanks)
Length: 11.74 m (38 ft 6 in)
Height: 4.26 m (13 ft 11¾ in)
Wing area: 30.3 m² (326 sq ft)
Weight: maximum 7475.5 kg (16 480 lb); empty 5225 kg (11 495 lb)
Powerplant: one 3000-kg (6615-lb) st SNECMA Atar 101 D2 axial-flow turbojet
Performance: maximum speed 1060 km/h (658 mph) at sea level; range 885 km (550 miles); service ceiling 15 240 m (50 000 ft)
Armament: two 30-mm (1.18-in) DEFA cannon
Crew: 1
Production: 150

Below: The fifth prototype Mystère II; a IIA became the first French aircraft to exceed the speed of sound in October 1952

Mystère IV, Dassault

FIRST FLIGHT 1952

Left: A Mystère IVA with its payload of bombs, rockets, drop-tanks, napalm, and cannon. Though the aircraft could not carry all these munitions at once it could use different combinations for a variety of ground-attack roles
Below: Mystère IVAs of ET 1/8 Saintonge, a squadron which was formerly known as Maghreb when it was based in Algeria

THE Mystère IV was generally similar in layout to the Mystère II from which it was evolved, but had a thinner wing (7.5% thickness/chord ratio) with more sweepback (41°), a larger fuselage and a more powerful engine. The first prototype Mystère IV flew on September 28, 1952, powered by the Hispano-Suiza-built Tay 250A turbojet, rated at 2850 kg (6283 lb) st, as were the first 50 production Mystère IVAs. From aircraft 51, the uprated Tay called the Verdon, was installed.

Production was initiated following an 'offshore' production order from the United States under the Military Assistance Program, placed in April 1953, with a further 100 aircraft ordered directly by France. Initially entering service as an interceptor with the 12ᵉ Escadre de Chasse and the 2ᵉ EC in 1955, it replaced the Ouragan. It remained in Armée de l'Air front-line service until replaced by the Mirage IIIC in the early 1960s. The Mystère IVA was also used by France's Tactical Air Command (FATAC) as a ground-attack fighter, its underwing hardpoints being able to carry a variety of bombs, rocket pods, air-to-ground missiles or fuel tanks. The type served with the 5ᵉ and 8ᵉ ECs until replaced by Jaguars in 1975. Some Mystère IVs remain in Armée de l'Air service as operational trainers with l'Ecole de Chasse de Tours, being replaced by the Alpha Jet in 1980. In all, Armée de l'Air received 242 production Mystère IVAs.

Israel was first to receive export models of the Mystère IVA, in two batches of 24 and 36 aircraft. The first aircraft arrived during April 1956, replacing Meteor F.8s, and were used in the October war

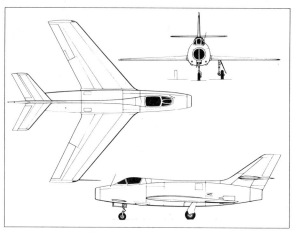

that year. They were found to be superior on several counts to MiG-15 Fagots flown by the Egyptians. Two squadrons were still in use during the June 1967 war. The Indian air force was the second export customer, taking delivery of 110 Mystère IVAs from 1957.

Apart from several paper projects, only two other versions of the Mystère IV flew. These were the three prototypes and 16 pre-production IVBs, with redesigned intake in the nose and rear fuselage modifications, powered by a Rolls-Royce Avon RA.7R with afterburning (first flight December 16, 1953); and the single two-seat Mystère IVN with a nose radome and chin intake (like the F-86D) for night and all-weather interception (first flown July 19, 1954), also powered by an RA.7R.

Mystère IVA

Type: single-seat fighter-bomber
Maker: Avions Marcel Dassault
Span: 11.12 m (36 ft 5¾ in)
Length: 12.85 m (42 ft 1¾ in)
Height: 4.59 m (15 ft 1 in)
Wing area: 32 m² (344.5 sq ft)
Weight: maximum 9500 kg (20 950 lb); empty 5870 kg (12 950 lb)
Powerplant: one 3500-kg (7716-lb) st Hispano-Suiza Verdon 350 turbojet
Performance: maximum speed 1120 km/h (696 mph) at sea level; range (clean) 917 km (570 miles); service ceiling 15 000 m (49 200 ft)
Armament: two 30-mm (1.18-in) DEFA cannon in lower forward fuselage, with provision for a retractable pack of 55 Matra air-to-air rockets; four underwing stores pylons for 907 kg (2000 lb) of bombs
Crew: 1

Production: 442

Sea Hawk, Hawker

FIRST FLIGHT 1947

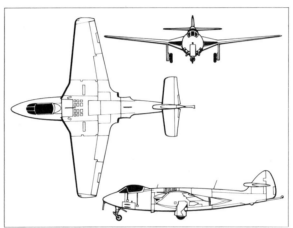

FGA.4

Type: single-seat naval fighter-bomber
Maker: Hawker Aircraft Ltd/Sir W G Armstrong Whitworth Aircraft Ltd
Span: 11.9 m (39 ft)
Length: 12.1 m (39 ft 7 in)
Height: 2.65 m (8 ft 8 in)
Wing area: 25.8 m² (278 sq ft)
Weight: maximum 7355 kg (16 200 lb); empty 4165 kg (9190 lb)
Powerplant: one 2270-kg (5000-lb) st Rolls-Royce Nene 103 turbojet
Performance: maximum speed 848 km/h (530 mph) at 12 200 m (40 000 ft); range (two drop-tanks in low-attack missions) 618 km (386 miles); service ceiling 13 560 m (44 500 ft)
Armament: four nose-mounted 20-mm (0.79-in) cannon; underwing provision for bombs or rocket projectiles
Crew: 1
Production: 524 (all types)

TOWARDS the end of 1944 preliminary details of the Rolls-Royce B.41 jet engine were made known to manufacturers. After discussions with the Ministry of Aircraft Production in December of that year, Hawker put forward the P.1040 project, with the engine in the centre fuselage exhausting through bifurcated jetpipes on either side of the rear fuselage. The idea was to put fuel in the rear fuselage. Hawker went ahead with Rolls-Royce, while the Air Staff and the Admiralty remained aloof. In October 1945 Hawker decided to proceed with the construction of a prototype. Naval Staff decided that the design showed promise, and in January 1946 it was tendered again as a naval interceptor, with the result that Specification N.7/46 was produced. Work proceeded on three prototypes and one test specimen.

The P.1040 flew at Boscombe Down on September 2, 1947. The aircraft had mid-wings picking up on stub wings integral with the fuselage and with engine air intakes in the wing roots. It was powered by a 2041-kg (4500-lb) thrust Nene I, and later a Nene II of 2268 kg (5000 lb) thrust. Controls were conventional and manually operated, with spring-tab ailerons.

The first naval prototype flew on September 3, 1948, and featured folding wings, catapult spools and full armament of four Hispano 20-mm (0.79-in) cannon. After preliminary carrier trials during the spring of 1949 the wing span was increased by 76 cm (30 in). In November 1949 more deck trials were undertaken, with satisfactory results.

The first production Sea Hawk F.1 flew on

November 14, 1951, powered by a Nene 101 engine and with a modified hood, and was used by the firm for stability and control trials. Lateral control was found to be below standard; this was cured by the introduction of power-boosted ailerons. No 806 Squadron at Brawdy was the first operational unit to receive Sea Hawks in March 1953 and later that year embarked in HMS *Eagle*.

In 1952 it was decided that production facilities at Kingston and Langley were not adequate to fulfil the orders received for both Hunter and Sea Hawk. Accordingly all Sea Hawk work was transferred to Sir W G Armstrong Whitworth Aircraft, at Coventry, also a member of the Hawker Siddeley Group.

The first AWA-built F.1 (the 36th) was flying late in 1953, and, after completing a batch of 40, the F.2 was introduced in early 1954 with fully powered ailerons and spring feel. The first fighter-bomber FB.3 flew in March 1954, followed five months later by the FGA.4 ground-attack fighter, equipped for the carriage of rockets or four 227-kg (500-lb) bombs. The last variant, the FB.6 with uprated Nene, saw operational service during the Suez crisis, and the Sea Hawk remained in front-line service until 1960. The Dutch Mk 50 was equipped with Sidewinder missiles, and the German Marinefliger Mk 101 and radar-podded Mk 102 night fighter had taller vertical tails. The Indian navy bought both new and secondhand Hawks which are still in front-line service and will not be replaced by British Aerospace Sea Harriers until after 1982.

Top: A cannon-armed Sea Hawk with its wings folded for stowage – the aircraft was later equipped to carry bombs and rockets for ground attack. Hawks saw action when aircraft from HMS *Albion*, *Bulwark* and *Eagle* attacked targets in Egypt during the operations at Suez in November 1956
Above left: With its arrester hook deployed and flaps and wheels down, one of the original Hawker-built Sea Hawk F.1s recovers during carrier trials

F-89 Scorpion, Northrop

FIRST FLIGHT 1948

IN response to a request issued by the US Army Air Force in December 1945, eight aircraft manufacturers came up with proposals for a jet-propelled night fighter. Two designs were selected, the Curtiss XP-87 Nighthawk and the Northrop N-24, which later became the F-89 Scorpion.

Of the two, the USAAF considered Northrop to have designed the better aircraft, but a contract for 58 F-87A and 30 of the all-weather reconnaissance version, the RF-87A, was awarded to Curtiss while Northrop was given an order for two prototypes of its design.

The first all-black prototype, XP-89, made its maiden flight on August 16, 1948 at Muroc (Edwards AFB), with the serial number 6678. The test pilot was Fred Bretcher. During the following months, test flights continued, demonstrating that the aircraft was easy enough to handle, but armament and radar had yet to be decided upon. The XP-89 flew with two Allison J35-A-13 axial turbojets, each developing 1701 kg (3750 lb) thrust, mounted side-by-side under the fuselage for easy removal and servicing. The shoulder-mounted wing was broad and unswept but it had a low thickness/chord ratio. The XF-89's most prominent feature was its main wheels, which had to be thin to fit inside the wing, and had to be of large diameter, to carry the weight. The fuselage consisted of two halves bolted to a central keel.

By March 1949, two wingtip tanks had been added. The US Air Force, formed in 1947, ordered 48 production aircraft, which now had Hughes E-1 radar in the nose. The first of the production

machines, the YF-89A, first flew on June 27, 1950. Unlike the black prototype, it was unpainted.

The F-89 was christened Scorpion by the air force because of its resemblance on the ground to the animal. Fighter interceptor squadrons of Air Defense Command and Alaska Air Command began to equip with F-89As in 1952, although accidents held up combat readiness and the aircraft was still deficient in some combat equipment, and still a fairly primitive machine despite its hydraulically-boosted control surfaces, including split ailerons that doubled as airbrakes.

The powerplant for production aircraft was two J35-A-21 engines, developing 2223 kg (4900 lb) thrust dry and 3084 kg (6800 lb) with Solar afterburners lit. The F-89A's fuel was contained in

Top: A Northrop Scorpion F-89D, its wingtip pods holding 104 70-mm (2.75-in) Mighty Mouse rockets. The nose-mounted Hughes E-6 radar could predict a target and direct the aircraft into range
Above: An F-89D fires a salvo of rockets on a range in the USA
Above right: An early F-89D with an airspeed indicator probe mounted in the nose

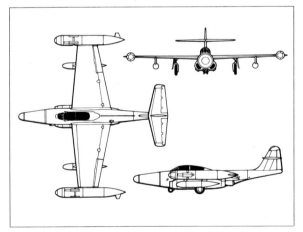

F-89D

Type: two-seat all-weather interceptor
Maker: Northrop Aircraft Corporation
Span: 18.19 m (59 ft 8 in)
Length: 16.41 m (53 ft 10 in)
Height: 5.36 m (17 ft 7 in)
Wing area: 52.2 m² (562 sq ft)
Weight: maximum 19 160 kg (42 240 lb); empty 11 387 kg (25 194 lb)
Powerplant: two 3270-kg (7210-lb) st Allison J35-A-35 or -47 afterburning turbojets
Performance: maximum speed 960 km/h (600 mph); range 2205 km (1370 miles); service ceiling 14 996 m (49 200 ft)
Armament: 104 69-mm (2.75-in) folding-fin rockets carried in two wingtip pods; provision for GAR-1 Falcon missiles in place of FFAR
Crew: 2
Production: 1050 (all types)

sump tanks, wing, and wingtip tanks. The F-89A weighed around 13 154 kg (29 000 lb) with maximum fuel. Armament consisted of six 20-mm (0.79-in) T-31 cannon mounted in the nose with underwing provision for bombs and rockets.

The F-89B was a modified F-89A with the more powerful A-33 engines. Most of the F-89As were brought up to F-89B standard, with improved equipment. The next production version was the F-89C which incorporated further improvements, particularly in radar and in the thrust rating of the two J35 engines which was increased to 2540 kg (5600 lb) dry. There were 164 of these delivered to the air force.

Production of the F-89D (Northrop N-68) began in 1953. It had the totally new Hughes E-6 radar

fire-control, matched not to guns but to FFARs (folding-fin aircraft rockets). The radar's ability to predict the position of the target, and to direct the Scorpion towards it automatically, made the F-89D a more lethal proposition. Instead of guns it carried 104 Mighty Mouse rockets, salvoed from two wingtip containers.

An F-89F version and an F-89G were planned, but never got off the drawing board. The F-89H was simply an F-89D, rebuilt to contain the Hughes E-9 fire-control system and carrying six Hughes Falcon guided missiles around the wingtip pods, with provision for Mighty Mouse rockets as well as unguided nuclear MB-1 Genie rockets on the wing pylons. About 300 F-89Ds were modified into F-89Hs, being redesignated F-89J.

CF-100, Avro Canada

FIRST FLIGHT 1950

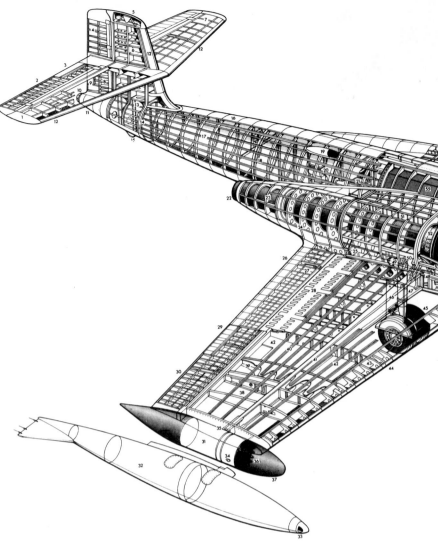

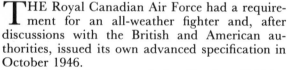

THE Royal Canadian Air Force had a requirement for an all-weather fighter and, after discussions with the British and American authorities, issued its own advanced specification in October 1946.

Avro Canada, part of the Hawker Siddeley Group, were given the task of designing this very advanced aircraft. Although the Rolls-Royce AJ.65 Avon was on order for the prototype CF-100, the Canadians wished to acquire as much advanced technology as possible, and the Gas Turbine Division of Avro Canada had produced a turbojet of its own design, the Chinook, from which stemmed the much larger Orenda, which made a highly successful first run in 1949. Progress with this engine was so swift that by the end of the year it had gone through the equivalent of the official type tests, and was obviously in the same league as the Avon and Sapphire.

The basic configuration of the CF-100 was conventional and straightforward: a long slender fuselage, a low unswept wing of relatively high aspect ratio, and a tricycle landing gear. The fuselage was full of fuel and the engines were added on each side, making the mid fuselage very wide. The crew of two sat in tandem. The main and steerable nose gears all had twin wheels.

The first, black-painted, prototype, No 18101, was the only CF-100 to be powered by Avon engines, because of the rapid progress made with the Orenda. The first aircraft had little equipment other than flight-test instrumentation. As a result it was light in weight, but nevertheless its take-off

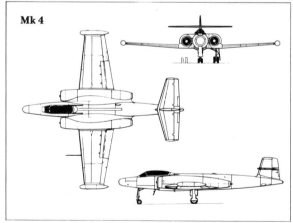

Mk 4

and climb performance was outstanding. All flight controls were powered. Airbrakes were fitted above and below the wing, ahead of the powerful double-slotted flaps. Martin-Baker ejection seats were fitted for the crew.

Roly Falk from Avro in England made the first flight in January 1950. The first Canadian-powered CF-100 with the Avro Orenda engine of 2722 kg (6000 lb) thrust flew on June 20, 1950, the first of a development batch of ten. One was fitted with dual controls, with the designation Mk 2T, but as no modification was made to the cockpit the view from the back was poor.

An order was received in September 1950 for 124 CF-100 Mk 3s. These were equipped with the Hughes Aircraft E-1 radar fire-control, matched to

CF-100 Mk 5

Type: two-seat all-weather interceptor
Maker: A V Roe Ltd
Span: 17.75 m (58 ft)
Length: 16.7 m (54 ft 2 in)
Height: 4.76 m (15 ft 6½ in)
Wing area: 54.9m² (591 sq ft)
Weight: maximum 16 800 kg (37 000 lb); empty 10 478 kg (23 100 lb)
Powerplant: two 3300-kg (7275-lb) st Orenda 11 turbojets
Performance: maximum speed 1110 km/h (690 mph); range 4000 km (2500 miles); service ceiling 16 461 m (54 000 ft)
Armament: eight 12.7-mm (0.5-in) machine-guns or 48 70-mm (2.75-in) rockets; 104 70-mm rockets
Crew: 2
Production: 692 (all versions)

CF-100 Mk 4B

1 Right tailplane construction
2 Right elevator
3 Trim tab
4 Rudder upper section
5 Communications aerial
6 Fin construction
7 Left tailplane
8 Rudder lower section
9 Rudder trim tab
10 Tail navigation lights
11 Tailcone
12 Leading-edge de-icing
13 Fin spar joints
14 Tailcone attachment frame
15 Tail bumper
16 Fuselage skinning
17 Rear fuselage construction
18 Fuselage frames
19 Air intake
20 Air conditioning plant
21 Radio equipment bay
22 Jet efflux
23 Nacelle tailpipe
24 Nacelle construction
25 Wing rear spar fixing
26 Right wing flap
27 Flap hydraulic jack
28 Herringbone airbrake
29 Aileron trim tab
30 Right aileron
31 Wingtip rocket pod
32 Wingtip fuel tank
33 Tip-tank navigation light
34 Rocket pod navigation light
35 Wingtip attachment
36 29 folding-fin 70-mm (2.75-in) rockets
37 Rocket pod frangable nose cone
38 Wing construction
39 Wing inner skin
40 Wing stringers
41 Main spar
42 Wing fuel tanks
43 Leading-edge construction
44 Leading-edge de-icing
45 Twin mainwheels
46 Undercarriage leg door
47 Main undercarriage leg
48 Main spar fixing
49 Undercarriage leg pivot
50 Retraction jack
51 Nacelle centre section construction
52 Jetpipe shroud
53 Engine mounting struts
54 Orenda 11 turbojet engine
55 Fuselage fuel tanks
56 Control duct along top of fuselage
57 Left engine nacelle
58 Airbrake hydraulic jack
59 Left airbrake
60 Left wing flap
61 Aileron trim tab
62 Left aileron
63 Aileron hydraulic jack
64 Wingtip rocket pod
65 Landing lamp
66 Wing inner skin
67 Leading edge de-icing boots
68 Pitot head
69 Left wing fuel tanks
70 Left engine cowlings
71 Sliding canopy cover
72 Canopy rails
73 Air intake
74 Engine mounting frame
75 Firewall
76 Engine driven gearbox
77 Engine bay construction
78 Nacelle lower fairing
79 Ventral gun pack
80 Ammunition boxes
81 Spent cartridge deflector plates
82 Eight 0.5-in (12.7-mm) Browning machine-guns
83 Gun muzzle fairings
84 Gun port
85 Right engine intake guard
86 Engine air intake
87 Intake anti-ice spray
88 Ammunition bay
89 Navigator's ejector seat
90 Radar display
91 ADF loop aerial
92 Left engine intake
93 Pilot's ejector seat
94 Nosewheel bay
95 Nosewheel door
96 Pressurized cockpit structure
97 Control column
98 Engine throttles
99 Windscreen frame
100 Gun sight
101 Nose electronics compartment
102 Rudder pedals
103 Nose undercarriage pivot
104 Nosewheel leg
105 Twin nosewheels
106 Nosewheel leg door
107 Nose radar bay construction
108 Hughes APG-40 radar
109 Fire control and interrogation radar
110 Radar scanner
111 Radome

eight 12.7-mm (0.5-in) Colt-Brownings mounted in a single belly pack for easy removal or replacement. The Mk 3 entered service in 1953 and soon became operational.

In 1951 the RCAF decided to follow the lead of the USAF and adopted rockets for their all-weather fighters. In partnership with Hughes Aircraft, a completely new armament system was evolved. A Mk 2 was modified as the prototype Mk 4, flown on October 11, 1952. The nose was much larger to house the powerful MG-2 (E-4) fire-control radar. The gun pack was retained, with wingtip pods that housed up to 30 Mighty Mouse rockets each. The new collision-course fire-control system was so promising that the last 54 aircraft were cut from the Mk 3 order, and the total orders for the Mk 4 rose to 510.

The Mk 4B was the next variant, fitted with the Orenda 11 of 3300 kg (7275 lb) thrust and the majority also had an all-rocket armament, the gun pack being replaced by a retractable box containing 48 rockets. It also had a one-piece canopy, as did some of the Mk 4As.

The final CF-100 version had 1.06 m (3 ft 6 in) added to each wingtip to improve the high-altitude performance. Designated Mk 5, they brought the total production figure for the CF-100 to 692.

From late 1956 to 1962 four RCAF squadrons of Mk 4Bs and Mk 5s were based in Europe as part of the all-weather defence provided by the AAFCE (Allied Air Forces Central Europe). Apart from the wing failure of a Mk 5 their service career was extremely satisfactory.

Top left: An Avro CF-100 on patrol along the Canadian seaboard. The elevators are mounted high on the tail which prevents any damage from the jet exhaust
Above: An Avro Canada CF-100 Mk 4, fitted with wingtip tanks and repainted with insignia of the Canadian armed forces
Left: A CF-100 Mk II takes off using six RATO (rocket assisted take-off) bottles. This enabled heavily loaded aircraft to use comparatively short airstrips

Saab 29

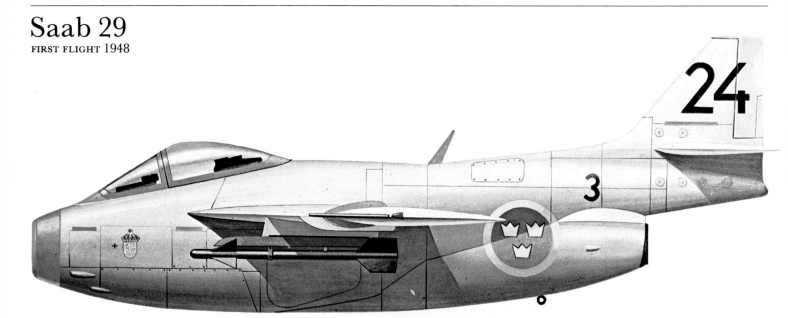

SWEDEN had no remarkable success in jet combat-fighter design until the Saab J29, which started out in mid 1945 as Project R1001. It was the first of several fighter aircraft which put Saab at the forefront of jet-fighter design and manufacture.

In November 1945, plans were devised for the aircraft to take the new de Havilland H-2 Ghost as powerplant. The fuselage was barrel-shaped. The laminar-flow wing section and tail boom were slender in contrast. The landing gear was unusual, in that the wheels inclined inwards and retracted into the fuselage.

Armament comprised four nose-mounted 20-mm (0.79-in) Hispano cannon and drop-tanks with underwing pick-up points for rockets. J29 wings had, in the earlier stages, been fitted to a Saab Safir light aircraft and flown in low-speed trials. The wings originally had airbrakes fitted to them, but because of aileron flutter which occurred at speeds in excess of 555 km/h (345 mph), these were replaced by brakes pivoting out from the fuselage.

The J29 prototype made its first flight on September 1, 1948, piloted by Squadron Leader Robert Moore. The powerplant was a Ghost 45 turbojet developing 1996 kg (4400 lb) thrust. The first production J29A day fighters were delivered to F13 wing of the Swedish air force at Norrköping in May 1951. Production aircraft were powered by the Svenska Flygmotor-built RM2 Ghost, with a thrust rating of 2268 kg (5000 lb).

Several versions were built; the A29A ground-attack aircraft; the J29B, which had increased fuel capacity; the S29C, an unarmed reconnaissance aircraft; the 29D, which was fitted with an after-burner; the J29E, which had improved perform-ance; and the J29F and A29F, which had still better performance. Production ended in April 1956, but there were later modification pro-grammes.

The J29 had great agility and was well liked by pilots. In May 1954, Capt K E Westerlund set a world 500-km (311-mile) circuit record, flying a J29B at a speed of 977 km/h (607 mph). In 1955, Major Hans Neij and Birger Eriksson flew two S29C aircraft in formation at 901 km/h (560 mph), setting up a world 1000-km (621-mile) record.

The Saab J29 remained in service until 1973, an outstanding record considering the short service lives accorded to so many combat aircraft. In all 661 aircraft were produced.

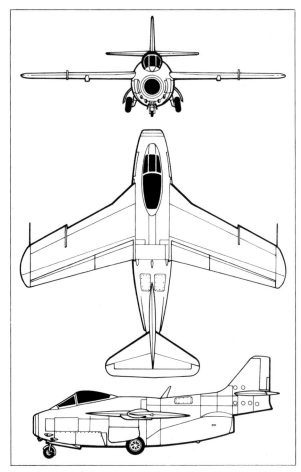

J29B

Type: single-seat fighter-bomber
Maker: Svenska Aeroplan AB (Saab)
Span: 11 m (36 ft 1 in)
Length: 10.13 m (33 ft 2½ in)
Height: 3.75 m (12 ft 3½ in)
Wing area: 24 m² (258 sq ft)
Weight: maximum 6060 kg (13 360 lb); empty 4300 kg (9479 lb)
Powerplant: one 2268-kg (5000-lb) st Svenska Flygmotor Ghost 50 turbojet
Performance: maximum speed 1060 km/h (658 mph); range 2700 km (1677 miles); service ceiling 13 716 m (45 000 ft)
Armament: four 20-mm (0.79-in) cannon; 24 76-mm (3-in) rockets
Crew: 1
Production: 661 (all types)

Top: The Saab J29 Tunnan (barrel) was the first swept-wing fighter in Europe. It is seen here in Swedish markings armed with Sidewinder AAMs
Above: A Saab J29F in service with the Austrian air force

J32 Lansen, Saab

FIRST FLIGHT 1952

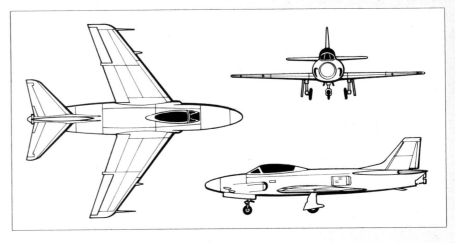

THE Swedish Air Board authorized the production of a new attack aircraft designated P1150 in December, 1948, designed around the Swedish STAL Dovern turbojet. The Dovern was later abandoned in favour of the Rolls-Royce Avon RA.7 (Series 100), which was licence-built by Svenska Flygmotor as the RM5. The wings, with a 35° sweepback and Fowler flaps, had been flight-tested on a modified Safir trainer, redesignated Saab-202. The first of four prototypes of what was now known as the Saab 32 Lansen (Lance) completed its maiden flight on November 3, 1952. It entered production in 1953, and on October 25 that year exceeded the speed of sound in a shallow dive.

The first production variant was the A32A for attack at land or sea targets. It entered Flygvapnet service with Attack Wing F17 in 1955, and went on to equip 12 squadrons by 1957. The Lansen proved a stable gun and missile platform, and from a centrally-located base could reach any land or coastal target in Sweden in an hour's flying time.

The A32A attack version was succeeded on the production line by the J32B, an all-weather fighter. Driven by the more powerful Avon Series 200 engine, built under licence as the RM6B with a new Swedish-design afterburner, giving 6890 kg (15 190 lb) st for take-off, the RM6B engine installation also required some slight enlargement of the air intakes to provide the greater mass of air-flow needed. The first J32B flew on January 7, 1957. The guns were changed for 30-mm (1.18-in) Aden cannon, integrated with Ericsson radar and the

Saab S6 computerized fire-control system. Four underwing hardpoints could carry various rocket pods, and from 1960 four Rb 324 air-to-air missiles (licence-built Sidewinders) were fitted as standard. The J32B entered Flygvapnet service in July 1958, going to the three squadrons of F12, followed by the three squadrons of F1, and to one squadron of F21. Some 120 J32B Lansens were built between 1958 and 1960.

The final variant of the Lansen was the S32C reconnaissance version, carrying cameras in a much modified nose. Powered by the RM5, the first aircraft flew on March 26, 1957. Production of the Lansen was completed during 1960. The last Lansen variant in service, the S32C was withdrawn from service in 1976.

J32B

Type: two-seat all-weather fighter
Maker: Svenska Aeroplan AB (Saab)
Span: 13 m (42 ft 7¾ in)
Length: 14.66 m (48 ft 0¾ in)
Height: 4.75 m (15 ft 7 in)
Wing area: 37.4 m² (402.6 sq ft)
Weight: maximum 13 600 kg (29 983 lb); empty 7438 kg (16 398 lb)
Powerplant: one 6890-kg (15 190-lb) st Rolls-Royce Avon 200 turbojet, licence-built by Svenska Flygmotor as the RM6B, rated at 5110 kg (11 250 lb) st (dry).
Performance: maximum speed 1114 km/h (692 mph) at sea level; maximum range with external fuel 3219 km (2000 miles); service ceiling 15 000 m (49 212 ft)
Armament: four 30-mm (1.18-in) Aden cannon in lower forward fuselage; underwing pylons for four Rb 324 Sidewinder ASMs
Crew: 2
Production: 450 (all types)

Left: A Saab J32B Lansen night-fighter rolls away during a patrol exercise on the Swedish border
Below: An S32C reconnaissance aircraft sporting dramatic and appropriate nose insignia. The Lansen was also employed as an attack aircraft with the designation A32A and an armament which included two RB04 air-to-surface missiles

Hunter, Hawker

FIRST FLIGHT 1951

IN 1946 the need for a Gloster Meteor replacement was under discussion and on January 24, 1947, a new specification F.43/46 was issued. This requirement called for a single-seat interceptor fighter capable of dealing with high flying high-speed bombers.

On closer examination of F.43/46 the Hawker design team, headed by Sydney Camm, decided to start on a private-venture fighter in 1947. This project was to be powered by a single Rolls-Royce AJ.65 axial turbojet, later to be known as the Avon. A new specification, F.3/48, was issued in March 1948 to cover the new Hawker project, which the firm had designated as the P.1067. As first envisaged, it weighed about 5443 kg (12 000 lb) with swept-back wings and tail surfaces, a nose inlet, T-tail, and two 30-mm (1.18-in) Aden cannons. The nose intake was dropped after it became apparent that it would cause difficulties with the installation of radar equipment and wing-root intakes were adopted. Wind tunnel results led to a mid-fin position being adopted for the tailplane. Armament was to be four 30-mm (1.18-in) Aden guns in a detachable pack to speed rearming.

The first prototype, WB188, made its maiden flight from the Aeroplane & Armament Experimental Establishment at Boscombe Down on July 20, 1951, piloted by Neville Duke. The second prototype was WB195, and, unlike the first, was almost to production standard, with the gun pack of four Aden cannon and gun-ranging radar. WB202, the third prototype, was fitted with the Sapphire engine. The prototypes carried out exhaustive flight trials and the ailerons, which the A & AEE had criticized as being heavy at high IAS (indicated airspeeds), were modified. Another problem was to find the optimum position for the air brake, to enable it to be used at any place in the flight envelope without causing any deterioration in the aircraft's use as a gun platform.

The first production Hunter WT555 was first flown on May 16, 1953, and together with two other production-line aircraft, went to Boscombe Down for CA Release trials from November 1953 to June 1954. In all, some 20 early production aircraft were involved in development work with the firm, Rolls-Royce and various ministry establishments. One of the more intractable problems with the Avon-powered F.1 was that the engine surged when the guns were fired at high altitude. This led to an altitude restriction on gun firing as no satisfactory remedy was found, though variable swirl vanes helped. The Sapphire-powered F.2 was unaffected by gun firing. Despite this defect the F.1 was very popular with pilots, who praised the handling qualities and strength. Three squadrons were equipped with the F.1 and two with the F.2.

The first prototype WB188 was fitted in 1953 with a new version of the Avon engine, the RA.7R, with 3234 kg (7130 lb) thrust dry, or 4355 kg (9600 lb) thrust with afterburner. WB188 was the only Hunter with this modification and it was known as the Mk 3. On September 7, 1943, Neville Duke flew it over a 3-km (1.86-m) course off the South Coast to set a new absolute speed record of 1170.9 km/h (727.6 mph).

The early Hunters were limited to the intercep-

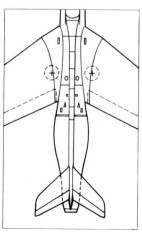

Top: A Kingston-built Hawker Hunter F.6. Some of the batch of 110 aircraft were later converted into FGA.9 versions
Above: XG 196 which operated with No 19 (F) Squadron RAF. It is carrying the earlier pattern of finned drop-tanks
Right: The area-ruled fuselage modification of the Hunter Mk 1
Far right: A pilot's eye view of Hunters of the Blue Herons RN aerobatic team

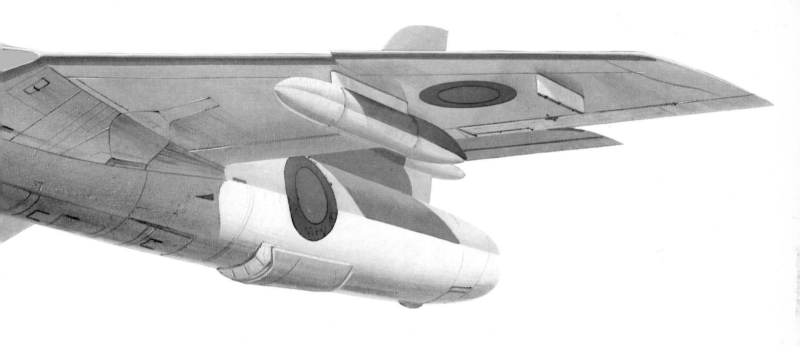

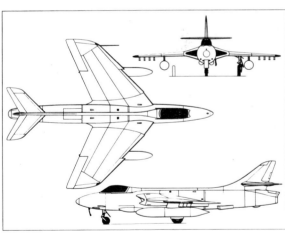

Hunter Mk 6 (F.6)

Type: single-seat fighter-bomber
Maker: Hawker Aircraft; Armstrong Whitworth Aircraft; Fokker; Aviolande; Fairey; SABCA
Span: 10.26 m (33 ft 8 in)
Length: 13.99 m (45 ft 10½ in)
Height: 4.01 m (13 ft 2 in)
Wing area: 31.59 m² (340 sq ft)
Weight: maximum 10 886 kg (24 000 lb); empty 5747 kg (12 670 lb)
Powerplant: one 4536-kg (10 000-lb) st Rolls-Royce Avon 203 turbojet

Performance: maximum speed (typical) 1143 km/h (710 mph); range 2961 km (1840 miles) at 829 km/h (515 mph); service ceiling 15 697 m (51 500 ft)
Armament: four 30-mm (1.18-in) Aden guns; two 454-kg (1000-lb) bombs or 16 rockets
Crew: 1
Production: 1972 (all types)

tor role by the lack of drop-tanks. This was rectified by the incorporation of strong wing points for store pylons and increased internal-fuel tankage in WT701, the 114th aircraft off the Kingston production line, and was the first F.4. First flown on October 20, 1954, service deliveries of the Mk 4 started in March, 1955, and by 1956 20 squadrons had been re-equipped. The first 156 F.4s still had the Avon 113 but later machines were equipped with Avon 115, which had been modified to alleviate engine surge during gun firing. This variant, with its increased capability, aroused considerable interest abroad and resulted in licence agreements being made with Fokker in Holland and Avions Fairey in Belgium, as well as export orders from, eventually, over a dozen countries.

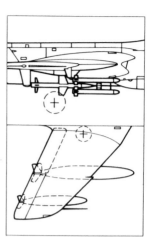

Hunter FGA.9

1 Radome
2 Radar scanner dish
3 Ram air intake
4 Camera port
5 Radar ranging equipment
6 Camera access panel
7 Gun camera
8 Ground pressurization connection
9 Nosewheel door
10 Oxygen bottles
11 IFF aerial
12 Electronics equipment
13 Nosewheel bay
14 De-icing fluid tank
15 Pressurization control valves
16 Cockpit front bulkhead
17 Nose undercarriage leg
18 Nosewheel forks
19 Forward retracting nosewheel
20 Nosewheel leg door
21 Cannon muzzle port
22 Gun blast cascade deflectors
23 Rudder pedals
24 Bullet proof windscreen
25 Cockpit canopy framing
26 Reflector gunsight
27 Instrument panel shroud
28 Control column
29 Cockpit section fuselage frames
30 Rearward sliding cockpit canopy cover
31 Pilot's right-side console
32 Martin-Baker Mk 3H ejection seat
33 Throttle control
34 Pilot's left-side console
35 Cannon barrel tubes
36 Pneumatic system air bottles
37 Cockpit canopy emergency release
38 Cockpit rear pressure bulkhead
39 Air conditioning valve
40 Ejection seat headrest
41 Firing handle
42 Air louvres
43 Ammunition tanks
44 Ammunition link collector box
45 Cartridge case ejectors
46 Batteries
47 Left air intake
48 Boundary layer splitter plate
49 Intake lip construction
50 Radio and electronics equipment bay
51 Sliding canopy rail
52 Air-conditioning supply pipes
53 Control rod linkages
54 Communications aerial
55 Fuselage double frame bulkhead
56 Boundary layer air outlet
57 Secondary air intake door, spring loaded
58 Intake duct construction
59 Forward fuselage fuel tank
60 Right intake duct
61 Right wing fuel tank
62 Drop-tank
63 Inboard pylon mounting
64 Leading edge dog-tooth
65 Drop-tank
66 Outboard pylon mounting
67 Wing fence
68 Leading edge extension
69 Right navigation light
70 Right wingtip
71 Whip aerial
72 Fairey hydraulic aileron booster jack
73 Right aileron
74 Aileron control rod linkage

75 Flap cut-out section for drop-tank clearance
76 Right flap construction
77 Flap hydraulic jack
78 Flap synchronizing jack
79 Right main undercarriage mounting
80 Retraction jack
81 Right undercarriage bay
82 Dorsal spine fairing
83 Main wing attachment frames
84 Main spar attachment joint
85 Engine starter fuel tank
86 Air conditioning system
87 Engine intake compressor face
88 Air-conditioning pre-cooler
89 Cooling air outlet louvres
90 Rear spar attachment frames
91 Aileron control rods
92 Front engine mountings
93 Rolls-Royce Avon 207 engine
94 Bleed air duct
95 Engine bay cooling flush air intake
96 Rear engine mounting
97 Rear fuselage joint ring
98 Joint ring attachment bolts
99 Tailplane control rods
100 Fuel piping from rear tank
101 Rear fuselage fuel tank
102 Fuel collector tank
103 Jetpipe mounting rail
104 Fin root fairing
105 Hydraulic accumulator
106 Tailplane trim jack
107 Fairey hydraulic elevator booster
108 Tailplane mounting pivot
109 Rudder hinge control rods
110 Right tailplane
111 Right elevator
112 Tailfin construction
113 Fin tip aerial fairing
114 Rudder construction
115 Rudder trim tab
116 Trim tab control jack
117 Tailplane anti-buffet fairing
118 Tail navigation light
119 Brake parachute housing
120 Tailpipe fairing
121 Left elevator construction
122 Tailplane construction
123 Detachable tailcone
124 Tailplane spar mounting frames
125 Jetpipe
126 Jetpipe access doors
127 Rear fuselage frame and stringer construction
128 Airbrake jack housing
129 Airbrake retracted position
130 Airbrake operating jack
131 Airbrake open position
132 Engine bearing cooling air outlet
133 Wing root trailing edge fillet
134 Flap housing construction
135 Left main undercarriage bay
136 Mainwheel door
137 Left main undercarriage retraction jack
138 Main undercarriage leg pivot mounting
139 Flap synchronizing jack
140 Hydraulic flap jack
141 Left flap
142 Rear spar
143 Aileron control rod
144 Aileron trim tab
145 Left aileron construction
146 Fairey hydraulic aileron booster
147 Wingtip construction
148 Left navigation light
149 Pitot tube
150 7.62-cm (3-in) rocket projectiles

151 Leading edge extension ribs
152 Wing rib construction
153 Main spar
154 Dowty main undercarriage leg
155 Shock absorber torque links
156 Leading edge dog tooth
157 Mainwheel doors
158 Dunlop-Maxaret anti-skid wheel brakes
159 Left mainwheel
160 Left wing fuel tank
161 Leading edge pin joint
162 ML twin stores carrier
163 9-kg (20-lb) practice bombs
164 Inboard wing pylon
165 454-kg (1000-lb) bomb
166 4 × 30-mm (1.18-in) Aden gun pack
167 Ammunition boxes, 100 rounds per gun
168 Link collector box
169 Gun gas purging air duct
170 Cannon barrels remaining in aircraft when gun pack is withdrawn

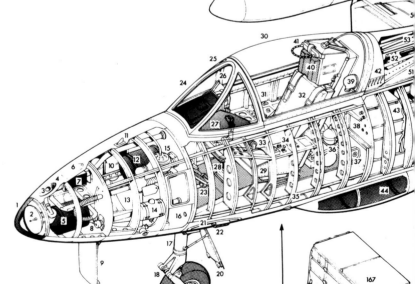

The advent of the Hunter 4 resulted in a number of trial installations being carried out with external stores, including 455-litre (100-Imp gal) drop-tanks, bombs and rocket projectiles. It continued in operational service until 1957 with the RAF when it was replaced by the F.6.

The Hunter F.5 was built at Coventry, powered by an Armstrong Siddeley Sapphire 101. Its relationship to the Mk 4 was exactly the same as that of the Mk 2 to the Mk 1. They equipped five home-based squadrons of Fighter Command, and remained in service until late in 1958.

The Hunter's life as an interceptor was extended by the installation of the Avon series 200 with 4536-kg (10 000-lb) thrust and designated F.6. Pitch-up problems with this far more potent version led to the adoption of extended leading edges, but by the end of 1958 the Mk 6 was entering service in the RAF.

A two-seater training version based on the Mk 4 with the RA.21 Avon first flew on 8 July, 1955. After lengthy trials with various hood fairings the T.7 went into production at Kingston, the first off the line taking to the air on October 11, 1957.

In addition to more than 80 marks of export Hunters many were rebuilt for the RAF and Royal Navy. The most important was the multirole FGA.9 with stronger airframe, drag chute and many other modifications. The FR.10 was a fighter-reconnaissance model, and in 1980 the Royal Navy still used the FGA.11 ground-attack trainer.

Far left: A Hunter FGA.9 armed with 24 76.2-mm (3-in) rockets
Left above: Fireflash air-to-air missiles mounted experimentally on Hunter F.4 XF310; one of the fastest Hunters had nose radar and Firestreak missiles
Left below: 1045-litre (230-Imp gal) and 454-litre (100-Imp gal) drop-tanks slung underwing

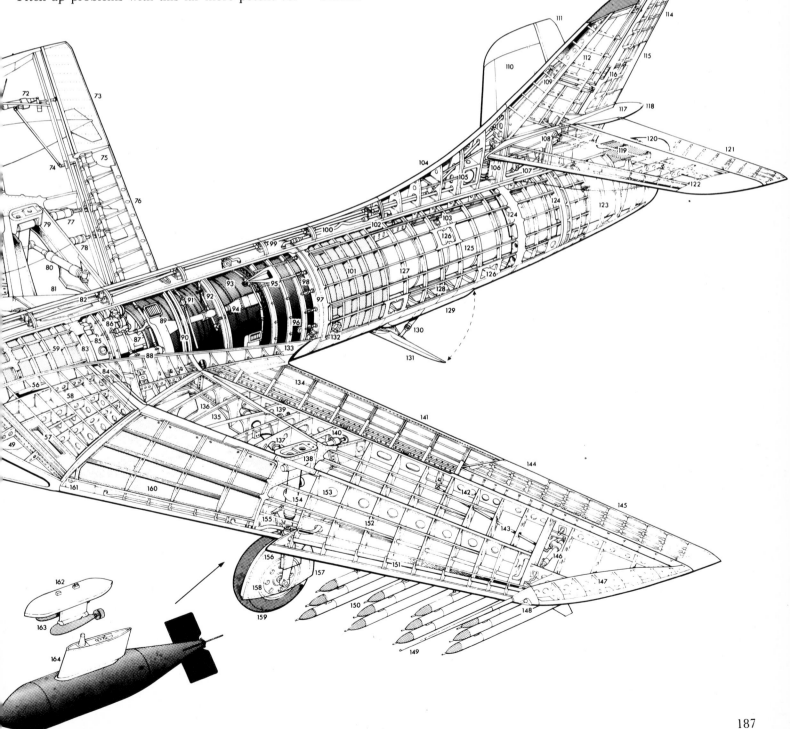

F-100 Super Sabre, North American

FIRST FLIGHT 1953

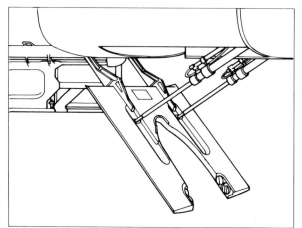

THE North American Super Sabre was note-worthy on several counts. It was the first operational fighter to exceed Mach 1 in level flight, and was also the first of the USAF's Century-series fighters. It had the distinction of holding the last subsonic world speed record of 1215.261 km/h (755.149 mph) and the first supersonic world speed record of 1323.061 km/h (822.135 mph).

The F-100 originated as the NA-180, dubbed Sabre 45 because of its 45° swept-wing, and was a North American private venture for two years of project design and development. The prototype design featured a slab tailplane located low on the rear fuselage, and an oval lip air-intake for the massive J57 two-spool afterburning turbojet, in addition to the 45° wing with inboard ailerons (to avoid twist and control-reversal) which meant there could be no flaps (though there were full-span slats). The first prototype YF-100A, with an XJ57-P-7 engine, made its maiden flight from Edwards AFB on May 25, 1953, piloted by George Welch.

The first production F-100A flew on October 29, 1953. The early production aircraft had a shorter fin and rudder of slightly increased chord, and were powered by the J57-P-7 turbojet. The armament comprised four 20-mm (0.79-in) M-39 revolver cannon, and two wing pick-up points carried long drop-tanks cleared for supersonic flight.

The first three production aircraft were sent to George AFB to begin the re-equipment of the 479th Fighter Day Wing, TAC towards the end of November, 1953, and this Wing became oper-

ational on September 29, 1954. Suddenly, with aircraft pouring off the Los Angeles assembly line, Welch was killed when an F-100A came apart in the air. After months of desperate investigation the roll-coupling cause was found, and all aircraft were rebuilt with taller fin and extended-span wings. The modified F-100As began to come off the production line in the spring of 1955. With the 104th production unit (the first F-100A-20-NA) changes were made to the cockpit, and with the 168th the J57-P-39 engine replaced the -7.

The F-100C, which followed the -A, was adapted as a fighter-bomber, with a stronger wing having six or eight pick-up points for bombs or other weapons to a total of 2722 kg (6000 lb) or four large fuel tanks. Provision was made for probe and

Top: An F-100 Super Sabre of the USAF Thunderbirds display team. An F-100D flown by Captain Merril A McPeak lost both wings during a vertical roll at an air show given by the Thunderbirds in 1967. The team was grounded and a $620 000 modification programme was required to correct the fatigue cracks
Above left: The speed brake has a relief valve to prevent deployment at too high a speed
Above right: The first F-100F during trials with the manufacturer

F-100D

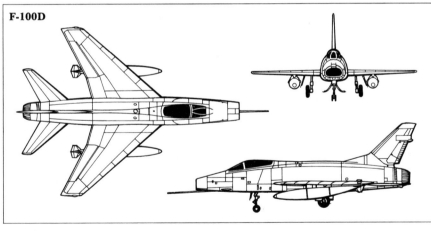

drogue type refuelling and also for 'buddy' refuelling using a hosereel in a pod. At a gross weight of 12 701 kg (28 000 lb), the F-100C had a clean speed of Mach 1.25 as shown on August 20, 1955, when the first aircraft of this variant established the first speed record above Mach 1 at 1323.061 km/h (822.135 mph). The powerplant used by the F-100C was, after the first few, the J57-P-21. The first production C flew from Los Angeles on January 17, 1955, piloted by Al White. A second production line was set up at Columbus, Ohio, whose first F-100C flew on September 8, 1955.

In 1956 production at both plants switched to the F-100D. Modifications to this version included an enlarged fin and rudder, a Minneapolis-Honeywell autopilot, underwing pylons for a maximum load of 3402 kg (7500 lb), and a wing with flaps and outboard ailerons. The final batches were fitted for zero-length rocket launching from atom-proof shelters. The Los Angeles plant built 940 F-100Ds and 334 were built at Columbus.

An F-100C was modified before delivery as a two-seater, with a 91-mm (36-in) extension to the fuselage for the tandem cockpits. It first flew on August 6, 1956, and was the prototype for the F-100F, a production combat trainer. This Super Sabre variant flew on March 7, 1957, and although it was fully equipped for operational use it carried only two M-39E cannon. A production run of 339 F-100Fs ended in October 1959. In the Vietnam war F-100Cs and Ds were used for ground-attack and top-cover operations.

F-100C

Type: single-seat supersonic interceptor and fighter-bomber
Maker: North American Aviation Inc
Span: 11.58 m (38 ft)
Length: 14.33 m (47 ft)
Height: 4.88 m (16 ft)
Wing area: 35.8 m^2 (385 sq ft)
Weight: maximum 12 701 kg (28 000 lb); empty 9526 kg (21 000 lb)
Powerplant: one 7710-kg (17 000-lb) Pratt & Whitney J57-P-21 afterburning turbojet
Performance: maximum speed 1323 km/h (822 mph) at 10 670 m (35 000 ft); range 920 km (575 miles); service ceiling over 15 250 m (50 000 ft);
Armament: four 20-mm (0.79-in) cannon; six underwing pylons for air-to-air or air-to-surface missiles, bombs or rockets
Crew: 1
Production: 476

Super Mystère B2, Dassault

FIRST FLIGHT 1956

Top: An SMB2 painted up for a Tiger Meet – an international NATO fighter competition
Far left: A factory-fresh SMB2
Left: An SMB2 of EC1/2 with its Cicogne insignia on the tail

THE Super Mystère was the last in the line of fighters evolved through the Mystère line, and was a transonic successor to the Mystère IVA. Similar in general design to the Mystère IVB, it had a revised cockpit, an improved air intake and a thinner, sharper swept-wing (45°) which bestowed the aircraft with a supersonic capability in level flight. The first prototype, the Super Mystère B1, flew on March 2, 1955, powered by a Rolls-Royce Avon RA.7R turbojet, rated at 4290 kg (9458 lb) st. The next day it exceeded Mach 1 in level flight, becoming the first European design to do so.

The Avon engine was substituted for a SNECMA Atar 101G for the pre-production model, which was designated the Super Mystère B2, and first flown on May 15, 1956. The first production model flew on February 26, 1957, and a total of 180 Super Mystère B2s were built for Armée de l'Air, the last being delivered during 1959. Armed with a pair of 30-mm (1.18-in) cannon and SNEB air-to-air rockets, the type was used as an interceptor, serving with the 5e, 10e and 12e Escadres de Chasse. With two underwing pylons for up to 908 kg (2000 lb) of stores on each, the Super Mystère B2 was a useful fighter-bomber. The type served operationally with Armée de l'Air until September 1977, being replaced in part by the Mirage IIIC, and in part by the Mirage F1C.

The only export sale for the Super Mystère B2 was 36 for Israel, which were delivered in 1958 and were used with success in a fighter-bomber role in the two Arab-Israeli wars since 1967. During the early 1970s, Israel retrofitted her surviving aircraft

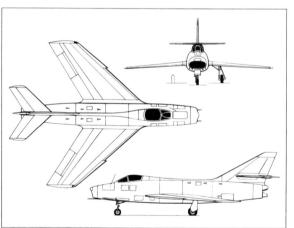

with a non-afterburning Pratt & Whitney J52-P-8A turbojet, rated at 4218 kg (9300 lb) st. This resulted in a longer rear fuselage than the standard model, and other airframe modifications were also made. The variety and weight of external stores were increased, and uprated avionics of Israeli manufacture fitted. The first public appearance of this version was in May 1973, and in mid 1977, 12 refurbished Super Mystère B2s were supplied to Honduras.

The French flew two prototypes of the Super Mystère re-engined with the Atar 9 turbojet, rated at 6000 kg (13 227 lb) st with afterburner, designated B4. The first prototype flew on February 9, 1958, but it did not enter production because of the higher performance offered by the Mirage III.

SMB2

Type: single-seat interceptor and fighter-bomber
Maker: Avions Marcel Dassault
Span: 10.5 m (34 ft 5¾ in)
Length: 14.04 m (46 ft 1¼ in)
Height: 4.53 m (14 ft 10¾ in)
Wing area: 35 m² (377 sq ft)
Weight: maximum 10 000 kg (22 046 lb); empty 6985 kg (15 400 lb)
Powerplant: one SNECMA Atar 101G turbojet, rated at 3400 kg (7495 lb) st (dry) and 4500 kg (9920 lb) with afterburner
Performance: maximum speed 1200 km/h (743 mph) at 12 192 m (40 000 ft); range at 10 973 m (36 000 ft) 870 km (540 miles); service ceiling 17 000 m (55 750 ft)
Armament: two 30-mm (1.18-in) DEFA cannon, with provision for 35 SNEB Type 22 68-mm (2.68-in) air-to-air rockets; two underwing hardpoints each for 907 kg (2000 lb) of bombs, rockets, fuel tanks and either AA30 or AS30 missiles
Crew: 1
Production: 188

F4D Skyray, Douglas

FIRST FLIGHT 1951

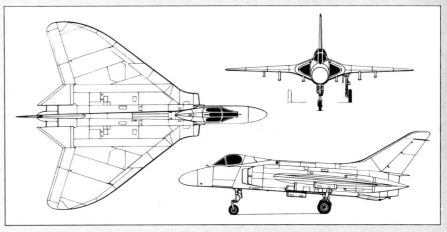

INFORMATION captured in Germany towards the end of World War II had aroused great interest in the work of Dr Alexander Lippisch on delta and modified delta wings.

The US Navy Bureau of Aeronautics selected a Douglas proposal for further studies on June 17, 1947, and awarded a contract to cover the initial design. Under the direction of Ed Heinemann and C S Kennedy of the El Segundo Division of Douglas, the design was continually refined and finally emerged as a highly swept mid-mounted wing of low aspect ratio, instead of the pure delta planform. Armament comprised four 20-mm (0.79-in) cannon mounted outboard of the wing drop-tanks. The engine was to be a Westinghouse J40 axial-flow afterburning turbojet, which should have given a maximum speed in excess of Mach 1 and an outstanding rate of climb. Accordingly on December 16, 1948, Douglas received a contract to construct test two XF4D-1 Skyrays.

Progress at El Segundo was fast, but engine development was a disaster and 2268-kg (5000-lb) thrust Allison J35-A-17 engines were temporarily installed in the prototypes. Robert Rahn made the first flight on January 23, 1951, at the Edwards AFB flight test centre, to be joined shortly after by the second prototype. As both aircraft were underpowered, they were used to evaluate handling. They were re-engined with the temperamental XJ40 engines and with the 5262-kg (11600-lb) thrust afterburning XJ40-WE-8 the performance was so promising that on October 3, 1953, a successful attempt was made on the world's absolute speed record, then British-held, to raise it to 1211.712 km/h (752.944 mph), and, a few days later, the 100-km (62-mile) closed circuit, at 1171.747 km/h (728.11 mph).

Severe difficulties with the J40 led to the cancellation of the engine programme, and the Skyray was redesigned to take the Pratt & Whitney J57 two-shaft turbojets of 4400 kg (9700 lb) thrust (6713 kg [14 800 lb] with afterburner). Eventually the F4D-1 was ordered into production with the J57-P-2 engine, Westinghouse APQ-50 radar (part of the Aero-13 fire-control system) and with numerous changes and refinements to systems and equipment. It did not enter squadron service until April, 1956. A US marine pilot broke five time-to-height world records in May, 1958, the time to 15 000 m (49 212 ft) being 2 min 36.05 sec.

F4D-1

Type: single-seat carrier-based fighter-bomber
Maker: Douglas Aircraft Co
Span: 10.21 m (33 ft 6 in)
Length: 13.79 m (45 ft 3 in)
Height: 3.96 m (13 ft)
Wing area: 51.75 m² (577 sq ft)
Weight: maximum 11 340 kg (25 000 lb); empty 7268 kg (16 024 lb)
Powerplant: one 6804-kg (15000-lb) with afterburning Pratt & Whitney J57-P-8 axial-flow turbojet
Performance: maximum speed 1162 km/h (722 mph) at sea level; range 1931 km (1200 miles); service ceiling 16 765 m (55 000 ft)
Armament: four wing-mounted 20-mm (0.79-in) cannon; six external pick-up points for up to 1814 kg (4000 lb) weapons, tanks or buddy packs
Crew: 1
Production: 419

Left: An early F4D-1, painted midnight blue, during qualification trials (mainly on the USS *Coral Sea*) makes a cat launch from the new *Forrestal*
Below: A US Navy Skyray – the type was known as the 'ten-minute killer' because of its fast climb rate

F11F Tiger, Grumman

FIRST FLIGHT 1954

THE F9F design was further extended after the Cougar by the Tiger. A swept-wing variant of the F9F-2 aircraft had already been built as the F9F-6, but the Grumman model G-98, of basically the same design configuration, was in fact a totally unrelated design. Compared with the Cougar, it was amazingly small. The G-98 had a thin, slightly tapered wing with folding tips, lateral air inlets, landing-gears which retracted fully into the area-ruled fuselage, low-mounted slab tailplane and a Wright J65 (Americanized Sapphire) powerplant with afterburner.

The G-98, which was to be the last of the Grumman 'cat' family of fighters, was ordered by the US Navy on April 27, 1953, designated F9F-8, in line with the common policy with airframes and engines of kidding Congress that a new design was merely a new version. The designation was changed to F9F-9 when -8 was used for a Cougar variant. Both the -9 fighter and -9P reconnaissance version were ordered into production. A J65-W-7 without afterburner was used for the maiden flight of YF9F-9 on July 30, 1954, to be followed by the second prototype in October. Supersonic speed was attained without afterburner! In January 1955 the second machine made its first flight with an afterburner, and other changes. The aircraft was redesignated F11F-1 in April 1955. By this time the first three production machines had flown, but without afterburners.

After cancellation of the reconnaissance version, Grumman built 42 F11F-1s on the first contract and 157 on a follow-up order. The second batch had a longer nose to take radar, but this was never installed. All orders were completed by December 1958. First deliveries were made to a navy day fighter unit in March 1957. Another five squadrons were divided between AIRLANT the Atlantic and AIRPAC the Pacific fleets, and the Blue Angels aerobatic team were also equipped with Tigers. In 1959 the F11F-1 began to be relegated to Advanced Training Command. Apart from its engine the Tiger was popular, but not able to fly the more complex missions of an F-8 or F-4.

The final variant was a company venture, the Super Tiger, which achieved Mach 2 on a J79-3A engine. Two were built, and fought the Mirage III and F-104 for the big German order in 1960 to equip fighter units of the new Luftwaffe won by the F-104G.

Above: The Grumman F11F-1 Tiger was remarkable for its small size and heavy armament of four cannon and four Sidewinder missiles
Left: F11F-1s of the US Navy Blue Angels aerobatic team trail coloured smoke during a display

F11F

Type: single-seat naval fighter
Maker: Grumman Aircraft Engineering Corporation
Span: 9.65 m (31 ft 7½ in)
Length: 13.69 m (44 ft 11 in)
Height: 4.04 m (13 ft 3 in)
Wing area: 23.3 m² (250 sq ft)
Weight: maximum 10 922 kg (24 078 lb); empty 6036 kg (13 307 lb)
Powerplant: one 5450-kg (12 015-lb) with afterburning Wright J65-W-18 turbojet
Performance: maximum speed 1432 km/h (890 mph) at 10 700 m (35 000 ft); range 2044 km (1270 miles); service ceiling 15 400 m (50 500 ft)
Armament: four fixed forward-firing 20-mm (0.79-in) cannon; 2 or 4 Sidewinder missiles
Crew: 1
Production: 39 (short nose), 157 (long nose)

Ajeet, HAL

FIRST FLIGHT 1975

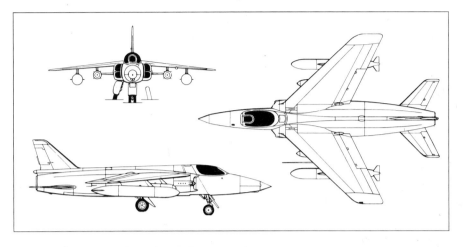

THE Ajeet (unconquered) or Gnat II was developed from the Folland (later Hawker Siddeley) Fo 141 Gnat F.1, which made its maiden flight on July 18, 1955. India signed a licence agreement to manufacture the type in September 1956 and HAL (Hindustan Aeronautics Ltd) produced the Gnat and its engine with progressively Indian content. The first all-Indian built Gnat flew on May 21, 1962, and by 1974 some 213 aircraft had been built (including UK-supplied Gnats). The type has enjoyed extremely successful service with the Indian Air Force.

HAL began studies to improve the performance of the Gnat in 1969, and in 1974 the Gnat II design was completed. The Ajeet, as the aircraft was renamed, is fitted with improved communications and navigation systems; more reliable longitudinal control; and an increased fuel capacity with a redesigned fuel system. This is in the form of integral wing tanks, housing the same quantity of fuel as was formerly carried in underwing tanks, which allows the aircraft the same range as a drop-tanked Gnat but with pylon-mounted weapons.

The last two Gnat F.1 airframes were built as Ajeet prototypes, the first flying on March 5, 1975 and the second on November 5, 1975. The electronics and hydraulic systems had previously been flight tested by two other Gnats (since brought up to Ajeet standard) while a third airframe was used for ground testing. The first production Ajeet flew on September 30, 1976, and deliveries began in 1978. The first unit to convert to the Ajeet, 9 Squadron, became operational on the type during

1979. The other five Gnat F.1 squadrons are expected to convert to the Ajeet as the aircraft become available. It is expected that Gnats with sufficient airframe life will be brought up to Ajeet standard.

Since 1975 work has been in hand for a two-seat version of the Ajeet. The overall length is increased to 10.44 m (34 ft 3 in) with two separate cockpit canopies enclosing the pilots, rather than the single clamshell type of the RAF's T.1 version of the Gnat. Two of the fuselage fuel tanks have been deleted to accommodate the extra pilot, but by removing the Aden cannon the trainer can carry 273 litres (60 Imp gal) internally. Pods on the inboard wing pylons carry 7.62-mm (0.30-in) machine-guns.

Ajeet

Type: single-seat fighter
Maker: Hindustan Aeronautics Ltd
Span: 6.73 m (22 ft 1 in)
Length: 9.04 m (29 ft 8 in)
Height: 2.69 m (8 ft 10 in)
Wing area: 12.69 m² (136.6 sq ft)
Weight: maximum 4170 kg (9195 lb); empty 2307 kg (5086 lb)
Powerplant: one 2118-kg (4670-lb) st HAL-built Rolls-Royce Olympus 701E single-shaft turbojet
Performance: maximum speed 1152 km/h (716 mph) at sea level; range low-level with two Arrow rocket pods and two 150-litre (33-Imp gal) drop-tanks 259 km (161 miles); ceiling 13 720 m (45 000 ft)
Armament: two 30-mm (1.18-in) Aden Mk 4 cannon; Vinten Type G90 gun camera; Ferranti Type 195 ISIS gunsight; four underwing store pylons, sample loads including two 227-kg (500-lb) bombs; four Arrow Type 122 rocket pods with 186.6-cm (2.6-in) rockets
Crew: 1
Production: expected to reach over 100

Right: The Ajeet extends its landing gear as an airbrake on a fast pass. The type has proved effective both as a trainer, lightweight fighter and ground-attack aircraft
Below: The Ajeet in an attractive overall high-altitude camouflage

F-102 Delta Dagger, General Dynamics

FIRST FLIGHT 1953

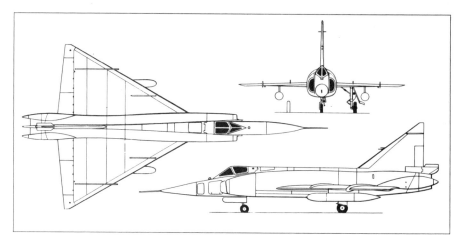

THE XF-102 was Convair's response to a 1950 USAF requirement for an all-weather interceptor, to incorporate the Hughes Aircraft MX-1179 fire-control system. This consisted of the MG-10 radar, computer and six Falcon missiles. It was the first time an airframe had been regarded as a mere portion of a weapon system.

The design was based on the company's XF-92A research aircraft. This was the world's first high-speed aircraft to fly with a delta wing and no horizontal tail, and resulted from the wartime researches of Dr Alexander Lippisch in Germany. Two prototype YF-102s were ordered, and the first flew on October 24, 1953. The initial flight trials showed it to be well below expectations and incapable of the stipulated supersonic speeds.

Using the recently discovered NACA Area Rule principle, the airframe was completely redesigned, with a much longer, waisted fuselage, bulges at the rear, taller tail and conically-cambered wings. The redesigned aircraft was designated YF-102A and made its first flight on December 20, 1954. Once ordered into full production, the first aircraft was handed over to the USAF in June 1955, and entered operational service a year later. In 21 months, a total of 875 F-102A Delta Daggers were delivered.

On November 8, 1955, a side-by-side subsonic trainer version, designated TF-102A, made its first flight. Some 63 of these were delivered before production of the Delta Dagger ceased in April 1958. During its career, the F-102 underwent several major modifications to ensure its combat efficiency was maintained. One of these was the addition of a sensitive heat-seeker ahead of the cockpit canopy, improving the aircraft's IR-target acquisition capability.

The F-102 Delta Dagger saw service with nine squadrons in Aerospace Defense Command as all-weather interceptors. In the 1960s retired Daggers were passed to 16 Air National Guard units. During the Vietnam War, F-102As were used for Quick Reaction Alert duties at many US air bases in South-east Asia.

By 1972 the Deuce (as it was known) had been withdrawn from active USAF service. Large numbers have been rebuilt by Sperry as remotely piloted QF-102 and unmanned PQM-102A versions, for threat evaluation and drone target use.

F-102

Type: single-seat all-weather interceptor
Maker: Convair Division of General Dynamics
Span: 11.6 m (38 ft 1½ in)
Length: 20.85 m (68 ft 5 in)
Height: 6.46 m (21 ft 2½ in)
Wing Area: 64.57 m² (695 sq ft)
Weight: maximum 14 288 kg (31 500 lb); empty 8641 kg (19 050 lb)
Powerplant: one 7802-kg (17 200-lb) st Pratt & Whitney J57-P-23 afterburning turbojet
Performance: maximum speed 1328 km/h (825 mph [Mach 1.25]) at 12 192 m (40 000 ft); range 2173 km (1350 miles); service ceiling 16 460 m (54 000 ft)
Armament: three Hughes AIM-4A/B/E beam-riding AAMs; three Hughes AIM-4C/D/F IR-homing Falcon AAMs; provision (originally) for 24 69-mm (2.75-in) Mighty Mouse spin-stabilized rockets
Crew: 1
Production: 1052 (all types)

Left: A Convair TF-102A Delta Dagger dual-control aircraft takes off during a training flight. The Deuce (as it was known) served with Air National Guard units after it was withdrawn from active service in 1972

F-106 Delta Dart, General Dynamics

FIRST FLIGHT 1956

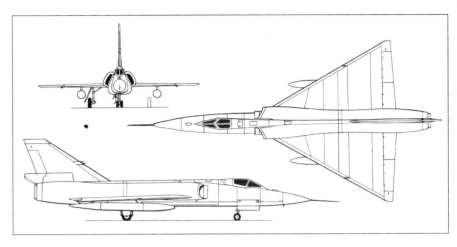

THE F-106 was the natural development of the Delta Dagger, and was originally designated F-102B. The aircraft was designed from scratch to Area Rule principles for minimum supersonic drag, and was provided with a new engine, avionics and weapons. The longer, sleeker fuselage combined with the more powerful J75 engine made the F-106 twice as fast at high altitude as the F-102, well in excess of Mach 2. The aerodynamic prototype, without the interception system, flew for the first time on December 26, 1956.

The new Hughes MA-1 interception system, although more complex and more expensive than that fitted to the F-102, was very much more capable. It was designed to be integrated with the nationwide SAGE (semi-automatic ground environment) defence system with a digital computer used to track and select targets, and aim and fire the weapons.

The initial armament of the F-106A was four Falcon AAMs and two Genie nuclear-tipped air-to-air unguided rockets. By 1970 the change in the threat made the USAF drop part of the missile armament in favour of a 20-mm (0.79-in) M61 rotary cannon, installed in the front of the missile bay. Other update features have included inflight refuelling capability, new avionics and sensors, improved ECCM (electronic counter-counter measures) and drop-tanks capable of being used at supersonic speeds.

After the first prototype, 16 pre-production aircraft were built and the first production F-106A entered USAF service with the 539th Fighter Interceptor Squadron in June 1959. In all, 277 Delta Darts were built, serving with 13 units within Aerospace Defense Command. A tandem-seat F-106B trainer version of the Delta Dart flew on April 9, 1958, and some 63 were delivered. Production was completed by July 1960. On December 15, 1959, an F-106A from Edwards AFB established a world record speed of 2455 km/h (1525 mph).

Originally conceived as an improved interceptor, the F-106A was expected to be replaced in 1964 but is still in USAF and Air National Guard service. Although several attempts have been made to find an Improved Manned Interceptor, the USAF is no nearer a decision. The F-15 Eagle remains the most likely choice, though it is very far from an optimum 1980s choice.

F-106A

Type: single-seat all-weather interceptor
Maker: Convair Division of General Dynamics
Span: 11.67 m (38 ft 3½ in)
Length: 21.56 m (70 ft 8¾ in)
Height: 6.18 m (20 ft 3⅓ in)
Wing area: 64.8 m² (697.8 sq ft)
Weight: maximum 17 350 kg (38 250 lb); empty 10 725 kg (23 646 lb)
Powerplant: one 11 130-kg (24 500-lb) st Pratt & Whitney J75-P-17 afterburning turbojet
Performance: maximum speed 2455 km/h (1525 mph [Mach 2.31]) at 12 192 m (40 000 ft); range 2735 km (1700 miles); service ceiling 1737 m (57 000 ft)
Armament: (typical) one AIR-2A and one AIR-2G Genie rocket; two each of AIM-4E/F/G Falcon AAM's; one internal 20-mm (0.79-in) M61 rotary cannon
Crew: 1
Production: 277 (F-106A), 63 (F-106B)

Above left: The F-106A which was designed from the start to the newly discovered area rule
Far left: The Delta Dart with drop-tanks; it carries internal gun, ECCM equipment and sensors as well as missiles
Left: The wedge-shaped cockpit canopy of a F-106A, opened during a ground inspection

F3H Demon, McDonnell

FIRST FLIGHT 1951

THE F3H Demon was an outstandingly advanced aircraft aerodynamically and structurally. It was a single-seat, single-engine aircraft with lateral air intakes and swept-wings and tail, advanced high-lift systems and a single large afterburning engine.

Powered by a Westinghouse XJ40-WE-6 (without afterburner), rated at 2848 kg (6500 lb) st, the first XF3H-1 prototype flew on August 7, 1951. It was lost shortly afterwards in the first of 11 accidents to occur during the flight trials.

While the prototypes were under construction, the US Navy refined its requirement from a day fighter to an all-weather and night-fighter. The resulting F3H-1N featured an enlarged nose housing Westinghouse APG-51 radar, and accommodated additional fuel.

The flight trials, however, showed the J40 underpowered, and the 58 production F3H-1Ns were powered by the J40-WE-22, rated at 3266 kg (7200 lb) st. Although delivered to the US Navy, they were never used operationally: 29 were converted to F3H-2N standard.

Once the fundamental shortcomings of the Westinghouse engine became apparent, the fuselage was redesigned to take the Allison J71, and the wing area was increased by 7.15 m² (77 sq ft) by increasing the chord forward of the main spar. Two F3H-1Ns were modified on the production line, and served as prototypes for the F3H-2 series, the first flight of which was on April 23, 1955.

Three versions of the F3H-2 were built, all of which retained the basic F3H-1N armament of four 20-mm (0.79-in) cannon mounted below the air inlet ducts. The F3H-2N was fitted with four AIM-9C Sidewinder IR-homing AAMs, and became the first operational version, when VF-14 received their first six aircraft in March 1956. In 1962, this type was redesignated F-3C. The F3H-2M was produced in parallel with the -2N, being equipped with four AIM-7 Sparrow I semi-active radar homing missiles. Later designated MF-3B, the first aircraft flew on August 23, 1955.

The final variant, the F3H-2, later designated F-3B, was configured as a strike fighter able to carry up to 2722 kg (6000 lb) of bombs or rockets, while retaining the capability to carry the Sparrow III AAM. The last Demons were withdrawn from service in August 1964.

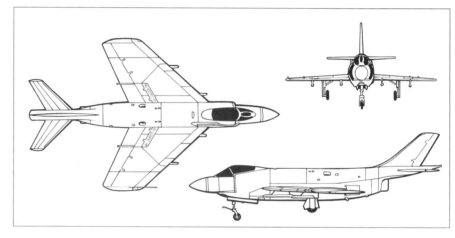

F3H-2N (F-3C)

Type: single-seat carrier-borne all-weather fighter
Maker: McDonnell Aircraft Co
Span: 10.77 m (35 ft 4 in)
Length: 17.98 m (59 ft)
Height: 4.44 m (14 ft 7 in)
Wing area: 48.22 m² (519 sq ft)
Weight: maximum 15 161 kg (33 424 lb); empty 9656 kg (21 287 lb)
Powerplant: one 6350-kg (14 000-lb) st Allison J71-A-2 afterburning turbojet
Performance: maximum speed 1170 km/h (727 mph); at sea level; range 2205 km (1370 miles); service ceiling 13 000 m (42 650 ft)
Armament: four 20-mm (0.79-in) cannon; four AIM-9C Sidewinder AAMs
Crew: 1
Production: 519 (all types)

Left: An F-3B Demon is readied for take-off aboard the USS *Coral Sea* during operations in March 1961

F-104 Starfighter, Lockheed

FIRST FLIGHT 1954

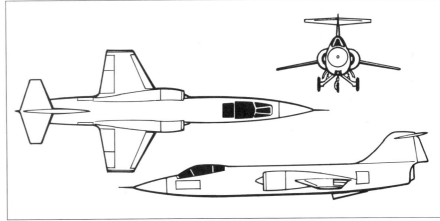

Far left: The unmistakable shape of an F-104G with its stub wings and long tapered fuselage
Left: Two West German F-104Gs take off during a test scramble in July 1979. German machines had numerous alterations including a Martin-Baker upward-ejection seat more suited to low altitudes in Europe

IN spite of being procured in small numbers for the USAF, the F-104 Starfighter was one of the most successful aircraft of the 1960s. Although it was perhaps a disappointment in its original fighter role, it sold worldwide as a tactical attack and reconnaissance aircraft.

The lessons learned in air battles with the MiG-15 over Korea provided the stimulus for the Lockheed Model 83, designed by C L 'Kelly' Johnson. The objective was flight performance at all costs. The first of two prototype XF-104s, as the Model 83 became, flew on February 7, 1954. Powered by a Wright J65-W-6 turbojet (derived from the British Sapphire), the XF-104 looked more like a manned missile than aircraft, with amazingly small thin wings and a downward ejection seat. The YF-104A and definitive F-104A were fitted with the more powerful General Electric J79-GE-3 engines, in a fully developed supersonic installation with shock-control cones in the inlets and variable primary and secondary nozzles. Normal armament was a pair of wingtip-mounted AIM-9 Sidewinder AAMs, and an internal 20-mm (0.79-in) M61 Vulcan rotary cannon.

The first J79-powered F-104A flew on February 17, 1956, fitted with the ASG-14T1 radar fire-control system. Although entering service with Air Defense Command in January 1958, they had to be withdrawn and modified with a ventral fin and GE-3B engine before resuming service. After being withdrawn some 18 months after entering service, 25 were supplied to Taiwan and 12 to Pakistan, where the type saw action in the Indo-Pakistan

Wars of 1965 and 1971. Another 27 were later re-engined with the more powerful GE-19 version of the J79, serving with the Air National Guard. A tandem dual-control version of the 104A, designated F-104B, made its first flight on February 7, 1957.

A multi-mission version for Tactical Air Command was the next version produced, the F-104C, powered by the J79-GE-7A turbojet. It also featured blown flaps, a flight-refuelling probe, and two underwing and centreline stores pylons. The 77 F-104Cs built served with the 479th Tactical Fighter Wing from 1959–65. The two-seat version of the C was designated F-104D. A derivative of the D was the F-104F, 30 of which were used by the Luftwaffe to train their pilots in the US.

In 1958–59 Lockheed developed a completely new version, the 104G, to meet a German requirement for a tactical strike and reconnaissance aircraft. Based on the F-104C with increased vertical tail area, the airframe was considerably strengthened. Instead of the Lockheed C-2 seat a Martin-Baker upward ejection seat was fitted, as well as, manoeuvering flaps, arrester hook, Nasarr multi-mode radar and an inertial navigation system. The so-called 'Super Starfighter' was powered by the J79-GE-11A turbojet, rated at 716 kg (15 800 lb) st.

The original contracts for German licence-production were modified during 1960–61 as Belgium, and the Netherlands, Italy, Canada and later Japan and other countries, all selected the F-104G for their air forces. A NATO Starfighter consortium was formed and production lines set up in

F-104S

Type: single-seat air-superiority fighter
Maker: Aeritalia, under Lockheed licence
Span: 6.68 m (21 ft 11 in) without tip tanks
Length: 16.69 m (54 ft 9 in)
Height: 4.11 m (13 ft 6 in)
Wing area: 18.22 m^2 (196.1 sq ft)
Weight: maximum 14 060 kg (31 000 lb); empty 6760 kg (14 900 lb)
Powerplant: one 8120-kg (17 900-lb) st General Electric J79-GE-19 afterburning turbojet
Performance: maximum speed 2330 km/h (1450 mph [Mach 2.2]) at 11 000 m (36 000 ft); range (ferry on internal fuel) 2920 km (1815 miles); service ceiling 17 680 m (58 000 ft)
Armament: two Selenia Aspide or Raytheon AIM-7E2 Sparrow III AAMs or an M61 20-mm (0.79-in) cannon; two AIM-9 Sidewinders
Crew: 1
Production: 2446 (all types)

north Germany, south Germany, Italy, the Netherlands and Canada. The first production F-104G flew from Burbank on October 5, 1960, and the first Lockheed-built Gs were delivered to the Luftwaffe in May 1961.

Canada had selected the Starfighter as its Sabre replacement in July 1959, and Canadair produced its own variation on the F-104G theme, designated CL-90, or CF-104 by the RCAF. The cannon was deleted, together with its sighting computer, and the Nasarr radar was optimized for air-to-surface attack. The CF-104 was powered by the Orenda-built J79-OEL-7, and had an increased internal fuel capacity. The first CF-104 made its maiden flight on May 26, 1961. After completion of CF-104 production, Canadair built an additional 110 F-104Gs which were supplied to third countries under the Military Assistance Program (MAP), including Denmark, Greece, Norway, Spain, Taiwan and Turkey.

Two-seat tandem trainer versions of the F-104G and CF-104 were produced, being designated TF-104G and CF-104D respectively. The cannon and associated equipment were deleted, but the stores pylons retained.

The final country to select the F-104G Starfighter and build the type under licence was Japan. Some two-seat F-104DJs were initially procured in a knocked-down state, and re-assembled in Japan by Mitsubishi. The same company went on to build the single-seat F-104J (a simplified G with Japanese equipment), the first production example of which flew on June 30, 1961.

In Italy, Fiat Aviation (now part of Aeritalia) continued development of the Starfighter, in collaboration with Lockheed, to produce an air superiority version. Designated F-104S, it was designed around the AIM-7 Sparrow III system, the guidance package of which displaced the internal cannon. It is also able to carry the Italian-developed rival to the AIM-7, the Aspide. The F-104S is powered by the uprated J79-GE-19 turbojet, and is equipped with the Autonetics R-21G radar updated to include moving-target indication and tracking, plus an increased ECCM (electronic counter-counter measures) capability. The first production F-104S flew on December 30, 1968, with deliveries in early 1969. The Turkish air force received 40 F-104S Starfighters, delivery of which was completed in mid 1976.

Many Starfighters were built or modified for the reconnaissance role by the addition of a sensor pod (as is available for the CF-104 and F-104S) or by removing the internal cannon and installing a camera pack (as on the RF-104G). Some Luftwaffe and Marineflieger aircraft are RTF-104Gs.

The Starfighter has been in service for over 20 years in spite of adverse publicity over its high attrition rate in the 1960s. It was not exactly what the USAF required, but its conception produced an airframe that was developed far beyond the original air-defence role, to the satisfaction of many air forces. With deliveries of the last batch of F-104S Starfighters to the Italian air force continuing in 1979, the F-104 and its variants should be in use to the turn of the century.

F-104S

1 Pitot tube
2 Radome
3 Radar scanner dish
4 R21G/H multi-mode radar equipment
5 Radome withdrawal rails
6 Communications aerial
7 Cockpit front bulkhead
8 Infra-red sight
9 Windscreen panels
10 Reflector gunsight
11 Instrument panel shroud
12 Rudder pedals
13 Control column
14 Nose section frame construction
15 Control cable runs
16 Pilot's side console panel
17 Throttle control
18 Safety harness
19 Martin-Baker IQ-7A ejection seat
20 Face blind seat firing handle
21 Cockpit canopy cover
22 Canopy bracing struts
23 Seat rail support box
24 Angle of attack probe
25 Cockpit rear bulkhead
26 Temperature probe
27 Nosewheel doors
28 Taxiing lamp
29 Nosewheel leg strut
30 Nosewheel
31 Steering linkage
32 AIM-7 Sparrow avionics (replacing M61 gun installation of strike model)
33 Inertial platform
34 Avionics compartment
35 Avionics compartment shroud cover
36 Cockpit aft glazing
37 Ram-air turbine
38 Emergency generator
39 Avionics compartment access cover
40 Fuselage frame construction
41 Pressure bulkhead
42 Ammunition compartment auxiliary fuel tank
43 Fuel feed pipes
44 Flush fitting UHF aerial panel
45 Anti-collision light
46 Right intake
47 Engine bleed air supply to air conditioning
48 Gravity fuel fillers
49 Fuselage main fuel tanks
50 Pressure refuelling adaptor
51 Intake shock-cone centre body
52 De-iced intake lip
53 Left intake
54 Shock-cone boundary layer bleed
55 Boundary layer bleed air duct
56 Auxiliary intake
57 Hinged auxiliary intake door
58 Navigation light
59 Leading-edge flap jack
60 Intake trunking
61 Fuselage main longeron
62 Wing root attaching members
63 Intake flank fuel tanks
64 Wing-mounting fuselage mainframes
65 Control cable runs
66 Electrical junction box
67 Dorsal spine fairing
68 Right inboard pylon
69 Leading-edge flap (lowered)
70 AIM-7 Sparrow AAM

71 Missile launch rail
72 Right outer pylon
73 Tip-tank vane
74 Tip-tank latching unit
75 Right wingtip tank
76 Fuel filler caps
77 Right aileron
78 Aileron power control jacks
79 Power control servo valves
80 Fuel lines to auxiliary tanks
81 Flap blowing duct
82 Right 'blown' flap (lowered)
83 Engine intake compressor face
84 Intake spill flaps
85 Aileron torque shaft
86 Hydraulic reservoir
87 Air-conditioning bleed air supply pipe
88 General Electric J79-GE-19 turbojet
89 Engine withdrawal rail
90 Right airbrake (open)
91 Fin root fillet
92 Elevator servo controls
93 Elevator/all moving tailplane hydraulic jacks
94 Push-pull control rods
95 Tailfin construction
96 Fin-tip fairing
97 Tailplane rocking control arm
98 Right tailplane
99 One-piece tailplane construction
100 Tailplane spar
101 Tailplane spar central pivot
102 Fin trailing-edge construction
103 Rudder construction
104 Rudder power control jacks
105 Rudder servo valves
106 Exhaust shroud
107 Fully-variable afterburner exhaust nozzle
108 Fin attachment joints
109 Fin-carrying mainframes
110 Afterburner duct
111 Nozzle control jacks
112 Steel and titanium aft fuselage construction
113 Rear navigation lights
114 Aft fuselage attachment joint
115 Brake parachute housing
116 Left airbrake (open)
117 Airbrake scissor links
118 Fuselage strake (both sides)
119 Emergency runway arrester hook
120 Airbrake jack
121 Air exit louvres
122 Primary heat exchanger
123 Wing root trailing edge fillet
124 Flap hydraulic jack
125 Flap blowing slot
126 Left 'blown' flap (lowered)
127 Aileron servo valves
128 Aileron power control jacks
129 Left aileron
130 Tip-tank fins
131 Left navigation light
132 Left wingtip fuel tank
133 Fuel filler caps

134 Outboard pylon mounting rib
135 Wing multi-spar construction
136 Inboard pylon mounting rib
137 Main landing gear leg door
138 Shock absorber strut
139 Swivel axle control rods
140 Left mainwheel
141 Leading-edge flap (lowered)
142 Leading-edge flap rib construction
143 Left outboard pylon
144 Missile launch rail
145 Left AIM-7 Sparrow AAM
146 Mk 82 226-kg (500-lb) bomb
147 Mk 83 454-kg (1000-lb) bomb
148 Bomb-mounting shackles
149 Auxiliary fuel tank
150 Left inboard wing pylon
151 Pylon attachments
152 LAU-3A 2.75-in (70-mm) FFAR pod (19 rockets)
153 AIM-9 Sidewinder AAM
154 Missile launch rail
155 Fuselage stores pylon adaptor

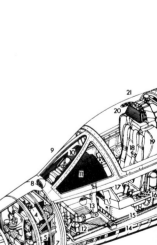

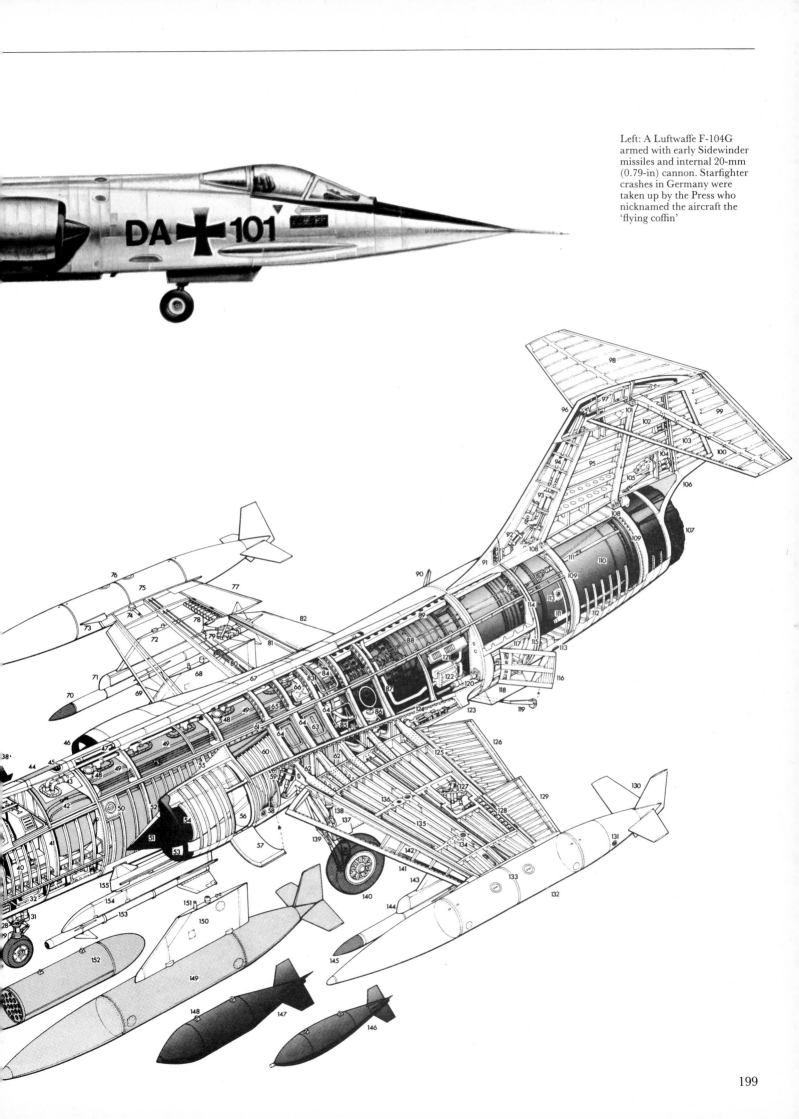

Left: A Luftwaffe F-104G armed with early Sidewinder missiles and internal 20-mm (0.79-in) cannon. Starfighter crashes in Germany were taken up by the Press who nicknamed the aircraft the 'flying coffin'

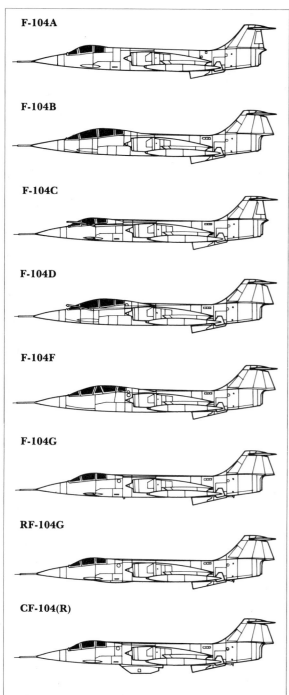

F-104A

F-104B

F-104C

F-104D

F-104F

F-104G

RF-104G

CF-104(R)

Above: The Starfighter was produced in numerous versions including reconnaissance, ground-attack trainers and interceptors. It has seen a progressive improvement in speed and load carrying. The F-104A had five external stores positions, but was able to lift only 141 kg (310 lbs) in contrast to the 1955 kg (4310 lbs) of the F-104G. With this improvement it was also able to reach a maximum altitude of 18 288 m (60 000 ft). The progressive improvement in powerplants from the J79-GE-3A, through the J79-GE-7 to the J79-GE- 11A has resulted in an increase in weight, but this has been more than compensated by the enhanced performance. Although new pilots had the unnerving experience of hearing the engine emit 'a lot of wierd noises ... groans, howls, screams' at high Mach numbers, it was, in the words of a veteran pilot, 'all quite normal'. The single engine gave the aircraft a small clean shape which allowed it to perform very well. However if the pilot lost power he was in an aircraft with 'the aerodynamics of a bath tub'

Far left: An F-104 sits on its Dowty Liquid Spring landing gear which makes it easy for groundcrews to have access to the fuselage interior
Top: A Royal Netherlands Air Force F-104G takes off
Above: A Canadian CF-104 deploys its tail-brake parachute as it comes in to land
Left: A German F-104G during a visit to an RAF station in September 1977

Javelin, Gloster
FIRST FLIGHT 1951

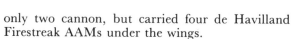

THE first prototype of the Gloster Javelin flew on November 26, 1951, experiencing severe rudder buffeting. It was later lost in June 1952, and the second prototype suffered a similar fate in August 1952. Three further prototypes, incorporating many modifications (especially to the wing and tail) followed, and the first production Javelin FAW.1 flew on July 22, 1954.

The FAW.1 was armed with four 30-mm (1.18-in) Aden cannon in the enormous wings, and the AI.17 radar was managed by a radar operator/navigator in the rear cockpit. Further problems delayed service entry until February 1956, when 46 Squadron at Odiham took delivery of their aircraft. The FAW.2 was a development of the FAW.1 with AI.22 (American Westinghouse APQ-43) radar in a shortened nose.

Chronologically the FAW.4 was the next variant, being an FAW.1 with an all-moving tailplane. The FAW.5 incorporated a new wing with increased internal fuel capacity, and the FAW.6 was basically a Mk 5 with radar of the FAW.2.

A dual-control version, designated Javelin T.3, was developed by Air Service Training. It was based on the FAW.4, with a new forward fuselage lengthened by 1.12 m (3 ft 8 in) to 18.29 m (60 ft), with the rear cockpit higher than the first to give forward view.

All versions up to the FAW.6 had been powered by Armstrong Siddeley Sapphire 102/103 turbojets, rated at 3765 kg (8300 lb) st. From the FAW.7, the Sapphire 200 series became available, with considerably higher thrust. The FAW.7 also had

only two cannon, but carried four de Havilland Firestreak AAMs under the wings.

The FAW.8 was the last new-build version. Basically an FAW.7, it was fitted with AI.22 (Westinghouse) radar, a Sperry autopilot, further wing modifications and a low-augmentation afterburner, increasing the available thrust to 6074 kg (13 390 lb).

The final version of Javelin was the FAW.9, an FAW.7 rebuilt to FAW.8 standard, with provision for a crude flight refuelling probe, but retaining the British AI.17 radar of the FAW.7. The first FAW.9s entered service with 25 Squadron in December 1960. Later most FAW.9s were 'plumbed' to carry four 1045-litre (230-Imp gal) drop-tanks from the missile pylons.

FAW.9

Type: All-weather fighter
Maker: Gloster Aircraft Co
Span: 15.87 m (52 ft 1 in)
Length: 17.3 m (56 ft 9 in)
Height: 4.95 m (16 ft 3 in)
Wing area: 86.21 m² (928 sq ft)
Weight: maximum 19 470 kg (42 930 lb); empty 13 154 kg (29 000 lb)
Powerplant: two 6074-kg (13 390-lb) st Armstrong Siddeley (later Bristol Siddeley, later Rolls-Royce) Sapphire 203/204 afterburning turbojets
Performance: maximum speed 1094 km/h (680 mph) at sea level; range 1497 km (930 miles); service ceiling 15 088 m (49 500 ft)
Armament: two 30-mm (1.18-in) Aden cannon; up to four de Havilland (later HSD) Firestreak AAMs
Crew: 2
Production: 435 (all types)

Above far left: The Javelin FAW.9 specially instrumented chase aircraft, XH879. It remained in use until 1975, at the Boscombe Down test centre
Above left: A Javelin of No 46 Squadron starting up its engines
Left: A Javelin FAW.8, XJ125, at the SBAC Show, 1959, carrying dummy Firestreak infra-red homing air-to-air missiles

MiG-21, Mikoyan

FIRST FLIGHT 1955

Left: A group of MiG-21 interceptors in a demonstration flight at the 50th anniversary of the October Revolution Aviation Festival, Domodedovo Airport, 1967
Below: A Syrian MiG-21F clear-weather interceptor, differing from initial production MiGs in having an uprated R-11 turbojet with full reheat, and a tailfin of increased chord

THE MiG-21 series of fighters (NATO codename Fishbed) are undoubtedly the most widely used and numerous combat aircraft in the world today. The original design was outlined in the immediate aftermath of the Korean War as a light, high-performance day fighter. Both the tailed delta and swept-wing configurations were flown on prototypes before the former was selected. The E-5 prototype of the MiG-21 had its maiden flight in 1955, and made its public debut at Tushino, Moscow on June 24, 1956. The initial armament was two 30-mm (1.18-in) NR-30 cannon, to which were added a pair of K-13 (NATO codename Atoll) AAMs (not unlike the AIM-9B Sidewinder I), the left cannon being deleted to provide space for the missile avionics.

The first major production version was the MiG-21F (F for forsirovanny, boosted), known as the Fishbed-C. Powered by a Tumansky R-11 turbojet rated at 5750 kg (12 676 lb) st with afterburning, it was armed with the single NR-30 cannon and two underwing pylons on which could be mounted either the K-13 Atoll or a UV-16-57 rocket pod. There was no radar except for gunsight ranging.

The MiG-21PF Fishbed-D incorporated airframe improvements with a larger less-tapered forward fuselage, and larger centrebody to house the R1L search/track radar (NATO codename Spin Scan A); other changes included larger main wheels and additional fuel. An uprated R-11 engine giving 5951 kg (13 120 lb) st with afterburning was installed, and the cannon deleted.

The Fishbed-E, identified in 1964, is similar to

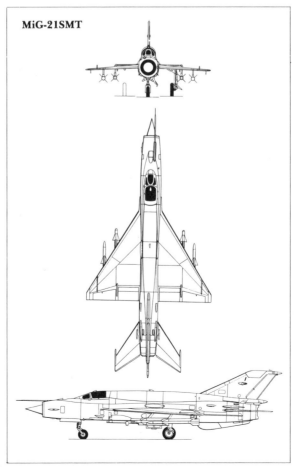

MiG-21SMT

MiG-21MF

Type: single-seat multirole fighter
Maker: Mikoyan-Gurevich design bureau
Span: 7.15 m (23 ft 5½ in)
Length: 15.76 m (51 ft 8½ in) including pitot boom
Height: 4.5 m (14 ft 9 in)
Wing area: 23 m² (247.57 sq ft)
Weight: maximum (with two K-13As and three drop-tanks) 9400 kg (20 725 lb); empty not available
Powerplant: one 6600-kg (14 550-lb) st Tumansky R-13-300 afterburning turbojet
Performance: maximum speed 2230 km/h (1385 mph [Mach 2.1]), above 11 000 m (36 000 ft) in level flight; range on internal fuel only 1100 km (683 miles); service ceiling 18 000 m (59 050 ft)
Armament: one GSh-23 twin-barrel 23-mm (0.9-in) gun; four underwing pylons and a centre-line pylon for the carriage of drop-tanks, rocket pods, bombs or K-13 Atoll/ Advanced Atoll AAMs
Crew: 1 (2 in Mongol)
Production: 10 000 (all types)

MiG-21MF

1 Pitot-static boom
2 Pitch vanes
3 Yaw vanes
4 Conical three-position intake
5 Spin Scan search-and-track radar antennae
6 Boundary layer slot
7 Engine air intake
8 Radar (Spin Scan)
9 Lower boundary layer exit
10 Antennae
11 Nosewheel doors
12 Nosewheel leg and shock absorbers
13 Castoring nosewheel
14 Anti-shimmy damper
15 Avionics bay access
16 Attitude sensor
17 Nosewheel well
18 Spill door
19 Nosewheel retraction pivot
20 Bifurcated intake trunking
21 Avionics bay
22 Electronics equipment
23 Intake trunking
24 Upper boundary layer exit
25 Dynamic pressure probe for q-feel
26 Semi-elliptical armour-glass windscreen
27 Gunsight mounting
28 Fixed quarterlight
29 Radar scope
30 Control column (with tailplane trim switch and two firing buttons)
31 Rudder pedals
32 Underfloor control runs
33 KM-1 two-position zero-level ejection seat
34 Left instrument console
35 Landing gear handle
36 Seat harness
37 Canopy release/lock
38 Right wall switch panel
39 Rear-view mirror fairing
40 Right-hinged canopy
41 Ejection seat headrest
42 Avionics bay
43 Control rods
44 Air-conditioning plant
45 Suction relief door
46 Intake trunking
47 Wingroot attachment fairing
48 Wing/fuselage spar-lug attachment points (four)
49 Fuselage ring frames
50 Intermediary frames
51 Main fuselage fuel tank
52 RSIU radio bay
53 Auxiliary intake
54 Leading-edge integral fuel tank
55 Right outer weapons pylon
56 Outboard wing construction
57 Right navigation light
58 Leading-edge suppressed aerial
59 Wing fence
60 Aileron control jack
61 Right aileron
62 Flap actuator fairing
63 Right blown flap–SPS
64 Multi-spar wing structure
65 Main integral wing fuel tank
66 Landing gear mounting/pivot point
67 Right mainwheel leg
68 Auxiliaries compartment
69 Fuselage fuel tanks Nos 2 and 3
70 Mainwheel well external fairing
71 Mainwheel (retracted)
72 Trunking contours
73 Control rods in dorsal spine
74 Compressor face
75 Oil tank
76 Avionics pack
77 Engine accessories
78 Tumansky R-13 turbojet (rated at 6600 kg [14 550 lb] with full reheat)
79 Fuselage break/transport joint
80 Intake
81 Tail surface control linkage
82 Artificial feel unit
83 Tailplane jack
84 Hydraulic accumulator
85 Tailplane trim motor
86 Tailfin spar attachment plate
87 Rudder jack
88 Rudder control linkage
89 Tailfin structure
90 Leading-edge panel
91 Radio cable access
92 Magnetic detector
93 Tailfin mainspar
94 RSIU (very-short-wave fighter radio) antenna plate
95 VHF/UHF aerials
96 IFF antennae
97 Formation light
98 Tail warning radar
99 Rear navigation light
100 Fuel vent
101 Rudder construction
102 Rudder hinge
103 Braking parachute hinged bullet fairing
104 Braking parachute stowage
105 Tailpipe (variable convergent nozzle)
106 Afterburner installation
107 Afterburner bay cooling intake
108 Tailplane linkage fairing
109 Nozzle actuating cylinders
110 Tailplane torque tube
111 All-moving tailplane
112 Anti-flutter weight
113 Intake
114 Afterburner mounting
115 Fixed tailplane root fairing
116 Longitudinal lap joint
117 External duct (nozzle hydraulics)
118 Ventral fin
119 Engine guide rail
120 JATO assembly canted nozzle
121 JATO assembly thrust plate forks (rear mounting)
122 JATO assembly pack
123 Ventral airbrake (retracted)
124 Trestle point
125 JATO assembly release solenoid (front mounting)
126 Underwing landing light
127 Ventral stores pylon
128 Mainwheel inboard door
129 Splayed link chute
130 Twin 23-mm (0.92-in) GSh-23 cannon installation
131 Cannon muzzle fairing
132 Debris deflector plate
133 Auxiliary ventral drop tank
134 Left forward air brake (extended)
135 Leading-edge integral fuel tank
136 Landing gear retraction strut
137 Aileron control rods in leading edge
138 Left inboard weapons pylon
139 UV-16-57 rocket pod
140 Left mainwheel
141 Mainwheel outboard door section
142 Mainwheel leg
143 Aileron control linkage
144 Mainwheel leg pivot point
145 Main integral wing fuel tank
146 Flap actuator fairing
147 Left aileron
148 Aileron control jack
149 Outboard wing construction
150 Left navigation light
151 Left outboard weapons pylon
152 Advanced Atoll infra-red guided AAM
153 Wing fence
154 Radio altimeter antenna

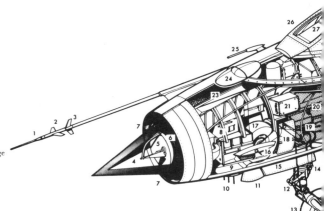

the C but with broad-chord vertical tail surfaces and a brake parachute housing at the base of the rudder. Provision is made for an underbelly pack housing a GSh-23 23-mm (0.9-in) twin-barrel gun.

The late-model version of the MiG-21PF was designated MiG-21FL (L for lokator, R2L Spin Scan B radar) and had the broad-chord vertical tail surfaces and parachute housing of the Fishbed-E. Primarily for export, this model was built under licence by HAL in India, as the Type 77.

The MiG-21PFS or PF(SPS) was similar to the Fishbed-D, but fitted with a flap-blowing system known as Sduva Pogranichnovo Sloya as standard.

The MiG-21PFM Fishbed-F embodied improvements previously incorporated in the PF/PFS series (M signifying an exportable version of an existing design). The fin leading edge was extended 450 mm (18 in) forward and the small dorsal fin fillet deleted. A simple ejection seat and sideways-hinged canopy were fitted. It was also produced in Czechoslovakia.

The Fishbed-G was a single prototype experimental STOL (short take-off and landing) version of the PFM, with a pair of vertically mounted lift jets in a lengthened fuselage. It was displayed at Domodedovo in July 1967.

A multirole version of the PFM, designated MiG-21PFMA Fishbed-J, introduced a deeper dorsal spine housing extra fuel, four underwing pylons and provision for the underbelly gun pack. Late models have the GSh-23 gun mounted internally in a shallow underbelly fairing and a zero-

Above: A MiG-21PF, an interim model equipped with radar warning which informed the pilot if his aircraft had been located by hostile radar. A parabrake is housed in a bullet-shaped fairing at the base of the rudder

Above right: An early MiG-21F of the Yugoslav air force displaying its centreline pod for extra fuel or ECM, and one of its K-13A AAMs

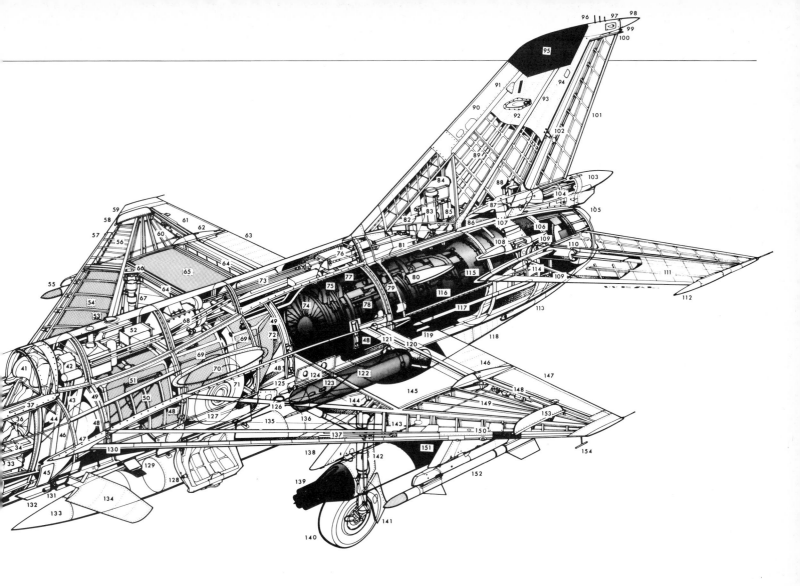

zero ejection seat. A derivative of this version, the MiG-21M, with the internal gun and R-11F2S-300 engine, succeeded the FL on the HAL production line as the Type 88. The first Indian M was handed over on February 14, 1973. A reconnaissance version of the J is codenamed Fishbed-H by NATO.

The MiG-21MF is also codenamed Fishbed-J as it is basically the PFMA re-engined with the Tumansky R-13-300. It entered service in 1970. The MiG-21SMT Fishbed-K is similar to the MF, but with a deep dorsal spine extending to the brake parachute housing, wingtip ECM pods and comprehensive avionics including tail-warning radar. Like the MiG-21PFMA and MF, it can carry both the IR-homing Atoll and radar-homing Advanced

Atoll missiles. It has been in Warsaw Pact service since 1971.

The third generation MiG-21bis Fishbed-L is a multirole air combat/ground-attack aircraft, built to improved standards with a new airframe and uprated avionics. It has a wider and deeper dorsal spine. When re-engined with the Tumansky R-25, rated at 7500 kg (16 535 lb) st with afterburning, the 21bis is codenamed Fishbed-N. Further avionics improvements, including Tacan-type navigation are incorporated. In service since the mid 1970s, the MiG-21bis is still in production.

Two-seat training versions of the Fishbed have been produced under the designation MiG-21U (codename Mongol). The Mongol-A is based on the MiG-21F with tandem seating and a sideways-hinging canopy, with the cannon armament deleted. The Mongol-B has the broad-chord vertical tail surfaces and deeper dorsal spine, with no fillet, and is the later production model. The MiG-21US (also Mongol-B) has the SPS flap-blowing, while the MiG-21UM is the trainer version of the Fishbed-J with the R-13 engine and four underwing pylons. It is again codenamed Mongol-B.

Although it is difficult to be exact, an estimated 10 000 examples of the MiG-21 of all versions have been produced worldwide, including an unlicenced version in China, known as the Shenyang F-8. MiG-21s of many variants have been supplied to or purchased by Afghanistan, Albania, Algeria, Angola, Bangladesh, Bulgaria, China, Cuba, Czechoslovakia, Egypt, Finland, East Germany, India, Indonesia, Iraq, Nigeria, North Korea, Poland, Romania, Somalia, Sudan, South Yemen, Syria, Tanzania, Uganda, Vietnam, the Yemen Arab Republic and Yugoslavia. Some examples are known to have been acquired by the United States via Israel. The Egyptian aircraft are being updated with inertial navigation, a weapon-aiming and head-up display by Ferranti and improved instruments by Smith Industries, supported by spares supplied by China.

The early marks of MiG-21 are known to be very effective day fighters, and have been described as 'sweet to handle'; but it is understood that some sub-variants have severe limitations due to adverse characteristics. However, it is most probable that the MiG-21 will be around for the remainder of this

Below: Boarding a MiG-21MF by night. This is the first version of the MiG-21 to use the Tumansky R-13 turbojet, which made extensive use of titanium in its construction

206

century. The West had a unique opportunity to evaluate the MiG-21 when an Iraqi pilot defected on August 16, 1966, with a MiG-21-13. The aircraft was flown by the Israeli air force chief test pilot who reported that it had a lower landing speed than the Mirage III and it had thicker armour. The cockpit was said to be cramped and this comment was born out by North Vietnamese pilots who had flown US F-5 fighters as well as MiG-21s. Despite the good armour protection the MiG-21 proved to be less rugged than the MiG-17 and caught fire and burned out more completely when attacked by Israeli aircraft. Indian pilots, however, seemed happy with the aircraft's ability to withstand battle damage but criticized the simple radar and fuel capacity. When they evalu-

ated a MiG-21F prior to licence production they stipulated changes including improved brakes, better-quality tyres, larger drop-tanks and the GP-9 gun pack with a predictor gun sight. During the India/Pakistan war of December 1971 they were pitted against Lockheed F-104A fighters and proved to have a better turning circle at low altitude and could accelerate faster. The ground-crews found them easy to maintain. The Indian aircraft is built by the HAL factory at Nasik near Bombay, while the Tumansky R-11 engine is produced at Koraput.

There are unconfirmed reports that two or three aircraft captured by the Israelis during fighting with Egypt were shipped to the USA for evaluation in the late 1960s.

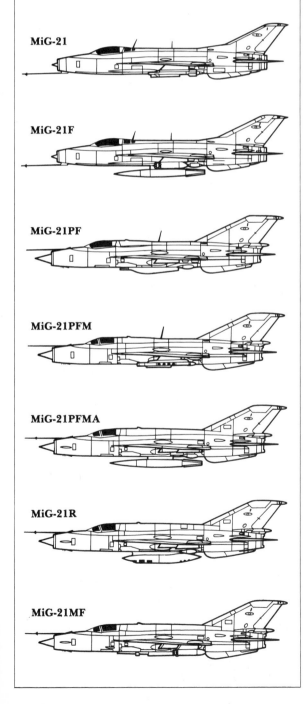

MiG-21

MiG-21F

MiG-21PF

MiG-21PFM

MiG-21PFMA

MiG-21R

MiG-21MF

Centre left: The MiG-21 has been built in numerous varieties equipped with reconnaissance or ECM pods, cannon or rocket pods. Only the initial MiG-21 has the narrow-chord fin
Left: Two MiG-21PFMs which introduced a conventional fixed windscreen with quarterlights, and simple ejection seat with the canopy hinging to the right. It also incorporated an ECM pod on the wing pylon

Above: A MiG-21F day fighter in service with the Finnish Ilmavoimat. This was one of the earliest production versions
Left: A STOL (short take-off and landing) version of the MiG-21PFM, showing the opened intake for the two vertical lift jets. These were inserted in the centre of the fuselage to shorten the take-off and landing

F8U Crusader, Vought

FIRST FLIGHT 1955

THE design of the Crusader began in 1952 in response to a US Navy requirement for a supersonic air-superiority fighter. Chance Vought was awarded a development contract for two prototypes of the XF8U-1 on June 29, 1953. The design incorporated a variable-incidence wing, which could pivot through 7° to enhance the angle of attack for landing without raising the nose.

The maiden flight of the XF8U-1, powered by a J57-P-11, was on March 25, 1955, when Mach 1 was exceeded. The second prototype flew in September 1955. The first F8U-1 (later redesignated F-8A) was delivered to the US Navy in March 1957, to equip VF-32. This version was armed with four 20-mm (0.79-in) Colt-Browning cannon in the sides of the forward fuselage, a pack for 32 70-mm (2.75-in) HVAR rockets (in early models) and two fuselage-mounted AIM-9 Sidewinders (in later models). An unarmed reconnaissance version, the RF-8A, followed on the production line. Power for the F-8A was the J57-P-12 or P-4A, rated at 7348 kg (16 200 lb) st with afterburning, which was capable of giving this version a maximum speed of Mach 1.67.

The F-8B (originally F8U-1E) featured a small interception radar above the chin intake, giving this model a limited all-weather capability. Addition of the higher-powered J57-P-16, offering a 317-kg (700-lb) increase in afterburning thrust, changed the F-8B to the F-8C (originally F8U-2). This version had an improved fire-control system together with four Sidewinders, in addition to the cannon.

The F-8D Crusader (originally F8U-2N) was given a better all-weather capability by the addition of a Vought push-button autopilot and extra avionics. It was powered by the J57-P-20 engine giving 8165 kg (18 000 lb) of thrust, enabling a level speed close to Mach 2 to be reached.

Progressive development of the Crusader next produced the F-8E (originally F8U-2NE), a multi-role aircraft. This featured the more advanced APQ-94 search/fire-control radar, plus four under-wing pylons enabling a maximum stores load of 2268 kg (5000 lb) to be carried.

The last new-build production version of the Crusader provided the type's first export success. France ordered 42 F-8E(FN)s in August 1963. To fit the small French carriers this version had

Below: A US Navy two-seat TF-8A Crusader trainer
Bottom: An F-8 Crusader at the moment of touchdown. The arrester hook has engaged the deck cable and a crewman is giving the pilot signals to cut power and fold wings

208

several modifications, including blown trailing-edge flaps, two-part leading-edge flaps, doubled ailerons and a 2° reduction in the angle of wing incidence. Provision was also made for two large Matra R 530 AAMs in addition to the Sidewinders. The first production F-8E(FN) flew on June 26, 1964.

Between 1965 and 1971 many early models of the Crusader were completely rebuilt. A total of 73 RF-8As became RF-8Gs; 61 F-8Bs became F-8Ls; 87 F-8Cs became F-8Ks; 89 F-8Ds became F-8Hs; and 136 F-8Es became F-8Js. The addition of boundary-layer control (flap-blowing) was among the modifications adopted for improved low-speed performance and handling. The French navy Crusaders have also been modernized to F-8J standard.

Vought also produced two other versions of the Crusader: a single example of a tandem two-seat combat trainer, the YTF-8A, which flew on February 6, 1962; and the F8U-3 all-weather fighter, which was a completely new design armed with three AIM-7 Sparrows and powered by a J75 engine. Development of the Crusader III, as it was known, was cancelled in favour of the F-4B Phantom II.

In late 1977, the Philippine government purchased 35 F-8H Crusaders from the United States. Twenty-five were completely refurbished by Vought, and the remaining ten airframes were cannibalized for a ten-year spares programme. First deliveries were in 1978, and the Philippine Crusaders entered service in early 1979.

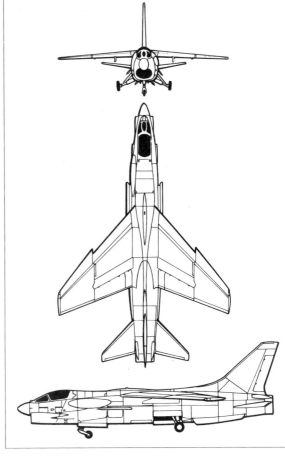

F-8E

Type: single-seat carrier-borne strike fighter
Maker: Chance Vought; Ling Temco Vought; Vought Corporation
Span: 10.72 m (35 ft 2 in)
Length: 16.61 m (54 ft 6 in)
Height: 4.8 m (15 ft 9 in)
Wing area: 34.84 m² (375 sq ft)
Weight: maximum 15 420 kg (34 000 lb); empty 8935 kg (19 700 lb)
Powerplant: one 8165-kg (18 000-lb) st Pratt & Whitney J57-P-20A afterburning turbojet
Performance: maximum speed 1859 km/h (1155 mph) at 10 973 m (36 000 ft); range (clean) 2253 km (1400 miles); service ceiling 17 680 m (58 000 ft)
Armament: four 20-mm (0.79-in) Colt Mk12 cannon; four fuselage-mounted AIM-9 Sidewinder AAMs; four underwing pylons each of a nominal 454-kg (1000-lb) capacity for bombs, Zuni rocket packs or AGM-12 Bullpup ASMs
Crew: 1
Production: 1261 (all types)

Above: A Vought F8U-1E (F-8B) with wings folded on board USS *Intrepid*
Left: Afterburner gas and catapult steam curl away from an F-8E as it takes off from the USS *Bon Homme Richard* during operations in the Gulf of Tonkin in 1967

F-101 Voodoo, McDonnell

FIRST FLIGHT 1954

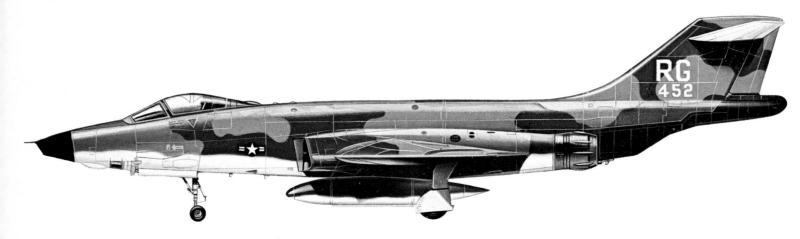

THE F-101 Voodoo was derived from the earlier XF-88 Voodoo. A modified XF-88A was produced following experience gained in Korea, and in January 1952 McDonnell was given a Letter of Intent for an advanced development. The resulting F-101 Voodoo was to become the most versatile supersonic fighter of its period.

As a result of predicted increase in fuel consumption, the F-101's fuselage was lengthened and widened to increase the fuel capacity and to enhance the range further, two drop-tanks were added under the fuselage, plus both probe/drogue and boom-receptacle inflight-refuelling capability. The all-moving tailplane was moved almost to the top of the fin, the wing area fractionally increased by lengthening the chord inboard, and other

aerodynamic refinements were made. The first flight of the F-101A Voodoo was made on September 29, 1954, during which it flew at a supersonic speed.

The 77 F-101As were armed with four 20-mm (0.79-in) M-39 revolver cannon. In addition they could carry either a 735-kg (1620-lb) or 1688-kg (3721-lb) nuclear weapon on the centreline. The MA-7 fire-control system was fitted, together with a LABS (low-altitude bombing system) computer for the toss release of the bomb. The F-101A Voodoo entered USAF service in spring 1957, equipping the 27th Tactical Fighter Wing, part of Tactical Air Command. That year an F-101A set a world speed record at a speed of 1943.4 km/h (1207.6 mph).

Above: An RF-101G in South-east Asian camouflage; the earlier RF-101A supplied clear photographs of missile bases in Cuba during the Missile Crisis in October 1962. With their six cameras they were also deployed in Vietnam during the early stages of the second Indo-Chinese war. The G and H were reconnaissance rebuilds

Above: An XF-88 Voodoo experimental fighter later developed into the much more powerful F-101
Right: The high tail which was one of the alterations to the F-101 airframe
Far right: An F-101A development prototype is readied for a flight at Edwards Air Force Base in California in 1955

As the F-101A was not stressed for its new low-altitude tactical role it was succeeded by the F-101C with a suitably strengthened airframe. The first F-101C flew on August 21, 1957, and entered service with the 81st Tactical Fighter Wing at RAF Bentwaters in the spring of 1958. In service, one of the cannon was removed in order to provide enough space for the Tacan (tactical air navigation) equipment.

Tactical reconnaissance versions of both the A and C model Voodoos were built as the RF-101A and RF-101C respectively, without armament but with a long camera-filled nose. Later Lockheed Aircraft Services converted surplus F-101A/C aircraft to the same role, becoming the RF-101G and H respectively.

The most numerous Voodoo was the F-101B all-weather interceptor, of which 480 were built. This had a new forward fuselage with a tandem cockpit, MG-13 radar fire-control system (with automatic search and track modes) and a flight-refuelling probe. The cannon armament was deleted, and an all-missile armament (typically two nuclear-tipped Genie rockets and four semi-active radar-homing or IR-homing Falcon AAMs) was installed in and beneath a missile bay in the lower fuselage. The first F-101B flew on March 27, 1957.

The first unit to be equipped with the F-101B was the 60th Fighter Interceptor Squadron, in 1959. In later years, the F-101B was updated with an improved fire-control system, and an IR-detector mounted forward of the windscreen in place of the flight-refuelling probe. With these modifica-

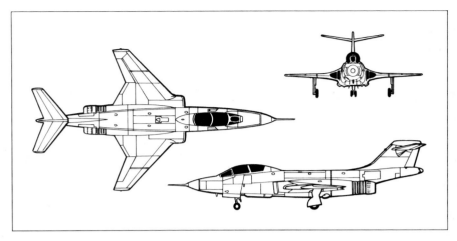

tions, the aircraft was redesignated F-101F. Some 60 F-101B/F Voodoos remained in Air National Guard service in 1980.

The TF-101B was a dual-control trainer version of the B model, produced alongside it. Some of these aircraft were later updated to F standard, becoming TF-101Fs.

The CAF (Canadian Armed Forces) was the only export customer for the F-101B, taking 56 CF-101Bs and ten CF-101F trainers in 1961/62. During 1970/71, the surviving 46 CF-101Bs, together with the ten CF-101Fs, were exchanged for 56 refurbished ex-USAF B models and ten TF-101Bs respectively. These aircraft remain in service with four Canadian squadrons, but will be replaced in the mid 1980s by the CF-18.

F-101B

Type: two-seat all-weather interceptor
Maker: McDonnell Aircraft Co
Span: 12.09 m (39 ft 8 in)
Length: 20.55 m (67 ft 5 in)
Height: 5.49 m (18 ft)
Wing area: 34.19 m² (368 sq ft)
Weight: maximum 23 768 kg (52 400 lb); empty 13 141 kg (28 970 lb)
Powerplant: two 6750-kg (14 880-lb) st Pratt & Whitney J57-P-55 afterburning turbojets
Performance: maximum speed 1825 km/h (1134 mph) at 10 670 m (35 000 ft); range 2495 km (1550 miles); service ceiling 15 850 m (52 000 ft)
Armament: three AIM-4D Falcon missiles; two AIR-2 Genie rockets
Crew: 2
Production: 807 (all types)

Saab 35 Draken

FIRST FLIGHT 1955

THREE prototype Saab 35 and three pre-production Saab 35As were ordered in August 1953, and the prototype made its maiden flight on October 25, 1955. The aircraft was powered by a Rolls-Royce Avon engine with simple afterburner.

The Saab 35A was ordered into quantity production in early 1956, being designated J35A (Adam) by the Flygvapnet (Royal Swedish Air Force). The initial batch of 65 J35As were powered by the RM6B (Avon 200), rated at 6804 kg (15 000 lb) with afterburning, and armed with a pair of 30-mm (1.18-in) Aden cannon in the wings plus four Rb324 Sidewinder AAMs. The aircraft entered service with wing F13 in 1960, which found them easy to fly and maintain, and very robust.

A refined model, designated J35B (Bertil), went into production in late 1961. This was equipped with the Saab S7 collision-course fire-control system (integrated with the Swedish Stril 60 air defence environment), had a slightly longer fuselage, improved canopy and retractable twin tailwheels (which were retro-fitted to the J35A). Powerplant and armament were the same as the J35A, many of which were later brought up to B standard.

An increase in engine power, by using the RM6C (Avon 300) followed, with the J35D (David), which also had increased internal fuel capacity and a Saab FH5 autopilot. First flown on December 27, 1960, the D model did not enter production until 1962, with service a year later.

The final production version for the Flygvapnet

Above left: A Saab J35F Draken of Air Wing F13, Royal Swedish Air Force, armed with Swedish-built Rb27 Falcon missiles
Above: A Saab RF35XD at the Paris Air Show in 1971
Below: A Danish TF35XD trainer with centreline and underwing pods. These Danish aircraft have a greatly increased attack capability

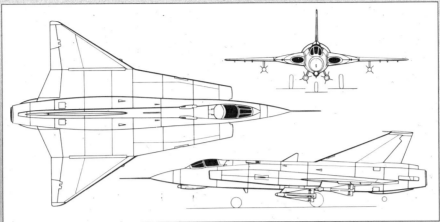

J35F

Type: single-seat interceptor/strike fighter
Maker: Saab-Scania (Aerospace Division)
Span: 9.4 m (30 ft 10 in)
Length: 15.35 m (50 ft 4 in)
Height: 3.89 m (12 ft 9 in)
Wing area: 49.2 m² (529.6 sq ft)
Weight: maximum 12 270 kg (27 050 lb); empty 8250 kg (1818 lb)
Powerplant: one 8000-kg (17 635-lb) Volvo Flygmotor RM6C (licence-built Rolls-Royce Avon 300 turbojet, with Swedish-designed afterburner)
Performance: maximum speed 2125 km/h (1320 mph [Mach 2]) at 11 000 m (36 090 ft) (clean); range (with external stores, but internal fuel) 1300 km (800 miles); service ceiling 20 000 m (65 600 ft)
Armament: one 30-mm (1.18-in) Aden M/55 cannon; two Rb27 Falcon (radar-homing) and two Rb28 Falcon (IR-homing) AAMs, with further provision for two or four Rb324 Sidewinder AAMs; the export Saab 35X has two Aden cannon plus nine stores stations, each with a capability of lifting 454 kg (1000 lb)
Crew: 1
Production: 606

was the J35F (Filip), which featured an improved version of the S7 fire-control system and provision for both the radar-homing and IR-homing versions of the Falcon AAM, built under licence in Sweden as the Rb27 and Rb28 respectively. Several hundred of this type were built.

The first attempt to export this outstanding aircraft met with failure. In 1960, a single Saab 35H (Helvetia) fitted with Ferranti Airpass II radar was produced for Swiss evaluation. The project was abandoned after Switzerland opted for the Mirage III.

In 1968, however, the Danish government selected the Saab 35X for the Royal Danish Air Force. Based on the J35F, the 35X has a greatly increased attack capability – with a maximum external load of 4500 kg (9920 lb) and with two drop-tanks and two 454-kg (1000-lb) bombs on a hi-lo-hi profile the radius of action is 1000 km (621 miles). A total of 46 aircraft (20 F35XD fighters, 20 RF35XD recce-fighters and six TF35XD trainers) were delivered from 1970–71. The F35XDs equip 725 Squadron, while the RF35XDs equip 729 Squadron, with the trainers being split between the two.

The final export customer for the Draken was Finland, ordering 12 Saab 35S in 1970. Prior to their acceptance, the Finns leased six Flygvapnet J35Bs, now designated J35BS, which they subsequently purchased. Later a further nine ex-Flygvapnet low-time Drakens were acquired: three Sk35C trainers and six J35F fighters. The 27 Drakens in Finnish service are flown by 11 Sqn.

Lightning, BAC

FIRST FLIGHT 1957

THE Lightning was developed from the English Electric P.1A supersonic research aircraft to Specification F.23/49, which made its maiden flight on August 4, 1954. The definitive fighter version, at first designated P.1B, was ordered for the RAF in November 1956. The first of 20 P.1B development aircraft, powered by two Rolls-Royce Avon 200 turbojets in a completely redesigned fuselage with a circular intake cone to house the radar, flew on April 4, 1957. The P.1B was officially named Lightning in October 1958. It had a distinctive superimposed engine configuration with angular swept wings and a wedge shaped tail.

By early 1961, Fighter Command's first unit, 74 Squadron, had been equipped with the production Lightning F.1 and declared operational. It was the RAF's first supersonic fighter, equipped with Ferranti Airpass monopulse radar able to track targets and launch the two de Havilland Firestreak heat-seeking AAMs againt a hostile target without visual contact. A pair of nose-mounted 30-mm (1.18-in) Aden cannon supplemented the missile armament.

After only 19 F.1s, improvements including Avon 210 engines and an inflight refuelling probe were made to produce the F.1A. The Lightning was next given updated avionics and a fully variable afterburner to produce the F.2 version. This first flew on July 11, 1961 and two RAF units, 19 and 92 Squadrons, were fully operational by mid 1963.

Then came the F.3 version, incorporating the AI.23 radar and Red Top missiles, while the gun

Above: The Lightning F.1 was the first RAF fighter to exceed the speed of sound in level flight. It will be replaced by the Tornado F.2 in 1985, but continues to operate alongside the Phantom as an air-defence fighter

Below: Lightning F.2s of 92 Squadron in Germany; later they were remanufactured to F.6 standard as F.2As

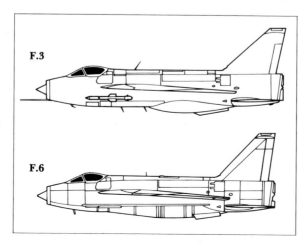

Above: An exhibition Lightning with RAF serial numbers, Saudi Arabian markings, and dummy Firestreak missiles

Right: The Lightning F.3 armed with two de Havilland Firestreak missiles and the Lightning F.6 with its ventral tank giving a deeper profile. It has twice the internal fuel of the F.1

F.3

F.6

armament was deleted. More powerful Avon 301 engines were fitted, and the fin area increased by 15% to compensate for the larger missiles. The first Lightning F.3 flew on June 16, 1962, and went on to equip four RAF squadrons. Some are still in service with the RAF's remaining Lightning units.

The first production F.6 flew on June 16, 1965, and is still the principal version in service today. Between 1968 and 1970, 31 Lightning F.2s, equipping the two RAF Germany squadrons, were rebuilt to F.6 standard, and redesignated F.2A. In the early 1970s, a pair of 30-mm (1.18-in) Aden cannon were retro-fitted to the forward part of the ventral tank of the F.6.

As part of an air-defence package deal in December 1965, Saudi Arabia ordered 33 F.53s (F.6s with two underwing pylons, each of 454 kg [1000 lb] capacity) and six T.55s (T.5s). In addition some five F.52s (ex-RAF F.2s) and two T.54s (ex-RAF T.4s) were provided on which to train. Delivery was completed in June 1968. Kuwait was the only other country to purchase the Lightning, receiving a dozen F.53s and two T.55s during 1968–69.

Although most of the RAF's Lightning squadrons were re-equipped with Phantom FGR.2s during the early 1970s, two squadrons were retained. Because of the so-called 'NATO fighter gap', it was announced in July 1979 that a third squadron of Lightnings would be brought back into service (using aircraft out of the mothballed reserve stock). The Lightnings will be replaced by the Panavia Tornado F.2 from 1984.

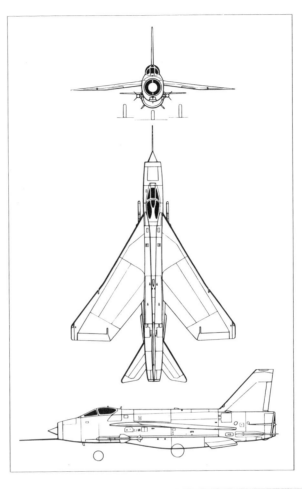

F.6

Type: single-seat all-weather interceptor
Maker: English Electric (later BAC, now British Aerospace)
Span: 10.62 m (34 ft 10 in)
Length: 16.84 m (55 ft 3 in)
Height: 5.97 m (19 ft 7 in)
Wing area: 44.08 m² (474.5 sq ft)
Weight: maximum 22 680 kg (50 000 lb); empty approx 12 700 kg (28 000 lb)
Powerplant: two 7393-kg (16 300-lb) st Rolls-Royce Avon 303 afterburning turbojets
Performance: maximum speed 2414 km/h (1500 mph [Mach 2.3]) at 12 192 m (40 000 ft); range 1290 km (800 miles); service ceiling over 18 288 m (60 000 ft)
Armament: two 30-mm (1.18-in) Aden cannon; two Red Top AAMs
Crew: 1
Production: 339 (all types)

MiG-19, Mikoyan

FIRST FLIGHT 1953

THE logical development of the MiG-15 and 17 designs, the MiG-19 was initially ordered on July 30, 1951, as the I-350, and flew for the first time on September 18, 1953. The initial day-fighter version (designated Farmer-A by NATO), of which some 500 were built from 1955, was armed with a single 37-mm (1.46-in) N-37 and two 23-mm (0.9-in) NR-23 cannon. Before long, this version was supplanted by the MiG-19S (stabilator), with an all-moving tailplane, an armament of three 30-mm (1.18-in) NR-30 cannon, a ventral airbrake and wing pylons for bombs or ASMs. NATO designated this version Farmer-B.

The adoption of the RD-9 turbojet, in 1956, led to an increased level Mach number from 1.1 to 1.3. Built in large numbers, this version was designated MiG-19SF and codenamed Farmer-C. Developed parallel with the C model was a limited all-weather version with a small Izumrud (emerald) radar, mounted in an intake centre-body, and a ranging unit on the top of the intake lip. This was designated MiG-19PF and codenamed Farmer-D. The final production version, the MiG-19PM Farmer-F differed from the PF by having the cannon armament deleted in favour of four AA-1 (Alkali) beam-riding missiles, mounted under the wings.

Although production of the MiG-19 ceased in the Soviet Union in the early 1960s, it still continues in China, following a manufacturing licence agreement signed in January 1958.

The first Chinese-built F-6 (MiG-19S standard) flew in December 1961, and was in general service by mid 1962. Since then, many thousands of F-6s have been built, including equivalents of the PF and SF versions. The Chinese also have developed a tactical-reconnaissance version, a two-seat trainer, TF-6, and the Fantan-A strike fighter.

Originally thought to be designated F-9, the Fantan-A is now known to be the F-6*bis*. Based on the F-6, all dimensions appear to have been increased by 10%.

As with most Soviet types, nations friendly to the USSR have received the MiG-19 including (in addition to Warsaw Pact countries), Afghanistan, Cuba, Indonesia, Iraq, North Korea, Uganda and Vietnam. The F-6 has been supplied by China to Pakistan, Tanzania and Egypt. It is generally believed that the MiG-19/F-6 will be an effective future combat aircraft in the Third World.

Above: A Farmer-A MiG-19 showing its ventral airbrake (as on later models), and fuselage-mounted 37-mm (1.46-in) N-37 cannon on the right side beneath the cockpit
Left: The four fuselage fuel cells could be supplemented by two 800-litre (176-Imp gal) underwing drop-tanks. The wing-mounted NR-30 cannon are situated close to the fuselage

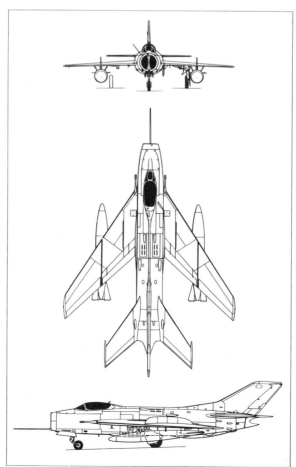

MiG-19SF

Type: single-seat fighter
Maker: Mikoyan Gurevich design bureau; Shenyang State Aircraft Factory
Span: 9 m (29 ft 6¼ in)
Length: 13.09 m (42 ft 11½ in)
Height: 4.02 m (13 ft 2¼ in)
Wing area: 25 m² (269.1 sq ft)
Weight: maximum 8700 kg (19 180 lb); empty 5760 kg (12 698 lb)
Powerplant: two 3250-kg (7165-lb) st Tumansky (Mikulin) RD-9B afterburning turbojets
Performance: maximum speed 1452 km/h (902 mph) at 10 000 m (32 810 ft); range with two 800-litre (176 Imp gal) drop tanks 2200 km (1367 miles); service ceiling 17 900 m (58 725 ft)
Armament: two wing-mounted and one fuselage-mounted 30-mm (1.18-in) NR-30 cannon; two wing pylons capable of carrying (typically) two 250-kg (550-lb) bombs, two 212-mm (8.35-in) ARS-212 rocket missiles, or two 800-litre (176-Imp gal) drop-tanks
Crew: 1
Production: estimated in thousands

Kfir, IAI

FIRST FLIGHT 1971

THE development of the Kfir (lion cub) by IAI was the ultimate result of the 1967 embargo by the French government on the delivery of 50 Mirage 5J fighter-bombers, which had been developed for and paid for by the Israeli government. The Kfir is a curious but effective blend of French aerodynamics (improved in Israel), American engine technology and Israeli avionics expertise. To begin the process, a J79 engine was installed in a two-seat Mirage IIIB, with much modification, and test flown in September 1971.

The Kfir is basically the airframe of the Mirage 5, with a longer nose and shorter rear fuselage to accommodate the J79 engine. Because of the higher external wall temperature of the J79, compared with the Atar 9C, thermal insulation plus a ram-air dorsal intake for cooling air are provided. In order to take higher operating weights, strengthened long-stroke oleo main gears are fitted. The cockpit was redesigned to include an Israeli-designed HUD and weapons sight, and a Martin-Baker JM6 zero-zero ejection seat. The Kfir is equipped with either the Elta EL/M-2001B or EL/M-2021 X-band pulse-Doppler target acquisition and tracking radar, with dual air-to-air or air-to-surface capability. Internal fuel tankage is more than on the Mirage 5, being estimated at 4000 litres (880 Imp gal). This initial production version, the Kfir-C1, equipped two squadrons of the Heyl Ha'Avir.

An improved version of the aircraft, the Kfir-C2, was revealed on July 20, 1976, and is understood to have entered production in 1974. The most significant change is the addition of non-retractable

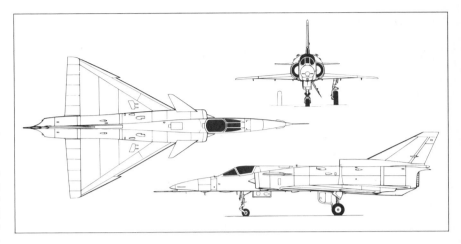

but detachable, swept-back canard surfaces aft of the engine intakes; but additionally, two small strakes are mounted either side of the extreme nose.

The Kfir-C2 is the standard production aircraft, initial C1 versions being updated to C2 configuration, and is also being offered for export by IAI. An order in 1976 for 24 Kfir-C2s by Ecuador was vetoed by the United States; but an order for 50 from Taiwan was granted approval in July 1978. Other export initiatives have been made to Austria and countries in South America.

A two-seat version of the Kfir was reported as being under development, with a first flight due in 1979, but the year went by without any further announcement.

Kfir-C2

Type: single-seat interceptor and ground-attack fighter
Maker: Israel Aircraft Industries
Span: 8.22 m (26 ft 11½ in)
Length: approx 16.35 m (53 ft 7¾ in)
Height: 4.25 m (13 ft 11¼ in)
Wing area: 34.85 m² (375 sq ft)
Weight: maximum 14 600 kg (32 188 lb); empty 6785 kg (14 960 lb)
Powerplant: one 8120-kg (17 900-lb) st General Electric J79-J1E afterburning turbojet (a modified J79-GE-17)
Performance: maximum speed (estimated) 2335 km/h (1450 mph [Mach 2.2]) over 11 000 m (36 100 ft); range (interceptor with two 600-litre [132-Imp gal] drop-tanks) 1070 km (664 miles); service ceiling over 15 240 m (50 000 ft)
Armament: two IAI-built 30-mm (1.18-in) DEFA 552 cannon; seven hardpoints for external stores; for interceptor role, Rafael Shafrir 2 IR-homing AAMs; for ground-attack role, a combination of bombs (including conventional and 'concrete-dibber' type), IMI rocket pods, napalm tanks, ECM pods, air-to-surface missiles (including AGM-45 Shrike, AGM-65 Maverick and GBU-8 Hobos) and 600-litre (132-Imp gal) drop-tanks
Crew: 1
Production: 180 (estimated) by January 1980

Left: This frontal view of the Kfir-C2 clearly shows the small nose strakes, and the swept-back fixed canards behind the engine intakes, which greatly improve manoeuvrability

Sea Vixen, Hawker Siddeley

FIRST FLIGHT 1951

THE first prototype de Havilland DH.110 flew on September 26, 1951, and on April 9, 1952, exceeded the speed of sound in a dive. The aircraft was of twin tail-boom configuration, with the crew compartment and twin engines in a nacelle. The pilot was under a canopy, offset to the left, while the observer was totally enclosed within the nacelle behind to the right. The powerplant was a pair of Rolls-Royce Avon RA.7 turbojets, each rated at 3402 kg (7500 lb) st.

A semi-navalized prototype flew in June 1955, and carrier-suitability trials were successfully completed by April 1956. The first fully-navalized production aircraft, with power-folding wings, hydraulically steerable nosewheel and a pointed nose radome for GE AI.18 radar, flew on March 20, 1957. Hatfield's DH.110 had become the Sea Vixen FAW.1, produced at Christchurch.

The Sea Vixen FAW.1 was the first Fleet Air Arm fighter to be designed as an integrated weapons system, and the first British fighter not to have a gun armament. Four de Havilland (later HSD) Firestreak IR-homing AAMs were the primary armament, while two retractable Microcell packs under the fuselage held 28 50.8-mm (2-in) FFARs. The Sea Vixen, with twice the rate of climb, a far greater service ceiling and endurance, was far ahead of the Sea Venom it replaced in service.

The first operational Sea Vixen unit was 892 Squadron, forming in July 1959 – ten years after design and eight years from first flight – and embarking in HMS *Ark Royal* in March 1960. In 1961, the decision was made to update the FAW.1 to take the new Red Top AAMs and increase the fuel capacity, by deepening the tailbooms and extending them forward of the wing. Two FAW.1s were converted as interim FAW.2 prototypes, the first of which flew on June 1, 1962.

The first 14 FAW.2s began life as FAW.1s, being converted on the production line, while a further 15 new-build FAW.2s were completed. The first production FAW.2 made its maiden flight on March 8, 1963, and the last Sea Vixen was completed in 1966. Between 1963 and 1968, however, some 65 FAW.1s were returned to Hawker Siddeley (which had absorbed de Havilland) and were rebuilt to FAW.2 standard.

The first unit to receive the Sea Vixen FAW.2 was 899 Squadron in December 1963, and a year later it became operational in HMS *Eagle*. In 1965, it took part in the blockade operations, off the coast of Mozambique, against Rhodesia. The remaining Sea Vixen FAW.1 units gradually re-equipped with the FAW.2; the last unit to get the FAW.2 was 890 Squadron in August 1967.

The Sea Vixens were, however, soon to begin their phasing out of service, following the Labour Government's 1966 decision to run down the aircraft carrier force. The last Sea Vixen unit in service was 899 Squadron, which disbanded in January 1972.

A few Sea Vixens were retained for trials and evaluation purposes, and some of 899 Squadron's aircraft were converted to RPV configuration by Flight Refuelling. Designated D.3, these are used as unmanned targets for live missile-firing.

Right: A Sea Vixen development aircraft takes off from an aircraft carrier, leaving the strop from the catapult in mid-air
Below: The Sea Vixen FAW.2, showing the tail booms extended forward of the wing to house extra fuel

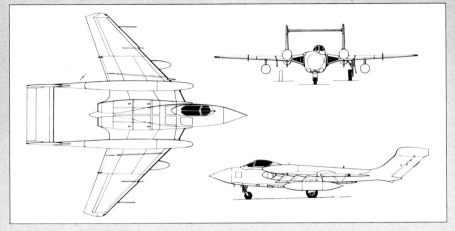

Sea Vixen FAW.2

Type: two-seat carrier-borne all-weather fighter
Maker: de Havilland Aircraft Co (later Hawker Siddeley Aviation, now British Aerospace)
Span: 15.5 m (51 ft)
Length: 16.94 m (55 ft 7 in)
Height: 3.28 m (10 ft 9 in)
Wing area: 60.2 m² (648 sq ft)
Weight: maximum 16 783 kg (37 000 lb); empty 11 793 kg (26 000 lb)
Powerplant: two 5094-kg (11 230-lb) Rolls-Royce Avon 208 turbojets
Performance: maximum speed 1030 km/h (640 mph) at sea level; range 1931 km (1200 miles); service ceiling 14 630 m (48 000 ft)
Armament: four wing-mounted HSD Red Top AAMs; a 2 × 14 Microcell under-fuselage pack of FFARs; alternatively various combinations of 227-kg (500-lb) bombs, 76.2-mm (3-in) air-to-surface rockets, AGM-12B Bullpup ASMs or drop-tanks
Crew: 2
Production: 150 (all types)

Yak-25, Yakovlev
FIRST FLIGHT 1953

BELIEVED to have flown for the first time in 1953, the Yakovlev Yak-25 (NATO codename **Flashlight**) was the Soviet Union's first production two-seat twin-jet all-weather fighter. It was selected from a wealth of rival designs tested during 1949–53 and made its first public appearance at Tushino in 1955. It formed the basis for a long series of heavier and more powerful aircraft for many other roles.

The Yak-25 featured a fully swept mid wing and a high-mounted swept tailplane. Initial production aircraft were powered by underslung Mikulin AM-5s, rated at 2200 kg (4850 lb), but from 1957 these were supplanted by a pair of Tumansky RD-9 turbojets. This version was redesignated Yak-25F, **Flashlight-A**. An unusual feature of the aircraft

was its bicycle-type main landing gear which featured a double-wheel main unit at about the centre of gravity, with a single nosewheel and wingtip outriggers. The pilot and radar operator were housed in tandem, the radome in the nose being a blunt, rounded shape, enclosing a bulky and rather primitive radar based to some degree on the US SCR-720 of World War II. The armament was a pair of 37-mm (1.46-in) cannon in the belly, with provision for a ventral pack of 55-mm (2.16-in) unguided air-to-air rockets.

A parallel development of the tactical-reconnaissance Yak-25R was codenamed **Flashlight-B**. This featured a glazed nose and single canopy. This type was first seen in 1956. A straight-wing variant intended as a Soviet air force counterpart to the US

220

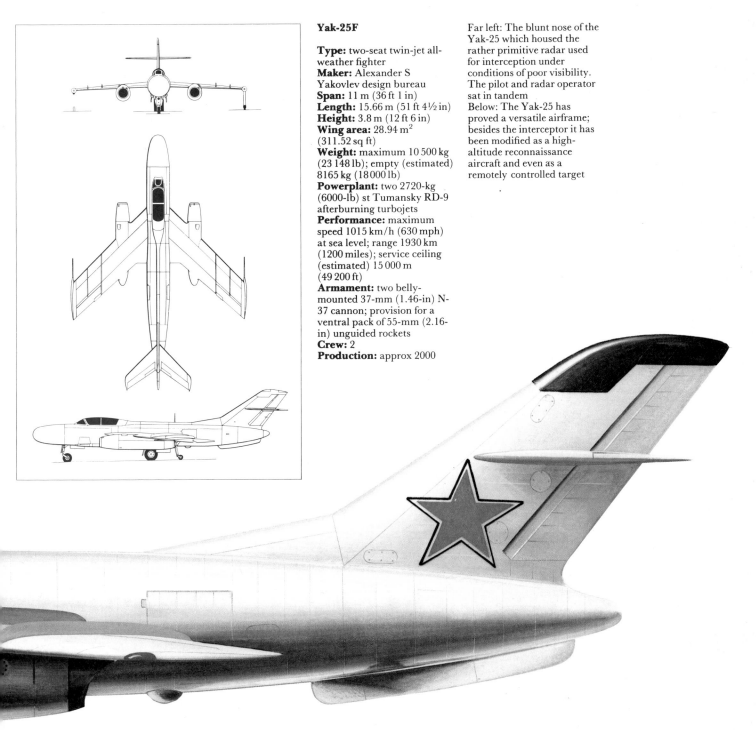

Yak-25F

Type: two-seat twin-jet all-weather fighter
Maker: Alexander S Yakovlev design bureau
Span: 11 m (36 ft 1 in)
Length: 15.66 m (51 ft 4½ in)
Height: 3.8 m (12 ft 6 in)
Wing area: 28.94 m² (311.52 sq ft)
Weight: maximum 10 500 kg (23 148 lb); empty (estimated) 8165 kg (18 000 lb)
Powerplant: two 2720-kg (6000-lb) st Tumansky RD-9 afterburning turbojets
Performance: maximum speed 1015 km/h (630 mph) at sea level; range 1930 km (1200 miles); service ceiling (estimated) 15 000 m (49 200 ft)
Armament: two belly-mounted 37-mm (1.46-in) N-37 cannon; provision for a ventral pack of 55-mm (2.16-in) unguided rockets
Crew: 2
Production: approx 2000

Far left: The blunt nose of the Yak-25 which housed the rather primitive radar used for interception under conditions of poor visibility. The pilot and radar operator sat in tandem

Below: The Yak-25 has proved a versatile airframe; besides the interceptor it has been modified as a high-altitude reconnaissance aircraft and even as a remotely controlled target

Lockheed U-2, Yak-25RD, is known as Mandrake. The first sighting of a Mandrake in the West was over India. It is also believed to have been used in the surveillance role along the Russo-Chinese border. The record-breaking RV is thought to be a Mandrake but nobody is certain as to what RV signifies – the most likely possibility is *rekord vysota*, record height, but it could stand for *razvedshchik vysota*, which means high altitude reconnaissance.

The Flashlight-C looked like a developed B with extended 'drooped' leading edges to the wings, an increased span (with wing fences deleted) and extended afterburning engine nacelles. This version was redesignated Yak-27P. Some versions retained the gun/rocket armament, while later

versions were seen with missile pylons under the wings. A reconnaissance version, designated Yak-26 is known as Mangrove, after being initially thought to have been designated Yak-27R, codenamed Flashlight-D. It is also thought that this version eventually served as the prototype for the Yakovlev Yak-28 fighter-bomber, which entered operational service with the Soviet air force in 1962–63.

Unlike most Russian-built aircraft, the Yak-25 has not been supplied to any other air force than that of the Soviet Union. Production of the Yak-25 series is thought to have ceased in the late 1950s, the initial type being the most numerous variant produced. Some may still be in use as radio-controlled target aircraft.

Yak-28P, Yakovlev

ESTIMATED FIRST FLIGHT 1961

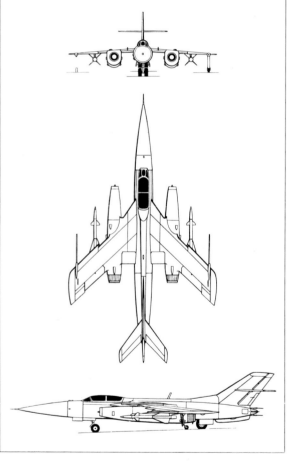

Yak-28P

Type: two-seat twin-jet all-weather fighter
Maker: Alexander S Yakovlev design bureau
Span: 12.95 m (42 ft 6 in)
Length: 21.65 m (71 ft 0½ in) (early models) 22.56 m (74 ft) (late models)
Height: 3.95 m (12 ft 11½ in)
Wing area: (estimated) 37.5 m² (403.65 sq ft)
Weight: (estimated) maximum 15 875 kg (35 000 lb); empty not available
Powerplant: two 5850-kg (13 120-lb) st Tumansky R-11 afterburning turbojets
Performance: (all figures estimated): maximum level speed 1180 km/h (733 mph [Mach 1.1]) at 10 670 m (35 000 ft); range 1930 to 2575 km (1200 to 1600 miles); service ceiling 16 750 m (55 000 ft)
Armament: one IR-homing and one semi-active radar homing AA-3 Anab missile
Crew: 2
Production: not available

THE Yak-28 series of aircraft were first seen in 1961, being successors to, and derived from, the Yak-25/26/27 series of multi-purpose aircraft. Retaining the configuration of the earlier series, the Yak-28 was a new design featuring a shoulder-wing of different form, new engines and revised landing gear with a steerable two-wheel nose unit and the main twin-wheel unit moved further aft. The new aircraft was much heavier than its predecessors, and since there were several versions on display, it was assumed that the new types, described as supersonic multi-purpose aircraft, were prototypes. At least three glazed-nose and several solid-nose versions of the Yak-28 were involved in the Tushino flypast of 1961.

The first three versions of the Yak-28 were tactical-bomber aircraft with glazed noses, shorter fuselage and shorter engine nacelles ahead of the wings. These bore the NATO codenames Brewer-A/B/C. A reconnaissance version is codenamed Brewer-D, while the Brewer-E is an ECM conversion of the earlier series.

The fighter version of the Brewer is codenamed Firebar, being developed in parallel, and designated Yak-28P. (The suffix P denotes *perekhvatchik*, interceptor, meaning the design has been adapted for the fighter role.) It differs from the Brewer in featuring a dielectric nose cone, housing an air-interception radar (NATO codename Skip Spin) with an effective range of approximately 40 km (25 miles), a tandem cockpit for the two-man crew (the windscreen being some 76 cm (2 ft 6 in)

Top: A Yak-28 in an experimental radiation-reflection camouflage
Left centre: The Yak-28P showing its centreline landing gear
Above left: A Yak-28P, with extended radome, takes off. The Russians have always required their aircraft to be able to operate from hastily prepared landing strips
Above right: The Yak-28U, training version. This does not carry the radar of the 28P and cannot instruct a complete aircrew

further forward), and the internal weapons bay of the Brewer deleted (it is assumed) in favour of extra fuel tankage. The codenames were allocated after confusion arose as to the specific roles of the aircraft.

The main armament of the Yak-28P is a pair of AA-3 (Anab) air-to-air missiles mounted on wing pylons, one missile being an IR-homer, the other being radar-guided. At the Domodedovo display in 1967 an aircraft was on display in the static park with two pylons under each wing – one for an AA-2 (K-13) (Atoll) missile plus one for an Anab.

It is assumed that this aircraft was a weapons development vehicle. It also featured a much longer nose radome, which has subsequently been seen on other Yak-28Ps in squadron service. The

longer radome is not assumed to indicate any increase in aircraft performance or radar capability. It is thought that tail-warning radar is fitted.

A trainer version exists in the form of the Yak-28U, called Maestro by NATO. This features two individual single-seat cockpits with the front canopy hinging to the right and the rear canopy sliding rearwards.

It is thought the Yak-28P entered series production in 1963–64, lasting until 1969–70. Several thousand of the whole Yak-28 series are thought to have been built. Latest estimates suggest that in excess of 300 28Ps, with uprated avionics and missiles and more powerful engines, are still in service with, and form a significant component of, the Soviet PVO (home-defence interceptor force).

Tu-28P, Tupolev
ESTIMATED FIRST FLIGHT 1957

THE largest fighter ever to be put into operational service anywhere in the world, this formidable supersonic interceptor was first seen at the Tushino air display in July 1961. It was designated Tu-102 by the Tupolev design bureau and is one of a number of supersonic aircraft, another being the Tu-105/Tu-22 (Blinder) bomber, developed from the Tu-98 series of technology development aircraft built by Tupolev in the late 1950s and codenamed Backfin. It is thought the Backfin made its first flight in 1955. It was originally thought to be a Yakovlev design.

It is interesting to note that the designation P (*perekhvatchik*, interceptor) is used. This suffix is applied to aircraft which have been designed for one role, and then adapted for use as a fighter. It is possible that as this is the only fighter to emanate from the Tupolev design bureau, its original role may have been as a reconnaissance or strike aircraft, possibly for anti-shipping use. The threat of USAF B-52 or B-70 bombers may have caused its adaptation as a fighter, and it is thought that it made its maiden flight in 1957. Its endurance is estimated at around three to five hours, although it could be considerably longer, with the use of auxiliary fuel tanks. A CIA-operated U-2 reconnaissance aircraft photographed a Tu-28 in 1959, but western intelligence experts had considerable trouble with its identification because of its resemblance to the Tu-98 Backfin. As a fighter, the Tu-28 would have a useful role patrolling those areas of the Soviet Union not fully covered by the SAM umbrella. Its powerful radar and AAM armament would be effective against low-flying enemy bombers attempting to penetrate through the radar cover.

Of conventional swept-wing configuration, the Tu-28P has the greatest internal fuel capacity of any known fighter, plus the largest AI radar (an I-band radar, codenamed Big Nose) known to exist. Codenamed Fiddler by the West (and referred to on some occasions by the US Department of Defense as the Tu-128), the Tu-28P is powered by two large axial-flow turbojets of an unknown type, rated at 12 250 kg (27 000 lb) st with afterburning. There has been speculation that models are fitted with afterburning turbofans, rated at 13 610 kg (30 000 lb). The jetpipes are mounted side-by-side in a bulged tail.

Above: A Tu-28P armed with AA-5 Ash missiles. Codenamed Fiddler, the Tu-28 has the largest AI radar known to exist, with the appropriate codename of Big Nose
Below: Three AA-5-armed production Fiddlers make a low pass during a Soviet aviation presentation

Above: One of the original Tu-28s seen in 1961, with large ventral bulge and two rear ventral fins
Right: Pilot and navigator go aboard a Tu-28P of the IA-PVO for a patrol mission

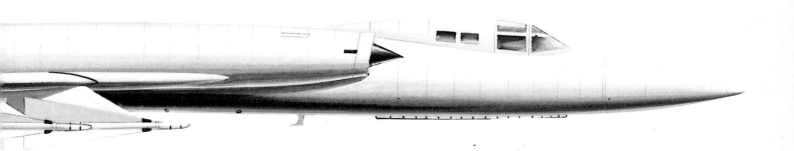

The wing, which is mid-set and with a small anhedral angle, has an increased chord on the inboard panels, which are separated from the increased-sweep trailing edge by large fairings for the four-wheel bogie main landing gears.

The sharply swept tail surfaces, when first seen in 1961, were supplemented by two ventral fins, but these have since been deleted. Also deleted since the 1961 sighting is a large, bulged under-fuselage fairing. The crew sit in tandem under upward-hinged canopies.

When first seen, the Tu-28's armament was two delta-winged air-to-air missiles (codenamed Ash), mounted under the wings. This has since been doubled to four missiles, two each of the radar-homing and IR-homing types. At no time has this aircraft been observed with a gun armament.

Although production is thought to have ceased by 1969, the Tu-28P is still in service. It is an ideal strategic patrol fighter to operate in conjunction with the Tu-126 (Moss) airborne warning and control aircraft. As the Tu-22 bomber is replaced in service by the Tu-22M/Tu-26 (Backfire), it is thought that the Tu-28P will be phased out of service in favour of an interceptor version of the Tu-22. Maximum front-line strength is thought not to have exceeded 150 Tu-28Ps, most of these being based in the Moscow military district. It is also possible that some have been converted for use as an EW/ECM aircraft, with specialized electronic equipment being housed in a ventral pack similar to the fairing seen on the type in 1961.

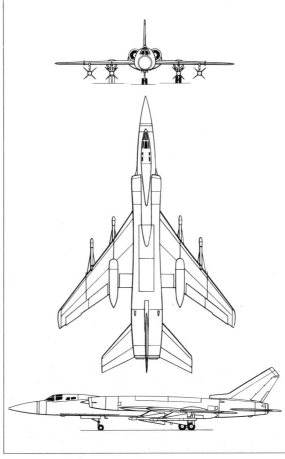

Tu-28P

Type: two-seat long-range all-weather interceptor
Maker: Andrei N Tupolev design bureau
Span: 20 m (65 ft)
Length: 26 m (85 ft)
Height: 7 m (23 ft)
Wing area: 75 m^2 (807.3 sq ft)
Weight: maximum 45 000 kg (100 000 lb); empty 25 000 kg (55 000 lb)
Powerplant: two 12 250-kg (27 000-lb) st axial-flow afterburning turbojets of an unknown type
Performance: maximum speed 1850 km/h (1150 mph, Mach 1.75) at 11 000 m (36 000 ft); range with maximum fuel 4989 km (3100 miles); service ceiling 20 000 m (65 620 ft)
Armament: two radar-homing and two IR-homing AA-5 AAMs
Crew: 2
Production: not available

All data are estimated

Mirage III, Dassault-Breguet

FIRST FLIGHT 1956

THE origins of the Mirage began in 1952, with an Armée de l'Air requirement for a light-weight interceptor to be powered by two small turbojets. The prototype Mirage I was powered by a pair of Dassault-built Armstrong Siddeley Vipers, rated at 998 kg (2200 lb). It made its first flight on June 25, 1955. Although exceeding Mach 1.15 in a dive, it was not until an SEPR liquid-propellant rocket, of 1497 kg (3300 lb) thrust, was installed under the rear fuselage, that the Mirage I achieved Mach 1.3 in level flight. Dassault was not happy with this low-powered aircraft, and after some work on the Mirage II, the company went ahead with the larger and heavier Mirage III, powered by a SNECMA Atar 101G, of 4000 kg (8820 lb) thrust. This version made its maiden flight on November 17, 1956, and although with provision for a SEPR rocket motor, it achieved a speed in excess of Mach 1.5 at 10 973 m (36 000 ft) on January 30, 1957, flying on the turbojet alone.

The Armée de l'Air soon grasped the potential of the Mirage III. The design was refined with a thinner wing and redesigned fuselage to house the new SNECMA Atar 9 turbojet, as the Mirage IIIA, and ten pre-production aircraft ordered. The first IIIA flew on May 12, 1958, and on October 24, 1958, became the first western European fighter to exceed Mach 2 in level flight. Additionally, it exhibited its ability to take off and land on a grass field in less than 870 m (2500 ft). The Armée de l'Air wasted no time, and 100 developed intercep-

Below: A Mirage IIIE of EC 2/4 La Fayette which received these aircraft in November 1966
Bottom left: The drag chute blossoms from a Mirage IIIE as it lands at a French base
Bottom right: A Mirage IIIC armed with an R.530 AAM. The type saw action in the Middle East both as a fighter and also as a day ground-attack aircraft

tor versions, designated Mirage IIIC, were ordered into production.

The IIIC could be fitted with either a pair of 30-mm (1.18-in) DEFA cannon or the SEPR 841 rocket motor for a faster climb and combat capability. The main armament was either two AIM-9 Sidewinder or a single Matra R.530 AAM, used in conjunction with CSF Cyrano I fire-control radar. The first IIIC flew on October 9, 1960, entering service in late 1961.

Export models of the Mirage IIIC were sold to Israel as the IIICJ, without rocket motors or missiles, in 1963; South Africa as the IIICZ; and one as a pattern aircraft for Switzerland, which built the IIIC with a Hughes Taran fire-control system and provision for HM-55 Falcon AAMs as

the Mirage IIIS under licence. Some 244 examples of Mirage IIICs were built.

A tandem two-seat trainer version, designated Mirage IIIB, first flew on October 20, 1959. The fuselage was some 0.6-m (23.6-in) longer than the IIIA, and although the radar was deleted, it could perform air-to-surface strike operations. A total of 174 IIIBs of all versions were built. The Mirage IIID is an improved trainer version, based initially on the Australian-built IIIO, but later adopted as the training version of the Mirage IIIE and 5 series.

The potential of the Mirage III was further exploited by developing a long-range intruder variant, designated IIIE. This had an increase of 0.3 m (11.8 in) in the fuselage length, to help house

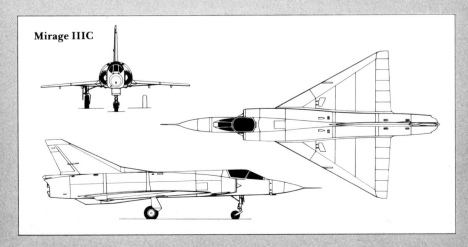

Mirage IIIC

Mirage IIIE

Type: single-seat fighter-bomber
Maker: Avions Marcel Dassault/Breguet Aviation
Span: 8.22 m (26 ft 11½ in)
Length: 15.03 m (49 ft 3½ in)
Height: 4.5 m (14 ft 9 in)
Wing area: 34.85 m² (375 sq ft)
Weight: maximum 13 500 kg (29 760 lb); empty 7050 kg (15 540 lb)
Powerplant: one 6200-kg (13 670-lb) st SNECMA Atar 9C afterburning turbojet plus provision for one 1500-kg (3307-lb) SEPR 844 rocket
Performance: maximum

speed 2350 km/h (1460 mph [Mach 2.2]) at 12 000 m (39 375 ft); range 2400 km (1490 miles); service ceiling at Mach 1.8 17 000 m (55 775 ft)
Armament: two fuselage-mounted 30-mm (1.18-in) DEFA cannon; one Matra R.530/Super R.530 AAM or two 454-kg (1000-lb) bombs on centreline pylon; two underwing pylons each capable of carrying one 454-kg (1000-lb) bomb, JL-100 rocket pod, Matra R.550 Magic or AIM-9 Sidewinder AAMs, and drop-tanks
Crew: 1
Production: 840 (of all Mirage IIIs)

the improved avionics installed, including Tacan (tactical air navigation), Doppler and the improved Cyrano II fire-control radar. The first prototype flew on April 5, 1961 and the first production delivery was made in January 1964. Most of the 523 IIIEs manufactured were for export, going to 13 air forces including Argentina (IIIEA), Brazil (IIIEBR), Lebanon (IIIEL), Pakistan (IIIEP), Spain (IIIEE), South Africa (IIIEZ) and Venezuela (IIIEV). The Government Aircraft Factories in Australia built a version of the IIIE with the Sperry twin gyro platform and a PHI 5C1 navigation unit, as the IIIO. The first two aircraft were supplied from France as patterns and 48 IIIOF interceptors, 50 IIIOA ground attack, plus ten IIID trainers, were built. A reconnais-sance variant of the IIIE with five nose-mounted cameras, is designated IIIR.

At Israel's suggestion, a clear-weather ground attack version, aimed at Middle Eastern countries, was developed. Designated Mirage 5, it had the radar and fire-control avionics removed, 500 litres (110 Imp gal) extra fuel installed and an increased stores capacity. Israel ordered and paid for 50 of these aircraft, but on the orders of the French government they were never delivered. This action prompted the Israeli development of the Kfir.

For the optimized ground-attack role, the Mirage 5 is armed with a pair of 30-mm (1.18-in) DEFA cannon, and can carry 4000 kg (8820 lb) of external stores on seven fuselage and wing hard-points. It can also be configured as an interceptor

Above: A Mirage IIICJ of the Israeli Defence Force with a Nord AS 30 tactical air-to-surface missile, two Sidewinder (or Shafrir) AAMs and two drop-tanks
Above right: A Mirage IIIE with a Martel AS.37 anti-radiation missile for use against enemy radars

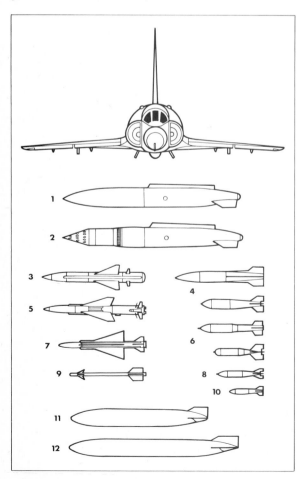

with two Sidewinder AAMs and 4700 litres (1034 Imp gal) of external fuel.

The first Mirage 5 flew on May 19, 1967, and although Israel never received them (they were issued to the Armée de l'Air), they were exported widely to Abu Dhabi, Belgium, Columbia, Egypt, Gabon, Libya, Pakistan, Peru, Saudi Arabia, Venezuela and Zaire. Some 480 Mirage 5s of all marks were ordered.

In 1975, the multi-mission Mirage 50 was unveiled at the Paris Air Show. Retaining the basic airframe of the Mirage III/5, it is powered by the uprated SNECMA Atar 9K50 turbojet, rated at 7200 kg (15 873 lb) st with afterburning, as fitted to the Mirage F1C. The Mirage 50 can carry the full range of armament and equipment developed for the III/5 series, plus the Agave or Cyrano IV multi-function radar, an inertial or Doppler navigation/attack system, and a head-up display. The Mirage 50, which offers better performance and manoeuvrability than the III/5, first flew on April 15, 1979.

Apart from the production aircraft, Dassault produced several experimental variants including the enlarged Mirage IIIV V/STOL (short take-off and landing) fighter, with a SNECMA TF306 turbofan for propulsion and eight Rolls-Royce RB.162 lift jets mounted in the centre-fuselage; the large high-wing T family; the swing-wing Mirage G series; and the Milan, a Mirage 5 with retractable 'moustache' foreplanes for shorter field length and better manoeuvrability.

Mirage III

Mirage IIIA-01

Mirage IIIA-05

Mirage IIIC

Mirage IIIE

Mirage IIIB

Far left: The centreline and underwing loads of the Mirage III
1 1700-litre (374-Imp gal) tank
2 1300-litre (286-Imp gal) tank with FFAR pod
3 Martel AS.37 missile
4 500-kg (1102-lb) bombs
5 AS.30 ASM
6 250-kg (551-lb) bombs
7 R.530 AAM
8 125-kg (265.5-lb) bombs
9 Sidewinder AAM
10 55-kg (121.2-lb) bombs
11 1300-litre (286-Imp gal) tank
12 1500-litre (330-Imp gal) tank
Centre: A Mirage 5 demonstrates its substantial carrying capacity with a load of 14 bombs. It can carry up to 4000 kg (8820 lb) of external stores
Left: The trainer, interceptor and attack versions of the versatile Mirage III

F-4 Phantom II, McDonnell Douglas
FIRST FLIGHT 1958

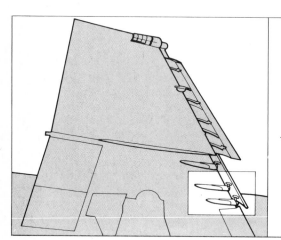
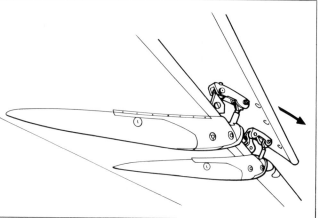

Above: An RAF FGR.2 of 41 Squadron. The first British unit to receive Phantoms was a Fleet Air Arm trials squadron in 1968
Far left: The position of the slats on an F-4 Phantom II
Left: A detail of the slat drive mechanism on the F-4E. The slats give a marked improvement in manoeuvrability, which was required for air actions over Vietnam and the Middle East
Right: US Marine Corps F-4Js climb vertically above a desert training area

PROBABLY the most famous, and certainly the second most numerous, fighter to be produced in the West since World War II, the Phantom II began life as a company-sponsored single-engined multirole attack aircraft, armed with four 20-mm (0.79-in) cannon, for the United States Navy. A letter of intent for two prototypes was issued on October 18, 1954. A change of mission to missile-armed fleet air defence was made on June 23, 1955, when the designation was changed to F4H-1. The prototype of the now twin-engined XF4H-1, christened Phantom II, made its first flight on May 27, 1958.

The first 23 development aircraft, and 24 production aircraft, were designated F-4A, and the US Navy's VF-121 took delivery of their first F-4As in December 1960.

The F-4B Phantom was the first major production aircraft for the US Navy and Marine Corps. Powered by a pair of General Electric J79-GE-8 turbojets, each rated at 4944 kg (10 900 lb) st (dry) and 7711 kg (17 000 lb) with afterburning, the F-4B was capable of Mach 2.27 at altitude. A Westinghouse APQ-72 radar served the basic armament of four AIM-7 Sparrow air-to-air missiles, semi-recessed under the fuselage, while 7257 kg (16 000 lb) of ordnance could be carried on pylons below the wings and fuselage.

Derivatives of the F-4B include the DF-4B 'mother' aircraft for drones and RPVs, the QF-4B unmanned supersonic target and the RF-4B reconnaissance version. When fitted with AN/ASW-21 data link communications, 12 F-4Bs were

redesignated F-4G. They were used briefly over Vietnam in 1965–66, then returned to F-4B.

After evaluation of the F-4B, the United States Air Force adopted the Phantom in March 1962, procuring a US Navy aircraft for the first time. Initially designated F-110A, the changes made to the B were minimal: installation of the J79-GE-15 engine, wider-tread low-pressure tyres, a KC-135 refuelling boom receptacle, APQ-100 radar and ASN-48 inertial navigation system. The first F-4C, as it was redesignated, flew on May 27, 1963.

The USAF also adopted the Phantom for reconnaissance duties by installing sideways-looking radar, IR-detection and sideways-looking cameras, with panoramic coverage, as the RF-4C. This had a longer nose, which increased the fuselage length by 0.84 m (2 ft 9 in). The RF-4B for the US Marine Corps was derived after the RF-4C, using the same reconnaissance systems. The RF-4E, originally developed for Germany, was a marriage of the RF-4C nose and the engines and airframe of the F-4E.

The F-4D version followed the F-4C into USAF service, being more closely tailored to their requirements. The main improvements were the APQ-109 radar and the ability to carry Falcon and Maverick missiles, plus the range of USAF precision-guided munitions. The first F-4D flew in December 1965; it was the mainstay of the USAF over Vietnam. Some F-4Ds went to Iran and South Korea.

The combat experience gained over Vietnam assisted in developing the F-4E. More powerful J79-GE-17 engines were fitted, together with the APQ-120 radar, a slotted tailplane and, most

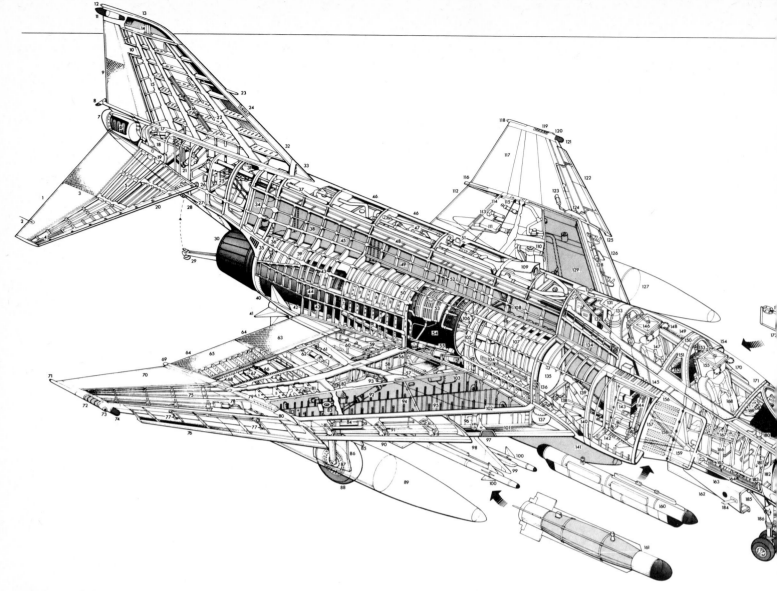

important, a nose-mounted M61 20-mm (0.79-in) rotary cannon. It made its maiden flight on June 30, 1967. Apart from becoming the major USAF variant, the F-4E also became the major export version, albeit with certain items of classified equipment deleted.

The F-4E has since been retrofitted with leading-edge manoeuvering slats, and from 1973, the Northrop TISEO system for long-range visual identification of targets.

Japan was the only country to licence-build the Phantom, and 127 were produced with tail warning radar and provision for the Mitsubishi AAM-2 missile as the F-4EJ.

In addition to the RF-4E, Germany also procured the air superiority F-4F, with leading-edge

slats and improved avionics. The RF-4Es, although initially unarmed, are going through a modification programme to give them a secondary ground-attack role.

The need for specialized ECM aircraft to attack hostile defences, especially surface-to-air missiles, led to the conversion of some F-4Cs to supplement the F-105G Wild Weasel aircraft used in the Vietnam War. Later both the F-4D and F-4E were evaluated for similar conversion as Advanced Wild Weasels. The F-4E was selected, and 116 were converted, taking up the 'vacant' -G suffix, as the F-4G (Advanced Wild Weasel).

To avoid confusion with the original F4H-1 designation of the Phantom, the next variant became the F-4J. This was developed for the US

Above left: An RAF Phantom FGR.2. The four large missiles are the new-technology BAe Sky Flash
Above: A Phantom RF-4C of the USAF 32nd TRS deploys its parachute as it lands at Alconbury, England

F-4E Phantom II

1 Right tailplane
2 Static discharger
3 Honeycomb trailing edge panels
4 Tailplane mass balance weight
5 Tailplane spar construction
6 Drag chute housing
7 Tailcone/drag chute hinged door
8 Fuselage fuel tanks vent pipe
9 Honeycomb rudder construction
10 Rudder balance
11 Tail warning radar fairing
12 Tail navigation light
13 Fin-tip antenna fairing
14 Communications antenna
15 Fin rear spar
16 Variable intensity formation lighting strip
17 Rudder control jack
18 Tailplane pivot mounting
19 Tailplane pivot seal
20 Fixed leading edge slat
21 Tailplane hydraulic jack
22 Fin front spar
23 Stabilator feel system pressure probe
24 Anti-collision light
25 Stabilator feel system balance mechanism
26 Tailcone cooling air duct
27 Heat resistant tailcone skinning
28 Arresting hook housing
29 Arresting hook, lowered
30 Right fully variable exhaust nozzle
31 Rudder artificial feel system bellows
32 Fin leading edge
33 Ram air intake
34 Fuselage No 7 fuel cell
35 Engine bay cooling air outlet louvres
36 Arresting hook actuator and damper
37 Fuel vent piping
38 Fuselage No 6 fuel cell
39 Jet pipe shroud construction
40 Engine bay hinged access doors
41 Rear AIM-7E-2 Sparrow air-to-air missile
42 Semi-recessed missile housing
43 Jet pipe nozzle actuators
44 Afterburner jet pipe
45 Fuselage No 5 fuel cell
46 Fuel tank access panels
47 Fuel system piping
48 Tailplane control cable duct
49 Fuselage No 4 fuel cell
50 Right engine bay construction
51 TACAN aerial
52 Fuselage No 3 fuel cell
53 Engine oil tank
54 General Electric J79-GE-17A turbojet engine
55 Engine accessories
56 Wing rear spar attachment
57 Mainwheel door
58 Main landing gear wheel well
59 Lateral control servo actuator
60 Hydraulic accumulator
61 Lower surface airbrake jack
62 Flap hydraulic jack
63 Right flap
64 Honeycomb control surface construction
65 Right aileron
66 Aileron power control unit
67 Flutter damper
68 Spoiler housing
69 Wing tank fuel vent
70 Dihedral outer wing panel
71 Rear identification light
72 Wingtip formation lighting
73 Right navigation light
74 Radar warning antenna
75 Outer wing panel construction
76 Outboard leading-edge slat
77 Slat control linkage
78 Slat hydraulic jack
79 Outer wing panel attachment
80 Right wing fence
81 Fuel vent system shut-off valves
82 Top of main landing gear leg
83 Outboard pylon attachment housing
84 Inboard slat hydraulic jack
85 Right outer pylon
86 Mainwheel leg door
87 Mainwheel brake discs
88 Right mainwheel
89 Right external fuel tank
90 Inboard leading-edge slat, open
91 Slat hinge linkages
92 Main landing gear retraction jack
93 Landing gear uplock
94 Right wing fuel tank
95 Integral fuel tank construction
96 Inboard pylon fixing
97 Leading-edge ranging antenna
98 Right inboard pylon
99 Twin missile launcher
100 AIM-9 Sidewinder air-to-air missiles
101 Hinged leading edge access panel
102 Wing front spar
103 Hydraulic reservoir
104 Centre fuselage formation lighting
105 Fuselage main frame
106 Engine intake compressor face
107 Intake duct construction
108 Fuselage No 2 fuel cell
109 Air-to-air refuelling receptacle, open
110 Left main landing gear leg
111 Aileron power control unit
112 Left aileron
113 Aileron flutter damper
114 Left spoiler
115 Spoiler hydraulic jack
116 Wing fuel tank vent pipe
117 Left outer wing panel
118 Rearward identification light
119 Wingtip formation lighting
120 Left navigation light
121 Radar warning antenna
122 Left outboard leading edge slat
123 Slat hydraulic jack
124 Wing fence
125 Leading-edge dog tooth
126 Inboard leading-edge slat, open
127 Left external fuel tank
128 Inboard slat hydraulic jack
129 Left wing fuel tank
130 Upper fuselage light
131 IFF antenna
132 Avionics equipment bay
133 Gyro stabilizer platform
134 Fuselage No 1 fuel cell
135 Intake duct
136 Hydraulic connections
137 Starter cartridge container
138 Pneumatic system air bottle
139 Engine bleed air supply pipe
140 Forward AIM-7 missile housing
141 Ventral fuel tank
142 Bleed air louvre assembly, lower
143 Avionics equipment bay
144 Variable intake ramp jack
145 Bleed air louvre assembly, upper
146 Radar operator's Martin-Baker ejection seat
147 Safety harness
148 Face blind seat firing handle
149 Rear cockpit canopy cover
150 Front canopy hinges
151 Inter-canopy bridge section glazing
152 Radar operator's instrument console
153 Canopy jack
154 Left intake
155 Pilot's Martin-Baker ejection seat
156 Intake front ramp
157 Right intake
158 Bleed air holes
159 Boundary layer splitter plate
160 ALQ-72 electronic countermeasures pod (replaces forward Sparrow missile)
161 HOBOS 908-kg (2000-lb) guided bomb
162 Nosewheel door
163 AIM-7E-2 Sparrow missile semi-recessed housing
164 Forward formation lighting
165 Air-conditioning plant
166 Battery
167 Pilot's right side console
168 Ejection seat safety harness
169 Engine throttles
170 Left intake front ramp
171 Forward cockpit canopy cover
172 Left inboard wing pylon
173 Pylon attachments
174 Triple ejector release unit
175 Mk 84 low profile 227-kg (500-lb) bombs
176 Extended bomb fuses
177 Windscreen panels
178 Pilot's lead computing sight and head-up display
179 Instrument panel shroud
180 Control column
181 Rudder pedals
182 Cockpit front pressure bulkhead
183 Refrigeration plant
184 Communications antenna
185 Nosewheel jack
186 Nose landing gear strut
187 Twin nosewheels
188 Nosewheel torque links
189 Landing and taxiing lamps
190 Air-conditioning ram air intake
191 Angle of attack probe
192 Ammunition drum, 639 rounds
193 Rain dispersal duct nozzle
194 ADF antenna
195 Gun bay frame construction
196 M61A-1 0.79-in (20-mm) rotary barrel cannon
197 Cannon fairing
198 AN/APQ-120 fire-control radar
199 Radar antenna mounting
200 Gun muzzle fairing
201 Radar scanner
202 Radome
203 Pitot tube

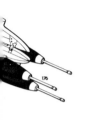

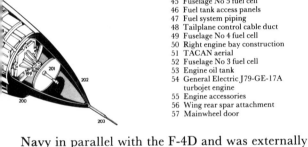

Navy in parallel with the F-4D and was externally similar. Internally, the pulse-Doppler AWG-10 fire control, with a new integrated missile-control system and the one-way ASW-25 digital data link, were fitted.

The first export customer for the Phantom was the UK, who ordered the F-4K in 1964. This version was powered by Rolls-Royce RB.168-25R Spey Mk 201 turbofans, with wider air-intake ducts, which were later updated to Mk 202/203 standard, rated at 9305 kg (20515 lb) st with reheat. Based on the F-4J, the K also had British avionics and an extra-extendable nosewheel undercarriage. Designated Phantom FG.1, 24 saw Royal Navy service from 1969-78, before joining the survivors of the 28 which went direct to the RAF.

The F-4M for the RAF was basically the same as the F-4K, but with the larger brakes and low-pressure tyres of the F-4C, and no fixed tailplane slot. Designated Phantom FGR.2 the RAF took delivery of 118 aircraft which were initially used for attack, but since 1974 have been adapted as the RAF's major air-defence aircraft.

Between 1972 and 1978, 226 F-4Bs were brought up to almost-F-4J standard as the F-4N, and in a similar way the F-4S is an upgraded F-4J, with leading-edge slats and structural strengthening. Production of the Phantom at McDonnell Douglas' St Louis factory ceased on October 26, 1979, after 5057 F-4s had left its gates. Although the F-15 Eagle is supplanting the Phantom in many USAF units, and the F-14 in US Navy units, the type is still a front-line aircraft in the US and abroad.

F-4E Phantom II

Type: all-weather fighter
Maker: McDonnell Douglas Corporation
Span: 11.77 m (38 ft 7½ in)
Length: 19.2 m (63 ft)
Height: 5.02 m (16 ft 5½ in)
Wing area: 49.2 m² (530 sq ft)
Weight: maximum 28 030 kg (61 795 lb); empty 13 757 kg (30 328 lb)
Powerplant: two 8120-kg (17 902-lb) st General Electric J79-GE-17A turbojets with afterburning
Performance: maximum speed with external stores over 2414 km/h (1500 mph [Mach 2.27]); combat radius (area intercept) 1266 km (786 miles); service ceiling (supersonic) 16 580 m (54 400 ft)
Armament: combinations of four AIM-4 Falcon, AIM-7 Sparrow, AIM-9 Sidewinder, AGM-45 Shrike or Walleye missiles, or two AGM-12 Bullpup missiles, on four semi-recessed under-fuselage mountings and four underwing pylons; provision for carrying 7250 kg (16 000 lb) of weapons on seven hardpoints below wing and fuselage; stores which can be carried include:- nuclear bombs, conventional bombs (free-fall, cluster and precision-guided), fire bombs, the MLU-10 landmine, flares, rocket pods, ECM pods, gun pods, the Pave Knife pod and AAVS IV camera pod; one nose-mounted 20-mm (0.79-in) M61A-1 rotary cannon
Crew: 2
Production: (F-4A) 47; (F-4B) 649; (RF-4B) 46; (F-4C) 563; (RF-4C) 505; (F-4D) 825; (F-4E) 1389; (RF-4E) 146; (F-4EJ [licence-built in Japan]) 127; (F-4J) 522; (F-4K) 52; (F-4M) 118

HF-24 Marut, HAL

FIRST FLIGHT 1961

THE HF-24 Marut (wind spirit) was the eventual result of a 1950 decision by the Indian government to develop its own combat aircraft. Detail design began in 1956 by a team led by Dr Kurt Tank, designer of the wartime Focke-Wulf aircraft. The prototype Marut eventually made its maiden flight on June 17, 1961, powered by a pair of non-afterburning Orpheus 703s mounted side-by-side in the area-ruled fuselage.

Although it had been hoped the Marut would become a high-performance interceptor, the power limitations of the Orpheus saw the role changed to ground attack. A batch of 18 pre-production Maruts were laid down, the first of which flew in March 1963, and on May 10, 1964, a token delivery of two of these aircraft was made to the Indian air force. Later a further 12 of this batch were handed over. The remaining four were retained by HAL for trials and development: one was used as a prototype Mk 1A in 1966, having an afterburner fitted to the Orpheus 703.

A two-seat tandem trainer version of the Marut, designated Mk 1T, was developed with minimal changes. The retractable Matra rocket pack was removed to permit the installation of a second Martin-Baker Mk 84C ejection seat, and dual controls fitted. It retains much of the operational equipment of the Mk 1, although the four Aden cannon are usually reduced to two on the Mk 1T.

When the German design team left HAL in 1967, an Indian team continued the development of the Marut. Their main concern has been to find a more powerful engine to give the Marut its intended Mach 2 performance. Several proposals have been reported, with designations of Mk II and Mk III, but so far no hard information has been released. The designation HF-73, previously used in connection with the Mk II, is now understood to apply to a new project. Thought to be a two-seat, twin-finned aircraft powered by a pair of RB.199 turbofans, this aircraft may replace the Mk II/III plans.

There are, however, firm plans to make the present fleet of Mk 1s into dedicated tactical air-support aircraft. This will involve fitting new avionics systems and a new powerplant. It is possible the same systems as used in the Jaguar International, now entering Indian air force service, will be adopted, together with its Adour engines.

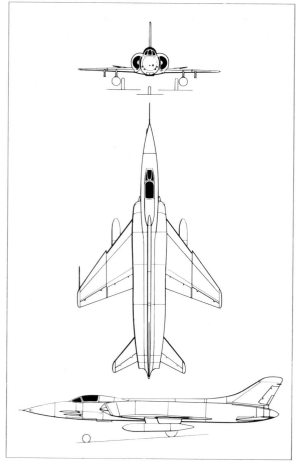

HF-24 Mk 1

Type: single-seat ground-attack fighter
Maker: Hindustan Aeronautics Ltd (HAL)
Span: 9 m (29 ft 6¼ in)
Length: 15.87 m (52 ft ¾ in)
Height: 3.6 m (11 ft 9¾ in)
Wing area: 28 m² (301.4 sq ft)
Weight: maximum 10 908 kg (24 048 lb); empty, equipped 6195 kg (13 657 lb)
Powerplant: two 2200-kg (4850-lb) st HAL-built Rolls-Royce Bristol Orpheus 703 turbojets
Performance: maximum speed 1112 km/h (691 mph) at sea level; range (on internal fuel) approx 1000 km (620 miles); service ceiling approx 15 240 m (50 000 ft)
Armament: four 30-mm (1.18-in) Aden Mk 2 cannon; a Matra Type 103 retractable pack (aft of nosegear unit) for 50 SNEB 68-mm (2.68-in) rockets; four underwing pylons, each of 454 kg (1000 lb) capacity, on which can be carried a combination of 454-kg (1000-lb) bombs, Matra Type 116 SNEB rocket packs, clusters of T10 air-to-surface rockets, napalm tanks, drop-tanks or other stores
Crew: 1
Production: 167 (all types)

Above and left: The attractive lines of the HF-24 Marut, an aircraft originally intended as an interceptor, but destined to be primarily a ground-attack fighter. It can carry a variety of bombs, rockets and napalm

Su-11, Sukhoi

FIRST FLIGHT 1956

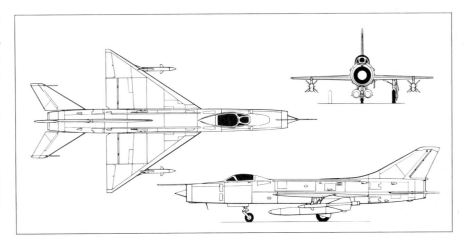

THE prototype of this Sukhoi fighter was first seen at the Tushino display in 1956. It was apparently based on the fuselage and tail unit of the Su-7B Fitter-A with a delta wing. The wing resembled that of the MiG-21, though the aircraft was much larger. One of the aircraft seen had a small conical radome above the nose air intake, while another had a conical centrebody in the intake. Both were codenamed Fishpot-A.

The second variant became the production version as the Sukhoi Su-9 Fishpot-B. The centrebody housed an R1L (Spin Scan) S-band radar, and examples seen at Tushino in 1961 had two fuel tanks mounted side-by-side under the fuselage, and were armed with four AA-1 (Alkali) AAMs.

A much improved Su-9 was developed and first seen in public at the 1967 Domodedovo display. Designated Su-11 and codenamed Fishpot-C, it was powered by an uprated version of the Su-9's Lyulka AL-7 turbojet. The nose was lengthened and less tapered than the Su-9 and the enlarged intake centrebody housed the Uragan 5B (Skip Spin) X-band radar. There are two slim duct fairings along the top of the centre-fuselage. The armament was changed from four Alkalis to two AA-3 (Anab) AAMs.

Although of almost identical tailed delta configuration, the Su-9 and Su-11 are larger and more powerful than the MiG-21. Unlike the MiG-21, which is a day-fighter, they have a limited all-weather capability, but their endurance, radius of action and armament (no guns have ever been seen on the Fishpot series) makes them less flexible aircraft in terms of operational use. They are pure all-weather interceptors.

The Su-11 Fishpot-C has a cleaner airframe than the MiG-21, lacking that type's ventral stabilizing fin and fairings forward of the leading edge of the wing roots, on the fuselage. The landing-gear track is wider on the Su-11 than the MiG-21, and there are four petal-type airbrakes mounted in pairs on the rear fuselage. The cockpit canopy slides backwards on the Su-11, while that of the MiG-21 opens forward at the base of the windscreen.

In 1977 it was estimated that 25% of the Soviet Union's interceptor force of 2500 aircraft comprised the Su-9 and Su-11. It is thought that many of these may now have been replaced by the Su-15 Flagon and MiG-23S Flogger-B.

Su-11

Type: single-seat all-weather interceptor
Maker: Pavel O Sukhoi design bureau
Span: 8.43 m (27 ft 8 in)
Length: 17.4 m (57 ft)
Height: 4.9 m (16 ft)
Wing area: 39.5 m² (425.1 sq ft)
Weight: maximum 13 608 kg (30 000 lb); empty 9070 kg (20 000 lb)
Powerplant: one 10 000-kg (22 046-lb) st Lyulka AL-7F-1 afterburning turbojet
Performance: maximum speed 1160 km/h (720 mph [Mach 0.95]) at sea level; 1270 km/h (790 mph [Mach 1.2]) at height, with two missiles and two drop-tanks; range 1125 km (700 miles); service ceiling 17 000 m (55 700 ft)
Armament: one radar-homing and one IR-homing AA-3 Anab AAM, mounted on underwing pylons
Crew: 1
Production: estimated 2000
All data are estimated

Left: Pilots and groundcrew run out to their waiting Su-11 fighters in a scene reminiscent of a World War II scramble

Su-15, Sukhoi
ESTIMATED FIRST FLIGHT 1964

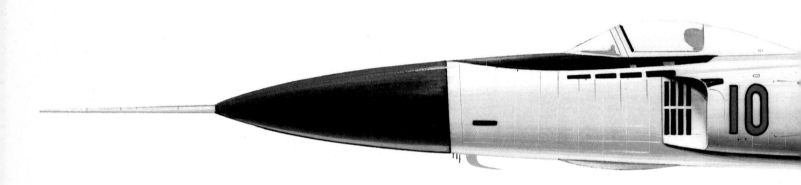

THE first examples of the Sukhoi Su-15, codenamed Flagon by NATO, were seen at the Domodedovo air display in July 1967. Ten aircraft were observed on that occasion, and the family resemblance to the Su-11 Fishpot-C in the wings and the tail areas was obvious. The twin-engine powerplant not only conferred an increase in performance, but left the nose area free for a much larger radar, in a conical radome. Unlike most Russian fighters the Su-15 has very high wing-loading and low power-loading.

The Su-15 was developed to meet a Soviet air force requirement for a Mach 2.5 interceptor to replace the Su-11. It is thought that the prototype Su-15 first flew in 1964. The first production version, the Flagon-A, had simple delta wings reminiscent of the Su-11, with an estimated span of 9.15 m (30 ft), and a conical radome. The powerplant is reported as being a pair of Tumansky R-11F2-300 turbojets, each rated at 6200 kg (13 668 lb) st with afterburning, as used in the MiG-21 series. The Flagon-A entered service in 1969, and only a small number are thought to have been produced.

A STOL (short take-off and landing) version of the Su-15, with three lift-jet engines mounted vertically in the centre fuselage, also appeared at the Domodedovo display in 1967. Codenamed Flagon-B, it remained only an R&D aircraft for rough-field testing. A tandem dual-control training version, designated Su-15U codenamed Flagon-C, is based on the Flagon-D.

Above: An Su-15 with airbrakes deployed and an underwing armament of AA-3 Anab AAMs
Below left: The STOL Su-15 landing during an air display in 1967 at Domodedovo Airport
Bottom left: The same aircraft at low speed during a demonstration flight
Below right: Three Flagon-A Su-15s during celebrations to mark the 50th anniversary of the October Revolution

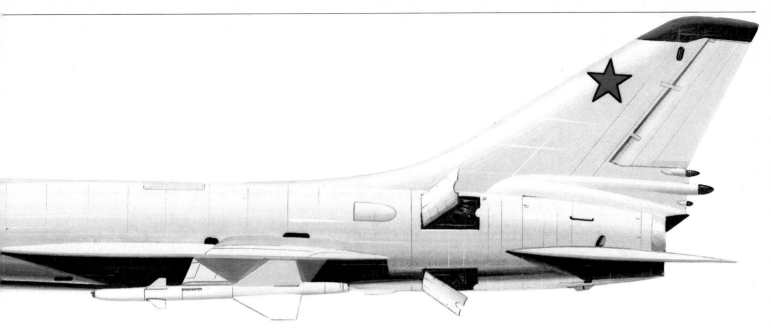

The first major production version of the Su-15 was the Flagon-D. Basically similar to the Flagon-A, the wings have compound sweep and increased span. The sweep is produced by reducing the angle of sweepback on the outer panels. A small unswept section between the two angles takes underwing missile pylons in order to accommodate the Anab missiles.

The Flagon-E takes the basic airframe of the D model with uprated avionic systems and the more powerful Tumansky R-13F-300 turbojets of the later model MiG-21s, each rated at 6604 kg (14 550 lb) st with afterburning. This version was also put into quantity production.

The latest version of the Su-15 in service is the Flagon-F, which is generally similar to the E model, but with an ogival radome, possibly to house a larger scanner. A further uprated version of the R-13F-300 turbojet gives the Flagon-F more power. The air inlets are fitted with variable ramps on the splitter plates, on which are vertical slots for boundary-layer control.

In 1979, it was estimated that of the PVO-Strany (the Soviet air defence organization) 2600-strong fleet of interceptors, about 1000 were the Sukhoi Su-15, in the Flagon-D/E/F versions. Some Flagons have been deployed to other Warsaw Pact countries in the past, and to Egypt in 1973, in small numbers, but all are now thought to be in Soviet service. There is some speculation that the Flagon-F may carry the Fox Fire radar and AA-6 Acrid missiles of the MiG-25 Foxbat.

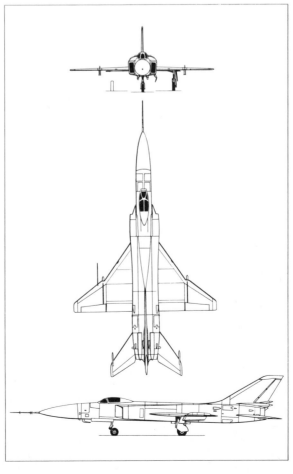

Su-15 Flagon-F

Type: single-seat long-range all-weather interceptor
Maker: Pavel O Sukhoi design bureau
Span: 10.53 m (34 ft 6 in)
Length: 20.5 m (68 ft)
Height: 5 m (16 ft 5 in)
Weight: maximum 16 000 kg (35 275 lb); empty 11 800 kg (26 000 lb)
Powerplant: two 7201-kg (15 875-lb) st Tumansky R-13F2-300 afterburning turbojets
Performance: maximum speed (with external stores) 2445 km/h (1520 mph [Mach 2.3]) over 11 000 m (36 000 ft); range 1450 km (900 miles); service ceiling 20 000 m (65 600 ft)
Armament: one radar-homing and one IR-homing AA-3 Anab AAM on underwing pylons; two side-by-side pylons under centre fuselage are available for either external fuel tanks or further weapons, (AA-6 Acrid or AA-7 Apex have been suggested, but not substantiated)
Crew: 1
Production: approx 2000

All data are estimated

MiG-23S, Mikoyan

ESTIMATED FIRST FLIGHT 1965

IT is thought the maiden flight of the variable-geometry aircraft codenamed Flogger was made in 1965. Its first public appearance was in July 1967, at Domodedovo, where it was initially thought to be a Yakovlev design. One or two squadrons of the Soviet air force took delivery of the initial Flogger-A version of what is now known to be the MiG-23. The experience of these aircraft led to a redesign of the first major production version, the MiG-23S, (Flogger-B).

A single-seat air-combat fighter with large tail surfaces and a high-power Tumansky afterburning turbojet, the Flogger's development owes much to the Mirage-G and F-111. The Flogger-B differs from the A model in having the tail further aft (except for the ventral fin) making an increased gap between the wing and tailplane, a larger dorsal fin and fixed inboard wing leading edges.

The Flogger-B is equipped with the High Lark search radar in the nose, which is thought to have a track range of 54 km (34 miles) and a search range of 85 km (53 miles). An undernose laser rangefinder is fitted, as is Doppler equipment and Sirena 3 radar warning equipment. In addition to a belly-mounted 23-mm (0.9-in) cannon, Apex and Aphid AAMs can be carried, plus other external stores.

Flogger-B is known to have entered service in quantity in 1973. At that time, the Secretary of the USAF described the Flogger's radar and missile systems as comparable with those of the latest F-4 Phantom. In the US Military Posture statement for FY1979, the Flogger-B was described as 'the first Soviet aircraft with a demonstrated ability to track and engage targets flying below its own altitude'.

A tandem two-seat version, used for both training and combat, designated MiG-23U, is codenamed Flogger-C. Flogger-D is the ground-attack version with many airframe features common to the MiG-23S, but now known to be designated MiG-27. The Flogger-F is the export version of the D model, having a mix of MiG-23/27 features. Examples of the MiG-23 and MiG-27 are in service with Algeria, Czechoslovakia, Cuba, Ethiopia, Iraq, Libya and Syria.

In the summer of 1978, six aircraft from Kubinka air base made goodwill visits to Finland and France. Similar to the Flogger-B, they lacked the cannon armament, underwing weapons pylons and laser rangefinder, while having a smaller dorsal fin fillet and were codenamed Flogger-G.

Above: The MiG-23S, fitted with High Lark search radar in the nose and an AA-8 Aphid on fuselage pylon
Left: A Flogger-G opens its canopy on the runway after landing in France during a goodwill visit in the summer of 1978

MiG-23S

Type: single-seat air-combat fighter
Maker: Mikoyan-Gurevich design bureau
Span: fully swept 8.17 m (26 ft 9½ in); fully spread 14.25 m (46 ft 9 in)
Length: 16.8 m (55 ft 1½ in)
Height: 3.96 m (13 ft)
Wing area: 36 m² (387.5 sq ft)
Weight: maximum 17 000 kg (37 480 lb); empty 10 000 kg (22 050 lb)
Powerplant: one 11 498-kg (25 350-lb) Tumansky R-29B afterburning turbojet
Performance: maximum speed 2445 km/h (1520 mph [Mach 2.2]) at height with external stores; range 1920 km (1200 miles); service ceiling 18 600 m (61 000 ft)
Armament: one 23-mm (0.9-in) twin-barrel GSh-23 gun in fuselage belly pack; weapon stations under the centre fuselage, one under each air inlet duct and one under each fixed inboard wing panel for AA-7 Apex and AA-8 Aphid AAMs, rocket pods, fuel tanks cr other external stores
Crew: 1
Production: estimated 1500 built (all MiG-23/27 types) by spring 1979

All data are estimated

F-5, Northrop

FIRST FLIGHT 1959

THE US Department of Defense's interest in the N-156F trainer began in May 1958, when the USAF authorized Northrop to build three prototypes. The first aircraft was ready in just over a year, due to its commonality with the T-38, and it made its first flight on July 30, 1959.

A lack of requirement for the N-156F caused the programme to be shelved after two prototypes had been built. The project came out of limbo in May 1964, when the Department of Defense selected Northrop's N-156F, now dubbed 'Freedom Fighter', to be supplied to 'favoured nations' under the Military Assistance Program (MAP). The N-156F was redesignated F-5A, and a two-seat trainer variant, externally generally similar to the T-38 Talon, became the F-5B. The partially completed third prototype was rebuilt to F-5A standard, and in October 1962 production orders for 71 F-5As and 15 F-5Bs were placed with Northrop. The first production F-5A flew on July 31, 1963, and the first F-5B on February 24, 1964.

The F-5A light tactical fighter was powered by a pair of General Electric J85-GE-13 turbojets, each rated at 1850 kg (4080 lb) st with afterburning, mounted side-by-side in the rear fuselage. The basic armament was two 20-mm (0.79-in) M-39 cannon, mounted in the upper fuselage forward of the windscreen, plus provision for a Sidewinder AAM on each wingtip. The four underwing and single under-fuselage hardpoints could carry 2812 kg (6200 lb) of ordnance. Wingtip fuel tanks could be mounted in place of the Sidewinders.

Initial deliveries to the USAF Tactical Air

F-5E

Type: single-seat light tactical fighter
Maker: Northrop Corporation
Span: 8.13 m (26 ft 8 in)
Length: 14.68 m (48 ft 2 in)
Height: 4.06 m (13 ft 4 in)
Wing area: 17.3 m² (186 sq ft)
Weight: maximum 11 193 kg (24 676 lb); empty 4392 kg (9683 lb)
Powerplant: two 2268-kg (5000-lb) st General Electric J85-GE-21A afterburning turbojets
Performance: maximum speed 1705 km/h (1060 mph

[Mach 1.6]) at 10 975 m (36 000 ft); range (with maximum fuel, reserves and tanks retained) at sea level 2483 km (1543 miles); service ceiling 15 790 m (51 800 ft)
Armaments: two 20-mm (0.79-in) M-39-A2 cannon in nose; two AIM-9 Sidewinder AAMs on wingtip rails; one under-fuselage and four underwing pylons can carry up to 3175 kg (7000 lb) of ordnance including Mk 82 GP and Snakeye 227-kg (500-lb) bombs, Mk 84 907-kg (2000-lb) bombs, LAU-68(7) 70-mm (2.75-in) rockets, AGM-65 Maverick and other laser-guided munitions; 1041-litre

(229-Imp gal) drop-tanks; the centreline hardpoint can carry a multiple ejection rack
Crew: 1
Production: 2225 delivered by January 31, 1980

Above: A US Navy F-5 in Aggressor camouflage takes off to simulate a Soviet MiG-21 in mock air-to-air combat near NAS Miramar, California

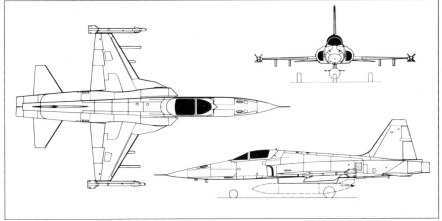

Command at Williams AFB, where all the air and ground crew of countries receiving the F-5 are trained, began in April 1964. Iran was the first country to put the F-5A into service in February 1965, and during the same year Taiwan, Greece, the Philippines, South Korea, and Turkey also took delivery of F-5s. In 1966, F-5As were delivered to Ethiopia, Morocco, Norway and Thailand. The Norwegian aircraft were designated F-5G. The Republic of South Vietnam received F-5As in 1967, and Libya took delivery in 1968.

Canada selected the CF-5A in 1965, and 115 aircraft, both single and two-seat (CF-5D) aircraft, were built under licence by Canadair. These aircraft had increased-power J85-CAN-15 engines and flight refuelling capability, and entered service in 1968. Venezuela has taken delivery of 20 surplus CF-5As from Canada. A further 105 aircraft were integrated into the Canadian production line for the Netherlands. These versions had increased fuel capacity, a Doppler navigation system and manoeuvering flaps, and were designated NF-5A/B. CASA also built the type under licence in Spain, producing 70 SF-5A/Bs designated C-9/CE-9 by the Spanish air force.

In mid 1968, the operational use of the F-5 was expanded by offering a four-camera reconnaissance nose unit. Greece, Iran, Norway, Spain and South Vietnam were among the countries to operate the RF-5A, as the sub-variant was designated.

In 1970 an upgraded version of the F-5 was selected by the US Department of Defense as the new International Fighter Aircraft to be supplied

Top: A US Air Force F-5 in a Warsaw-Pact-style camouflage to simulate a MiG-21 in training exercises
Above: A US Navy F-5E Tiger II in an Aggressor colour scheme
Right: A Tiger II displays some of its armament including retarded bombs, napalm, rockets, cannon ammunition and underwing tanks

Left: An Aggressor aircraft with one wingtip-mounted Sidewinder
Below: A bomb-laden F-5 taxies along a grass strip. The Tiger II or Freedom Fighter can operate from unprepared fields and is very stable with its short, wide landing gear. For very short strips an arrester hook can be fitted
Right: A two-seat F-5B fighter-trainer version of the F-5A in the markings of the Republic of Korea. It retains the fire-control system but has had one M-39 gun deleted. Deliveries began in 1976 and the aircraft has proved a popular export design

under MAP as the successor to the F-5A. The new aircraft, named Tiger II, was the result of feedback from F-5A users, and incorporated modifications from the Dutch, Norwegian and Canadian aircraft, in addition to increased-power J85-GE-21A engines.

Designated F-5E, the Tiger II has a slightly wider fuselage, which increases wing span, and tapered wing leading-edge extensions between the inboard leading edge and fuselage. Provision for assisted take-off, runway arrester gear, AN/APQ-159V X-band pulse radar, a two-position nose leg (for increased angle of attack on the ground) and developed manoeuvering flaps were all incorporated into the F-5E.

The first flight was made on August 11, 1972, and deliveries to the USAF began in spring, 1973. A two-seat version, designated F-5F, with the fuselage lengthened by 1.08 m (3 ft 6½ in) and the right-hand M-39 cannon deleted, was also produced, flying on September 25, 1974. A reconnaissance nose, based on that of the RF-5A, can also be incorporated. The fighter has a lead-computing optical gunsight using inputs from the airborne radar for AAMs and cannon, and gives a roll-stabilized manually-depressible reticle aiming reference for ground attack. It includes a 'snapshoot' capability for attacking violently manoeuvring or fleeting targets.

Customers to date include Brazil (whose aircraft have a large dorsal fin to accommodate an ADF antenna), Chile, Indonesia, Iran, Jordan, Kenya, Malaysia, South Korea, Saudi Arabia, Singapore, Sudan, Switzerland (building 72 F-5E/Fs under licence), Taiwan (also building 200 aircraft), Thailand and the Yemen Arab Republic. It is thought that some of the aircraft built for Egypt, but not delivered, will be supplied to Pakistan.

A company-funded development of a dedicated reconnaissance version of the F-5E, with a lengthened nose, was given approval in March 1978. The prototype aircraft, designated RF-5E, made its maiden flight on January 29, 1979. Various combinations of cameras and sensors can be fitted in pallets. The right-hand M-39 cannon is deleted, but the wingtip mountings for Sidewinders retained. No sales had been made by mid 1980, but many of the 25 nations flying F-5s had expressed interest.

In the summer of 1978, Northrop did the engineering development on a further variant of the F-5E. The work was originally done for Taiwan, and consisted of re-engining the F-5E with a single General Electric F404 turbofan, rated at 7257 kg (16 000 lb) st with afterburning, in place of the two J85 turbojets, and installing an F-16-type radar. Development was suspended in October 1978, following a presidential veto on the sale of the aircraft to Taiwan. However, in early 1980, the type (which is provisionally known as the F-5G, not to be confused with the Norwegian version of the F-5A) is one of the contenders for the US export fighter to replace the F-5E series. Should the decision go in Northrop's favour, the F-5 series will certainly be extended for at least another twenty years.

Top: An F-5E in service with the USAF 527th TFS (Aggressors) about to take off at Alconbury, England. It has one Sidewinder on the right wingtip

Above: The F-5A Freedom Fighter on display at the Paris Air Show in 1967. It has been widely exported to countries allied to the United States–and captured South Vietnamese aircraft have been operated by Vietnamese pilots against the Chinese. They report that the aircraft is easier to fly than Soviet fighters

242

MiG-25, Mikoyan
ESTIMATED FIRST FLIGHT 1964

INITIALLY developed to counter the threat of the USAF Mach 3 B-70 Valkyrie strategic bomber (which was cancelled in 1961), the MiG-25 Foxbat is one of the most potent interceptors in service today. In the form of the E-266 research aircraft, it set many world records in rate-of-climb, payload-to-height and closed-circuit speed categories over the period 1965–73.

The first public sighting of this twin-finned twin-engined single-seat fighter was at the Domodedovo display in 1967. Codenamed Foxbat-A, the interceptor is fitted with a powerful fire-control radar, codenamed Fox Fire, and has provision for four underwing air-to-air missiles, usually the radar-homing and IR-homing versions of the AA-6 Acrid type, the largest AAMs ever put into service.

The defection of Lieutenant Viktor Belenko to Japan, in September 1976, gave the West its first opportunity to examine a MiG-25 Foxbat-A in detail. The airframe is reported as being constructed mainly of stainless steel, with titanium being used in areas of extreme heating, such as wing and tail surface leading edges. This makes for an extremely heavy aircraft, and consequently the amount of internal equipment is somewhat limited.

Although effective, the Fox Fire radar (with an estimated range of 100 km [62 miles]) is bulky and, like other 1950s-designed radars is built with valve, rather than solid-state, circuitry. A high-quality airborne computer, when used in conjunction with a ground-based flight-control system, enables the Foxbat to be vectored onto its target automatically over long ranges. Most of the high electrical power output is used by its extensive ECM suite, which includes the Sirena 3 radar warning system.

It has been reported that the MiG-25 has detected a simulated cruise missile target flying below 60 m (200 ft), while itself flying at 6000 m (19 685 ft), at a range of 20 km (12.5 miles).

The MiG-25U Foxbat-C is a trainer variant with a separate raised cockpit, but no search radar or reconnaissance sensors. The Foxbat-D is a MiG-25R with no cameras and a larger sideways-looking radar than the Foxbat-B.

It is reported (via Lieutenant Belenko) that a developed interceptor version which has a strengthened airframe to permit supersonic flight at lower altitudes, uprated engines, improved avionics and two extra missile mountings (on the fuselage) has been developed.

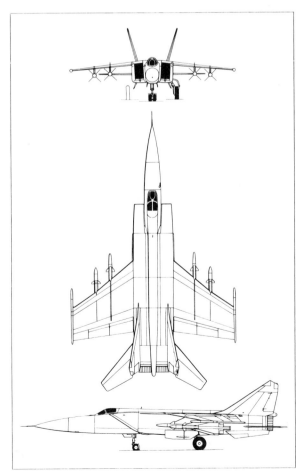

MiG-25

Type: single-seat all-weather interceptor
Maker: Mikoyan-Gurevich design bureau
Span: 13.95 m (45 ft 9 in)
Length: 22.3 m (73 ft 2 in)
Height: 5.6 m (18 ft 4½ in)
Wing area: 56 m² (603 sq ft)
Weight: maximum 36 200 kg (79 805 lb); empty 20 000 kg (44 100 lb)
Powerplant: two 11 000-kg (24 250-lb) st Tumansky R-31 afterburning turbojets
Performance: maximum speed with missiles 3113 km/h (1934 mph [Mach 2.8]) at 12 000 m (39 375 ft); range 2600 km (1610 miles); service ceiling 24 400 m (80 000 ft)
Armament: four air-to-air missiles on pylons, two under each wing; usually one radar and one IR-homing version of AA-6 Acrid under each wing, or one AA-7 Apex and one AA-8 Aphid under each wing (the improved interceptor version may have an internal 23-mm (0.9-in) GSh-23 cannon installed)
Crew: 1
Production: approx 1000

All data are estimated

F-14 Tomcat, Grumman

FIRST FLIGHT 1970

THE VFX, later designated F-14, has three main roles: fighter sweep and escort duties for a carrier-launched strike force, in company with ECM and AEW aircraft; the air defence of carrier task forces by combat air patrols (CAP) and deck-launched interceptions (DLI); and the third role of secondary attack of ground tactical targets, supported by the forces of its first role.

The F-14 is a variable-geometry aircraft, the optimum sweep of the wing being controlled automatically, as a function of Mach number and altitude, by a Mach sweep programmer, with twin outward-canted vertical tail surfaces. Small fore-planes (glove vanes) are positioned in the forward fixed leading edge of the wing, and they extend automatically at supersonic speeds to control centre-of-pressure shifts.

The heart of the F-14's weapons system is the Hughes AN/AWG-9 radar, used in conjunction with the Hughes AIM-54 Phoenix AAM, which is unique to the Tomcat. The radar is able to track 24 targets at once at ranges up to 161 km (100 miles) and engage six of them simultaneously with the Phoenix missiles. For close-in fighting, air combat missiles (Sidewinder) and the internal gun can be used. With these weapons combined with the Tomcat's automatic wing sweep, Grumman claim the aircraft to be unrivalled and able to out-manoeuvre all previous combat aircraft.

The initial contracts called for 12 development aircraft, and the prototype F-14A Tomcat made its maiden flight on December 21, 1970, but was lost on its second flight. Flight testing resumed on May 24, 1971 with the second Tomcat. Including the development aircraft, the US Navy's procurement plans call for 521 F-14 Tomcats. The first two operational squadrons, VF-1 and VF-2, were deployed on board USS *Enterprise* in September 1974.

In the mid 1970s, Grumman and the US Navy were involved in renegotiation of the F-14 contracts, because of vast cost overruns. At one stage, Grumman claimed it would incur a loss of $105 million. By 1975 these difficulties had been resolved and production continued.

The F-14B programme to re-engine the Tomcat with Pratt & Whitney F401 afterburning turbofans was shelved as a result of budget problems. Two F-14As were re-engined with the F-401, rated at 12 247 kg (27 000 lb) st with afterburning, the first of which flew on September 12, 1973.

A parallel programme to equip the F-14B with new weapons and avionics, as the F-14C, was shelved. It is possible some work will be done to upgrade F-14A avionics, with a redesignation to F-14D. The only other F-14 development programme has been to test a tactical air reconnaissance pod system (Tarps), which is mounted 0.38 m (1 ft 3 in) off the centreline. This may be procured to replace the RF-4B/RF-8G/RA-5C aircraft.

The only export sale of the Tomcat has been to Iran, with an order of 80. The first Iranian Tomcat flew on December 5, 1975, and all 80 had been delivered by the end of 1978.

Problems with the TF30 engine have led to proposals to replace it with the General Electric F101-DFE, while cost escalation of the F-18 has put new impetus behind F-14 production.

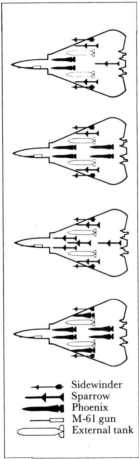

Sidewinder
Sparrow
Phoenix
M-61 gun
External tank

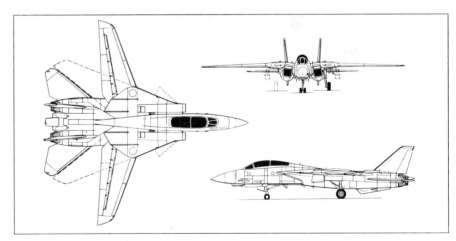

Above: A Grumman F-14A
Tomcat development aircraft.
The instrumentation probe on
the nose was used to give
accurate air-data
Left: F-14A Tomcats with
empty underwing pylons on
the deck of USS *Enterprise*.
This carrier participated in
the abortive 1980 mission to
rescue American hostages
from Iran

Left: A Tomcat with the full
load of six Phoenix AAMs
under the fuselage and on
wing pylons
Above: An unusual head-on
view on the ground with
swing-wings at full sweep
Above right: Four alternative
weapon loads carried by the
Tomcat
Right: A close up of the
cockpit with the fairings and
cooling gills associated with
the M61A-1 cannon mounted
on the lower left side of the
Tomcat

F-14A

Type: two-seat multi-mission
carrier fighter
Maker: Grumman Aerospace
Corporation
Span: fully swept 11.65 m
(38 ft 2½ in); fully spread
19.45 m (64 ft 1½ in)
Length: 18.89 m (61 ft
11¾ in)
Height: 4.88 m (16 ft)
Wing area: 52.49 m² (565 sq
ft)
Weight: maximum 33 724 kg
(74 348 lb); empty 17 830 kg
(39 310 lb)
Powerplant: two 9480-kg
(20 900-lb) st Pratt &
Whitney TF30-P-412A

afterburning turbofans
Performance: maximum
speed 2486 km/h
(1565 mph [Mach 2.34]) at
12 200 m (40 000 ft); range
with external fuel over
3200 km (2000 miles);
service ceiling above 15 240 m
(50 000 ft)
Armament: one General
Electric M61A-1 20-mm
(0.79-in) Vulcan cannon;
four AIM-7 Sparrow or four
AIM-54A Phoenix AAMs
mounted under the fuselage,
and two underwing pylons
with two AIM-9 Sidewinder
AAMs, or one Sparrow/
Phoenix and one Sidewinder
on each pylon

Crew: 2
Production: 422 (F-14A) by
1980, plus 30 approved for
FY80

Mirage F1, Dassault-Breguet

FIRST FLIGHT 1966

THE Mirage F1-01 prototype first flew on December 23, 1966, exceeding Mach 2 on its fourth flight on January 7, 1967, though it soon crashed. The French government ordered three pre-series F1s in September 1967, the first of which flew on March 20, 1969, reaching Mach 1.15. Mirage F1-03 flew in September 1969. By the time the third pre-series aircraft F1-04 flew on June 17, 1970, with a full electronics suite and an extended leading edge, giving a 'dog-tooth', it was representative of the initial production version. This was designated Mirage F1-C, and was an all-weather interceptor, fitted with Thomson-CSF Cyrano IV fire-control radar in the nose, and many of the systems of the Mirage IIIE. With the capability to carry external ordnance, a secondary attack role is possible.

By removing much of the electronics and replacing them with extra fuel tankage, the ground-attack/air combat Mirage F1-A version was produced. A tandem two-seat trainer version, the Mirage F1-B, made its maiden flight on May 26, 1976.

The first production Mirage F1-C flew on February 15, 1973, and was handed over to the Armée de l'Air on March 14, 1973. The first unit to re-equip with the F1-C was the 30e Escadre at Rheims, becoming operational in early 1974. By January 1980, 214 Mirage F1s of all variants had been ordered for l'Armée de l'Air.

The sole prototype F1-E, used was as a testbed for the M53 engine, which now powers the Mirage 2000 and Super Mirage 4000. The designation F1-

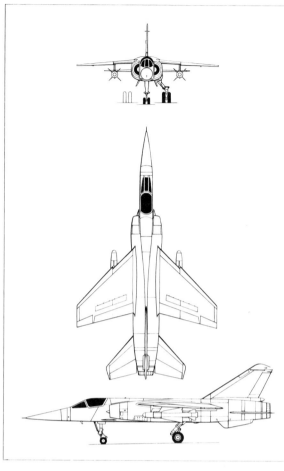

Mirage F1-C

Type: multi-mission fighter
Maker: Avions Marcel Dassault-Breguet Aviation, with SABCA/Sonaca of Belgium
Span: 8.4 m (27 ft 6¾ in)
Length: 15 m (49 ft 2½ in)
Height: 4.5 m (14 ft 9 in)
Wing area: 25 m² (269.1 sq ft)
Weight: maximum 15 200 kg (33 510 lb); empty 7400 kg (16 314 lb)
Powerplant: one 7200-kg (15 873-lb) st SNECMA Atar 9K-50 afterburning turbojet
Performance: maximum speed 2335 km/h (1450 mph [Mach 2.2]) at 12 000 m (39 375 ft); range 900 km (560 miles); service ceiling 20 000 m (65 600 ft)
Armament: two 30-mm (1.18-in) DEFA 553 cannon in lower forward fuselage; one centreline, four underwing and two wingtip weapon stations for max 4000 kg (8820 lb); typical interception armament one radar-homing and one IR-homing Matra R.530/Super 530 AAMs on the inboard underwing pylons, plus one AIM-9 Sidewinder or Matra R.550 Magic AAM on each wingtip
Crew: 1
Production: approx 340 by end of 1979

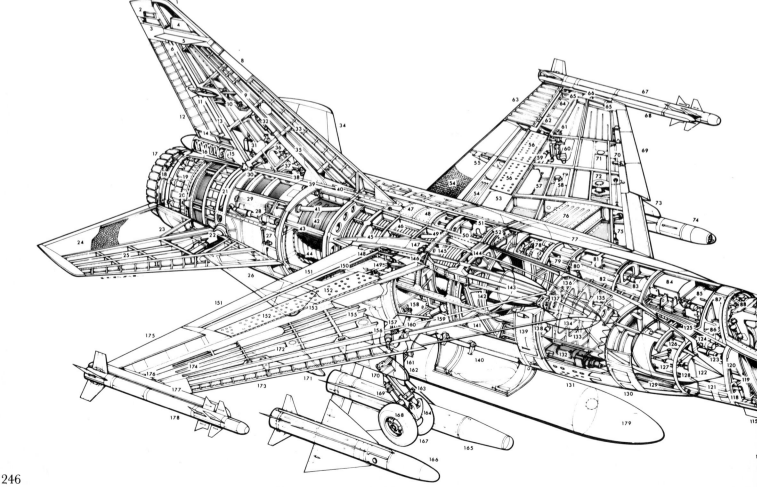

E is now used for an Atar 9K-powered export version of the F1-C with a more comprehensive navigational attack system.

The most recent development of the aircraft was announced in February 1979. The Armée de l'Air is to procure some 30 Mirage F1-Rs, which will replace the Mirage IIIR/RDs of 33e Escadre de Reconnaissance at Strasbourg. The F1-R is expected to become operational by 1983.

Despite the failure to sell the Mirage F1 into Europe, the type has a very successful export record to typical French clients, with some 500 being on order by January 1980. Among the customers are the air forces of Ecuador (F1-BJ/EJ), Greece (F1-CG), Iraq (F1-BQ/EQ), Kuwait (F1-BK/CK), Libya (F1-AD/BD/ED), Jordan (F-1B/E), Morocco (F1-CH), South Africa (F1-AZ/CZ) and Spain (F1-BE/CE). South Africa has a licence-production agreement with AMD-BA, but it is not known whether Atlas Aircraft has put the F1 into production. A reported sale to Egypt, funded by Saudi Arabia, was never completed, the Mirage IIIEE being supplied instead.

In L'Armée de l'Air service the Mirage F1-C also equips 5e Escadre at Orange and 12e Escadre at Cambrai, each escadre comprising two escadrons. It is possible a third escadre will be established at Cambrai, as an OCU (operational conversion unit) with the F1-B. During 1978–79, 24 F1-Cs were re-manufactured to F1-200 standard with flight refuelling equipment, the probe being positioned forward of the windscreen.

Above: A Mirage F1-C of the French Normandie-Niemen squadron, which originated in the USSR during 1942 and was given the name Niemen by Stalin. This F1 is without missile attachments but has two 30-mm (1.18-in) DEFA 553 cannon in the lower front fuselage

Mirage F1C

1 Glass-reinforced plastic antenna housings
2 Rear navigation light
3 IFF antenna
4 VHF 1 antenna
5 VOR/LOC antenna
6 Rudder upper hinge
7 Tailfin structure
8 UHF antenna
9 Main fin spar (machined)
10 Rudder control linkage
11 Rudder central hinge fairing
12 Rudder
13 Fin rear spar
14 VHF 2 antenna
15 Parachute release mechanism
16 Brake parachute
17 Exhaust secondary nozzle
18 Exhaust primary nozzle
19 Pneumatic nozzle actuators
20 Jet pipe mounting link
21 Fuselage aft support frame (tailplane trunnion/fin rear spar)
22 Tailplane mounting trunnion
23 Trunnion frame
24 Honeycomb trailing-edge structure
25 Multi-spar box structure
26 Ventral fin (left and right)
27 Elevator control rod
28 Elevator servo control unit and linkage
29 Hydraulic lines
30 Tailfin rear spar attachment
31 Rudder trim actuator
32 Rudder servo control
33 Fin leading-edge structure
34 Left tailplane
35 Main fin spar lower section
36 Spring rod
37 Servo control quadrant
38 Rudder pulley bellcranks and cables
39 Main fin spar/fuselage attachment
40 Fin root fittings
41 Sealed-sheath hydraulic line
42 Tailplane
43 Engine fitting and removal rail
44 Inside fuel tank skin (milled structure)
45 Wingroot fairing
46 Rear lateral fuselage fuel tanks
47 Engine mounting access panel
48 Control run access panel
49 Filler/cross-feed system (rear/forward lateral fuselage fuel tanks)
50 Aileron linkage
51 Compressor bleed-air pre-cooler
52 Main wing/fuselage mounting frame
53 Wing skinning
54 Inboard flap composite-honeycomb structure
55 Flap tracks
56 Perforated spoiler panels (two)
57 Spoiler actuator
58 Wing tank fuel lines
59 Aileron trim jack
60 Aileron servo control
61 Aileron operating rod
62 Aileron inboard hinge
63 Left aileron
64 Aileron outboard hinge
65 Missile attachment points
66 Missile ignition box
67 Matra 550 Magic air-to-air missile
68 Missile adaptor shoe
69 Drooping leading edge
70 Slat hinges
71 Pylon mounting point (outboard)
72 Pylon mounting point (inboard)
73 Left inboard weapons pylon
74 Matra 530 air-to-air missile (infra-red homing head)
75 Leading-edge slat actuator
76 Forged high-tensile steel main wingroot fitting
77 IFF antenna
78 Engine duct ventilation
79 Central fuselage fuel tank
80 Aileron control rod
81 Avionics bay
82 Electrical/hydraulic leads
83 Inverted-flight accumulator
84 Amplifier
85 Main radio/electronics bay
86 Water separator and air-conditioning turbo-compressor
87 Canopy hinge
88 Canopy actuating jack
89 Martin-Baker Mk 4 ejection seat
90 Clamshell jettisonable canopy
91 Gunsight
92 One-piece cast windshield frame
93 Instrument panel
94 Control column
95 Instrument panel shroud/gunsight mounting
96 Heated, bird-strike proof windshield
97 Pitot heads
98 Radar attachment points
99 Thomson-CSF Cyrano IV fire-control radar
100 Radar scanner
101 Glass-reinforced plastic radome
102 TACAN antenna
103 Front pressure bulkhead
104 Rudder pedals
105 Aileron control bellcrank
106 Control column base
107 Elevator control bellcrank
108 Retraction jack fairing
109 Nosewheel retraction jack
110 Oleo-pneumatic shock-absorber
111 Twin nosewheels
112 Nose gear bogie
113 Guide link
114 Steering/centring jack
115 Nose gear door
116 Pilot's seat
117 Nose gear trunnion
118 Elevator linkage
119 Angled rear pressure bulkhead
120 Battery (24 volt)
121 Gun trough
122 Air intake shock-cone
123 Heat exchanger
124 Shock-cone electric motor
125 Boundary-layer bleed
126 Shock-cone guide track
127 Screw jack
128 Right air intake
129 DEFA cannon barrel
130 Auxiliary air intake doors
131 Right airbrake
132 Right DEFA 30-mm (1.18-in) cannon
133 Forward fuselage integral fuel tank
134 Wingroot fillet
135 Fuel lines
136 Machined frame
137 Wing forward attachment point
138 Landing gear door actuator/linkage
139 Ammunition magazine
140 Pre-closing landing gear door (lower)
141 Main landing gear well (right)
142 Main wing/fuselage mounting frame
143 SNECMA Atar 9K50 turbojet
144 Main wing attachment points
145 Machined frame
146 Wing rear attachment point
147 Engine mounting trunnion
148 Inboard flap guide track
149 Flap actuator and linkage
150 Honeycomb trailing-edge structure
151 Double-slotted flaps
152 Perforated spoiler panels (two)
153 Spoiler leading-edge piano hinge
154 Multi-spar wing box tank structure
155 Pylon mounting point (inboard)
156 Main gear actuator
157 Leg door link
158 Main gear trunnion
159 Landing gear hydraulic truss jack
160 Landing gear rocking bellcrank and actuator
161 Messier main landing gear leg
162 Right inboard weapons pylon
163 Up-lock
164 Rocker beam
165 Matra Super 530 air-to-air missile
166 Matra 530 air-to-air missile (semi-active radar guidance)
167 Twin mainwheels
168 Hydraulic multi-plate disc brakes
169 Oleo-pneumatic shock-absorber
170 Main landing gear bogie beam
171 Right outboard weapons pylon
172 Pylon mounting point (outboard)
173 Leading-edge structure
174 Auxiliary spars
175 Right aileron
176 Machined end rib
177 Missile adaptor shoe
178 Matra 550 Magic air-to-air missile
179 Auxiliary fuel tank

McDonnell Douglas F-15 Eagle,

FIRST FLIGHT 1972

IN December 1969, McDonnell Douglas were awarded a contract for 18 single-seat F-15A and two TF-15A two-seat trainers for development. A twin-finned, twin-engined, single-seat aircraft with tremendous performance, the F-15 Eagle has emerged as one of the best fighters available today. The Eagle is powered by a pair of F100 afterburning turbofans developed specially for the aircraft by Pratt & Whitney (and later adopted as the powerplant for the F-16). It is armed with an internal M61 cannon (initially a new 25-mm [1-in] gun using caseless ammunition was specified, but the project was dropped after development problems) and four Sparrow AAMs, controlled by the Hughes APG-63 lightweight pulse-Doppler radar.

Since its first flight on July 27, 1972, the F-15 has proved to be an exceptional aircraft for interception and air combat, with the advantage of also being able to carry an effective attack weapons load over long ranges though its fuel burn is tremendous.

The USAF's requirement was initially said to be 729 F-15 Eagles by 1983, plus the 20 R&D aircraft, the first order in 1973 being for 30 aircraft. Up to FY79 funding, some 582 had been ordered. The first Eagle to be handed over to the USAF, on November 14, 1974, was a two-seat F-15B. (Initially designated TF-15A, the first F-15B had flown on July 7, 1973.)

An ingenious way to increase the range of the F-15, while maintaining an aerodynamically clean shape has been found by the use of special conformal pallets, called Fast (fuel and sensor, tactical) packs. These low-drag pallets can accommodate 2268 kg (5000 lb) of fuel, and are designed to the full stress factors and limits of the aircraft. The fuel capacity can be traded off against other systems, such as reconnaissance sensors, ECM equipment, laser designators or low-light-level television. The external stores stations remain available with Fast packs fitted, and the Sparrow missiles, usually fitted to the edge of the bottom fuselage, can be attached to the corners of the Fast packs.

From mid 1979 all Eagles delivered to the USAF had provision for an extra 907 kg (2000 lb) of internal fuel and the ability to carry the Fast packs. These aircraft are designated F-15C and D, equating to the single- and two-seat versions respectively. From mid 1980, the F-15C/Ds have the capability of their APG-63 radar increased by the use of programmable signal processors and an increased capability computer.

As of December 31, 1979, 476 Eagles had been delivered to the USAF, serving with four tactical fighter wings in the United States, the 36th TFW at Bitburg, Germany and the 32nd TFS at Soesterburg in the Netherlands. Eagles were coming off the production line at St Louis at the rate of ten per month in 1979.

On the exports side, the F-15 has been sold to three countries: Israel has received 25 out of the 35 ordered (including four refurbished R&D aircraft) and these have already been used in combat; Saudi Arabia, 60; and Japan 100 F-15Js, all but eight being built under licence, with Mitsubishi as the prime contractor.

Above: An overall-grey F-15A seen in Britain in September 1978. It is fitted with a centreline fuel tank
Left: An F-15A with underwing tanks–it can carry up to 2313 kg (5100 lb) on each of the two inner wing pylons
Right: An Eagle armed with four AIM-7F Sparrow AAMs lands with dorsal airbrake open
Below: The F-15 Eagle as it appeared with square wingtips during its evaluation by the US Air Force
Above right: An F-15 Eagle of the Israeli Air Force at Tel Aviv

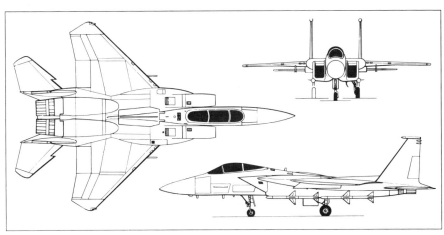

F-15A

Type: single-seat air-superiority fighter
Maker: McDonnell Douglas Corporation

Span: 13.05 m (42 ft 9¾ in)
Length: 19.43 m (63 ft 9 in)
Height: 5.63 m (18 ft 5½ in)
Wing area: 56.5 m² (608 sq ft)
Weight: maximum 25 401 kg (56 000 lb); empty approx 12 700 kg (28 000 lb)
Powerplant: two 10 800-kg (23 810-lb) st Pratt & Whitney F100-PW-100 afterburning turbofans
Performance: maximum speed over 2575 km/h (1600 mph) at height; range without Fast pack 4631 km (2878 miles), with Fast pack 5560 km (3450 miles); service ceiling 18 288 m (60 000 ft)

Armament: one General Electric M61A-1 20-mm (0.79-in) Vulcan cannon; four AIM-7F Sparrow AAMs; one centreline pylon stressed for 2041 kg (4500 lb) for fuel tank, reconnaissance pod or tactical weapon; two inner-wing pylons stressed for 2313 kg (5100 lb) for tanks or weapons, with provision for mounting two AIM-9 Sidewinder AAMs laterally on the pylon; two outer-wing pylons stressed for 454 kg (1000 lb) for weapons or ECM pods
Crew: 1
Production: 924 built and under order

F-16, General Dynamics

FIRST FLIGHT 1974

IN April 1974, the US lightweight fighter pro-gramme received a change of emphasis. The increased cost of the F-15 led to the adoption of a 'high-low mix' policy by the USAF: the F-15 being the 'high' end, and a new air combat fighter (ACF) being the 'low' end, to be procured in larger numbers than the F-15. Spurred on by foreign interest in the USAF's selection, from the governments of Belgium, Denmark, Norway and the Netherlands, it was announced that the General Dynamics YF-16 had been selected for full-scale engineering development.

The F-16 represents a fresh approach to fighter design, having a flared wing-body shape and the F-15's F100 engine, with a simple fixed intake below the fuselage. The pilot lies back in a reclining seat, and flies the aircraft with a side-stick controller in place of the conventional control column. It is a simple day air-combat fighter, armed with a 20-mm (0.79-in) M61 cannon and wingtip AIM-9 Sidewinder AAMs.

The prospect of a European order meant the original air-superiority role had to be expanded to give equal emphasis on the air-to-surface mission, to include radar and limited all-weather navigation capabilities. Six single-seat F-16A and two twin-seat F-16B trainers were ordered as pre-production aircraft; the first development F-16A flew on December 8, 1976, and the first F-16B on August 8, 1977. The initial orders were for 116 F-16s for Belgium, 58 for Denmark, 72 for Norway and 102 for the Netherlands. Of the 348 ordered, 58 were to be two-seaters.

During weapons development trials the second prototype YF-16 had demonstrated its ability to carry and fire both the AIM-7 Sparrow and Sky Flash AAMs. Company-funded trials have produced an F-16B Wild Weasel variant, which although not fulfilling any USAF requirement, has sparked interest with other customers of the F-16.

In October 1976 Iran ordered 160 F-16s, but this was later cancelled, following the fall of the Shah in January 1979. In January 1977 the USAF increased its buy by 738 aircraft, and as part of the three-way arms deal of August 1977, Israel is to receive 75 F-16s.

The first production F-16A flew on August 7, 1978, and was handed over to the USAF ten days later. It entered operational service with the USAF at Hill AFB in January 1979. The first European aircraft flew from the Belgian line in December 1978, and entered Belgian air force service in January 1979. The first Dutch aircraft, an F-16B, flew in May 1979, and was handed over to the Royal Netherlands Air Force on June 6, 1979. The first Norwegian F-16, also a two-seater, was first flown on December 12, 1979 and handed over on January 15, 1980. Israel received its first aircraft on January 31, 1980.

General Dynamics is also proposing a simplified version of the F-16 as a follow-on fighter for the F-5E supplied under Mutual Aid Programs. This version would be powered by a J79 turbojet of 8165 kg (18 000 lb) thrust, in place of the F100 turbofan. Structural changes would be limited to the rear fuselage and air intake, which would be re-sized to be compatible with the smaller J79.

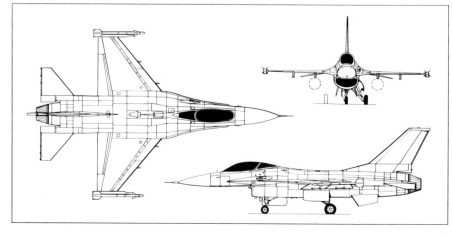

F-16A

Type: single-seat lightweight air combat fighter
Maker: General Dynamics Corporation
Span: 9.45 m (31 ft) over wingtip missile rails
Length: 14.52 m (47 ft 7⅔ in) excluding nose probe
Height: 5.01 m (16 ft 5⅓ in)
Wing area: 27.87 m² (300 sq ft)
Weight: maximum 16 057 kg (35 400 lb); empty 6607 kg (14 567 lb)
Powerplant: one 10 800-kg (23 800-lb) st Pratt & Whitney F100-PW-100(3) afterburning turbofan

Performance: maximum speed over 2124 km/h (1320 mph) at 12 200 m (40 000 ft); service ceiling over 15 240 m (50 000 ft); radius of action over 925 km (575 miles)

Armament: one General Electric M61A-1 20-mm (0.79-in) Vulcan cannon; one under-fuselage hardpoint stressed for 1000 kg (2200 lb); two inboard hardpoints for 1587 kg (3500 lb); two centre underwing hardpoints for 1134 kg (2500 lb); two outboard underwing hardpoints and two wingtip stations for 113 kg (250 lb);

typical loads include wingtip-mounted AIM-9 Sidewinder AAMs, drop-tanks, bombs, cluster weapons, rocket and flare pods, precision guided munitions, ECM and laser-designator pods
Crew: 1
Production: 1169 of all types ordered or built by Spring 1980

Top: A prototype YF-16 in company livery and armed with AIM-9 Sidewinder missiles
Above left: A development F-16A with a load of nine bombs under each wing
Above centre: An AIM-7 Sparrow streaks away from an F-16A during weapons trials. These cannot yet be used from the F-16. In July 1980 the F-16 was officially named the Fighting Falcon (Falcon as a single name is registered by Dassault for its business jet)
Above: The first F-16B to be delivered to the Israeli air force at Fort Worth

251

F-18 Hornet, McDonnell Douglas

FIRST FLIGHT 1978

THE rising costs of the F-14 Tomcat in 1974 led the US Navy to consider a low-cost multi-mission lightweight fighter, under the VFAX programme. The McDonnell Douglas/Northrop entry (the YF-17 fighter evaluated by the USAF) was selected for full-scale development (FSD) to meet naval requirements and was redesignated F-18 Hornet in January 1976. Production of the F-18 is split between McDonnell Douglas, as prime contractor, and Northrop who build the centre and rear fuselage as principal sub-contractor on a 60:40 basis. Although of conventional metal construction, much use is made of graphite/epoxy composites for doors, access panels and the speed brake. The F-18 is powered by a pair of General Electric F404 afterburning turbofans.

The maiden flight of the Northrop YF-17 (sometimes referred to as the prototype F-18) was on June 9, 1974. The first true Hornet, a YF-18, made its first flight on November 18, 1978. The FSD programme calls for 11 Hornets, including two TF-18A two-seat trainers, and initially 800 production aircraft were required. However, in early 1979, political blocking of the AV-8B Advanced Harrier for the US Marine Corps caused the requirement to be raised to 1377 Hornets (including the 11 FSD aircraft), of which every ninth aircraft will be a two-seater. (Should AV-8B funding be restored, this requirement may again be reduced.) The first production batch of nine F-18 Hornets was authorized in FY79, with 25 for FY80.

It can serve in the fighter role as the F-18, and

Below left: A prototype F-18 with a mixture of company livery and service insignia. By mid 1980 the programme was hit by cost-escalation and even appeared vulnerable to cancellation
Below: The first F-18A on its 100th flight. The wide track landing gear and arrester hook can be seen

F-18

1 Radome
2 Radar scanner
3 Scanner drive mechanism
4 Gun muzzle
5 Gun gas vents
6 Cannon barrels
7 Radar package sliding rails
8 Low voltage formation lighting
9 Hughes AN/APG-65 multi-mode radar package
10 Infra-red sensor housing
11 Ammunition drum
12 Angle of attack probe
13 Gun mounting
14 Flight refuelling probe, extended
15 Refuelling probe hydraulic jack
16 M61, 0.79-in (20-mm) rotary cannon
17 Ammunition feed track
18 Communications antenna
19 Cockpit front bulkhead
20 Pressurization valve
21 Frameless windshield panel
22 Instrument panel shroud
23 Pilot's sight and Kaiser head-up display
24 Control column
25 Rudder pedals
26 Wing leading edge extension (LEX)
27 Nosewheel bay
28 Nosewheel doors
29 Retractable step
30 Catapult strop link, landing position
31 Strop link, launch position
32 Twin nosewheels
33 Catapult launch signal lights
34 Landing lamp
35 Cleveland nose landing gear leg
36 Avionics bay
37 Control runs
38 Engine throttle controls
39 Pilot's left side console
40 Cockpit rear bulkhead
41 Martin-Baker SJU-5/A ejection seat
42 Right side console
43 Ejection seat firing handle
44 Cockpit canopy
45 Canopy open position

46 Canopy jack
47 2nd seat structural space provision (TF-18)
48 Forward fuselage fuel tank, deleted for TF-18
49 Honeycomb panel construction
50 Liquid oxygen container
51 Nose landing gear retraction strut
52 Centreline drop tank
53 Avionics bays
54 LEX frame construction
55 Left navigation light
56 Air conditioning ducting
57 Intake splitter plate
58 Air conditioning intake
59 Bleed air holes
60 Boundary layer control slot
61 Main fuel tanks
62 Communications aerial
63 Bleed air outlet louvres
64 Right leading-edge extension
65 External fuel tank
66 Laser spot tracker pod (LST), right fuselage station
67 Right inboard wing pylon
68 Pylon mounting
69 Mk 83 low drag general purpose (LDGP) bombs (A-18)
70 Bomb ejector rack
71 Right outer wing pylon
72 Pylon fixing
73 Leading-edge dog tooth
74 Wing fold hinge line
75 Outboard leading-edge actuator
76 Drooping leading-edge
77 Right wingtip missile launcher rail
78 AIM-9L Sidewinder air-to-air missile
79 Outer wing panel folded position
80 Right drooping aileron
81 Right double-slotted flap
82 Flap guides
83 Wing integral fuel tank
84 Hydraulic flap jacks
85 Graphite/epoxy dorsal fairing panels
86 Fuel delivery piping
87 Fuselage longeron
88 Boundary layer bleed air duct
89 Air-conditioning plant
90 Left intake
91 Intake ducting
92 Leading-edge flap hydraulic jack

93 Flap sequencing control unit
94 Control cable runs
95 Wing attachment pin joints
96 Rear fuselage fuel tank
97 APU exhaust duct
98 Right engine bay
99 Fin attachment fixing
100 Fin construction
101 Fuel jettison pipe
102 Graphite/epoxy skin
103 Anti-collision light
104 Steel leading-edge strip
105 Honeycomb panel
106 Aerial tuners
107 Electronic countermeasures aerials (ECM)
108 Fin tip antenna housing
109 Communications aerial
110 Radar warning receiver
111 Tail navigation light
112 Fuel jettison
113 Low voltage formation lighting
114 Honeycomb rudder construction
115 Rudder hydraulic jacks
116 Airbrake open position
117 Right tailplane
118 Left fin tip antenna housing
119 Low voltage formation lighting
120 Airbrake housing
121 Airbrake hydraulic jack
122 Right engine tailpipe
123 Exhaust nozzle shroud
124 Variable area exhaust nozzle
125 Nozzle actuators
126 Afterburner duct
127 Left tailplane
128 Graphite/epoxy skin panels
129 Honeycomb construction
130 Steel leading edge strip
131 Deck arresting hook
132 Tailplane pivot
133 Tailplane hinge lever
134 Hydraulic servo actuator
135 Left engine bay
136 Engine access doors
137 Engine accessories
138 Main engine mounting
139 General Electric F404-GE-400 low bypass turbojet
140 Engine compressor face
141 Airborne auxiliary powerplant (APU)
142 Airframe mounted auxiliary drive gearbox

143 Left flap actuators
144 Flap sequencing control
145 Flap guides
146 Left double-slotted flap
147 Graphite/epoxy flap skins
148 Honeycomb panel construction
149 Wing fold actuator
150 Aileron hydraulic jacks
151 Left drooping aileron
152 Fixed portion of trailing edge
153 Left wingtip AIM-9 Sidewinder
154 Missile launcher rail
155 Honeycomb leading-edge construction
156 Outboard leading-edge actuators
157 Outboard wing panel construction
158 Wing fold hinge line
159 Left outboard pylon fixing
160 Left outboard pylon
161 Bomb ejector rack
162 Mk 83 LDGP bombs
163 Leading-edge dog tooth
164 Multi-spar wing panel construction
165 Left wing integral fuel tank
166 Inboard pylon fixing
167 Cleveland main landing gear leg
168 Pivoted axle beam
169 Left mainwheel
170 AIM-7F Sparrow air-to-air missile
171 Forward-looking infra-red pod (FLIR), left fuselage station

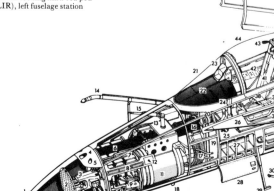

the attack/strike role as the A-18. One of the significant features of the Hornet which enables it to be used in both roles, with minimum differences in equipment, is the Hughes APG-65 multi-mode radar, which is equally effective in either the air-to-air or air-to-surface mode. In air combat, it has demonstrated its ability to display up to eight target tracks while retaining ten in its memory. In the air-to-surface mapping mode, it uses Doppler beam sharpening to enhance the resolution.

The only other major change for the A-18 version will be the carriage of forward-looking infra-red (FLIR) and laser designator pods in place of the fuselage-mounted Sparrow missiles. It is intended that an RF-18 reconnaissance version of the Hornet will be developed to replace the RF-4Bs and RF-8Gs currently in service.

The CF-18 Hornet was selected by the Canadian armed forces for its new fighter aircraft on April 10, 1980, and the type has been short-listed by Australia for its tactical fighter programme in competition with the F-16. Spain, Greece, Israel and Turkey are also interested.

When the production deal was concluded between McDonnell Douglas and Northrop, the latter retained the rights to produce and market a specifically land-based version of the Hornet, known as the F-18L. This retains the APG-65 radar and F404 engines, and is 80 to 90% common to the Hornet. Although it seemed in mid 1979 that the F-18L was a prime contender for the USAF's proposed Enhanced Tactical Fighter, the requirement appears to have faded.

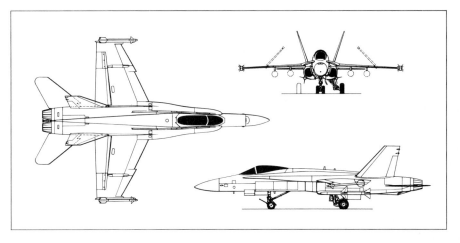

F-18A

Type: single-seat carrier strike fighter
Maker: McDonnell Douglas Corporation, Northrop Corporation
Span: 11.43 m (37 ft 6 in)
Length: 17.07 m (56 ft)
Height: 4.66 m (15 ft 3½ in)
Wing area: 37.16 m² (400 sq ft)
Weight: maximum 22 710 kg (50 064 lb) (catapult limit); empty (provisional) 9336 kg (20 583 lb)
Powerplant: two 7257-kg (16 000-lb) st General Electric F404-GE-400 afterburning turbofans

Performance: maximum speed over 1915 km/h (1190 mph [Mach 1.8]) at height; range 1480 km (920 miles), on attack mission 1019 km (633 miles); service ceiling approx 15 240 m (50 000 ft)
Armament: one General Electric M61 20-mm (0.79-in) Vulcan cannon; nine external weapons stations with a theoretical capacity of 8165 kg (18 000 lb) of ordnance, comprising two wingtip launch rails for AIM-9 Sidewinder AAMs, four underwing pylons for fuel tanks, AAMs, ASMs, bombs or rocket pods, a centreline

pylon for fuel tanks or weapons, and two nacelle fuselage stations for either AIM-7 Sparrow AAMs or Martin Marietta sensor pods
Crew: 1
Production: 1377 ordered with a probable requirement in excess of 1500 with foreign orders

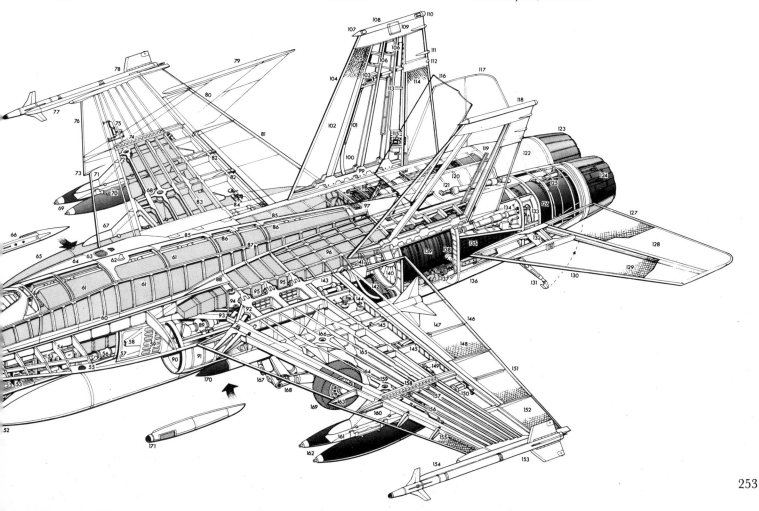

Mirage 2000, Dassault-Breguet

FIRST FLIGHT 1978

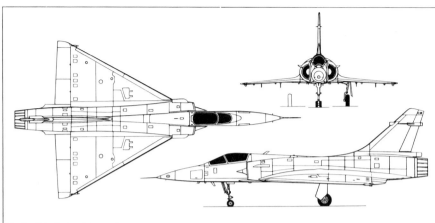

Top left: The Mirage 2000-01 at the SBAC Show at Farnborough in September 1978
Above: A view of 2000-01 showing the small canard strakes mounted on the air inlets
Left: The tail of 2000-01 showing the M53-2 variable nozzle. This engine was fitted to the prototypes but production versions will have the more powerful M53-5

Mirage 2000

Type: single-seat interceptor/air-superiority fighter
Maker: Avions Marcel Dassault – Breguet Aviation
Span: 9 m (29 ft 6 in)
Length: 15.33 m (50 ft 3½ in)
Height: 3.4 m (11 ft 1¾ in)
Wing area: not available
Weight: maximum 9000 kg (19 840 lb); empty not available
Powerplant: one 8500-kg (18 740-lb) st SNECMA M53-2 augmented afterburning turbofan fitted on the prototypes; production aircraft are intended to have 9000 kg (19 840 lb) st M53-5 afterburning turbofan
Performance: maximum speed 2445 km/h (1520 mph [Mach 2.3]); range with external tanks over 1500 km (932 miles); service ceiling over 20 000 m (65 600 ft)
Armament: two 30-mm (1.18-in) DEFA cannon; five under-fuselage hardpoints and two hardpoints under each wing; typical interception armament two Matra Super 530 AAMs on the inboard pylons, and two Matra 550 Magic AAMs on the outboard pylons; the projected strike version would carry up to 5000 kg (11 025 lb) of external stores
Crew: 1
Production: 5, orders for 4, plans for 127

All data are estimated

THE Mirage 2000 was developed as an interceptor and air-superiority fighter, and is expected to be equally suitable for low-level interdiction, close support and reconnaissance. The blended delta wing/fuselage offers a substantial structural weight gain, increased internal volume for both avionics and fuel, and a significant reduction in drag over conventional wings.

The large fin ensures that the pilot will have full control of the Mirage 2000 at high angles of attack. The addition of two small canard strakes mounted on the air intake ducts helps improve longitudinal control, and to some extent lateral control, by stabilizing the airflow at high angles of attack. Other modern concepts used in the Mirage 2000 include control-configured vehicle (CCV) technology and fly-by-wire transmission, plus the use of carbon-fibre and boron composites.

The Mirage 2000 is powered by the SNECMA M53 augmented turbofan, though this cannot offer the power needed for front-rank air-combat manoeuvrability with thrust/weight ratio exceeding 1 at sea level. The heart of the aircraft's weapons system is a new pulse-Doppler radar, known as RDI, being developed by Thomson-CSF in collaboration with EMD. It is reported as offering a range of 100 km (62 miles), the capability to detect targets at altitude and good ECCM (electronic counter-counter-measures) characteristics.

Five prototypes are being built, the first of which made its maiden flight on March 10, 1978. Although initial plans call for 127 air-defence versions, only four production Mirage 2000s were ordered in the 1979 budget. Dassault envisage the air-defence requirement to rise to 200 aircraft, and hope to sell a further 200 to the Armée de l'Air.

In the Spring of 1977, the Chief of Staff of the Armée de l'Air, General Maurice Saint-Circq summed up the technological advances the Mirage 2000 would bring. It would be able to fly at Mach 2.2 at 18 000 m (59 000 ft); offer low-speed characteristics to match the Mirage F1; have a rate of climb double that of the Mirage III, enabling it to attack a high altitude target penetrating at Mach 3 some five minutes after brake release; and finally offer a range 30% better than the Mirage III, after take-off from a 1200-m (3940-ft) long strip, which would enable it to maintain a combat air patrol for three times as long.

Tornado F.2, Panavia

FIRST FLIGHT 1979

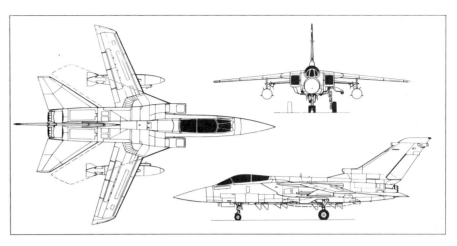

THE Tornado F.2 is the air-defence variant of the Panavia Tornado multirole combat aircraft (MRCA) developed jointly by Germany, Italy and the United Kingdom. The largest European industrial programme ever undertaken, a tri-national company, Panavia Aircraft, was formed to build the Tornado. This consortium comprised British Aerospace (42.5%), Messerschmitt-Bölkow-Blohm (42.5%) and Aeritalia (15%). Project definition of MRCA began in May 1969, and on July 29, 1976 the three governments signed a Memorandum of Understanding for the production of 809 Tornados (as the MRCA had been christened). The first prototype Tornado made its maiden flight from Manching, Germany, on August 14, 1974.

Full-scale development of an air-defence variant of the Tornado, for the exclusive use by the RAF, was authorized on March 4, 1976. Of the 385 Tornados being produced for the RAF, 165 are to be the air-defence variant. The first of three prototype Tornado F.2s made its maiden flight from the British production centre at Warton on October 27, 1979, during which it reached a speed of Mach 1.2.

The F.2 version of the Tornado enjoys some 80% commonality with the interdictor-strike version (RAF designation GR.1) but does differ in several important areas. An increase of 1.36 m (4 ft 5½ in) in the fuselage has been made, partly by a longer nose radome, and partly by the need to stretch the fuselage aft of the cockpit to allow the carriage of four Sky Flash AAMs in staggered

tandem pairs. This extension allows an additional 909 litres (200 Imp gal) of fuel to be carried.

The Tornado F.2 is equipped with a Marconi Avionics track-while-scan pulse-Doppler AI radar, known as Foxhunter, able to detect targets at distances in excess of 185 km (115 miles). It can track several targets simultaneously, while the Sky Flash AAMs offer 'snap-up, shoot-down capability' in the face of heavy ECM at ranges in excess of 40 km (25 miles).

It is expected that the first Tornado F.2s will start replacing Lightnings in RAF service from 1984, although in view of the RAF's 'fighter-gap', it might now be possible to bring that date forward by about a year. Once the Lightnings are replaced, the Tornado will take over from the Phantom.

Tornado F.2

Type: two-seat long-range interceptor
Maker: Panavia Aircraft GmbH (British Aerospace, MBB and Aeritalia)
Span: fully swept 8.6 m (28 ft 2½ in); fully spread 13.9 m (45 ft 7¼ in)
Length: 18.06 m (59 ft 3 in)
Height: 5.7 m (18 ft 8½ in)
Weight: maximum (GR.1 with external stores) 26 490 kg (58 400 lb); empty, equipped (GR.1) 9980 to 10 430 kg (22 000 to 23 000 lb)
Wing area: 30 m² (322.9 sq ft) estimated GR.1
Powerplant: two Turbo-Union RB.199-34R-04 turbofan engines, uprated from the -04 ratings of approximately 4082 kg (9000 lb) st (dry) and 7257 kg (16 000 lb) with afterburning
Performance: maximum speed at height (GR.1, clean) in excess of Mach 2 2124 km/h (1320 mph); radius of action, loiter for more than two hours, with sufficient fuel for interception including 10-min air combat 555 to 742 km (345 to 461 miles); service ceiling approximately 15 250 m (50 030 ft)
Armament: one 27-mm (1.06-in) IWKA-Mauser cannon, in right lower forward fuselage; two AIM-9L Sidewinder AAMs, mounted outboard of the inner-wing pylons; four BAeD Sky Flash mounted in staggered tandem pairs, semi-recessed under the belly; fuel tanks and ECM pods can be carried on the two underwing or under-fuselage stations
Crew: 2
Production: 165 on order for RAF (there is speculation from informed sources that an additional batch, perhaps 40, may be ordered)

Left: Four Sky Flash fit recessed under the longer fuselage of the F.2

Mirage 4000, Dassault-Breguet

FIRST FLIGHT 1979

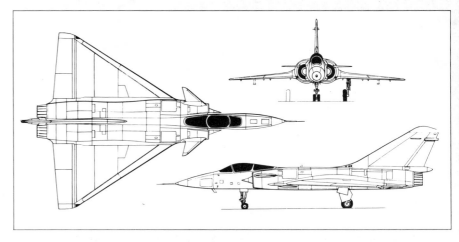

WHEN the announcement of the cancellation of the Avion de Combat Futur and go-ahead for the Mirage 2000 was made, in December 1975, Dassault-Breguet said it would proceed with a scaled-up version of the 'Deux Mille'. This was to be a twin-turbofan aircraft, funded by the French industry, intended for interception and low-level penetration attacks on long-range targets. With no requirement from the Armée de l'Air, this was to be for export only; potential customers were to be assured that it would outperform any aircraft in its class either in production or under development.

Originally called the Delta Super Mirage, a mock-up of what is now designated the Super Mirage 4000 was unveiled in December 1977. In the same class as the F-15 Eagle, the exact details of dimensions, weights, performance and armament remain classified. However, the installation of a pair of M53 turbofans, as fitted to the Mirage 2000, are intended to give the Super Mirage 4000 a thrust/weight ratio above 1:1 for the interceptor role, though this will have to wait until the M88 engine is available, probably not before 1986.

The prototype aircraft made its maiden flight on March 9, 1979, during which it achieved a speed of Mach 1.2. On its sixth flight on April 11, 1979, Mach 2.2 was reached. For these early flights, a loaded weight of 20 000 kg (44 000 lb) has been reported. As with the Mirage 2000, extensive use of carbon-fibre and boron components has been made in the foreplanes, access panels, control surfaces, fin and rudder.

The air-intake strakes of the 'Deux Mille' have been enlarged to foreplanes (similar to the IAI Kfir, another Mirage derivative), while the fly-by-wire active control system makes a rearward CG (centre of gravity) possible, useful in improving combat manoeuvrability. A blister-type canopy ensures a 360° field of vision, and the aircraft has a large nose radome for an as-yet unspecified radar.

Although only the one prototype is available, it seems incredible that an aircraft of this type is being proposed as a private venture. It has taken three major governments working together for ten years to produce the less-powerful Tornado. One can only speculate at the stimulus for the Super Mirage 4000, since the most likely potential customers, the Armée de l'Air, South Africa and Saudi Arabia, have all explicitly denied involvement.

Right: The Super Mirage 4000 at the Paris Air Show of 1979
Below: The Super Mirage in company livery; it had no radar but M53-5 uprated engines

Super Mirage 4000

Type: single-seat interceptor/strike fighter
Maker: Avions Marcel Dassault – Breguet Aviation
Span: 12 m (39 ft 4½ in)
Length: 18.7 m (61 ft 4¼ in)
Height: not available
Wing area: 73 m (786 sq ft)
Weight: maximum 20 000 kg (44 092 lb)
Powerplant: two 9000-kg (19 840-lb) st SNECMA M53-5 augmented afterburning turbofans
Performance: maximum speed over 2335 km/h (1450 mph [Mach 2.2]); range approx 2000 km (1250 miles); service ceiling over 20 000 m (65 600 ft)
Armament: two 30-mm (1.18-in) DEFA cannon; 11 external hardpoints for a variety of air-to-air and air-to-surface ordnance
Crew: 1
Production: one prototype demonstrator

All data are provisional

Index

Page numbers in bold refer to the main entry of the aircraft

Right: Grumman F6F Hellcat
Top right: BAC F6 Lightning
Centre right: Vought F8E
Crusader
Bottom: De Havilland
FAW.20 Sea Venom

Picture Credits